THE TASTEMAKER

The
TASTEMAKER

CARL van VECHTEN

and the

BIRTH of MODERN AMERICA

....

EDWARD WHITE

FARRAR, STRAUS AND GIROUX   *New York*

Farrar, Straus and Giroux
18 West 18th Street, New York 10011

Owing to limitations of space, illustration credits can be found
on pages 375–77.

Library of Congress Cataloging-in-Publication Data
White, Edward, 1981–
    The Tastemaker : Carl Van Vechten and the Birth of Modern America /
    Edward White. — First edition.
        pages   cm
    Includes bibliographical references and index.
    ISBN 978-0-374-20157-9 (hardback) — ISBN 978-0-374-70881-8 (ebook)
    1. Van Vechten, Carl, 1880–1964.   2. Authors, American—20th century—
Biography.   3. Photographers—United States—Biography.   I. Title.

PS3543.A653 Z95 2014
813'.52—dc23
[B]
                                                        2013034003

Designed by Jonathan D. Lippincott

Farrar, Straus and Giroux books may be purchased for educational, business,
or promotional use. For information on bulk purchases, please contact the
Macmillan Corporate and Premium Sales Department at 1-800-221-7945,
extension 5442, or write to specialmarkets@macmillan.com.

www.fsgbooks.com
www.twitter.com/fsgbooks • www.facebook.com/fsgbooks

10 9 8 7 6 5 4 3 2 1

For Mum and Dad

Americans are inclined to look everywhere but under their noses for art.

—*Carl Van Vechten*

Contents

· ·

THE TASTEMAKER

Prologue

. . . .

Concealed within rural Connecticut's verdant undergrowth, two young men—one white, the other black—stripped naked in the heat of a July afternoon in 1940. They had done this before; they knew the routine. Standing face-to-face, each reached out to place his hands on the other as the sunlight, breaking through the foliage above them, dappled their skin. Soon they settled into a pose and held it, frozen in place, until the click of a camera shutter pierced the quiet.

Ten feet away stood the photographer, Carl Van Vechten, a slightly stooped white man just turned sixty with thinning, slicked-back, snowy hair, high-waisted pants, and a stare as direct as the lens he held in his manicured hands. He had long been looking forward to today's shoot, which was taking place on the grounds of a friend's country estate. It was an opportunity to take a moment's respite from the relentless flow of happenings in his beloved New York City, the metropolis that had been his muse for the last thirty-four years of a prolifically creative life. More to the point, the two men posing for him that day were his favorite models, and it was a rare treat to have them both together like this. As he peered at them through his view-finder, his greatest obsessions snapped into focus: the beauty of male bodies; the wonders of racial difference; the preciousness of a life lived in the service of beauty, art, and pleasure. Despite the serious expression that gripped his features whenever he stepped behind the camera, this shoot, like the hundreds of others he was to do over the next two decades, was not a professional engagement; the photographs would not be bought or exhibited. It was just for fun. In Van Vechten's life, almost everything was.

Today, nearly a half century since his death, Carl Van Vechten's name means nothing to most Americans. New Yorkers may have seen it engraved on a pillar in the Great Hall at the New York Public Library on Fifth Avenue at Forty-second Street, in acknowledgment of his status as a major benefactor. Eighty or so blocks uptown, he might just garner the odd flicker of recognition as a bullhorn for the Harlem Renaissance of the 1920s or perhaps as the author of *Nigger Heaven*, a salacious novel of 1926 that unveiled the intimate lives of black Americans to their incredulous white compatriots and stoked a passion for Harlem nightlife that became a definitive part of Jazz Age New York. The book's title was as startling then as it is now, and the furor it caused has frequently overshadowed everything else Van Vechten achieved.

A list of those achievements makes extraordinary reading. Carl Van Vechten was a polymath unparalleled in the history of American arts. From the 1910s onward, he was, at various times, the nation's most incisive and far-seeing arts critic, who promoted names as diverse as Gertrude Stein and Bessie Smith long before it was popular to do so; a notorious socialite who held legendary parties; a controversial novelist who captured the dizzying panorama of Prohibition Era New York and topped the bestseller lists in the process; a celebrated photographer who took thousands of portraits of underappreciated artists as well as many of the world's most famous people; a de facto publicist for great forgotten names, including Herman Melville; and one of the most important champions of African-American literature, vital in progressing the careers of Langston Hughes, Nella Larsen, and Chester Himes.

Like many legendary New Yorkers, Van Vechten was an interloper. He grew up roughly one thousand miles from Manhattan, in the prosperous, provincial town of Cedar Rapids, Iowa. He was an odd-looking boy, willowy and sallow with entrancing chestnut-colored eyes, the prominent front teeth of a donkey, and the dress sense of a romantic poet. In Cedar Rapids, the Van Vechten men, all workaholics who made their fortunes from respectable business concerns, embodied the masculine ideals of the era, ran their homes with firm-handed benevolence, and joined clubs, lodges, and committees to shape their community. Young Carl bucked the trend. If it had not been for the unmistakable forehead and jawline—two solid curves of bone as smooth and thick as sculpted marble—it would have been difficult to know that he was a Van Vechten at all. He was lazy in school, had no interest in politics or sports or the other manly pursuits of the day, and sublimated his unspoken homosexual desires into a fantasy world of music, literature, and theater. His one burning desire was to ditch the life of a bourgeois midwesterner for the glamour and grime of the big cities. When asked what he was going to do when he grew up, he did not name a sensible profession or an earnest vocation like the other boys at school. He knew the art of living was to be his calling. "I'm going to live in Chicago; I'm going to live in New York; I'm going to live in London; I'm going to live in Paris," he declared. He wanted to see the world and have the world see him.

When Van Vechten began his urban adventures at the start of the twentieth century, the United States was convinced of its manifest destiny as a political and economic powerhouse, yet culturally it languished in the shadow of the European civilization it aimed to usurp. With the patronage of industrial magnates, museums, opera houses, and symphony halls were built in towns and cities across the country, often in eager imitation of places seen on pilgrimages to Paris, London, Florence, Venice, and Rome. Many Americans became anxious that cultural life in the nation's cities was drab and derivative, a pale imitation of European traditions. Others feared that the urban way of life was simply inimical to the American project. In his hugely popular book of 1885, *Our Country*, the Congregationalist minister Josiah Strong expressed the fears of many socially conservative Americans when he identified the city as "a serious menace to our civilization" because of its multiethnic populations of young, single people led astray by godless entertainments and fleshly pleasures. When the Democratic candidate William Jennings Bryan campaigned in the presidential election of 1896, he too tapped into the generic fears about an American republic run from the cities. Cedar Rapids was one of the many stops on his mammoth nationwide campaign circuit during which he railed against the avarice of Wall Street, the corruption of Washington, the un-American values of East Coast cultural elites, and all the other cancers that, in his view, were destroying traditional ideals of thrift, industry, and piety.

In the first forty years of the twentieth century Van Vechten played a vital role in helping the United States accept its cities as the fount of a new and distinctively American culture that would be envied and imitated the world over. As a critic, novelist, photographer, and promoter he valorized modern art and the cultural life of the city in the industrial age, in particular New York, a place he depicted as a modernist phantasmagoria in which any experience was possible. Van Vechten was always on the scene, connecting himself to Greenwich Village poets and Broadway legends, setting trends and starting crazes. "For him Manhattan never loses its *Arabian Nights* glamour," said Van Vechten's friend the writer and editor Emily Clark in 1931. "It is the eighth, and most wonderful, wonder of the world." For more than half a century he prowled its various neighborhoods in flashy silk shirts, rings, and bracelets, in search of sexual adventure, exotic entertainment, and the company of brilliant individuals from assorted backgrounds. His stated ambitions in life were to avoid responsibility and stay one step ahead of boredom. Whether it was an evening at the opera or a gin-fueled night at a gay speakeasy in Hell's Kitchen, he did just that, immersing himself in spectacle and sensation.

At the height of his fame and cultural influence in the 1920s, his diaries sometimes read like a guide to the attractions of the city. An evening in a Chinese restaurant and a Yiddish theater would be closely followed by lunch at the Algonquin Hotel with H. L. Mencken and Sinclair Lewis and an eight-hour tour of Harlem cabaret clubs. Open the diaries at any page, and the record of a remarkable day is waiting to be found. On February 16, 1927, for example, Van Vechten went with Langston Hughes to the lavish home of A'Lelia Walker, the queen of Harlem high society, for one of her legendary parties attended by black poets, NAACP activists, jazz singers, socialites, and

sexual adventurers, before hopping in a cab to the downtown apartment of the *Vanity Fair* cartoonist Ralph Barton. Charlie Chaplin
happened to be there that evening, and over the finest bootleg liquor that money could buy, they gossiped for hours about the movie
business, Van Vechten having recently returned from a monthlong
sojourn in Hollywood. At five in the morning, Chaplin drove Van
Vechten home; after a couple of hours' sleep another hectic day began.
Nights like this, ones that would glow forever in the memory for
most people, were part of Van Vechten's weekly routine of pleasure
seeking. As he never tired of telling people, his own parties were the
best in town, and he prided himself on being the consummate host,
concocting guest lists and entertainments of exotic and jarringly
disparate elements in exactly the same way that he mixed his delicious, powerful cocktails. Van Vechten was dazzled by the wealthy,
seduced by the beautiful, and thrilled by the talented; his soirees
featured equal parts of each, of all ethnicities and sexual orientations.
As millionaire entrepreneurs befriended showgirls, Paul Robeson
might sing, or George Gershwin play the piano. Now and then passions soared and guests stripped naked as they danced or spat insults
over their martini glasses. No matter the character of a particular evening, Van Vechten delighted in the sight of his creation, the diverse
components of urban America in beautiful collision right there in his
front room.

Nothing gave him such joy as breaking taboos and transgressing
established notions of good taste; he treated it as evidence that he
was being true to himself, living the life of a liberated individual
and not buckling under the will of others. Steadfastly obeying one's
inborn instincts, no matter how peculiar, was the thing that bound
his wide-ranging artistic interests together. He was captivated by
Gertrude Stein because of the sheer unusualness of her writing and
the strength of her unconventional personality. His adoration of
African-American culture similarly stemmed from his fascination with
what he thought was an inner, irreducible blackness, a quality he
claimed to have spotted in Paul Robeson, Langston Hughes, and
Ethel Waters, all of whom he publicly feted. His creed of following
one's inherent nature meant he refused to be ashamed of his complex

sexuality, though it was also a symptom of his immense self-absorption. He held as an article of faith that the feelings and opinions of other people should supersede his desires only in truly exceptional circumstances, a fact that caused years of pain and discomfort for his wife, Fania Marinoff, a woman he claimed to love with all his heart but whom he repeatedly treated as an addendum to his life rather than the center of it, neglecting her in favor of his many friends and lovers. His high self-regard meant that he held others to standards of conduct that he never adhered to himself, and he was quick to lash out or sulk ostentatiously when he felt slighted. "If people have no sense of obligation and no sense of values I let them drift or stew in their own juice," he once confessed about his attitude toward friends who had lost his favor. "I can cut him [sic] off without a shilling. It's very easy for me."

Through his life of indulgence and excess, and in promoting his bespoke pantheon of celebrities, Van Vechten was one of the leading figures of a brash, iconoclastic generation of writers, artists, and thinkers that helped Americans to see that art and beauty existed amid the hum and buzz of their own cities and not just in the galleries and theaters of ancient European capitals. To an extent, his life and legacy have been overlooked simply because the extraordinary range of his interests and the idiosyncrasies of his character are too unwieldy to handle. A white champion of the African-American cause who used the n-word; a devoted husband who kept a retinue of young male lovers; a disciple of European modernism who hated to leave Manhattan; an aesthete with aristocratic leanings who loved the cheap thrills of Coney Island: the man is simply too contradictory to slot snugly into the established narrative of the American Century. Yet that is precisely why he is so important; his life was simultaneously atypical and emblematic. To his detractors—and there have been plenty of them—he was a flippant, egotistical, name-dropping drunkard, a fantasist and mythmaker who perpetuated grotesque racial stereotypes and wallowed in the immoral grime of city life. At times he was all these things. But he was also a modernist pioneer who lived a fast-paced cosmopolitan existence in its fullest aspect and a prophet of a new cultural sensibility that promoted the primacy of the individual, sexual freedom, and racial tolerance and dared put the blues on a par with Beethoven. Across those decades when the United States began to push itself from its nineteenth-century moorings into a chaotic but exciting new era, Van Vechten's hyperindividualism and radically eclectic tastes were perfectly suited to flourish.

ONE

The Gilded Age: A Tale of Yesterday

．．．

From the beginning of their adventure in America, the Van Vechtens did things their way—with force, panache, and little regard for what others might think. The trend started with Teunis Dircksz Van Vechten, a twenty-eight-year-old farmer, who sailed with his wife and infant son from the Netherlands to the shores of the New World in the summer of 1638. Along with a dozen other farmers and merchants, the family set out from the tiny Dutch island of Texel aboard the *Arms of Norway* on May 12 and arrived in New Amsterdam nearly three months later on August 4 ready to transform the fecund, open land before them into their fortune.

After two years working as a laborer for another colonist, Teunis acquired the tenancy of a farm on the Rensselaerswijck patroonship, a vast manorial estate given by the West India Company to Kiliaen van Rensselaer, a diamond merchant from Amsterdam. Teunis was soon making a fine living for himself and his family, amassing enough money to buy a 50 percent stake in a nearby brewery. Like many Dutch pioneers of the time, the Van Vechtens were pulled toward America rather than pushed from Europe. It was the promise of prosperity and the prospect of adventure, not the need for sanctuary from religious persecution or crushing tyranny, that tempted them across the ocean. For that very reason, some found life on Rensselaerswijck hugely frustrating, as the impositions of the colony's rulers often seemed more exacting than those of the royal government back home. Yet few of the colonists made such a fuss as Teunis, who bridled at any attempt to impinge on his liberty.

If the patroonship records can be believed, Teunis was a hothead, an old-fashioned brawler, who liked to settle disagreements with his sharp tongue and sizable fists. But he was also a man of strong principle, whose lack of deference frequently enraged authorities. In 1651 he was prosecuted for publicly humiliating one official—the director of the patroonship no less—calling him "an old grey thief and a rascal." More serious, he threatened to stab the Reverend Johannes Megapolensis with a knife; punishment, he said, for being "an informer." Perhaps it had been Megapolensis who let slip that Teunis was selling produce at a price not sanctioned by the patroonship, a crime for which he received a further prosecution. There were other moments when the disdain for Old World bondage was less about taking a stand and more about indulging a wicked sense of humor. In September 1648, Teunis ordered a young employee at his brewery to fire a musket four times during the middle of the night, seemingly for the amusement of watching Jean Labatie, the self-important Frenchman in charge of the nearby Fort Orange, panicked into action.

These acts of rebellion were coupled with plenty of arduous endeavor. The Van Vechtens thrived in the New World, and by 1685 their coffers had grown sufficiently for Teunis's grandson Michael to buy a plot of around nine hundred acres in the vicinity of the Raritan River in New Jersey, where he built a large family home. Nearly a century later, the house played a crucial role in the Revolutionary War, when it was willingly loaned by its owner, Derrick Van Vechten, to Quartermaster Nathanael Greene during the Middlebrook campaign against the British in the winter of 1778–79. Derrick Van Vechten had a reputation for throwing first-rate entertainments, and those he gave for Greene did not disappoint. At one soiree a high-spirited George Washington took a shine to the quartermaster's famously beautiful wife. "His Excellency and Mrs. Greene danced upwards of three hours without once sitting down," reported Greene, "a pretty little frisk." A lively, star-studded party in support of a revolutionary cause; Van Vechtens past and future would have been proud.

•

In the eight decades that elapsed after the Revolutionary War, the scope of American civilization drifted decisively westward, and at least one branch of the Van Vechten family drifted with it. By the time Carl Van Vechten was born in 1880, the family name was fast becoming one of the most important in the burgeoning state of Iowa.

In 1877 a fire razed the general store Van Vechten's parents, Charles and Ada, ran in Minneapolis, so they moved south to Cedar Rapids, where Charles's brother Giles had recently opened a bank. Known as the Parlor City because of its reputation for being a well-ordered and respectable community, Cedar Rapids was booming. Although founded in the 1840s, its real genesis moment came in 1859, when the arrival of the railroad transformed what had been a small town of just a few hundred people into an important player in the industrialization of Iowa farming. By the 1870s large grain-processing and meatpacking firms, including Quaker Oats in 1873, had set up in Cedar Rapids, transporting produce to Chicago and beyond in enormous quantities. The town boasted around ten thousand inhabitants when Charles and Ada arrived with the children; by the end of the century it was more than double that figure, making it one of the largest settlements in Iowa and one of the fastest-growing communities in the Midwest.

For industrious men like the Van Vechten brothers, Cedar Rapids held glittering prospects. After working as the cashier in his brother's bank for seven years, Charles struck out on a lucrative career in the insurance industry, an occupation he maintained well into his eighties. Throughout that time he strived hard to maintain a leading presence in the community. The fabric of civic life in Cedar Rapids was sewn together by voluntary associations of spirited individuals committed to the service of God and country, and Charles was involved in many of them; he sat as chairman of the cabinet at the First Universalist Church of Cedar Rapids and was a Mason, a Rotarian, and a member of the Knights Templar. The journalist William Shirer grew up in the Cedar Rapids of the early twentieth century and described it as "churchy, Republican, wholesome," a pithy but accurate sketch of the ordered and genteel society that the elder Van Vechtens helped form.

Carl's arrival into the world came as something of a surprise to his parents. Born on June 17, 1880, he was by far the youngest of Charles and Ada's three children. Emma, their daughter, was thirteen when Carl was born; their son Ralph, already a strapping specimen of all-American masculinity, was nearly eighteen. Just entering middle age and assuming their years of child rearing were fast coming to an end, Van Vechten's parents were, he said, "very surprised to have a visit from the stork," though the new baby was greeted joyously by the entire family.

Ada was besotted with her little boy, whom she regarded as a gift from the heavens. At thirty-nine she savored the pleasures of motherhood that she had been too anxious and inexperienced to enjoy with her first children. She set about recording every moment of Carl's young life as best she could in a journal solely devoted to his first three years. She studied him diligently as his personality developed, noting his burgeoning talents, the flourishing of his soft, cherubic features, and the joy that he brought her. "My little boy's birthday," her entry for June 17, 1882, reads. "Two years old, and oh what happy years they have been." His specialness to Ada peeks through the numerous photographs she had taken of him too. At eighteen months she sat him alone before the camera, posed on a crushed velvet armchair, wearing a black dress with a white lace collar, wisps of his long hair falling over his ears. He was a gorgeous, fat-cheeked baby with brown eyes like little pools of melted chocolate; it is easy to see why Ada found him so adorable. This was one of the first of many photographs that Ada arranged for Carl throughout his childhood, and it was she who introduced him to the camera's unique ability to extract and preserve beauty.

Other members of the family joined Ada in her efforts to make Carl feel precious and worthy of singular attention. During her pregnancy Ada's brother Charlie made a grand sentimental gesture, promising to write a special letter to the new baby every Christmas until he turned twenty-one. It seemed like a good idea at the time, and at first Charlie wrote charming letters about all the marvelous things that Santa might bring and how lucky Carl was to have been born a beautiful baby boy in the United States at a time of peace and plenty. But each year it became harder to find homespun wisdom

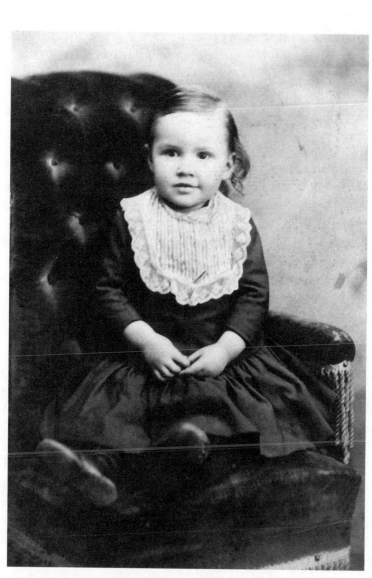

Carl Van Vechten, December 17, 1881

worth committing to paper. Fearful that Carl might feel hurt or rejected, Ada could not bear the idea that her brother should stop the letters, so Charlie was compelled to continue the tradition. By the boy's ninth Christmas, Charlie said, the chore was enough to make a man "tear wildly at his hair and roll his eyes upward in a pitiful way."

Among them, Ada, Charles, and the rest of the family spun around Carl a silken cocoon of genteel comfort. The family home, an elegant but restrained example of the Queen Anne architectural style so fashionable among the wealthy middle class in the late nineteenth century, had been gifted to Van Vechten's parents by Uncle Giles, whose success in banking had helped him build a considerable fortune. Giles's own house was a grand white-brick building with turrets, tall chimneys, and enormous bay windows "surrounded by great oak trees, their spreading branches shading the well-kept lawn." In his 1924 novel, *The Tattooed Countess*, which drew upon his childhood for its setting, Van Vechten evoked Giles's house as a midwestern temple to an age of prosperity, temperance, and moral certainty. Charles never matched his brother's tremendous wealth—worth millions in today's money—but a combination of astute investment and hard work ensured that he and Ada always kept a beautifully furnished home, maintained by a retinue of three or four domestic servants, and Carl of course was treated to the finest of everything.

The family began each day at 7:30 a.m. sharp with a vast hourlong breakfast, the sort of honest, gargantuan meal that drove back the frontier and furred up the arteries all at once. Bowls of fresh fruit and oatmeal preceded a main course of sausages, bacon, eggs, fried steaks, and potatoes in cream, with pancakes, buckwheat, corn, and doughnuts thrown in for good measure, all augmented by pots of steaming tea and coffee and thick milk delivered each morning fresh from the udders of Uncle Giles's Jersey cow. The surrounding Iowan countryside offered a rural paradise for curious children. Immediately outside the town center there was a scraggy patchwork of mills, silos, grain elevators, and the other grimy apparatus of Cedar Rapids's fortune. But beyond that no suburbs, only the Corn Belt: fields and open meadows, lightly pocked by a scattering of small farmsteads among a flourish of brooks, maples, willows, and wildflowers. Van Vechten's connection to this landscape was forged early and remained his whole life. In its rolling, twisting hectares of green and pale yellows that shimmered and rippled in the summer breeze like an incoming tide he saw a deeply undervalued beauty that was "essentially American" and affected in him "a kind of inspiration associated with great rivers, high mountains, or that mighty monster, Ocean," that others revered in more overtly dramatic locations. Old family photographs, some taken by Van Vechten himself, capture long summer days at Indian Creek, five or so miles from town, where he spent hours observing the wildlife, swimming in the warm, glistening waters, and camping out with his brother.

It would be hard to imagine a more indulged child in the state of Iowa. Van Vechten admitted he had probably been spoiled rotten as a boy. As the years passed, the material comforts and Ada's swaddling adoration fostered a self-centered and importunate nature within Carl. His idea of playing with other children was bossing them around, and delayed gratification was an entirely alien concept to him. "I hated interference, objections of any kind," Van Vechten recalled of his childhood, though he could have easily been talking about his adult self. He made that observation in 1921 while looking at a deep scar that ran across his palm, a legacy of the time he grabbed a kitchen knife by the blade from his mother's hand, "in a fury at not compelling her immediate attention."

Perhaps the impatience and egotism that caused his livid outbursts and squawking tantrums are not uncommon in children. The obsessiveness that began to exhibit itself around the age of twelve almost certainly is. It was at this time, during vacations at Uncle Charlie's house in Michigan, that Van Vechten's cousin Roy introduced him to collecting birds' eggs. Roy was a studious young man, a bespectacled teenage oologist whose idea of a fun weekend was shinning up trees to study the nesting patterns of the eastern meadowlark. Taking just one egg from a nest, he maintained, was pointless. Only by taking a clutch—that is, the entire contents of a nest—could one hope to learn anything of value. Back home in Cedar Rapids, Van Vechten followed Roy's lead, not out of intellectual curiosity but rather to satisfy the acquisitiveness that was a fundamental part of his personality. He recalled that "my mother, picturing the despair of the mother bird, begged me to leave at least one egg in each nest." He never did. Often the need to own and control the beautiful things in his orbit was so insistent it overruled all appeals to both heart and head, even when it risked hurting those who loved him the most.

A half century of ardent collecting began with those clutches of eggs. It was, ironically, a birdlike quality, a magpie's irresistible attraction to objects of ornament and beauty. Long after the ardor for birds had wilted, bangles and rings, objets d'art, precious first editions, rare recordings, silk shirts, and brightly colored neckties in their hundreds all became collecting fixations of his. Anything elaborate and exquisite, anything new or novel he scooped into his embrace, as man and boy. Even when he could not justify the expense, he spent extravagantly on the latest things: a Victrola phonograph; a sharp new suit; a sleek portable typewriter. During one of his trips to Europe just prior to the First World War, he procured an object apparently unfamiliar to Americans at the time, a timepiece that instead of resting in a pocket was attached to a dainty leather bracelet and worn around the wrist. Returning from another overseas vacation some years later, he disembarked his ship surrounded by porters hauling his twenty-five pieces of luggage onto the dockside, the spoils of a frenzied shopping tour of the markets and department stores of Paris and London.

Guided by the same acquisitiveness, as a child he gathered a peculiar menagerie of pets: pigeons, thrushes, field mice, canaries, pigs, turtles, chameleons, and, so he claimed as an adult, even an alligator all passed through his protection at one point or another. None of them survived long, and when they died, he was never very bothered. In fact, even the deaths of family members troubled him relatively little as a boy. The passing of his grandmothers, both of whom lived in Cedar Rapids, one of them in his home, caused him no great anguish, and the same was seemingly true when his cousin Roy died tragically young and in blackly ironic circumstances, in an elevator accident in a hospital where he was receiving treatment for an illness. It was not until the age of twenty-five when his mother died that Van Vechten endured the common experiences of bereavement. "Death, up to that time, had meant very little to me," he admitted. "People died, and I didn't seem to have any feeling about it," he said before adding that "I'd begun to think I didn't care whether people died or not."

It is a remarkable admission that illuminates Van Vechten's understanding of his place in the world and his connection to others. He was a solitary little boy with a striking capacity for self-reliance, and as the only child in a large, extended family of doting adults he was made to feel precious and unique. Even his siblings coddled him. Because of the age gap, Ralph and Emma were more like a devoted aunt and uncle than a brother and sister with whom to squabble and compete for their parents' affection. As a consequence, from an early age he valued those around him, and especially other children, less for their friendship and more for the purpose they might serve in allowing him to pursue his interests. Roy of course was useful for his collecting tips. Others gained favor by patiently sitting through performances of his model theater or posing for photographs he took with the family's box camera. If children would not act as he wished them to, there was always some new fad to amuse him or some new thing to collect and possess and invariably an older relative on hand to provide it.

Nevertheless, during his adult years Van Vechten often found cause to recast his indulgent and peaceful upbringing as deathly stifling. In the 1910s and 1920s, such lamentations were a common cry of modernist writers and artists. Theirs was a generation of pioneers, according to their shared mythology; the herald of a new age in binary opposition to the United States of the nineteenth century, which had been a dry and dusty landscape inhabited by creatures fossilized under the weight of bland materialism and puritanical instincts, the word "puritan" often decoupled from its theological definition and used as a shorthand for anything that seemed prudish and old-fashioned. In her 1926 biography of her husband and fellow writer, George Cram Cook, Susan Glaspell declared that the Iowa they both experienced in the 1890s "was not civilized. It knew nothing about success in life itself as apart from success in profession or business." Cook himself, according to Glaspell, identified a "Puritanic distrust of pleasure and beauty" in the young people he encountered in Iowa City around this time.

Those observations could have been lifted directly from Van Vechten's description of Cedar Rapids in his novel *The Tattooed Countess*, in which he ridicules the people he grew up among as either vicious gossips or well-meaning bores stuck in a Victorian cage of brittle and contrived manners. According to the novel's teenage antihero, a clear facsimile of the young Van Vechten, his fellow townsfolk were hideously repressed, unable "to be themselves, to do what they want to do, to live for love or whatever it is they want to live for." Undoubtedly a germ of truth existed at the heart of the caricature. "It was the day of the quilting party," as one who lived through the era described it, "of the Sunday promenade in the cemetery, of buggy-riding, of the ice-cream festival and the spelling bee," and polite society in places like Cedar Rapids often betrayed an acute suspicion of the pleasures enjoyed in the surging metropolises. The late-nineteenth-century craze for phosphate soda fountains and ice-cream parlors, for example, came about largely as godly alternatives to the saloon, and the extravagant *Wild West* shows of Buffalo Bill helpfully sanitized the history of the western frontier, reminding town dwellers of the virtuous individuals who had tamed the wilderness so future generations might enjoy its bounty. What was missing from Van Vechten's sketch of the Midwest that he had known were the subtle but insistent currents of radicalism that washed over him since birth, courtesy of his parents, neither of whom bore any relation to the vapid, small-minded hicks of *The Tattooed Countess*.

His mother may have been guilty of mollycoddling her youngest child, but she was in almost all other ways a formidable and inspirational woman. Cedar Rapids got its first public library thanks to her, when she seized on an initiative launched by Andrew Carnegie to partially fund the building of public libraries for communities across the United States. The cultivation of the mind as a means of individual and social progress was a principle very dear to Ada. Before her marriage to Charles, she had studied at Kalamazoo College, where she became a committed supporter of women's suffrage decades before the cause gained its first flourish of respectable, mainstream prominence. In later life Van Vechten suggested that during her time at Kalamazoo his mother had become friends with Lucy

Stone, the pathbreaking suffragist who shocked the United States by refusing to take her husband's name after marriage. More likely, Ada befriended the similarly named Lucinda Hinsdale Stone, who, along with her husband, James Stone, turned Kalamazoo into one of the country's first coeducational colleges. Hinsdale Stone acquired the sobriquet "Mother of Clubs" because of her pivotal role in creating institutions such as the Ladies Library Association, an attempt to advance the issue of women's rights through education. The influence clearly rubbed off on Ada. Along with Giles's wife, Emma, who at one point served as the president of the Women's Club of America, she established various groups for local women to join, exposing them to issues beyond the stereotypical female concerns of homemaking and child welfare.

Also important to Ada were the civil rights of black people, a passion she shared with Charles, and which they both pressed upon their children. Among the Van Vechtens' small retinue of domestic servants were two African-Americans—a laundry maid and a gardener—whom the children were instructed to address as Mrs. Sercey and Mr. Oliphant, rather than by their first names, as would have been customary. This was no slight eccentricity. Even in a community in which support for the party and causes of Lincoln was solid, as was the case in Cedar Rapids, it was a bold statement, which must have seemed willfully perverse to conservative neighbors. In 1909 Charles went much further, teaming up with a young black teacher called Laurence Clifton Jones to found the Piney Woods School for Negro Children in Mississippi, investing thousands of dollars of his own money. Charles believed that he had a moral duty to use his money for philanthropic ends, reforming the world around him by educating minds. He did this in large ways and small. In the 1940s Van Vechten still had a gift his father gave him on his eleventh birthday, a copy of *Cudjo's Cave*, an abolitionist novel by J. T. Trowbridge. Van Vechten eventually donated that same book to his own philanthropic mission designed to combat racism, the James Weldon Johnson Collection at Yale University. His father's influence was slow-burning, however, and despite Charles's best efforts, he could not completely insulate his son from the misguided attitudes of the day. To his embarrassment, Van Vechten recalled that as a young child he avoided the touch of anyone with very dark skin, afraid their color might leave a stain on his pale skin, like black ink spilled on a white cotton tablecloth.

Underpinning all their civic action was Charles and Ada's Christian Universalist faith, which Van Vechten conceded shaped his family's life in subtle but profound ways. The core Universalist conviction that all humans, irrespective of their conduct on earth, will ultimately find reconciliation with an ever-forgiving and beneficent God had significant implications on the development of nineteenth-century social and political ideas in the United States, allowing all manner of radical causes to flourish under its wing. In the debate about women's rights, the Universalist Church blazed a trail by making the suffragist Olympia Brown an ordained minister in 1863. Around the same time, some members of the Universalist Church were also involved in operating the Underground Railroad, which helped slaves escape the South to claim their freedom in the North. Above all, Universalists maintained a strong faith in the essential good within all people and in the individual's capacity to positively affect the world around him. From his parents' measured religious philosophy Van Vechten learned early that having the courage to be different was a laudable, if not sacred, quality.

It was a vital lesson too because as he grew, Van Vechten felt his differentness from those around him with increasing acuity. Physically he stood out from the crowd by his early teens. The plump softness of infancy had been stretched into a tall, ungainly frame, and his pinched, downturned mouth now gave his face a look of severity. And then there were the front teeth that became a trademark in his years of fame and infamy: huge, angular, misshapen, and apparently resistant to dental intervention of any sort. But the oddness was much more than skin deep. While other boys spent their playtime as cowboys and Indians, or reenacting Yankee victories in the Civil War, Van Vechten's obsessiveness was turned inward, constructing a cavernous interior world of music and literature.

As an adult he claimed that before puberty he had made his way through *Tristram Shandy* and the complete works of Shakespeare

Carl Van Vechten, aged three, with his parents, Ada and Charles (seated), his brother, Ralph, and his sister, Emma, November 7, 1883

and Ibsen, had adored Beethoven, and could play Mozart concertos on the piano. He proudly told friends that because Cedar Rapids was such an uncultured place his musical education was autodidactic. Nobody else in town even knew what a concerto was, while he was mastering concertos through sheet music, he snorted priggishly. Even his brother, Ralph, who played the violin well, was not "sophisticated enough to know that string quartets existed."

These were shameless exaggerations. It was true that he had obvious musical talent, a fact that helped him greatly in his later career as a music critic, and was also a voracious reader, but he was no child prodigy. As often with Van Vechten's tall stories, there is an important, greater truth tucked beneath the tissue of embellishments. Being a sophisticate among the hayseeds was a crucial part of the story that Van Vechten told about himself over the years, the central pillar upon which his adult personality was constructed. In an unpublished autobiographical sketch written in his early twenties, he claimed that by the age of ten his love for music and literature was so intense and all-consuming that it made him acutely aware that he was fundamentally unlike the other children in Cedar Rapids—especially the boys. The essential differentness he felt because of his artistic passions was a metaphor for another awakening he experienced around the same time but that as a child he neither understood nor would have been permitted to talk about: that of his nascent attraction to other males.

In the environment of the 1880s and 1890s it is easy to see how the two could become linked in his mind. The arts were often considered feminine concerns, while healthy American boys were expected to have the backwoodsman at their core; Tom Sawyer was closer to the model of precocious male youth than Mozart. Van Vechten wrote in *The Tattooed Countess* that Gilded Age society did not understand "boys with imagination and the creative impulse; they are looked upon with vague disgust and suspicion." Even Uncle Charlie, who shared his appreciation of literature, teased him a little about his artistic temperament, warning him in a Christmas letter not to waste too much of his time on poetry. Far better, he ragged, to channel his creative energies into the great new American art form of advertising slogans. "They have some practical common sense in them," Charlie said. "Everybody reads them. <u>And they pay</u>. What line of Shakespeare do you think ever had such wealth creating possibilities within its compass as the immortal, 'Good morning. Have you used Pears' Soap?'" Business was a manly pursuit, but the arts needed to be treated with caution, on the whole best left to girls, sissies, and foreigners.

At the age of eleven or twelve Van Vechten witnessed in the crypt of the Grace Episcopal Church in Cedar Rapids a local sixteen-year-old boy called Herbie Newell perform the skirt dance, a variation on the cancan first made famous by English music-hall star Lottie Collins. In his recollection of the performance the specter of sexual awakening hangs in the ether. He had never seen anything like it: Newell, dressed as a woman, "excelled in female impersonation," gracefully kicking up the "thirty or forty yards of soft material" that swirled around his waist. Throughout his personal and professional lives, performances of dance and female impersonation were two of the key ways in which Van Vechten explored his sexual attraction to men. Both created brash and unapologetic visions of maleness transported beyond the gender norms of the early 1900s, and dance had the bonus of providing a socially acceptable means of publicly admiring the male body. Newell's dance was expressive and unconventional, a strange contortion of masculinity. It was the moment when Van Vechten's appetite for creative expression, his inchoate sexual feelings, and his sense of being unusual soldered together as a single, inseparable entity. Like him, Newell was clearly different from most other boys and did not belong in Cedar Rapids; he was "headed for the Broadway stage and stardom."

As it turned out, Herbie Newell never made it to New York. In fact, the closest thing that Cedar Rapids had to Broadway stars for Van Vechten to dote on were the Cherry Sisters, five chaste, teetotal, tone-deaf siblings whose bizarrely awful musical act elevated them to the status of national celebrities for a brief moment at the end of the nineteenth century. The sisters moved to Cedar Rapids as adults, having grown up in neighboring Marion and spent twenty years touring their execrable self-written material, apparently oblivious that the huge audiences they drew came mainly to laugh at their ineptitude and po-faced self-delusion. In the big cities of the East they became a novelty hit because audiences saw in them all the worst stereotypes of the Midwest: pious, parochial rubes, uncultured and living in the past. It was those stereotypes that Van Vechten perpetuated in later life, casting the Midwest as a cultural desert, diametrically opposed to the vibrant and fertile cities in which he made his name as a cosmopolitan trailblazer.

The scene of the sisters' most infamous performance was on home turf, in Cedar Rapids's Greene's Opera House, run by the father of Louise Henderson, one of Van Vechten's childhood friends. The next day's *Cedar Rapids Gazette* featured a devastating review. "Imagine two hundred leading citizens jumping to their feet, waving hats, umbrellas, brooms and handkerchiefs, reaching toward the stage and shouting themselves hoarse in mockery of approval at the appearance before them of the greenest, gawkiest females that ever faced the footlights, and doing nothing but tramping out on the stage with a basket of flowers and with less grace than an elephant would eat soup." Clearly the patrons of Greene's Opera House were accustomed to far more accomplished acts. In fact, when the Cherry Sisters made their bows there, the place was an Iowan cultural institution, an eighteen-hundred-seat theater built in 1880 as a booster-ish statement of Cedar Rapids's growing wealth and an attempt to connect the town to the cultural current of the rest of the nation. No full-length opera was ever performed there, of course; the name was a misnomer popular of theaters of the time, and the ornate decor similarly attempted to emit an air of cultivation that bore little relation to the bills of pantomime and polite variety that were its stock-in-trade. Regardless of its clumsy pretensions, this was Van Vechten's favorite place in the whole of Cedar Rapids, a refuge of fantasy and magic in which exciting new worlds animated before his eyes and were crucial in developing his artistic sensibilities.

Greene's had opened at a propitious moment. For much of the nineteenth century, theater in the United States had been regarded as either a snobbish interest of a tiny elite in the East or a low, immoral distraction for single men, not far removed from the brothel and the saloon. In the 1880s vaudeville emerged: variety theater as professionally run as any of the great industries and designed to make the theater "as 'homelike' as it was possible to make it," in the words of the impresario B. F. Keith, so that it "would directly appeal to the support of ladies and children." Cedar Rapids's location as a railroad hub meant that it instantly became one of the key stops on the new theater circuit, though not always one that the performers relished playing. Cedar Rapids's audiences had a reputation for giving instant and bracingly honest critiques. When the Marx Brothers performed a skit based on *The Spirit of '76* at another Cedar Rapids venue, the Majestic Theatre, there were boos and catcalls from swaths of the audience, incensed by what they considered an insult to the flag. The young Van Vechten was nowhere near as discriminating. During his formative years a litany of theatrical talent whizzed through the town for one-night-only performances, sprinkling a film of stardust over Cedar Rapids as it went. From his favored vantage point of the balcony at Greene's, Van Vechten saw many of vaudeville's biggest stars, as well as celebrated names from outside the variety tradition. Richard Mansfield appeared as the caddish dandy Beau Brummell, Lillian Russell in *American Beauty*, and Otis Skinner in *Romeo and Juliet*; all three were celebrated names who packed theaters in New York and Chicago with ease. Van Vechten devoured everything the producers served up, from Shakespeare to minstrelsy; from Stephen Foster and John Philip Sousa to the productions of the American Extravaganza Company, which put on spectacular *Arabian Nights*–style pantomimes with evocative titles such as *Fantasia* and *Superba*.

Beyond the pure escapism, Greene's offered a glimpse of another America far away from the cornfields and church socials of Iowa, one brightly illustrated by a collage of multiethnic cultures and propelled by the brutal dynamism of urban life that was swiftly enveloping the nation. Young Carl saw a production of *A Trip to Chinatown*, a hit musical that revolved around fast-living members of the Bohemian Club, wealthy San Francisco bachelors who patronized fancy restaurants and dallied with young single ladies. Despite being set in California, the show featured a popular song, entitled "The Bowery," that helped establish the infamy of New York's vice districts in the late 1800s. Sissieretta Jones, an African-American singer otherwise known as Black Patti after the Italian soprano Adelina Patti, appeared with the Black Patti Troubadours, a revue company of dozens of black singers and dancers and acrobats, one of whom was a then unknown Bert Williams. There was even a demonstration of Edison's revolutionary Vitascope motion picture technology at which Van Vechten and a thousand other astonished patrons watched a Native American tribal ceremony, a round from Jim Corbett's victorious bout against Charley Mitchell in Florida, water cascading down New Jersey's Paterson Great Falls, and Loie Fuller dancing on the Parisian stage, the wonders of modern machinery summoning them all to appear under the same roof.

Van Vechten documented his passions in scrapbooks—another collecting obsession that stayed with him for life—spending hours filling their pages with magazine cuttings, theater programs, newspaper reviews, and a vast collection of cigarette card photographs of the biggest stars of the day. Actresses rather than actors, enchanting in their bustles and gowns, their hair pinned elaborately and their cheeks dusted with rouge, held his fascination. The charismatic comedian Della Fox was a particular favorite, but there were also less conventional heroines (or heroes), such as Richard Harlow, a hulking two-hundred-pound female impersonator, further testament to Van Vechten's interest in men who refused to be *men*. The scrapbooks were his attempt to possess beauty in much the same way that a lepidopterist pins butterflies to a board. Held in stasis between the covers of his books, the luminaries of the theater who swept into town never really left: they and the glamour they exuded were with Carl, always.

As a teenager he photographed his own moments of theatrical fantasy, getting friends to re-create poses from magazines or shows he had seen. He had Louise Henderson stand on a chair on his back porch, pretending to be an opera singer, while another female friend lay among flowers like Shakespeare's Juliet laid to rest. These were the adolescent prototypes of the famous Van Vechten studio portraits, studied and deliberate encapsulations of beauty and talent. As child and adult Van Vechten used his camera lens to eschew the banal and ugly, focusing on perfect little moments of make-believe to be captured for posterity.

In those sepia images, and in the dark of Greene's auditorium, an intangible presence reverberated like a new elemental force; through the taffeta drapery of the Gilded Age, the bright lights of a new world flickered before Van Vechten's eyes. Very soon the drapes would be torn down and the illumination would be total.

TWO

The Cosmopolitan Standard of Virtue

● ●

Eighteen ninety-three was a year of panic and exhilaration. In February an unprecedented credit crunch triggered the most devastating economic crisis in the nation's history, closing five hundred banks and destroying the livelihoods of millions. Weeks later Chicago, the great financial success story of the late 1800s, defied the gloom by opening the World's Columbian Exposition, an electrified jamboree of American power and potential to celebrate the four hundredth anniversary of Columbus's landing. The fair entertained millions but ended in horror and tragedy, doubling as the site of the assassination of Mayor Carter Harrison, Sr., and the grisly deeds of H. H. Holmes, the United States' first documented serial killer. By fall any Gilded Age illusions that Americans could stroll blithely into the modern world shielded by a parasol of genteel manners and Christian values were blown away.

The summer before the exposition Van Vechten, aged twelve, visited Chicago for the first time with his father. He had never encountered a great industrial city, and his first impressions were mixed. He was repulsed by its crowded, dirty streets, unlike anything he was used to in Cedar Rapids or Grand Rapids, the largest towns he had experienced before then. When his father took him away from the city's beating heart and out onto the cleaner, calmer waters of Lake Michigan, he saw the outline of the exposition buildings in mid-construction and thought them among the most wonderful things he had ever seen. He wrote his mother about them and also about the great traffic of tall steamships transporting lumber along the Chicago River. It was, he gasped, a truly beautiful sight. What he discovered in that trip was the hustle, dynamism, and spring-heeled ambition for which Chicago had become world renowned. In a grandiloquent echo of Van Vechten's own observations, the muckraking journalist Lincoln Steffens captured the atmosphere best when he declared Chicago "First in violence, deepest in dirt; loud, lawless, unlovely, ill-smelling, irreverent, new; an overgrown gawk of a village, the 'tough' among cities, a spectacle for the nation—I give Chicago no quarter and Chicago asks for none."

Van Vechten's fascination with Chicago intensified a year after his first visit, when his parents took him back to experience the exposition, the event that sealed Chicago's reputation as a place of dizzying excess. The exposition had a huge impact on Americans of the time, hailed by many as the greatest spectacle ever seen on American soil. For visitors, like Van Vechten, from smaller towns in the Midwest, the delights of the exposition offered an opportunity to feel part of the nation's growing international eminence, in an event that would command attention around the globe. Most felt themselves lucky to be able to attend at all, but Van Vechten was allowed to luxuriate in all the wonders of the exposition over several days, another treat provided by his parents' deep pockets.

Certainly there were enough attractions to make repeat visits worthwhile. At a cost of ten million dollars, the exposition swallowed over six hundred acres, turning swaths of barren marshland into an oasis of wonderment, an American Eden, not in the lush tranquillity of a garden but on the crude outskirts of a metropolis. Without doubt, its crowning glory was the White City, a custom-built district of sumptuous boulevards lined with white stucco buildings, the very ones that Van Vechten had gazed at from his boat on Lake Michigan, each of which housed a different array of mesmerizing exhibits. The Electricity Building demonstrated a zeal for technocratic solutions to the world's problems; the Manufactures and Liberal Arts Building evinced high-minded but practical sophistication; the Woman's Building reflected an earnest commitment to moral purity. There was no trace here of Burnham and Root's audacious skyscrapers that were Chicago's signature architectural style: all of the White City's buildings were reverent Romanesque constructions, a bold physical statement that Chicago belonged to an ancient tradition of progress, achievement, and beauty.

Naturally enough, the family was keen to introduce Van Vechten to the White City, that beacon of pure-minded sophistication. In the Palace of Fine Arts he was marched around the galleries to look at canvas after canvas of Greek and Roman mythological scenes and idyllic landscapes of pastoral calm and order. This was meant to be where Americans received a definitive lesson in what constituted good art and good taste; usually something European and godly were the fundamentals. The painting Van Vechten best remembered fitted into that category: *Invading Cupid's Realm*, a scene of a half-naked young woman being attacked by a group of cupids, some firing arrows toward her chest, while others pull on the flowing skirt that hangs loosely from her hips. The painting was by William-Adolphe Bouguereau, an academic French artist then revered by the artistic establishment and reviled by the impressionists. It has been suggested that Bouguereau intended the work to be an allegory for the metaphorical violence being wrought upon him and his peers by an impudent younger generation of French artists, led by his onetime pupil Henri Matisse. It would not have pleased the custodians of good taste to know that the pubescent Van Vechten's eye was caught not by the painting's classical representation of beauty but because "until then I had seen comparatively few pictures of naked women." Not for the first or last time, a sexual frisson had defined his moment of artistic revelation.

Indeed, all of Van Vechten's key memories of the exposition were linked to the illicit thrill of seeing naked flesh, usually forbidden but sanctioned here in many forms. Outside the refinement of the White City, the exposition resembled a fantastical county fair. In true Chicago style, this was the first world's fair to dedicate an entire precinct to entertainments without high-minded objectives, just thrills and empty escapism, set in an area dubbed the Midway Plaisance. The Midway featured an array of amusements from the crudity of greased poles and coconut shies to the extravagance of the world's first Ferris wheel. There was no space for indigenous American music in the White City—only Europe's classical traditions were permitted there—but it was everywhere on the Midway. Sousa's marching bands were a huge hit, and many visitors got their first exposure to ragtime. This was the folk culture of the American city: democratic, uncomplicated pleasure seeking, packaged in glitz and sold for five cents per ride. Along with twenty-seven million other visitors, Van Vechten was seduced and spent hours there wandering through the spectacles. The attractions that burrowed their way deepest into his memory were the exotic dancers who thrust and swiveled their hips, twisting shawls provocatively around their exposed shoulders and naked midriffs in a way "novel to most Americans of the period," he recalled, "and absolutely enthralling to me. The lady who could make an apple bound and bounce about by the movements of her abdomen especially delighted me." He was far from alone. The dancers, supposedly from places such as Java, Turkey, and Egypt, and whose risqué performances were justified on the pretext of providing an education in anthropology, were the talk of the fair. One journalist, unable to conceal his excitement, advised potential visitors that "you will see the female abdomen execute such feats as never before entered your wildest and most unrestrained imaginations to conceive." For Van Vechten, it was a second moment, shortly after Herbie Newell's skirt dance, in which sex and dance were fused, although this time there was nothing coded or elliptical in the performance; this was a blatant expression of carnality.

The significance of those first exposures to Chicago in 1892 and 1893 poke through in an unfinished autobiographical novel that Van Vechten wrote in his early twenties, a piece of juvenilia of negligible literary merit, in which he first set down the events of his life through the mythological lens that he employed thereafter. Although much of it cannot be unquestioningly accepted as a factual record of his early years, it seems emotionally authentic, capturing his idea of himself in relation to the world around him. In the first chapter of his tale he describes himself as an extravagantly gifted child who was drawn by fate to leave his midwestern home for the rowdy charms of Chicago, the mecca in which he would fulfill his urban destiny. It was self-absorbed hyperbole, of course, yet the rhetoric does suggest that his discovery of Chicago was a turning point, firing his imagination and giving him a tangible focus for his daydreams of life beyond

Cedar Rapids. New York sounded magical from all he had read about it, but he had never stepped foot on Broadway like his idols who dashed in and out of town on the railway, or on Fifth Avenue, like Carnegie, Rockefeller, or the other names that littered his father's copies of *The Atlantic Monthly*. He had, however, experienced Chicago, seen its filth-encrusted streets, heard the screeches of its streetcars, and witnessed the warp and weft of urban culture weaving one between the other, the unthinking pleasures of the Midway and the highbrow ambition of the White City, each as fascinating as the other.

Stalking his teenage years, the vision of Chicago deepened his withdrawal into a world created from his imagination and the scraps of insight that books afforded. Out went the distant childhood fantasies of *The Swiss Family Robinson* and *Arabian Nights*; in came contemporary adventures, animating an urban universe of conflict, speed, and excitement. *Confessions of a Young Man*, George Moore's scabrous account of city life, and the witty provocations of George Bernard Shaw's *Plays: Pleasant and Unpleasant* dropped into his world like incendiaries fizzing from the sky, setting his mind alight with the possibilities of an existence that spurned Victorian probity for art, self-expression, and the freedoms of the city.

A life like that could not have been pursued in Cedar Rapids—not openly at least. The older he got, the more Van Vechten came to believe that the town was not governed by gentility, honor, and respectability, as it wanted to believe, but by shame and hypocrisy. It was not, he thought, that the people in Cedar Rapids were any less lustful, crude, or imperfect than the people he had read about in books, merely that they chose to hide their true selves behind a facade. Increasingly, he became aware of extramarital affairs glossed over and vices indulged under the cover of darkness. His own brother, Ralph, had once been involved in what Van Vechten described years later as the town's "fast life," caught up in a passionate affair with Mahala Dutton, a vivacious epicurean who refused to behave like a demure lady of narrow interests and tepid emotions. After Ralph's death, in 1927, Dutton told Van Vechten that his brother had lived "a frightfully stupid life," chasing career success and money rather than the emotional honesty that had always been her guiding principle.

Van Vechten adored Dutton for her attitude toward life, and she was the closest thing he had to a role model during his teens, the first in a long line of flamboyant women to capture his imagination and shape his unconventional personality. His parents may have been remarkably freethinking in certain ways, but the significance they attached to maintaining an impeccable public reputation through the accumulation of wealth and status within Cedar Rapids made them frightfully conservative in his eyes. Dutton, one of the few prominent women in town of whom his mother did not approve, who was not "quite respectable enough," in his words, to be admitted into the clubs that Ada established, conducted herself in a very different manner. Respectability was never Dutton's concern: she was decadent, glamorous, and theatrical; she believed that attending to one's needs and desires was the primary business of life, and she never seemed to care when her affairs or her modish fashion sense set tongues wagging.

Aside from Dutton, female companionship was a constant part of Van Vechten's teenage years. His closest friend was Anna Snyder, a highly intelligent Gibson Girl of glacial temperament who shared his love of music and literature as well as his dissatisfaction with the emotional narrowness of life in Cedar Rapids, and though there was something faintly romantic about their connection, during this period it was entirely chaste. That his adolescent relationship with Anna, or any other girl, never blossomed into anything more than friendship intensified his feeling that he was somehow different from those around him. He felt only the weakest sense of physical attraction to girls. Even thinking of females as belonging to a different sex seemed strange, but he was unsure of why that might be. Neither at school nor at home were any of the facts of life explained to him, and he had not learned about sex in the tentatively hands-on way that many boys did, the way Ralph had done: finding a "high-spirited" girl with whom one could "twitch a garter, and probably go further," as the writer Henry Seidel Canby remembered the convention of the day.

Twitching garters was about as familiar to Van Vechten as rustling cattle. He began to exhibit on the outside the jumbled feelings of difference, superiority, and rebellion gestating on the inside, acquiring a wardrobe of tight-fitting clothes, growing his fingernails long, and cultivating a demeanor of aloofness that consciously marked him out as a misfit. The rakish appearance of the disaffected youth at the center of *The Tattooed Countess* was based on his own trademark outfit: "a brown derby hat, a chocolate-shaded coat with padded shoulders, very tight tan trousers, a very high, stiff collar with an Ascot tie, and pointed, patent-leather boots," and with long fingernails protruding from his starched cuffs. Dressed in his finest attire, he found being in front of the camera as enjoyable as being behind it and he developed the pose that he re-created hundreds of times over the decades, the one he used to communicate the mythology he wove around him: his mouth gripped shut, teeth hidden from view; his anvil of a jawbone jutting out defiantly; his stare fixed and predatory, like a tiger waiting to pounce. Plenty of teenagers acquire a shell of physical vanity and narcissism; Van Vechten never shook loose of his. In the 1950s he told one friend that he suspected that he had first dallied with cameras because he so adored being photographed, and fancied the idea of spending his time taking pictures of himself.

To most of his classmates he must have seemed deeply odd. In his unpublished autobiographical sketches he wrote that a group of girls at his high school gossiped about him, through giggles and sideways glances. He refrained from stating explicitly what about him they found so amusing, but the implication was that his effeminate strangeness identified him as a "sissy"—nothing like his brawny elder brother—and therefore an object of ridicule. The Van Vechten of later years was strident and unapologetic in his camp eccentricities and paraded his unconventionality. At this vulnerable stage in life that was much harder to do. More than anything he craved escape to Chicago, the city of his waking dreams, where he figured he would find other people like him. Eventually, he got his wish when he secured a place to study at the University of Chicago in 1899.

•

Coming to Chicago as a single young man, rather than as an adolescent under the guidance of his parents, Van Vechten discovered a city of even more distant extremes than the Columbian Exposition had revealed. At the end of the nineteenth century nowhere better represented the hopes and fears for the American future than Chicago. Around the world it had become famous for its love of business and its bluster and drive, and infamous for the endemic corruption that infused every aspect of its existence. To the journalists and novelists who tried to capture its excesses, here was a city that made Dickensian London look quaint. Fears about rampant prostitution, buccaneer capitalists, white slavery, black street gangs, and the collapse of public morals—what the Chicago novelist Theodore Dreiser famously called "the cosmopolitan standard of virtue"—gripped the city. Both social scientists and evangelical preachers urged Chicago to tackle its dissipations: the former through reform; the latter through salvation. "In no other city of the world," Van Vechten noted some years later, "is such anxiety manifested for the welfare of the soul," although it was not a topic he devoted much thought to. In the seven eventful years he lived there, he saw all possible sides of Chicago life but never showed the faintest interest in the great moral debates that dominated public discourse.

Perhaps his own religious education partly explains his lack of interest. The Universalist belief that all humans will be eventually reconciled with God irrespective of their conduct on earth seemed to translate itself in Van Vechten's mind into a form of moral complacency, a laissez-faire attitude to life and its problems that was subsequently amplified by the cynical detachment of the decadent authors he read in his early twenties, Oscar Wilde most notably. To his parents, of course, Universalism provided a profound optimism about man's potential for doing good in the world, but they instructed their children to view the fervor of the Third Awakening—the name given to the evangelical revival that swept American cities during Van Vechten's youth—with hostility and suspicion. When Van Vechten was taken to Chicago for the first time in 1892, he wrote his mother about an incident on a train when his father fell into conversation with a fellow passenger. The topic of religion was somehow raised, and the man mentioned that he happened to be a Baptist.

Van Vechten assumed that this revelation would be enough for his father to bring the conversation to an end and was surprised when Charles did not do so. In public Charles was able to tactfully mask his opinions for the sake of social concord, a skill his youngest son never mastered, but in the privacy of his home he taught his children to deride religious zealotry.

Van Vechten may not have been interested in the struggle for Chicago's soul, but by enrolling in the University of Chicago he became an unwitting participant in it. The influential reformer Jane Addams believed that Chicago's greatest failing was its inability to channel the spirit of adventure of its huge single male population into high art and away from the city's profusion of commercialized leisure and popular entertainment, "all that is gaudy and sensual . . . the flippant street music, the highly colored theater posters, the trashy love stories, the feathered hats, the cheap heroics of the revolvers displayed in the pawn-shop windows."

The university was one of a number of formidable cultural institutions opened in the 1890s designed to edify young minds just as Addams urged. In his opening semester Van Vechten could have been a poster child for the movement. Within weeks of his arrival he saw his first opera, Charles Gounod's *Faust*, starring Nellie Melba at the Auditorium, the zenith of Chicago's cultural establishment and, for the rest of his college days, the chief venue of his education in classical music. The Auditorium was the home of both the Chicago Opera as well as the Chicago Symphony Orchestra, and the New York Metropolitan Opera brought one production there each season, starring some of the finest international talents. To be surrounded by music of this type and quality was Van Vechten's dream come true. Barely a week passed throughout his four years of college when he did not attend several recitals, concerts, or opera performances. In particular the vivid, all-encompassing spectacle of the opera burrowed its way into his heart, though the high cost of frequent attendance meant he occasionally took to the stage as a supernumerary, standing silently at the back of a scene as a Roman soldier or a toiling peasant. This was not exactly a regular way of hearing the opera, but the Auditorium's ambitious attempts to rival the reputation of New York's Metropolitan Opera meant there was often a need for supernumeraries to fill the stage in its lavish productions. It was a great compromise for Van Vechten too. He found more pleasure in watching others perform than in performing himself, but being close to the first-rate talents who appeared at the Auditorium thrilled him, as if the pages of one of his scrapbooks had come to life around him.

The kinetic force driving Chicago's thriving music scene was the German-born conductor Theodore Thomas. An unapologetic elitist of the highest order, Thomas sacralized European high culture and believed that great art must by definition be *difficult* art. In the Auditorium, his audiences would get what they needed, not what they wanted. Chicago's taste-shaping magazine *The Dial* approved. "If you do not like it now," it said in reference to Thomas's insistence on playing the unpopular Wagner, "pray that you may learn to like it, for the defect is yours." Dictatorial snob though he may have been, it was thanks to Thomas that Van Vechten was introduced to a host of innovative modern composers, including Wagner, Dvořák, and Richard Strauss, obscure names to most Americans of the day, but very familiar to Van Vechten when barely into his twenties. The advanced state of his musical knowledge, as well as Thomas's notion that classical music was an exceptional art that required hard work and self-sacrifice in order to be properly appreciated, fitted perfectly with Van Vechten's sense of his specialness, a feeling that was gradually swallowing his entire sense of self. In a creative writing assignment, English being the one class he made any effort in during his undistinguished college career, Van Vechten wrote a short story titled "Unfinished Symphony," in which a sweet, uncomplicated young woman called Marian Ormesby pretends to like classical music in order to win the heart of the cultured and urbane Harvey Jerman, a thinly veiled self-portrait of Van Vechten. For a time Harvey is enchanted with Marian, delighted to have found a female companion capable of sharing his passions and his understanding of the emotional complexities of great art. But when Marian decides she can continue the charade no longer and reveals that her love of music has been a ruse, the spell is broken, their bond immediately dissolved; it was the allure of Marian's apparent cultivation that ensnared Harvey rather than the girl's looks or personality. It was how Van

Vechten saw his place in the world: not one of the regular people but a member of a special breed whose lives are inextricably bound to art.

Though the adolescent feelings of differentness and superiority calcified, the environment of a big city college helped Van Vechten shed some of the awkward aloofness of his teenage years. Surrounded by people with similar interests, he made friends quickly and even felt some excitement at the prospect of joining the Omega chapter of Psi Upsilon, one of the most prestigious fraternities at the university. Its members "came from the leading families around Chicago," according to the fraternity's official annals, but also had a reputation for creating a public nuisance. In 1899 the famed Chicago satirist George Ade published "The Fable of the Copper and the Jovial Undergrads" in the *Chicago Record*, depicting Chicago fraternity men as "drunken ruffians" in the guise of "well-bred young men," prone to smashing windows, starting fights in the street, and insulting policemen. This was not Van Vechten's world at all, but he felt the need to join Psi Upsilon to please his father, who was keen that he should become a well-connected, clubbable man of the world, as the other Van Vechten men were. Rather predictably, by the start of his senior year Van Vechten's commitment to the fraternity had waned decisively. He enjoyed the impressive banquets shared with chapters from other colleges, but when one of the boys put ice cubes in his bed or played some other jape, his enthusiasm dissipated, the practical jokes feeling uncomfortably like bullying.

However, close contact with young men did hold certain attractions for a sexually curious boy away from home for the first time. In the fraternity house, he became especially close to Edwin Boehmer, a slender, slightly fragile-looking boy with soft, feminine features and wavy blond hair that peaked in an unruly quiff. He and Van Vechten spent many evenings together, sharing jugs of foaming pilsner in the Little Vienna district and sitting up late by the fire in the fraternity house to talk about sex. Being the more experienced of the two, Boehmer did most of the talking, Van Vechten providing an eager audience for his tales of petting and fornication. Things may have progressed further than gossip and dirty stories too. In his perfunctory diary entries Van Vechten notes the numerous occasions on which Boehmer stayed the night in his room, a device used later in his life as shorthand for a sexual assignation. Whether they were lovers is unclear, but the intimacy they established strongly suggests this was more than plain friendship. Boehmer was not the only boy who caught Van Vechten's eye either. He confessed to his diary that he was in love with a fellow student by the name of Wid Norton, though the crush was apparently never acted upon.

It was a sexual awakening, but not one limited to his homosexual urges. At exactly the same time that he explored his interest in men for the first time, he embarked upon a number of embryonic romances with women. Most of it was chaste and sweetly innocent. He accompanied young ladies in voluminous evening gowns to formals, the dances organized by the university as a means of regulating social contact between the sexes, and enjoyed going on picnics and walks with coed classmates in Jackson Park. At this point he was too young, inexperienced, and sheltered to know exactly how his sexual identity was configured, and neither does it appear to have been something that bothered him very much. To judge from the scraps afforded by his diaries, letters, and unpublished creative writing, Van Vechten spent little time wrestling with his feelings but simply followed wherever the path of self-exploration led him, supremely confident in the rightness of his instincts.

Since leaving Cedar Rapids, he had kept in close contact with his old friend Anna Snyder, who had left town to study at Wellesley before returning after graduation to become a teacher. When they reunited during vacations, their old bond seemed stronger than ever before, charged now with a sexual dimension. Two weeks after his twenty-first birthday Van Vechten poured his heart out to his diary, saying that it caused him pain to depart from her and that there was nothing in the world he would not give her, she need only ask. Staying with his parents over Christmas that year, he found himself embroiled in a strange love triangle with Snyder and her Wellesley classmate Elsie Stern. In some quiet corner, they held a séance during which Van Vechten appears to have had sex with Snyder as Stern watched. On other nights Van Vechten made out with Stern, but it was Snyder, he said, who had his heart.

Rapidly the carapace of innocence that Cedar Rapids had

constructed around him was breaking up. Leaving home, he had been not just a virgin but remarkably ignorant about sex. He claimed that at the age of nineteen, the only woman he had ever kissed was his mother. When he found himself immersed in the freedoms and temptations of an industrialized city, that all changed: "I picked it up fast," he admitted. Little wonder, when some of his earliest sex education lessons appear to have come from the Levee, Chicago's red-light district, which had the undesirable reputation of being the most depraved locale of any city in the United States.

Just south of Chicago's Loop district and bordering the large African-American neighborhoods known as the Black Belt, the Levee was the center of Chicago's notoriously illicit nightlife, with street after street of gambling dens, cabaret clubs, gin palaces, and saloons, many lit up with new electric lighting, their enticing glow beckoning young men and women inside for some disreputable fun. In the Levee, fifty cents could buy access to just about any sexual adventure imaginable. Prostitutes of both sexes and various ethnicities walked the streets, posed topless in brothel windows to rustle up business, and offered their services at such places as the Bucket of Blood and the Why Not? The mind boggles on what exactly went on behind those closed doors. Prostitution was so rife there that the madams who ran its most profitable brothels were fixtures of newspaper gossip columns, and the stretch of State Street between Van Buren and Twenty-second Streets, was given the name Satan's Mile, such were the number and variety of bordellos on its path. Over the course of the six years he lived in Chicago, Van Vechten came to know the sins of the Levee better than most. If his diaries can be believed—and often they provide Van Vechten at his most factual and dispassionate—the boy who left home a sexual ignoramus was, by his second year in the big city, intimately acquainted with the world's oldest profession. In a diary entry from December 1901 he mentions going to Twenty-second Street, the southern tip of the Levee, where he encountered a young woman by the name of Violette, returning home at two in the morning. He gives no further details, but in 1901 young men who went to Twenty-second Street to meet women late at night generally did so for only one reason. A number of subsequent entries mention further trips to the Levee with male friends, including one futile attempt with his fraternity brother Denis Campau to rediscover Violette. In all likelihood the inexperienced Van Vechten was guided by Campau, whom, like Edwin Boehmer, Van Vechten admired for his worldliness. To Anna Snyder, Van Vechten confessed that he and Campau shared a "philandering spirit," and it was Campau who provided lyrics for "Love Songs of a Philanderer," one of Van Vechten's undergraduate attempts at musical composition.

Whether or not Campau coaxed Van Vechten into Chicago's red-light district, Van Vechten claimed to have played a notable part in an extraordinary chapter of the Levee's unpalatable story when he worked as a pianist at the Everleigh Club, the most sumptuous and exclusive brothel in town. Run by Ada and Minna Everleigh, two sisters originally from Omaha, the Everleigh Club combined degeneracy, elegance, and extravagance in a most Chicagoan way. Situated at South Dearborn and Twenty-second Streets, the Everleigh Club operated less like a whorehouse and more like an ultraexclusive private members' establishment, admitting only respectable, sober men prepared to pay a minimum of fifty dollars for an evening's entertainment. The staff, whose duty it was to see that the gentlemen got value for their money, was a cohort of young ladies with steady temperaments and unfailing good manners, fitted out in the latest expensive designs from Paris. The club's interior was suitably lavish. Leading off from its sweeping mahogany staircases were dozens of ornately decorated rooms, including a library, a ballroom, and a banqueting hall, all furnished with cut-glass chandeliers, plush carpets, and silk sheets. Everyone from John Barrymore to the heavyweight champion Jack Johnson to Prince Henry of Prussia passed through on trips to the city, and Chicago's literary leading men, including Edgar Lee Masters and Theodore Dreiser, were regulars too.

The centerpiece of the whole establishment was the Gold Room, in which stood a gold piano custom made for the Everleigh sisters at the eye-watering cost of fifteen thousand dollars. The resident piano professor was the improbably named Vanderpool Vanderpool, resplendent in finely cut evening wear and a lustrous head of tousled white hair. If Van Vechten's stories were true, it would have been

from him that he assumed piano-playing duties when Vanderpool
went for meal breaks. However, there is very little to corroborate his
testimony. In the writer Charles Washburn's detailed account of the
Everleigh Club, originally published in 1934, he made no mention
of a piano player who would have fitted Van Vechten's description,
and more recent histories of the club account only Scott Joplin as an
occasional substitute for Vanderpool. When asked as an old man for
details by one inquisitive friend, Van Vechten could not remember
the name of the Everleigh Club and gave its address, incorrectly, as
Custom House Place, evidence, perhaps, of a failing memory or that
the story had been a fabrication to begin with. It is very possible
that he had stitched together stories of various experiences to form
a tale that perfectly fitted the image of himself that he wanted to
project, a tactic he employed time and again over the years. He certainly played the odd piano recital at college; he frequented the
racier parts of town too and in the coming years became acquainted
with the Everleigh Club in his capacity as a journalist. These elements may well have fused themselves into a story that Van Vechten
could use in order to associate himself with the great emblem of
Chicago's cosmopolitan wonders, the place where sex, music, wealth,
beauty, flamboyance, and notoriety all met.

In his lifelong exploration of the illicit and forbidden, there were
two great taboo subjects that obsessed him. Sex was one; race was
the other. Chicago offered endless opportunities to traverse the early-
twentieth-century lines of racial division. The city's black vaudeville
scene was, like its classical music, arguably the most dazzling in the
country and a vital precursor to its legendary blues and jazz movements that gained international acclaim decades later. Van Vechten
had glimpsed African-American entertainment at Greene's Opera
House when Sissieretta Jones or some other polite black vaudeville
act came to town. What went down in the nightclubs and theaters
of the Black Belt was an altogether different experience: not sanitized for middle-class white spectators but expressed with verve for
working-class blacks. With Denis Campau in tow—two eager young
white faces conspicuous among the majority black audiences—Van
Vechten got to know venues such as the Dreamland Café and Lincoln Gardens, where he saw many of the most influential African-

American musicians and stage performers: the pianists James "Slap Rags" White and Millard Thomas, the vaudeville legends Williams and Walker, and the daring, cross-dressing Whitman Sisters. When he saw George Walker and his wife, Aida Overton Walker, perform the cakewalk at one South Side venue, it stayed with him forever as an iconic image of American art. Their cakewalk was "one of the great memories of the theatre," he wrote years later, praising its physical and technical brilliance as if recalling a prima ballerina at the Bolshoi. "The line, the grace, the assured ecstasy of these dancers who bent over backward until their heads almost touched the floor, a feat demanding an incredible amount of strength, their enthusiastic prancing, almost in slow motion, have never been equaled in this particular revel, let alone surpassed."

Slumming was a popular pastime for many bourgeois thrill seekers by 1900 in both Chicago and New York, a pseudoeducational entertainment that mirrored the new journalistic fad of poking a lens into the ghetto to see "how the other half lives." Adventure of this sort was almost certainly part of Van Vechten's motivation for investigating the Black Belt. Tests of physical courage were of little interest to him, but social danger—the buzz of breaking a taboo by keeping unusual company or straying into places convention dictated he should not go—was irresistible. But ultimately he went because he was fascinated by the shows, which displayed an extravagance and energy that he could not find in even the best white vaudeville acts. According to his own reminiscences, after one show he befriended one of his heroines, the singer and dancer Carrie Washington, who went by the stage name of Carita Day. She was the wife of Ernest Hogan, one of the great black pioneers of the American entertainment industry, whose legacy is often obscured by his song "All Coons Look Alike to Me," an enormous hit that sealed his reputation as a first-rate songwriter but whose title and lyrics, both of which he composed, later made him wince. When Hogan's revue *The Georgia Minstrels* opened in Chicago, Van Vechten was dazzled by Day, who shone in the lead role. Managing to meet her after the show, he made her acquaintance and even convinced Day and Hogan to perform at a fraternity house party.

As it happened, it was the fraternity that had first led him into the social world of the Black Belt. Shortly after joining the Omega chapter of Psi Upsilon, he struck up an unlikely friendship with its housekeeper, a middle-aged black woman named Mrs. Desdemona Sublett. She was a hefty, good-looking woman who fixed her hair tightly with curlers, and the boys of the fraternity found her forceful personality tremendously entertaining. To Van Vechten she was more than a mere amusement; she was mesmerizing. A devout Christian and member of the African Methodist Episcopal Church, Mrs. Sublett could often be heard praying in the loud, uninhibited tones of her evangelical faith. Van Vechten had been raised to associate Christian worship with a quiet, sober dignity that tended to sublimate raw emotion rather than draw it to the surface, as seemed to happen when Mrs. Sublett spoke to God. The religious faith at the center of her prayers was irrelevant; for all Van Vechten cared, Mrs. Sublett could have been invoking the devil or reciting entries from the telephone directory. It was her performance that excited him: the passion she summoned to enliven the mundane events of her everyday life. No white person he knew ever did this. Having grown up in an environment committed to racial equality, Van Vechten was able to communicate with her in a way the other socially privileged boys of the fraternity could not, and the two formed a close bond. Before long Van Vechten was missing fraternity parties to accompany her to the heart of black Chicago for church socials, wedding anniversary parties, and other "colohed affahs," in his words, where he was the only white person in attendance.

At some of these parties he took to the piano, though his repertoire of classical masterpieces made little impression and usually could not be heard over the noise of laughter and conversation. His pride was stung when he played Moszkowski's Waltz Opus 34 and discovered that only one small girl had been paying any attention. Despite this, he loved the crowded, convivial rooms Mrs. Sublett led him through and the warmth of the people he encountered within them, "uncultured and uneducated," he noted with unintended condescension, but "intensely good hearted, humorous, interesting and even clever." The things he most liked about them were attributes he believed belonged almost exclusively to black people: emotional expressiveness and a warm sensuality that he saw reflected in the

MRS. DESDEMONA SUBLETT

Mrs. Desdemona Sublett is one of the
pioneers in Illinois club work. She is
an active member of the Civic League
of Quinn Chapel, the Board of Man-
agers of the Phyllis Wheatley Home
Association and has held many of the
most important office in the State
federation. At the last meeting she
was appointed chairman of the Pioneer
Workers.

Desdemona Sublett, c. 1922

pleasing tones of their skin and the contours of their bodies, particularly the "dusky matrons with ample bosoms." He said that these women rekindled his childhood longing for a nurturing southern mammy, and he claimed that when he told them this, they responded with delight and pride, as if he had made some special connection with them thanks to his instinctive understanding of true blackness.

After several months of this socializing Van Vechten believed that he was able to project blackness, as if he had possessed some kind of magic cape that he could slip on in order to vault the social chasm that stood between blacks and whites. Although as pale-skinned as his Dutch name suggests, he claimed that when with Mrs. Sublett he was "invariably taken for a coon" by black people. It is the kind of rhetorical flourish that makes one suspect a good deal of his accounts were the product of either a febrile imagination or an inflated ego. Yet as is so often the case with Van Vechten, the literal truth is incidental; the important point is that for the first time he had experienced the power of social contact as a way of hurdling the seemingly insuperable barriers that existed between different groups of Americans. In his own mind at least, by simply attending the right parties at the right time, he had found it possible to erase centuries of rancorous history and become an honorary Negro. Touching, even inspirational, as that conviction was, it was also incredibly naive.

As he left college, Van Vechten reflected on his time in Chicago and concluded that the city had allowed him to live the lives of any number of people: a Buddhist, a Catholic; a pillar of virtue, and a pitiful thief; on some days a high-minded sophisticate, on others a good ol' boy who lived for corn bread and liquor. He was never actually any of those things, of course. It was a poetic way of expressing that Chicago allowed him to be the person he wanted to be, to escape the restraints of convention and unite disparate strands of American identity within one body. In the ferment of the twentieth-century city, he had found a place to belong.

THREE

That Shudder of Fascination

• •

Considering that Van Vechten eventually became famous for his frivolity and elegance, it is jarring that it was the newspaper trade of Chicago that provided his introduction to American public life when he graduated from college in the summer of 1903. In the Progressive Era of the early 1900s Chicago had a reputation for producing the most ruthless muckrakers in the United States. Eugene Field, Finley Peter Dunne, Theodore Dreiser, and George Ade headed a sparkling generation of polemicists, satirists, and investigative reporters who were untiring in their chase of a story. In a dingy backroom of Koster's saloon on a narrow street known as Newsboy's Alley, a group of those mavericks set up the Whitechapel Club, an impudent reference to the stalking ground of Jack the Ripper that captured the spirit of their profession. A coffin-shaped table dominated the clubroom with souvenirs of their greatest scoops lying around: the skull of a murdered prostitute; photographs of decapitated Chinese pirates; a blood-soaked Indian blanket salvaged from a gunfight out west.

Van Vechten would have appreciated the luridness of the Whitechapel Club, but he was no muckraker; he had no desire to speak truth to power or to save souls via the printing press. In his early twenties, the closest thing he had to a vocation was creative writing. "I cannot remember the time when I was not trying to write," he reflected in 1932. At college he had been delighted to be tutored by Robert Herrick, a writer of precise, tightly structured fiction and a prominent figure of the Chicago school of "realist" novelists, whom Van Vechten described as "the first novelist I ever met and a hero to me for many years on that account." His own efforts at writing fiction were anemic imitations of his heroes—namely, George Bernard Shaw, Oscar Wilde, and George Moore, whose work he devoured as a student. Literary greatness would have to be worked at.

Van Vechten's first exposure to journalism came at the end of his sophomore year in the summer of 1901, when he got a temporary job as a reporter for the City News, a wire service established by a number of newspapers to cover the bread and butter of daily news and a de facto training stable for up-and-coming reporters. He was employed to gather stories rather than write them up, and in this job a college education was less valued than a fellow's ability to keep his wits about him as he chased down whatever tales of intrigue came his way. For Van Vechten, a typical day's work might require reporting on assaults, petty crime, or the two great deadly hazards of inner-city Chicago, house fires and streetcar accidents. An entry from his diary of July 1901 mentions a legal case he was reporting on for which he arrived at a dilapidated house to discover a woman teetering at the top of the stairs with a cut to her head, blood coursing down her face. The green boy who had arrived from Iowa in 1899 would have been well out of his depth in those circumstances, but now he discovered that he had a flair for handling the unusual and the unexpected.

The job did nothing to improve his writing, but every day provided the chance to encounter a different set of characters and to gain an education in the workings of the real world. The work was exciting, dangerous, and unpredictable, a paid extension of the nighttime adventures he went on in the Levee; Eddie Boehmer even joined him on a couple of assignments. He enjoyed the job so much that he set his mind on quitting his final year of college to enter journalism full-time. Only his father's stern interjections deterred him from doing so. Charles favored as a career choice for Carl the family concerns of banking and insurance, where money and a steady future were plainly available. Carl's brother, Ralph, had also dabbled in newspaper reporting before he took to a lucrative career in finance. Charles hoped the same would happen with his younger son.

Van Vechten's first full-time job came immediately after graduation in the summer of 1903, as a rookie reporter on the best-known newspaper in the city, the *Chicago American* owned by the real Citizen Kane himself, William Randolph Hearst. Depending on whom you asked, the *American* represented either the apex of Chicago journalism or its nadir. Hearst established the paper in 1900 with the objective of crushing the pro-Republican *Chicago Tribune* and bolstering his chances of landing the Democratic nomination for the 1904 presidential election. Consequently, the *American* was run in accordance with the principles of yellow journalism, a mixture of lurid sensationalism and aggressive political agendas that had dominated the circulation war between Hearst's *New York Journal* and Joseph Pulitzer's *New York World* in recent years. On Hearst's watch, news was not something to be reported but something to be made. As he declared, "the modern editor of the popular journal does not care for facts." A good story was always valued over veracious journalism, and any employee who failed to appreciate that was swiftly replaced. Shortly before Van Vechten arrived, the journalist William Salisbury began work on the *American*, believing its mission was not just to report events but to shape the future of a fast-changing nation, "to enlighten and uplift humanity" and "to reform Chicago as it was reforming New York and San Francisco." How wrong he was. Not long into the new job, Salisbury was suspended, unpaid, for a week for failing to include in his report of a house fire the extraordinary details that a rival newspaper had related about the same incident. When he protested that the other newspaper had clearly fabricated its account of a great human ladder used to evacuate the victims of a fire that had actually taken place in a one-story building, he was told the facts of the story were irrelevant: "never allow any of the old conservative newspapers to outdo the *American* in 'features.'" From the moment he arrived Van Vechten knew that if one wanted to get ahead at the *American*, it was advisable to leave journalistic principles at the hatstand.

Like many of his colleagues, Van Vechten found his abiding memory of the *American* was the thunderous noise that enveloped its offices, the Madhouse, as those who worked there habitually called it. Located in a rickety old building at the former premises of the

Steuben Wine Company at 216 West Madison Street, the entire operation existed on a single floor. It was "the most terrific din you ever heard," Van Vechten said, remembering how the staccato clacking of mechanical typewriters, the brassy ring of candlestick telephones, and the yells of journalists racing toward the next deadline strained above the constant grind of the printing presses that churned out multiple editions each day. The usual workforce comprised around twenty reporters, but staff turnover was prodigiously high, and the pressure to deliver compelling stories even higher. As William Salisbury remembered it, most of the eager young newshounds who came through the Madhouse were dismissed before their colleagues were even aware of their existence. It says much for Van Vechten's talents for the dark arts of yellow journalism that he survived for more than two years.

Chief among his early assignments was securing photographs to accompany human interest stories—not shooting photographs of his own but rooting out preexisting ones and encouraging their owners to part with them. This practice was common at the time, especially on Hearst titles where vivid pictorial content was considered vital. "I was so successful at this I was kept at it interminably," Van Vechten later grumbled, but it was in performing this duty that he first discovered his remarkable powers of persuasion, using "guile" to get photographs from grieving relatives and irate victims of crime without the slightest trace of guilt or awkwardness. "I suppose sometimes I even lied to get photographs," he later admitted. It was a risky business. One time he found himself at the family home of a girl who had "either been killed or ravished"—Van Vechten, telling the story years later, could not remember which—attempting to procure a photograph from the victim's parents. Photograph in hand he was about to leave when the girl's brother rushed into the room and drew a gun on him, held it to his head, and demanded the picture be returned. Fortunately, the family priest was also on hand and convinced the man to lower his pistol. Van Vechten made his escape unscathed.

In an attempt to stay ahead of his rivals on the juiciest stories, Hearst split into two parts the job of the crime reporter, which in Chicago had been the most prized journalistic position during the

1890s. Instead of having one intrepid figure to investigate a story and spin a gripping article from his findings, on the *American*, nimble young reporters were dispatched to unravel a lead and straightaway send the details back to the office for skilled rewriters to turn into copy. For a time Van Vechten's brief was to cover events at the Harrison Street police station in the Loop, a notorious holding pen for violent criminals, pimps, prostitutes, drunks, and the mentally ill. He spent a bleak Thanksgiving of 1903 trawling through the misery contained within its cells in search of a subject to tug at the readers' heartstrings, eventually settling on a man in acute distress, sweating and shaking uncontrollably with alcohol withdrawal. A few weeks later came an even more depressing assignment when, on the afternoon of December 30, he was sent to report on a fire that had engulfed the Iroquois Theatre on West Randolph Street. The scene was hideous: at least six hundred people had been killed, many burned to death, others suffocated by the smoke or trampled in the mass panic. Reporters from all the city's newspapers scrambled to the nearest telephones to contact their editors and rewriters with the latest information only to find the lines had gone dead. It turned out that the first man on the scene, a ruthless young journalist named Walter Howey, working for Van Vechten's old employer the City News wire service, had sabotaged the local public telephones in an attempt to protect his exclusive. When Van Vechten eventually left the site of the tragedy later that night, the flames still licking the walls of the theater, he went home and wept. When he was an old man, his memories of the *American* were patchy and confused, but he never forgot the things he saw that night, how "on the sidewalk corpses were piled up like cordwood, with legs or arms burned off, or just simply smothered." The first weeks of 1904 were spent wading further into the pain and grief of others as he staked out the overcrowded makeshift morgues to find the most heart-wrenching stories of the unfortunates who had perished. The stark horror of the whole episode shook him and revealed something about the job that he would much rather have left concealed: that beneath the excitement and danger of the stories he covered were other people's lives, full of all their messy, complicating emotions, their sorrow, anger, and despair. The bubble of self-absorption in which he had spent much of the first twenty-three years of his life was pricked. Never before had he been forced to confront the interior lives of other people on such a scale. It was not an agreeable experience and one he hoped he would not have to repeat too often.

Van Vechten's crime reporting brief gifted him with a sense of the wild diversity that industrialization had brought to the United States and an insight into how the whole organism of a city functioned, the connections between its synapses and its sinews. It also sharpened his facility for flitting between different cultural and social groups, a common theme of his later endeavors. In the course of his duties on the *American* he encountered brothel madams and society ladies, police chiefs and violent criminals. Van Vechten's esteemed colleague Jack Lait once explained that as a journalist on the *American* he collated a "chorus of opinion," a bookful of contacts from all walks of life who could furnish an instant opinion on any conceivable issue. It was, he said, "a staff equal to any symposium in any emergency," and when he was promoted to a more senior editorial job, he passed it to "my next typewriter neighbor, Carl Van Vechten."

By the time he received Lait's contacts, Van Vechten had been given the task of writing some stories of his own. He handled the new responsibilities well, embellishing the formula of yellow journalism with a hint of his own mordant wit. Full of shocking facts—many of which, one suspects, were not really facts at all—and contrived outrage, his articles succeeded in conjuring something fantastical out of the mundane. He wrote about a young woman who sued an ex-fiancé for calling off their engagement when he discovered she had a glass eye and about a well-to-do young lady who ditched her millionaire suitor in favor of a Texan miner; a more serious piece exposed the fraudulent leader of a religious cult whose followers fasted themselves to the point of death. His editor also gave him the responsibility of writing the society gossip column, for which he invented a preposterous imaginary sidekick named Angel Child through whom he was able to voice catty observations about Chicago's upper crust. With puckish delight and a homosexual innuendo presumably lost on most of his readers, he once reviewed the performance of a brawny baseball-loving University of Chicago student who so convinced in a female role in a recent operatic production that young men rushed to the stage and threw violets at his feet. In a Christmastime edition, he filed the story of little Louis Simmons, a six-year-old boy who died after opening his presents on Christmas morning, under the headline XMAS TOYS BOY'S DEATH MESSENGER. Van Vechten quoted the child's mother, who said, "I have never seen him so happy before, and I think that it was joy that killed him." On the surface readers were entreated to wring their hands in sympathy. But there is a certain relish in the way Van Vechten reported the lament of this grieving mother: death in the attainment of pure pleasure seemed a gloriously decadent way to go.

Tabloid rag though it may have been, the *American* was an important stage in Van Vechten's development as a writer. The stories he wrote contain traces of the mischievous absurdity and gossipy satire that were to characterize his best novels of the 1920s. Just as significant, it was while working on the *American* that Van Vechten received a thorough training in how to put facts in the service of a story, an approach that he drew on extensively in his work as a music, dance, and drama critic in the 1910s. His best writing in that latter period succeeded because it thoroughly described his experience of the event rather than just the qualities of those performing. When reviewing a play, he would evoke the entire sensory environment inside the theater, sometimes down to the body odor of the people sitting next to him and the taste of the apple pie he had eaten in the restaurant across the street a half hour earlier. Most of his readers took these details as they were presented: intelligently observed and factual accounts of specific events. But Van Vechten never felt any obligation to facts. In a valedictory message in his final book of critical essays in 1925, he conceded that his work had always been "creative rather than critical," his objective being to evoke a sensation or an atmosphere rather than write a report of factual accuracy. With no ethical qualms he would embellish anecdotes, fabricate dates, invent conversations, and alter facts if it suited him to do so. The time he spent working on the *American* at the beginning of his career encouraged him to view objectivity and the truth as obstructions to good writing.

Van Vechten would have been reluctant to admit that a direct relationship might have existed between his elegant essays on music and dance and the tittle-tattle he wrote for tabloid newspapers. He was never embarrassed by his years in Chicago, exactly. Rather, this chapter of his life inserted a messy complication into his grand personal narrative, a kink in what could otherwise be written as an archetypal modern tale of the midwestern ingenue who comes to New York and discovers his creative identity amid opera, ballet, Greenwich Village bohemia, and modern art.

When he spoke to Columbia University's Oral History Research Office in 1960, he admitted that his experiences on the *American* had given him a marvelous education in the ways of the world. "That was some life," he recalled; "what I didn't know before then, I learned there." Yet in virtually the same breath, he spoke of how he outgrew the city: "I learned to dislike [it] heartily," he said, explaining that "there are lots of ways of amusing yourself [in Chicago] until you get tired of them. I got tired of them eventually." There was more to Van Vechten's sudden displeasure with Chicago than his capricious nature, tossing the city away once the novelty had worn off as he had with his pets and birds' eggs. The start of his dissatisfaction with the place actually coincided with the most traumatic event of his life so far. In November 1905 his mother died, and he felt the suffocating weight of grief for the first time. More than half a century later he recalled it as being a defining moment in his life, though even at the age of eighty he still sounded surprised that the passing of another person could have had such a profound effect on him. "I didn't get over it for weeks or months," he said. Only very rarely did the deaths of those in his life have any lasting emotional impact on him, evidence of his essentially egocentric character. The elderly Van Vechten claimed that he used his response to a person's death as a yardstick for measuring his feelings for him or her. "It's one way I can tell when I'm really fond of people," he said. "I think that's rather interesting and probably not the experience of most people, because some people at least make themselves believe they care a great deal when a friend died. I usually didn't." His mother's death was clearly an exception.

Ada's passing forced him to take stock of his own life. In a peculiar way the experience challenged his belief in his uniqueness; it made him feel "human or normal, whatever you want to call it," he confessed. He was twenty-five now, more than two years out of college, and saw no route for progress at the *American*. Writing the society column was fun as far as it went, and his reporting duties allowed him access to some fascinating aspects of life, but what he really wanted was to immerse himself in his passion for music and the stage; that alone would provide an environment in which his specialness would thrive.

Once he would have thought Chicago the perfect place for that type of escape. When Theodore Thomas passed away in January 1905, there was a tangible sense that Chicago's golden age of orchestral concerts and opera had died with him. New York, on the other hand, was just about to enter a phenomenally exciting period as Oscar Hammerstein announced his plans to open an enormous new opera house to rival the Metropolitan. All his life Van Vechten claimed that he had been sacked for "lowering the tone of the Hearst papers" when he insulted the wife of one of the paper's senior figures through his society column. That story was another exaggeration: he had been reprimanded for causing embarrassment but not dismissed. How much better for his rebellious self-image, though, to give the impression that an act of daring had cast him out into the cold. Neither William Randolph Hearst nor the great city of Chicago, the anecdote implied, could handle a personality as large and audacious as his. New York alone was capable of that.

"New York, my dear, you would love, with its thousand and one queer places and restaurants." In January 1907, Van Vechten wrote these words to a childhood friend, Leah Maynard, about all the wonderful things that could be found only in this incredible city, his new home. New York was alive with possibilities for artists and innovators of all stripes. Between shifts as a singing waiter at the Pelham Café a young Irving Berlin was writing his first Tin Pan Alley songs, while Alfred Stieglitz proselytized photography as the great visual art of the new century, finding mesmeric shapes and patterns in the city's huddled masses. On the Lower East Side the "nickel madness" reigned, working-class immigrants filling their days and nights with the impossibly futuristic technology of moving pictures, the flickering, fast-cut images mimicking the mad pace of the modern world. Mack Sennett was still a year away from breaking into the movies, but he was a regular face on New York's vaudeville stage along with Chinese conjurers, Armenian belly dancers, blackface minstrels, and Hungarian escapologists. On the tiny island of Manhattan, every conceivable sensation could be found.

The cultural event that gripped Van Vechten that year was a scandalous new opera from Europe. *Salome*, adapted by Richard Strauss from Oscar Wilde's controversial play of the same name, tells a tale of lust, incest, and murder, in which King Herod's niece and stepdaughter unleashes her powers of seduction to win John the Baptist's head on a plate in revenge for his refusal of her sexual advances. The publication of Wilde's play had been a crucial feature of Europe's art nouveau movement of the 1890s, especially the editions augmented by Aubrey Beardsley's vivid illustrations, his "whiplash line" in sensuous concert with the violent carnality of Wilde's text. By the time of its debut performance in Paris in 1896 Wilde was serving a sentence of hard labor for the crime of homosexuality, transforming a play that had previously been considered indecorous into something that was regarded as a work of genuine subversion. Upon its premiere in Dresden in 1905, *Salome*, the opera, generated even greater excitement, partly because of Wilde's narrative, partly because of Strauss's unconventional music—Strauss's own father described listening to it as having "one's trousers full of maybugs"— and partly because of its infamous nine-minute-long dance of the seven veils, a provocative striptease performed by Salome at the request of her stepfather, that many considered the depth of depravity. The archbishop of Vienna excoriated Strauss for having put his name to such inestimable filth and lobbied to have the whole thing banned. So when the news broke that New York's proudly conservative Metropolitan Opera was to make *Salome* the focal point of its 1907 season, there was widespread disbelief. American producers were known for eschewing operas considered controversial, challenging, or unconventional. For the Metropolitan and its audience, this was uncharted territory.

Like almost everyone else in the United States, Van Vechten had never heard a bar of *Salome* before its premiere, but the very idea of it thrilled him. Thanks to Theodore Thomas's ambitious orchestral programs, he had been exposed to Strauss in Chicago, an experience denied most New Yorkers at that point. He had also read Wilde's play and had enviously received a detailed account of the opera from Anna Snyder after she attended a performance in Germany during a trip to Europe. In New York with no particular plans or prospects, Van Vechten hustled the way a Hearst journalist should and used this secondhand knowledge to convince the new editor of *Broadway Magazine*, his fellow Chicagoan Theodore Dreiser, that he was the man to introduce New Yorkers to the most incredible theatrical event of their times. In a 1950 essay on his memories of Dreiser, Van Vechten claimed that the afternoon he arrived at Dreiser's office to pitch his services was their first meeting and that it had come about through the involvement of a mutual acquaintance, though he could not remember whom. Given Van Vechten's and Dreiser's links to Chicago, that person may well have been one of Van Vechten's well-connected fraternity brothers. There is the outside possibility that their paths may have crossed at the Everleigh Club too, as Dreiser was one of its most committed patrons. In any event, Dreiser commissioned Van Vechten to write an article entitled "Salome: The Most Sensational Opera of the Age." It lacked the insight and flair of his later work, but it was the first phase of his reinvention from tabloid hack to an insider of the star-studded world of New York opera.

The second phase began soon after when he was hired as a staff reporter by *The New York Times* in November 1906 and swiftly promoted to assistant music critic in early 1907. To Van Vechten's glee, the new position afforded him access to the city's great artistic events, including *Salome*. He wrote Leah Maynard that being present at *Salome*'s New York debut was a life-changing event; he feared that no future theatrical event could ever match it. That first night, on January 22, was like no other he, or any other American theatergoer, had ever experienced. His boss, the *Times*'s lead music critic, Richard Aldrich, captured the strange ambivalence of the audience, "tense with a sort of foreboding as well as with evident and insistent interest." He reported "a stifling and heavily erotic atmosphere" in the auditorium, "repulsive yet strangely fascinating."

The eroticism that Aldrich described was the thing that defined Van Vechten's memory of the night. Nine years later he wrote an essay on Olive Fremstad, the soprano who played the title role of Salome, in which he evoked the excitement he felt in watching her from the dark of the auditorium. She did not merely perform the role; she seemed to live it. So committed was she to inhabiting the character of Salome that she even spent time at a morgue, to familiarize herself with the experience of holding a dead man's head in her hands. Her performance enthralled Van Vechten. "Her entrance was that of a splendid leopard," he wrote, "standing poised on velvet paws on the terrace, and then creeping slowly down the staircase." Frequently he evoked sexual activity through the stalking behavior of cats: slow-moving elegance followed by a sudden pounce, both beautiful and savage. He extended the metaphor in his description of the final scene in which Fremstad took the Baptist's severed head in her hands and kissed it passionately on the lips. Van Vechten took a perverse pleasure in the breaching of a carnal taboo:

> I cannot yet recall her as she crept from side to side of the well in which Jochanaan was confined, waiting for the slave to ascend with the severed head, without that shudder of fascination caused by the glimmering eyes of a monster serpent, or the sleek terribleness of a Bengal tiger. And at the end she suggested, as perhaps it has never before been suggested on the stage, the dregs of love, the refuse of gorged passion.

He had never seen the pains and ecstasies of human experience explored like this before, in such a vivid and unambiguous way. The fact that so many in the audience were outraged by what he found electrifying only added to his enjoyment. When the time came for the dance of the seven veils, performed by the prima ballerina Bianca Froelich, it was more than many could stand. Dozens of ladies

Olive Fremstad as Salome at the Metropolitan Opera House, January 1907

apparently averted their gaze for the whole of the dance, and similar numbers of men avoided embarrassment by removing themselves from the auditorium altogether, at least until Froelich was through with her writhing. In his essay on Fremstad, Van Vechten deliberately underlined his divergence from the Diamond Horseshoe, the group of wealthy, conservative patrons who dominated the Metropolitan, by suggesting that the dance actually dulled the erotic intensity of the opera as a whole. Froelich's dancing on the first night, he said, was tame compared with the wild manner in which she had torn off her layers in the dress rehearsal. And in any case, Fremstad should have been allowed to do the dance herself; what she lacked in technique she would have made up for in sexual passion.

Several highly influential patrons of the Metropolitan were so disgusted by the production that they issued an ultimatum: cancel the production or lose their patronage. Van Vechten was sent to interview Olive Fremstad in her suite at the Wyoming Hotel, probably his first one-to-one interview with an opera star. With every ounce of her "overpowering and dominating temperament," as Van Vechten once described the singer, Fremstad defended the opera to the hilt, praising Strauss's innovative brilliance. Significantly, she could find no kind words for Oscar Wilde, whose association with the opera was a chief cause of complaint, the stench of his homosexuality trial still clinging to his name. "Salome is the worst sort of degenerate," Fremstad argued, "but Strauss makes something more of her at the last, where she gets her idea of what love means . . . Strauss tells me this. Wilde tells me nothing." Van Vechten thought that an absurd claim. He knew that an attempt to separate Strauss's depiction of Salome from Wilde's was senseless; the one flowed directly from the other. Eight days after its one and only performance, the directors of the Metropolitan Opera House announced that *Salome* was canceled with immediate effect. In the piece he wrote about the decision in the *Times*, Van Vechten suppressed his dismay and quoted the board in also laying the blame for the whole episode on the late Oscar Wilde. "We take issue with the statement that Strauss's music is of the same character and tendency as Wilde's text," it said, as if Wilde's play were an afterthought of Strauss's, rather than his sole inspiration. Clearly, to defend Strauss's inventive music could be seen as dedication to one's art; to defend the product of a deviant mind such as Oscar Wilde's was sure to provoke disgust.

The entire controversy was Van Vechten's first experience of art's capacity to polarize with such power, forcing one to take a side either for or against an artwork not simply for the quality of its content but for its underlying philosophy. *Salome* shocked so thoroughly not only because its stripteases and severed heads offended moral sensibilities but also because it emphatically challenged a long-standing assumption that the purpose of art should be to venerate goodness. As with many artists of the art nouveau era, which bridged the romantic and the modern, moral instruction was never a goal for Wilde or Strauss, who were far more interested in using art to explore the reality of the human condition, no matter how unpalatable. Van Vechten was in complete agreement. In time, he would take up his pen "in defence [*sic*] of bad taste"—that is, in support of individual expression free from moral censure. For now he had neither the critical skills nor the seniority at the *Times* to do so. Still, there was no doubt whose side Van Vechten was on: Wilde's and Strauss's instinct that there was beauty to be found in ugliness appeared self-evident. The great cities of the United States had already taught him that much.

Opera in New York was not usually such a combustible environment as it was in those opening weeks of 1907. For the majority of his career at the *Times*, Van Vechten's role was less music critic and more celebrity-watching gossip columnist as he covered the comings and goings of European opera singers, usually portrayed in the press as a species separate from drab, businesslike Americans. He fueled speculation about the love life of Geraldine Farrar, gasped at the fashion trends set by Mary Garden, gave dramatic insights into rivalries between chest-thumping tenors, and reported with astonishment the vast riches that these stars were raking in year after year thanks to the New York public's fixation with the opera. Making the most of his yellow journalism training, he quickly became accomplished at turning the most trivial episodes into news stories. CARUSO'S MUS-TACHE OFF declaimed the headline above his report of the momentous occasion when Enrico Caruso shaved off his mustache: "Can he sing without it?" Other earth-shattering scoops included Nellie Melba's decision to charge a dollar per autograph and the profligacy of Henry Clay Frick, the steel magnate, who paid one hundred thousand dollars for a box at the Metropolitan, before splashing out thousands more to have it redecorated.

Van Vechten enjoyed the froth and found the showy self-importance of the opera celebrities he met highly entertaining. At a time when journalists were given the kind of access to performers and rehearsals that is unheard of in the early twenty-first century, Van Vechten's working week was inhabited by the world-famous, and he assiduously cataloged his association with them in his scrapbooks. Some he even photographed, including Luisa Tetrazzini—the Italian soprano and prima donna in every sense—as she left *The New York Times* building in her customary silk turban and chinchilla fur coat. The photographs were an extension of the theatrical pictures he had taken in his youth and a precursor to the celebrity portraits he spent the last thirty years of his life obsessively shooting. It was less the person he was capturing, more the fame attached to him or her, another handful of glitter for his collections. Even so, the fact that these high-powered celebrities posed for him, no matter how informally, shows that he felt comfortable in their company, and they in his. The tartness of his usual personality was sugarcoated in their presence: more deferential, less abrasive. The hustler from Chicago was turning into a silver-tongued Manhattan schmoozer.

Luisa Tetrazzini took to Van Vechten so warmly that she allowed him to ghostwrite an article for her in *Cosmopolitan* magazine, detailing her life and her rise to fame. Van Vechten also clicked with Fyodor Chaliapin, a Russian bass whom he described as "exuberant," "like a great big boy, a sophomore in college, who played football." Chaliapin possessed only rudimentary English when Van Vechten first interviewed him in the dining room of the Savoy Hotel one dreary Sunday morning. But the barrier of language was swiftly overcome by their shared love of drinking and eating. "I spik English," Van Vechten recalled as his interviewee's first words. "How do you do? et puis good-by, et puis I drrrink, you drrink, he drrrrinks, et puis I love you!" The interview started shortly before midday and continued until late into the evening, though not much in the way of newsworthy comment was gathered. At one point, back in his room at the Brevoort Hotel after a whole day of drinking and eating, Chaliapin supposedly performed his party trick of singing along with a record of "La Marseillaise," managing to drown out the sound of the phonograph altogether, so powerful was his voice. "The effect in this moderately small hotel room can only be faintly conceived," said Van Vechten afterward, his ears ringing with the memory.

The nodal point of this sparkling pageant was not an exotic foreigner but Oscar Hammerstein, the millionaire cigar manufacturer turned theater impresario, who opened the Manhattan Opera House with the aim of breaking the monopoly of the Metropolitan and smashing the elitism and conservatism that its wealthy patrons exerted over opera in New York. For four years between 1906 and 1910 Hammerstein produced remarkable performances and elevated New York to one of the great opera capitals of the world. As a reporter from the *Times* Van Vechten was one of a select group who got to see Hammerstein up close during the four years of his reign. Helped immeasurably by the fact that a friend of his from Chicago, Anna Pollock, was Hammerstein's press agent, Van Vechten was a frequent guest at the rooms above the Victoria Theatre on Broadway where Hammerstein lived, "gilded, but shabby, dusty and dingy, and always crowded" with antique furniture, papers, and various detritus strewn around him. The only thing that seemed clean in those disheveled quarters was Hammerstein himself, always immaculately turned out in the finest tailoring. Through Pollock, Van Vechten filed a number of puff pieces about Hammerstein, such as the unlikely sounding one about a couple from Winnipeg, Manitoba, who came all the way from Canada to hear *Rigoletto* at the Manhattan with their eighteen-month-old baby, whom they deposited at the cloakroom for the evening. Van Vechten quoted Hammerstein as saying that the Manhattan could not "check all children who come with their mothers. However, it can be arranged occasionally if the baby is as good as this one."

Frequently, and his recollections of both Hammerstein and Chaliapin are cases in point, one wonders whether Van Vechten's anecdotes about the New York opera at this period capture the personalities of the real people he knew or merely the caricatures of their public images, the one-dimensional "stars" about whom he wrote in the *Times* and felt so proud to know. To an extent, this reflects a hazard of Van Vechten's testimony on just about anything in his past. An engaging and vivid storyteller though he may have been, he was certainly no infallible witness, and his years of writing gossip for newspapers undoubtedly exacerbated a natural tendency to embroider the truth for the sake of a good yarn. In this case, the profound influence his early years in New York had on him distorted Van Vechten's memories of the era, encouraging him to depict its personalities as larger and more magnetic than almost any he encountered at any stage of his life. He admitted as much in an interview in 1960: "some of the artists of that period, like Fremstad and Mary Garden, were so much better than anything we've had since, that it's very hard for me to get interested in opera any more." In the late 1910s Van Vechten wrote brilliant dissections of the craft of performance in various arts; no other critic in the United States came close to producing the same enthusiasm and depth of insight about such a breadth of music and dance, from the blues to Schoenberg. Yet when he turned his attention to the personalities of the performers in question, he frequently resorted to caricatures, gossipy dinner party anecdotes wheeled out by an inveterate name-dropper. There was always a part of Van Vechten that remained the stage door autograph hunter, the little boy from Iowa dazzled by the fame of the big stars, rapt by the spectacle of the show.

FOUR

A Certain Sensuous Charm

· ·

Within a year of arriving in New York Van Vechten had fully embraced the decadent notion that life itself was a work of art. Spending well beyond his means, he set about beautifying himself with suits and silk shirts from Fifth Avenue and eye-catching jewelry. *Salome* had affected him profoundly, and something of its dissolute, daring atmosphere enveloped him; the Wildean notion of sophistication, a knowing worldliness combined with a quixotic love of physical beauty, became the central value of Van Vechten's existence. However, as an elderly man Van Vechten concluded: "You don't pick up sophistication by wanting to"; it was not something that could be simply bought and slipped on like a fur coat. It could be acquired only through the loss of innocence and the steady accretion of experience of every sort—mind and body.

While the Metropolitan Opera and the Manhattan took care of his mind, his body was attended to in less respectable establishments, usually under the cover of darkness. The historian Lewis Erenberg credits the explosion of nighttime pleasure districts in American cities at the start of the twentieth century as the key cultural break with the nineteenth century because they provided perfect arenas in which young adults could "burst out of domestic controls and get closer to real desires." This was definitely true for Van Vechten, whose yearning for sexual adventure, interracial company, and rebellion against good taste all were catered to in New York's most debauched nocturnal playgrounds.

Portrait of Carl Van Vechten by Martha Baker, 1906

When Van Vechten arrived in New York, the hub of entertainment was Manhattan's Tenderloin district, at the southern end of which was a large African-American community known as Black Bohemia that gave Van Vechten the chance to expand on his adventures in the Black Belt of Chicago. At clubs like the Haymarket and Café Wilkins, he was able to hear the city's hottest ragtime musicians—both Scott Joplin and Eubie Blake were regulars—and as a very old man Van Vechten insisted that he once dined in the Tenderloin with one of his all-time heroes, Bert Williams, of the legendary Williams and Walker double act. The appeal of these places, though, was much more than good music and celebrities. Like most of Chicago's Black Belt, Black Bohemia existed only in the peripheral vision of the city's moral guardians, meaning that in its most popular nightspots blacks and whites could carouse together in ways they never could on the street in the light of day. Shrouded from the stern, judgmental gaze of the authorities, venues in this part of town also afforded nonheterosexual men and women, like Van Vechten, the chance to socialize, flirt, and even make pickups in relative safety.

Similar experiences were to be had in Greenwich Village, just then beginning to acquire a reputation for dissidence and bohemian living. By night in the Village, the winding streets and poor working-class Italian communities living cheek by jowl with the recent influx of artists and political radicals made the neighborhood feel very different from any other that Van Vechten had previously encountered, vaguely resembling the tales that he had heard about the Left Bank. In the ramshackle basement bars and dingy restaurants, the environment was different from the Tenderloin—more discussion of the sexual theories of Sigmund Freud and Havelock Ellis than dancing to ragtime tunes—but the same opportunities existed for taboo encounters. Given his sexual interest in men and his past experiences in the Levee, Van Vechten would have almost certainly been familiar with the fleshpots of the Bowery too. At the Bowery's "fairy" clubs, like Paresis Hall, male prostitutes worked the room in search of clients, while customers were entertained by effeminate men onstage performing acts of female impersonation. Some clubs even dared flout the laws against transvestism—masquerading as a woman could be

punishable by several weeks' incarceration—and allowed male entertainers to do full drag shows. Van Vechten's fascination with
cross-dressing that started with Herbie Newell's skirt dance led him
to numerous drag balls in Harlem in the 1920s—he even judged
one once—and he would have enjoyed a Bowery show too.

The popular stereotypes of homosexuality of the time revolved
around caricatures of limp-wristed inverts, half-male creatures
mincing their way up and down Broadway. In reality, of course, gay
men expressed their sexuality in many more subtle ways that often
went entirely unnoticed by the straight majority. As Van Vechten
discovered, New York had a thriving gay social world, but almost
none of it was out in the open. Outside the clubs and brothels of the
Bowery, homosexuality crept in the shadows and scrambled itself
into secret codes. In most places, if Van Vechten wanted to signal
his interest in another man, he would likely have followed the sort
of discreet tactics that many gay men of the time employed. A fleeting moment of eye contact held just a fraction longer and steadier
than normal might start it off, perhaps followed by an inquiry about
the time or a request for a match to light a cigarette. If the other
fellow responded to his attentions with a smile and a line of conversation, then he knew that things might be taken further. Like
many others, Van Vechten also gave little clues to his sexual interest
in men through his physical appearance. His silk shirts and ties, his
immaculately groomed hair, the occasional flower worn in his but-
tonhole, and a discreet bracelet gave him the merest hint of the
"fairy" caricature, colorful and a little showy, just enough to communicate his difference without attracting censure or antagonism.
The biggest but also subtlest clue was the intaglio ring depicting the
classical scene of Leda being raped by a swan he wore on the little
finger of his left hand. The myth of Leda acquired something of a
cult among many writers and artists of the fin de siècle era, a symbol of forbidden desire and taboo practices that some homosexual
dandies displayed as a sign that they existed outside the sexual
mainstream.

Van Vechten enjoyed the secretive culture of New York's clandestine gay world. The thrill of being a select member of a closed community getting up to things that would enrage public decency was

one of his central pleasures. Throughout his adult life it seemed that the more forbidden an assignation, the more exciting it was, whether it be with tough-looking sailors, effeminate teenagers, or black call boys. Not just on his person but throughout his creative work as essayist, novelist, and photographer he played with codes endlessly, leaving clues and references that those in the know would instantly pick up on. It was an obsession that hovered somewhere between risqué humor and an act of defiance, a refusal to bury his identity beneath conventional morality. In one of his novels, *Firecrackers*, written in 1925, a character named Paul Moody, who bears many superficial similarities to Van Vechten, buys two red neckties, sartorial shorthand for homosexuality. When he gives them to a helpful messenger boy as a gift, the boy accepts them "but not without grumbling that he wouldn't be caught drowneded [*sic*] in a red tie." Years after that, when Van Vechten's days and nights were taken up with photography, he had dozens of homosexual men—friends or artists he admired—come to his studio to have their pictures taken. In the poses of the subjects, their outfits, the props they held, or the floral backdrops placed behind them, Van Vechten left a sign to make the viewer aware that they were looking at another cherished face in his vast gallery of gay men, giving visibility to a hidden minority as well as to his own sexuality.

Though he was an avid cruiser for most of his adult life, his most lasting homosexual relationships came through introductions made by other homosexual friends. In 1906 the lesbian writer and activist Edna Kenton, an old friend from Chicago, freshly arrived in New York, introduced Van Vechten to Avery Hopwood, a promising young playwright whose innocent, baby-faced appearance was comically out of step with his hedonistic personality and incorrigibly irreverent sense of humor. Gertrude Stein said she detected in Hopwood "the air of a sheep with the possibility of being a wolf." Soon after meeting, he and Van Vechten forged an intense bond expressed through private jokes, gossip, and sexual innuendo that resulted in crescendos of shrieking laughter and often had the effect of making those outside their circle of two feel alienated and uneasy, wondering whether the joke was at their expense. Alice Toklas once described their combined presence as "gay, irresponsible and brilliant." The

Portrait of Avery Hopwood by Florine Stettheimer, c. 1915–18

double meaning of "gay" may well have been deliberate, for it was an open secret in their circle that Van Vechten and Hopwood's early friendship periodically strayed into a romantic and sexual intimacy, or "dead sweet affectionateness," as their mutual friend Mabel Dodge euphemistically describes it in her memoirs. Wherever they went, they were the self-appointed life and soul, playfully competing to see who could be the wittiest, most daring bon viveur. Twenty years before it became a defining characteristic of New York life, a spirit of irreverent levity enveloped them as they glided across the city at night. Their drinking habits preempted the atmosphere of the 1920s too. Frequently they got so drunk together that one or the other would subject nearby innocents to a tirade of insults, a habit that lost both of them numerous friends over the years.

Hopwood lived the life of a homosexual man as openly as was possible amid the considerable constraints of the time and only pursued relationships with other men. Van Vechten, however, continued to be romantically involved with the opposite sex. He was able to feel physically attracted to certain women, but his sincere need for female companionship was much more emotional than physical. "Women, seemingly, have had more influence on me than men," he observed in his final years, thinking of how bold, charismatic women, such as Mrs. Sublett; Mahala Dutton, the glamorous older woman from Cedar Rapids; and, later, Gertrude Stein, had captivated his attention and steered his life in new directions. It surely started with his mother, another headstrong woman, whose adoration of her precious baby boy inculcated in him the belief that he was somehow set apart from others. As an adult he rarely felt attracted to females in the same powerfully magnetic way that he was drawn to other males, but he hungered for their love, adulation, and physical affection just as urgently.

In the years he spent chasing stories at the *American*, his relationship with Anna Snyder had evolved from occasional adolescent fumbling into a steady and heatedly passionate long-distance romance. "I am determined to be a villain," Snyder telegrammed Van Vechten in advance of a visit to Chicago in 1904; "in other words—Stratford Hotel—six o'clock—Friday. And may the gods forgive me!" At the end of what had clearly been an eventful stay she sent another telegram, assuring him, "I do care and that it has been the best week ever." From a vacation in Europe, Snyder wrote to outline her vision of their life together in a union that would joyously overturn the conventions of the society in which they were raised. Comparing the "pure passion" of their relationship with *La Bohème*, which she had just heard for the first time, she painted a picture of "a bohemian domesticity," governed only by love and mutual adoration. Intimacy, honesty, and art would be the basis of their relationship, a new sort of marriage.

"Bohemian domesticity." The phrase is strikingly evocative of their relationship yet also intriguingly vague, an attempt, perhaps, to reconcile Snyder's need for a conventional marriage with Van Vechten's unconventional sexual identity. That she must have known about Van Vechten's strong sexual interest in men seems a virtual certainty and not only because his outward appearance semaphored it. Long before their wedding their letters to each other contained cryptic references to Van Vechten's "nature," something he said he could neither ignore nor conceal. Considering how they danced around the issue on paper, it is difficult to know whether Snyder realized the full implications of this, though at times it obviously played on her mind. "Do you remember once saying to me that you were much like your friend Campau in regard to his 'philandering spirit'?," she asked with forced casualness in one letter. "If I really thought so I think I should prefer never to see you again." In the months leading up to their wedding, she teased him that "all the men you seem most to fancy personally and admire, are of slender years." It is a delicate turn of phrase, but one that reverberates with the defense used by Oscar Wilde in his obscenity trial of 1895, in which he described his relationship with Lord Alfred Douglas as a manifestation of a Hellenic ideal, "a great affection of an elder for a younger man" of the sort that laced itself through the great art of Western history. Van Vechten was one of the many young men of the early twentieth century whose understanding of their homosexual desires was partially achieved through Wilde's argument, his physical attraction to men emboldened and validated by an artistic and intellectual lineage that stretched back to Michelangelo and Plato. As a middle-aged man, Van Vechten's attachment to this classical model of homosexual love was manifested in his predilection for taking lovers young enough to be his sons and capturing the physical beauty of youth in many of his photography sessions. Snyder noticed that even at the age of twenty-six Van Vechten liked to put himself in the role of the older man, the one with wisdom to impart and control to exert. His experience of being the ingenue "with all the joy, glamour and hope of life before him," as Wilde put it, came in his connections not to men but to older women. His relationships with Mahala Dutton and Mrs. Sublett, for example, lacked an overt sexual dimension, allowing him to exhibit his vulnerabilities and submit himself to their tutelage. With other men, however, he displayed a desire for status and dominance, an expression of the traditional masculinity of the powerfully built, high-achieving males in the Van Vechten family.

If Snyder's bohemian domesticity encompassed a reluctant accommodation of her fiancé's roving eye, an arrangement of that sort would not have been out of place in the fashionable neighborhoods of downtown Manhattan where Van Vechten was mixing. The writers Neith Boyce and Hutchins Hapgood, who became close friends of Van Vechten's around 1912, were intellectually committed to having an open marriage in which the autonomy of either partner would not be restricted by sexual jealousy or dependency of any kind. In one of Boyce's unpublished short stories a Village artist called Eugene encapsulated the ideal perfectly, in an echo of the imprecise aspirations that Snyder voiced in her letters to Van Vechten. "This wouldn't be an ordinary marriage," says Eugene. "Neither of us wants that—domestic atmosphere and all that . . . We can go on independently of one another."

Whatever the exact arrangement, Van Vechten agreed with Snyder that theirs would be a blissful wedded life of a sort that folks in Cedar Rapids could not possibly conceive. He was not madly in love with Snyder, but he was swept up in the story of their romance, their shared narrative of being freethinking rebels struggling against provincialism. Moreover, he basked in the strength of Snyder's feelings for him. Her letters professed him the sole focus of her erotic and romantic fantasies, her soul mate and her reason for living. The attention was exquisite. Accustomed as a child to having his every whim tolerated and indulged, as a man he needed desperately to be fussed over and worshipped by his lovers, his flaws instantly forgiven and his indiscretions just as swiftly forgotten. If his specialness went unrecognized, he could offer nothing in return. "I could never be in love with anybody who wasn't in love with me," he once admitted. When he felt Snyder had not expressed her adoration in sufficiently effusive terms, he sulked and lashed out in rebuke. After one particularly petulant episode Snyder asked, "I am not writing you love letters—is that your complaint? Do you care more for symbols than realities?" Frequently that was just so. Their correspondence often reads like the love letters of precocious teenagers rather than those entering their late twenties. For all his supposed sophistication, there remained at Van Vechten's core an emotional immaturity, both childlike and childish.

Playing at rebellious star-crossed lovers, Van Vechten and Snyder hatched a plan to marry in London in the summer of 1907, without their families present. Displaying less bohemianism and more bourgeois pragmatism than she would have liked to admit, Snyder briefly wobbled over the plan, fearing the reaction of her parents as well as the cost and the practicalities of life immediately after the wedding. Her fiancé, however, was immovable. He was already jealous enough of her European travels and desperately wanted to see the opera in Munich and Paris as well as the music halls of London, the next stage in his cosmopolitan education. He insisted that the wedding must go ahead; Snyder eventually relented. Of course Van Vechten had nowhere near enough money to fund his grand tour out of his wages from the *Times*, a little more than fifty dollars per week, all of which was spent as soon as it was made. To cover the cost, he cashed in the small bequests left him by his grandmothers. Carl's spending and accumulation of debt were a constant source of concern for his father, but Charles was delighted about the wedding, despite some sadness that he would not be permitted to attend. "It shall be a day of joy," he wrote in congratulation, adding that Van Vechten's mother would have been more pleased than anyone: "you must never forget how much she loved you."

Having married in Christ Church in Woburn Square, the newlyweds took in the highlights of the theatrical season in England, France, and Germany as part of a lengthy honeymoon. Paris was the undoubted climax. In Van Vechten's imagination the city was an almost mythical place akin to Babylon and Atlantis, and he was overwhelmed by his first encounter with it. "It would be difficult to exaggerate my emotion," he related several years later in his novel *Peter Whiffle*, as though describing a scene from a belle epoque painting rather than Paris itself: "the white wine, the bearded students, the exquisite women, all young and smiling and gay, all organdie and lace and sweet-peas, went to my head." Though he returned to the city many times, he maintained "the first night was the best and every other night more or less a pale reflection of that, always, indeed, coloured a little by the memory of it."

Back in New York the new Mr. and Mrs. Van Vechten moved into a suitably bohemian home when they took a room at the Maison Favre boardinghouse on West Fortieth Street, which backed onto the Metropolitan Opera House. The accommodation was not remotely luxurious, but it was a discernible improvement on the dingy room Van Vechten had been renting at a similar establishment on West Thirty-ninth Street for the last year. Edna Kenton was a frequent guest at many of the parties the Van Vechtens threw at their new home and thought it one of the best social spots in New York. Reminiscing about those times, she told Van Vechten how she loved "your indecent and unforgettable tales, with your wonderful blush coming swiftly after, and Ann's great big eyes brimming with laughter with you, and at the world." Van Vechten had equally fond memories. "It wasn't formal and it wasn't rich, but it was delightful."

Roughly a year into his marriage, in May 1908, Van Vechten's career received a huge boost when the *Times* awarded him the coveted position of Paris correspondent. Living on the fashionable rue Jacob, he and Snyder ensconced themselves in Left Bank society, befriending an array of prominent figures, including Polaire, the Algerian-born star of Parisian theater, as famous for her corseted thirteen-inch waist as for her acting talent; the American opera singer Bessie Abott; and James Hazen Hyde, the multimillionaire spendthrift, who had recently moved to France in the wake of a corporate scandal in which he was centrally implicated. The lifestyle was pleasing, but Van Vechten was unsuited to the job and often felt out of his depth. While interviewing the English author Elinor Glyn at the Ritz, he asked Glyn who should play the leading man in the forthcoming stage adaptation of her novel *Three Weeks*. The great lady said she did not know, but whoever it was must have class and must be a European. "No American, with his vulgar padded shoulders," she insisted. As Van Vechten reached self-consciously for the shoulder pads beneath his suit jacket, Glyn said, "I didn't mean you, dear boy. It isn't *your* fault that you haven't centuries of breeding behind you." It was a silly remark, the sort of throwaway witticism that Glyn was famous for. The fact that Van Vechten remembered it decades later and that it was one of the very few anecdotes he told about what should have been an immensely exciting time in his young life indicates the general sense of unease he felt in the job. With little knowledge of politics, and even less interest, he was unable to file the breadth of stories required of a foreign correspondent. His stories showed Paris not as one of the world's great political and financial capitals but as a playground for exceptional creatures and their exuberant lifestyles. The European jaunts of prominent Americans appeared frequently in his features, with details of the luxury and splendor the Vanderbilts and the Barrymores treated themselves to during their months abroad. The few stories about diplomatic rows and developments in the business world, when they did come, were clearly not enough to convince Van Vechten's employers that he should be kept on in such a wide brief, and he was recalled after a year in the post. "I don't think I was exactly what they wanted," he admitted, dryly. It was a chastening experience, one of the few that knocked his usually formidable self-confidence. He returned to New York in the summer of 1909 to continue his duties under Richard Aldrich: filing routine copy on the opera and mopping up the review work that Aldrich thought unworthy of his own attentions.

In the long run, being pulled back from Paris was highly fortunate. On his return to New York Van Vechten discovered the city at the start of an exciting cultural moment, the first of many to which he managed to tie himself. In recent months Alfred Stieglitz had displayed the paintings of Henri Matisse at 291, the first exhibition of modern art in America, while a group of New York painters known as the Eight put on a show of their work at the Macbeth Gallery, transferring to the canvas realistic depictions of the gritty panorama of urban American life of the sort that Theodore Dreiser, Stephen Crane, and Upton Sinclair had already committed to the pages of their novels. Soon after, twenty-two-year-old Van Wyck Brooks published *The Wine of the Puritans*, an excoriating attack on an American culture that viewed all art, "ritual, pleasure, light-heartedness . . . as symbols of opposition to the stern economic need." The desperate need for a revitalized national culture, unencumbered by the weight of foreign traditions, was a central seam of Herbert Croly's *The Promise of American Life* too, the work of political philosophy that best embodied the vaulting ambition of the Progressive Era.

When one looks back on this moment from the distance of more than a century, it appears to be an obvious turning point in American cultural history, the first shoots of a modern, urban artistic culture distinctive to the United States that would refute Henry James's old accusation that Americans had "the elements of modern man with *culture* quite left out," the sort of snobbish sentiment that Elinor Glyn had aimed at Van Vechten in Paris. Yet at the time few mainstream critics paid this moment of foment much attention. In fact, a recurring theme of Van Vechten's own work across the six and a half years he spent at the *Times* was the United States' supposed artistic retardation. He once quoted Chaliapin's raging against the close-minded American critics who objected to the crude realities of life appearing onstage, and in his interview with Harold Bauer, Van Vechten noted the English pianist's frustration that Americans apparently needed to pigeonhole art in order to appreciate it. In another of Van Vechten's articles, Luisa Tetrazzini expressed her bemusement at the American obsession with the size and shape of opera singers.

It was to Van Vechten's immense credit, then, that when Isadora Duncan took to the New York stage in November 1909, he was one of the few who recognized that she represented something new and important, although at first he struggled to say exactly what. Duncan's barefoot dances, inspired by the art of ancient Greece and informed by the techniques of ballet, had become a sensation across Europe, where she was hailed as the savior who had reinvented tired old European traditions with her American idiosyncrasies, in equal parts muscular, individualistic, naive, and exhilaratingly modern. Van Vechten was acutely aware of Duncan's European reputation. In the artistic circles in which he mixed on the Left Bank, Duncan, one of the few Americans to be considered a great artist, was lionized. This may have been in Richard Aldrich's mind when he decided that Van Vechten should take responsibility for reviewing Duncan's performances at the Metropolitan in November 1909, though his main reason was that he thought the whole thing rather beneath him. Like the majority of established newspaper critics in the United States, Aldrich considered dance more akin to a vaudeville entertainment than a "proper" art form like the opera.

Van Vechten was woefully underqualified for the job of reviewing the work of Isadora Duncan, who at that moment was the United States' most important modern artist. "I was almost totally ignorant of the finer points of any kind of dancing," he remembered of those assignments, although the deficiency was not his alone. Because dance was barely considered an art form, there was no critical tradition for Van Vechten to draw upon; in the process of writing his reviews late at night he had to invent a critical vocabulary to describe Duncan's performances right there at his typewriter. He was undoubtedly glad of the opportunity, but given his bruising experience of Paris, he was also apprehensive about how to describe things that neither he nor his readership was used to being critiqued. His anxiety bled onto the page. Grasping futilely for the appropriate language and reference points, he decided not to attempt a dissection of Duncan's technique but rather to convey the spirit of her work, its underlying artistic philosophy, which, visceral and unfettered as it was, seemed profoundly unusual to American audiences of the time, though, ironically, it was exactly this that made Europeans think of her choreography as quintessential of the United States. He may have been influenced in his approach by some of the writing about Duncan that had appeared in more obscure New York publications in recent months. Writing in Stieglitz's *Camera Work* magazine,

Isadora Duncan dancing "La Marseillaise," 1917

Charles Caffin had critiqued Duncan's dances in highly impressionistic terms, likening them to the paintings of Matisse. Both, he said, were masters of invoking the rhythms of the natural world, "the corporeality of things," as Caffin put it, submerged beneath a swamp of materialism, from the scent of flowers to the rush of running water. There are faint echoes of that in Van Vechten's reviews, in which he exalted the "life and gaiety and motion" of Duncan's dancing, describing how in one of the "wildest of her dances she closed with arms outstretched and head thrown back almost out of sight until she resembled the headless Nike of Samothrace."

Inexpert as these first efforts were, Van Vechten captured Duncan as an exuberant manifestation of a new type of art, though he struggled with some of her boldest experiments. With a tone of unconcealed astonishment he condemned as "a sacrilege" her use of music "never designed for dancing," such as Beethoven's A Major Symphony. It was evidence that modern art could befuddle him as much as many of the older, more conservative critics. As Paris correspondent he once filed a story in which he described the painting of Matisse as like that of "an inartistic child." Rarely would he admit to ever having held a conservative opinion on matters of art, preferring to fuel the notion that he had emerged from the womb as a maven of the broadest tastes. However, he did concede that although he enjoyed Duncan's approach, its precise meaning had him stumped at first. "Like any other new art," he wrote in a paean to Duncan in 1914, "it is not to be understood at first and I confess in the beginning it said nothing to me."

Duncan was in fact the first of three American female dancers to perform homecoming shows in New York that winter, and Van Vechten was asked to review them all. The second was Loie Fuller, who appeared at the Metropolitan just two weeks later. There was a connection there with Van Vechten's earliest memories of dance, for Fuller's routines were theatrical embellishments of the skirt dancing he had seen as a child. On this occasion it was the lithe, sinuous dancers who darted around Fuller's flowing skirts that caught his eye. Thamara de Swirksy, a Russian dancer, performed bare-legged in a modern American manner with "a more sensuous appeal than most dancers of the classic type," while Rita Sacchetto thrilled with

her "dance of madness in Chopin's *Tarantelle*." Flailing and writhing to the frenzied music, Sacchetto threw herself to the floor "completely exhausted, only to rise again to intensified emotion."

The sight of these barefoot young women expressing intense
emotion through the angles of their bodies brought to mind the atmosphere of *Salome*. In the aftermath of that controversy the American dancer Maud Allan achieved great success in Europe with a
routine she called a Vision of Salomé, which interpreted the themes
of *Salome* through dances of her own. When Allan brought the routine to New York for the first time in January 1910, Van Vechten's
review noted that in the last two and a half years the antics of Salome
had lost much of their ability to outrage: "there were no exclama-
tions of shocked surprise," he told his readers of Allan's performance, "no one fainted, and at the end there was no very definite
applause." By this point Van Vechten's confidence of expression was
beginning to catch up with his critical instincts, and he treated the
Times's readers to perhaps the most evocative descriptions of dance
yet to appear in an American newspaper. He wrote of Allan's "grace,
a picturesque personal quality" that gave her movements an enchanting elegance. "Bare-limbed and scantily draped in filmy gauzes, di-
aphanous in texture and unvivid in colour, she floats from one pose
to the next, emphasizing the plastic transitions with waving arms
and raised legs and sundry poses of the head."

He had no critical grounding in dance, but he did have an intui-
tive feel for it. Memories of dance—the dance of the seven veils, the
cancan from Paris, cakewalks from Chicago nightclubs, even Herbie
Newell—underpinned his education in art and his experiences of
cities on two continents. He was able to express what had so beguiled
Europeans about these American women's dancing, their energy
and individualism, those elemental forces of American modernity.
His name was still unknown to the public—the *Times* gave bylines
only to senior critics—but among his peers his reputation was greatly
enhanced, considered by many to be the city's leading critic of
dance. In those reviews he exhibited the kernel of the abilities that
characterized his subsequent achievements: a gift for recognizing and
expressing the ineffable brilliance of an artist and a moment of performance and, in so doing, binding himself to their greatness.

•

After the ignominy of his Paris experiences, the steps he made as a dance critic were a much needed fillip to a career that had stumbled. At home with his wife the future looked distinctly less promising. In the summer of 1911 Van Vechten's marriage effectively shattered when Anna Snyder left him behind in New York to take an extended break in Europe. From Paris she wrote to him in an attempt to re-kindle their dwindling relationship. "I not only love you," she as-sured him, "I desire you." No matter the strength of her feelings, the marriage had been doomed from the very start. Try as she might, Anna could not share her husband with Avery Hopwood or anyone else, and she felt neglected and marginalized by all of Van Vechten's friends and the full, passionate life he lived outside their home. By the beginning of 1912 the gap between Snyder's expecta-tions of her husband and Van Vechten's behavior had become a chasm. In January Van Vechten received a letter from Elsie Stern Caskey reassuring him that she had convinced Anna to "suppress the tale" of some transgression of his, the precise details of which she only elliptically referred to, though it was likely a homosexual liaison. Stern Caskey reassured Van Vechten that his reputation would survive this incident, but only if he learned to control him-self. "Do everything you can to talk and act discreetly," she im-plored, as "the people you are seen with etc. are going to be the deciding point. You can't afford to antagonize anyone, nor to disre-gard public opinion." Those were wise words: convictions for sod-omy in New York at the time typically resulted in a jail sentence of between four and seven years.

It is possible that Stern Caskey's letter referred to a much darker episode that had taken place roughly four years earlier. In his mem-oirs Bruce Kellner, a protégé of Van Vechten's, claims that many years after their wedding Anna Snyder confided to a friend that by the time she and Van Vechten married in England in 1907 she was pregnant with his child. With his phobia of responsibility there was nothing on earth that Van Vechten would have wanted less than to be a father, and Snyder's letters about their "bohemian domesticity" do not sound as though she had motherhood on her mind. Consequently, if she was pregnant, it is likely that Snyder either had an illegal abortion or carried the baby to full term and had it adopted. Intriguingly, around roughly the same time a married couple who had once worked for Van Vechten's father adopted a baby. Charles not only paid for the child's college education but also offered him a job upon his graduation. There is no paper trail that can either prove or disprove the supposition that this child was Snyder and Van Vechten's, but if true, it is easy to comprehend how the emotional strain of secretly putting their baby up for adoption could have contributed to the disintegration of their relationship.

The marriage in tatters, Van Vechten apparently chose audacious means to secure a definitive split. At the time the only legitimate cause for divorce in New York was adultery, which had probably been one of the root problems in this case, but obviously, to testify to homosexual affairs in a court of law was out of the question. To get around the problem, he hatched a plan. One evening, having hired a room in a hotel, Van Vechten went out to procure a prostitute from Times Square. With the young lady back at the hotel, a friend, Paul Thompson, walked in on the couple accidentally on purpose, thereby being able to truthfully testify that he had witnessed Van Vechten committing adultery.

After five years of marriage the divorce was finalized in August 1912. The split came as a shock to nobody. Uncle Charlie wrote Van Vechten a congratulatory letter when he heard the news. Charlie thought the unhappiness in their marriage had been plainly obvious, not because of anything that Van Vechten had said but because of "the things you have not said, which a young husband would naturally have spoken or written." Many years later Van Vechten gave a remarkable verdict on Snyder and the value of their relationship: "she influenced me in many ways and was very good for my progress." The solipsism of that statement reveals a fundamental truth about Van Vechten's view of his relationships with others, whose value to him was frequently determined by their capacity to aid his interminable process of self-development. Once he had set his mind on erasing somebody from his life, the break—for him at least—was clean. "I can stop a relationship immediately" is how he assessed his ability for such coldly clinical behavior, striking a discernible note of pride. "I'm very hard."

Before the divorce was official, Van Vechten had a new lady in his sights, a twenty-five-year-old Broadway actress named Fania Marinoff. According to the accounts that Marinoff gave to others during her life, she was brought as a child with her Jewish family to America from Odessa, smuggled beneath the skirts of her stepmother on an overcrowded passenger ship only to live undernourished and uneducated in the slums of Boston. At the age of eight she was sent away to be cared for by an older brother, Michael, who, along with his wife, treated her abysmally, working her feverishly hard around the home and locking her up alone in the dark, rats scurrying around her feet, for hours at a time. At the age of twelve Marinoff was paying her own way in the world, working as an actress in the Camilla Martinson St. George Company, a touring theatrical group that bolstered its income during fallow periods by doubling as a sort of itinerant brothel, although Marinoff herself did not turn tricks. By the time she met Van Vechten she had established herself as a bright young thing of the legitimate theater, taking prominent roles in hit Broadway shows, and was tipped for stardom. The tale sounds Dickensian and may well have been exaggerated or embellished in parts; Marinoff shared Van Vechten's flair for mythologizing, and like many actresses of the time, she spent most of her life claiming to be several years younger than she was.

Marinoff was a striking young woman: high cheekbones framed cupid's bow lips and large dark eyes, which looked out imploringly from milk-white skin. Van Vechten was immediately smitten by her looks and her personality. She was vivacious and assertive, the polar opposite of the languid and introspective Anna Snyder, with the added distinction of being an independent, self-made woman, who was urban to the core. "Artistic" might be the kindest way to describe her temperament; Van Vechten himself labeled her "a maid of many moods, and a few minutes after a violent discussion she is all smiles and charm." To Marinoff the whole world was a stage. "If there was a door, she'd go through it," one friend, paraphrasing a line from a Noël Coward play, fondly remembered her predilection

Fania Marinoff

for making a grand entrance. She had "prompt responses for every-thing," remarked another, less fondly. "If one took her to a picture-show she screamed with delight; if some one gave her a new kind of cake she screamed with joy . . . one suspected her reactions of being rather studied, for surely no one could go on reacting so violently for so long without the process becoming automatic." The gasps and shouts and trills of enthusiasm were an expression of shyness and insecurity rather than self-confidence. The hugs and kisses she liberally dispensed were a means of keeping others at arm's length, and very few friends ever saw the extent of the anxieties that plagued her, which ranged from a fear of abandonment to a fear of the dark. She was, in short, a born performer of tremendous emotional com-plexity, a perfect match for Van Vechten.

The two first met through a mutual friend at Claridge's on July 15; a second meeting occurred by chance on August 10. On August 15, they took a room at the Brevoort Hotel and spent the night to-gether for the first time. It was the start of an intense affair, even more tempestuous than the relationship Van Vechten experienced with Snyder. In the normal course of their days together they would go from kissing and cuddling to screaming at each other in the street in a matter of minutes, with the arguments ending as suddenly as they had started. When Marinoff was out of town working in the theater, letters volleyed back and forth to New York, Van Vechten's as giddy and garrulous as those of a lovesick teenager, displaying a tenderness unexpected of a cynical and worldly newspaperman who had just ended a disastrous marriage in unusual circumstances. "Dar-lingest Angel baby," he began one letter in early 1913. "You are the only one—of that I am sure." In mischievous moments, of which there were plenty, he sent his darling "Fan-Fan" warmest love from "Tom-Tom," his pet name for his penis.

Trying to sort people who lived a century ago into neat little piles of straight, gay, and bisexual by transposing their relationships to a post-Stonewall world is a difficult, and perhaps futile, exercise. This is almost certainly true with Van Vechten. That, from an early age, he had strong sexual attractions to men that outweighed any similar feelings he may have had for women is undeniable. But it does not follow that his intimate relationships with women were therefore fraudulent. These were not loveless shams of respectability to cover the dark and painful secret of the love that dare not speak its name. Beneath the bohemian exterior Van Vechten had some thoroughly conventional needs and yearned for the domestic stability that his parents had enjoyed. Until his death he kept a sequence of his parents' heartfelt love letters, written shortly before their wedding. "I must have kisses for breakfast, kisses for dinner and kisses for supper," Charles wrote Ada, whose love, he said, had "a spring like influence over me." Their nurturing relationship as husband and wife was one Van Vechten idealized and craved for himself. He could not feel fulfilled without a steady female companion in his life, a wife to adore him, to love him and reassure him, and at times he enjoyed the physical intimacy that came with these more conventional relationships.

To borrow a cliché from our own time, Van Vechten wanted it all: companionship and worship from an adoring wife who desired him, but also the freedom to follow his sexual urges wherever they led him. He was still on some level the greedy boy who found compromise impossible and would not be satisfied until he had taken every egg from the bird's nest. Anna Snyder had been swamped by his demands and felt ignored and taken for granted. Marinoff, whose whole life was deeply unorthodox and filled with atypical relationships, seemed better suited to a romance that deviated from societal norms. She was also an independent woman with a thriving career who would not wilt in the shadow of Van Vechten's enormous personality. Around a year after their first meeting Van Vechten told Marinoff that she was everything he had always dreamed of, "the only one I have ever found who completely satisfies me." It was the kind of disingenuous hyperbole he was to lavish upon her repeatedly over the fifty-two years that they were together. He loved her, and in the moment of uttering such fierce devotion he probably believed every word of it. But clearly she did not "completely satisfy" him in every way, and Marinoff knew it. From their earliest days together she was aware of Van Vechten's homosexual desires and probably accepted that he would sometimes have sexual encounters with men. Maybe her willingness to share him with others stemmed from a belief in free love, the "New Woman," and other radical ideas about gender roles that were fashionable in the circles in which she and Van Vechten mixed. Many couples of their acquaintance, believing that traditional marriage curbed the freedoms of the individual to an intolerable extent, tried similar companionate arrangements. The fact that Marinoff herself appears to have remained monogamous during the long course of their relationship suggests hers was a compromise she knew she had to make in order to remain beside the man she so passionately loved.

Van Vechten was overjoyed to have Marinoff in his life, taking care of his emotional needs and some of Tom-Tom's physical ones. She was not, however, the right person to aid his "progress," his next step on the road to true sophistication. In a crude assessment of her capabilities he once waspishly declared that "Fania's native intelligence is great; her opinions are frequently worthless." Enlightenment would come instead from a dazzling new source.

FIVE

How to Read Gertrude Stein

* *

In March 1913 Van Vechten interviewed John C. Freund, the editor of *Musical America* and one of the nation's leading authorities on classical music, about how the United States might create art as great as that produced by its cousins in Europe. The key, according to Freund, was women. Just as reformers such as Frances Willard and Jane Addams sought to improve society by imbuing it with civilizing values, by opening salons in their own front rooms, the nation's ladies could foster exciting new arts scenes, full of domestic virtue. "Any one or two dozens of great women in New York . . . could establish the first one," Freund assured his interviewer. It must have amused Van Vechten that Freund appeared unaware that at that very moment a great New York woman was doing just as he suggested, though the things her salon promoted were a long way from the idyll of feminine purity that Freund had in mind.

The woman in question was Van Vechten's remarkable new friend Mabel Dodge. After years of living in picturesque luxury in Italy and France, Mabel had begrudgingly moved to New York with her husband, the acclaimed architect Edwin Dodge and their son, John, in the summer of 1912, finding the United States' most sophisticated city monolithic, gray, and lifeless. In the spacious rooms of her Fifth Avenue apartment, the second floor of an imposing brownstone, she passed her time daydreaming of the Renaissance splendor of Florence and the art nouveau glamour of Paris. "We have left everything worthwhile behind us," she raged. "America is all machinery

and money-making and factories—it is ugly, ugly, ugly!" She decided it was her duty and destiny to release this city into a new plain
of experience.

The change began beneath her very feet. First, she ordered every
inch of her apartment be painted and papered a brilliant white.
Gleaming white marble mantelpieces and long white curtains were
brought in too, along with yard upon flowing yard of white Chinese
silk, "a repudiation of grimy New York." While Edwin and John
were attending football games, she crisscrossed the city in a chauffeur-
driven limousine, peering out at the passing shopwindows, dashing
out of the car only when a divine chandelier, chaise longue, or work
of colored glass came into view, spending no more time on the
mean, functional streets of New York than was absolutely necessary.
On the second floor of 23 Fifth Avenue, Mabel created a pristine
haven of sophistication. Now all she needed were some heavenly be-
ings to share it with.

According to Dodge, she and Van Vechten first met at a dinner
party hosted by a mutual friend. Sitting opposite him at dinner, Mabel was instantly captivated by Van Vechten, who struck her as a
large "porcine" man dressed fussily in a frilly white shirt with "finely
textured red skin," the teeth of a "wild boar," and "brown eyes, full
of twinkling, good-natured malice." Van Vechten was equally intrigued by the exotic but taciturn Mabel. After dinner he sought
her out and made her laugh by discreetly making "affectionate fun"
of their hosts. "He seemed amused at everything; there wasn't a
hint of boredom in him," Mabel recalled. At the end of the evening
she offered him a lift in her limousine. Instead of wanting to go
home to bed, Van Vechten asked to be taken to the Metropolitan
Opera House. "I have to meet some fellows in the lobby at the last
act and see what we're going to say about it tomorrow," he explained,
trying to suppress a smile. "After all, one takes one's job seriously,
I hope."

Van Vechten became a constant presence at the Dodge household,
often arriving in the morning to take Mabel to watch rehearsals at
the Metropolitan or the Manhattan. Unperturbed by his "warm
friendships for other men," for a time Mabel explored the possibility
of taking Van Vechten as her lover. It was only when the intensity of

Van Vechten's attachment to Marinoff became apparent that Mabel settled for a close, if peculiar, friendship. "He was the first person who animated my lifeless rooms," Mabel said, though he was far from the last.

From the early months of 1913 Mabel opened up her home to New York's most influential people. On any given night a hundred or more extraordinary characters ascended the polished wooden staircase of 23 Fifth Avenue to enter Mabel's immaculate chamber of white. Poets from Greenwich Village in scuffed shoes and frayed cuffs were followed by suave, well-fed art dealers, feminist radicals, free love evangelists, college professors, and Marxist agitators. In they filed like rare, exotic beasts stepping onto a bohemian Ark, each of them different from the last, all of them vital to the same outlandish project. They were there for one of Mabel's Evenings, a chance for New York's fractured array of radicals and dissidents to argue, debate, and create. Each Evening was themed by some vital current issue. There were Evenings on "sex antagonism," cubism, "dangerous characters," birth control, female suffrage, "art and unrest," revolutionary socialism, and Freudian psychoanalysis. At Mabel's salon the unthinkable was commonplace; the unsayable, routinely said.

Van Vechten adored the Evenings. He had no interest in the radical political ideas or the unsettling philosophical positions that were posited, but he loved the beautiful surroundings and the spirit of transgression that prevailed. He drank in the atmosphere as greedily as he did the champagne that sparkled and fizzed in Mabel's thin-stemmed crystal flutes. The tiniest sensual details buried themselves into his memory: "Curtis Cigarettes, poured by the hundreds from their neat pine boxes into white bowls, trays of Virginia ham and white Gorgonzola sandwiches, pale Italian boys in aprons, and a Knabe piano." The adornments that pleased him most were the clusters of exceptional people who spun like luminous tops across Mabel's luxurious Angora rugs. "The groups separated, came together, separated came together," Van Vechten wrote in re-creating the scene for a novel in 1922. "I talked with one and then another, smoking constantly and drinking a great deal of Scotch whisky." At Mabel's salon suffragists learned about mother complexes and penis

Mabel Dodge, c. 1910

envy; anarchists were introduced to spiritualism; bohemian artists discovered the mind-expanding power of peyote. In one corner Emma Goldman could be found in heated conversation with "Big" Bill Haywood, the irascible leader of the Industrial Workers of the World, while a Broadway celebrity like Avery Hopwood shared fine wine and cigars with Alfred Stieglitz in another. All the time Mabel floated on the periphery, sphinxlike, watching.

This was Mabel's genius, Van Vechten said: her ability to create a charged environment from thin air; her trick of bringing together incongruous groups of people and watching silently from the sidelines as they argued, joked, and got drunk together. It appealed to his sense of mischief as well as to his decadent instincts. The fact that the salon became an object of notoriety throughout the city, the physical embodiment of Greenwich Village degeneracy, added an extra edge. Newspaper reporters made their way into the apartment one evening and recounted the most heinous sights, of "women in low-necked gowns" smoking cigarettes and consorting with "men with long, black, flowing locks," all of which was shorthand for sedition and sexual perversion.

Despite the salon's reputation for radical politics and the mingling of unlikely groups, the attendees were still capable of being shocked, as Van Vechten proved when Mabel once allowed him to organize the program of entertainment. Inspired by his visits to the cabaret clubs in the Tenderloin, he arranged for a duo of black vaudeville entertainers to put on a little show at the salon, which for all its radicalism was a solidly white environment. Mabel and her bohemians were apparently horrified at what they witnessed. "The man strummed a banjo, sang an embarrassing song and she cavorted," Mabel said. "They both leered and rolled their suggestive eyes and made me feel first hot and then cold, for I had never been so near this kind of thing before, but Carl rocked with laughter and little shrieks escaped him as he clapped his little hands."

Van Vechten had expected and hoped for that response. The fact that many high-minded whites found African-American entertainment vulgar was one of the reasons he loved it. As far as he was concerned, an appreciation of black culture was a revolt against mainstream tastes and a means of confounding societal expectations.

He was far from the first white bohemian to see blackness in this way, and he would certainly not be the last. In the early nineteenth century minstrel performers such as Stephen Foster, Dan Emmett, and Frank Brower ran away from home and toured the country with their blackface acts as a means of repudiating the values and norms of the communities in which they had been raised. Van Vechten's situation was very different, of course, but still, his connection to black people and their culture provided him innumerable ways of rejecting the conventions of society or rebelling against his upbringing, an adolescent urge that persisted in him until late middle age. Even his habit of using the word "nigger" to refer to black people was an immature act of defiance against his parents. Of course such language was not uncommon among white people of the time, but Van Vechten should have known better. After all, he had grown up in a household where racial equality was passionately supported and where racial epithets were strictly taboo; Charles Van Vechten despised the word "nigger" and would not allow it to be spoken in his house. Consequently, when Van Vechten used the word, he did so deliberately and precisely—not because he ever wanted to cause hurt or offense to black people but because the word for him held the allure of the forbidden, a quality he associated with much African-American culture.

Still, the revulsion that the appearance of black entertainers provoked among Mabel's salon of self-proclaimed radicals demonstrates how strongly his ideas about American art and culture differed from many of those around him. Mabel, for instance, had started her salon to shake New York out of what she perceived to be a very American slumber of anodyne mass culture and commercialized frippery. Her tastes were radical but not remotely demotic, and she sometimes despaired of Van Vechten's crudity, his resistance to drawing distinctions between low and high culture. She dismissed as cheap, vacuous, and soulless many of the things he loved best: backstreet entertainments, popular song and dance shows, and the hedonism of uncomplicated pleasures. For her the objective of all art was intellectual and spiritual enrichment. Van Vechten, on the other hand, had grown to love the arts for their capacity to stimulate the senses, to excite, to arouse with novelty and sensation.

Despite their very different sensibilities, Van Vechten credited Mabel with setting his life on a new course. "I think I owe more to her, on the whole, than I do to any other one person," he once reflected. Given the combustibility of their friendship over the years, that was a remarkable admission. They periodically fell out over slights and indiscretions, real and imagined, causing silent feuds that dragged on for years before lines of communication were opened once again as if nothing had happened. During the détentes theirs was an extraordinary friendship sustained through an engrossing exchange of letters in which they joked, gossiped, and bickered. From the 1920s onward their correspondence also became an arena in which they jostled for primacy, each attempting to persuade the other of the superiority of his or her taste. But in that first year and a half of their acquaintance there was no debate about who was the senior figure. Mabel was the latest of Van Vechten's female mentors to instruct him in the art of living. It was she who proved to him definitively that Americans were equal to Europeans in terms of their creative genius. Trivial though it might sound, she also taught him techniques for being the perfect host, managing to appear both withdrawn and omnipresent at the same time, a skill that was crucial to Van Vechten's public reputation as an important figure on the New York arts scene in the decade following the First World War.

Perhaps, though, the greatest lesson Mabel taught him was how to bolster one's profile by championing the work of others. That particular lesson started the day she handed him a book, slim and elegantly bound in ornate Florentine wallpaper, containing the text of *Portrait of Mabel Dodge at the Villa Curonia* by Gertrude Stein, at that point a noted member of the Parisian avant-garde and friend to Picasso, Renoir, and Matisse, yet virtually anonymous in the United States. Written by Stein in the summer of 1912 at Mabel's home in Italy, Van Vechten's copy was one of a small number that Mabel had privately printed and dispersed to her flourishing crowd of New York acolytes. Beginning with one of Stein's most famous lines—"The days are wonderful and the nights are wonderful and the life is pleasant"—*Portrait of Mabel Dodge at the Villa Curonia* is a typical example of Stein's playful, disorientating prose in which words dance and jut from the page, their objective being to create a mood through sound and rhythm. In promoting the book, Mabel introduced Stein to numerous influential Americans, but she was motivated to do so as much by the prospect of enhancing her own reputation as a modernist trendsetter as by her love of Stein's work. Stein, who was herself an immensely ambitious woman who carefully constructed her public reputation, suspected as much, and jealousy, distrust, and rivalry enshrouded their subsequent relationship.

When Van Vechten took up Stein's cause, his reasons were a mixture of sincere admiration for Stein's writing and a desire to attach himself to the stirrings of an exciting new moment in American arts. Immediately he was drawn to the euphony of her writing, and with his keen musical ear and his critical background he frequently described his interest in Stein through musical metaphors, stressing the rhythmical and phonological dimensions of her work. Beyond the words on the page, he was fascinated by Stein, the person, the writer who had the requisite chutzpah to break all the rules, to dump convention and dedicate herself to crafting something so resolutely unusual. To discover that the most radical voice in English literature was a middle-aged Jewish American lesbian in self-exile in France, whose home was decorated with canvases painted by the mercurial imaginations of Europe's experimental visionaries, was too perfect for words. As with his attachment to African-American culture, the exoticism of Stein's writing remained a strong attraction his entire life. In the 1920s, when he began to write bestselling novels, he incorporated a number of Stein's devices and affectations in homage to the great lady in whose shadow he felt his generation of American writers toiled. Most notably, he refused to include speech marks in his writing, to the enduring irritation of his critics, who thought it a ridiculous affectation, an unsubtle shorthand to let readers know that they were in the presence of a genuine sophisticate.

Spotting an opportunity to use his position at the *Times* to glue himself to the burgeoning cult of Stein that was stirring among the members of Mabel's salon, he worked to publish an article about her, this American "cubist of letters," as he described her. After having had pieces rejected by various publications, he managed to persuade the *Times* to print a short profile of Stein, peculiarly, in its

Monday morning financial section. In it, he described Stein as the creator of a new type of literature, comparing her writing with the paintings of Picasso. "This is post-impressionist, or cubist, or futurist literature," he explained to New York's presumably confused bankers and stockbrokers reading that morning; "it is impressionistic, emotional literature . . . a new attempt at feeling a thing." He quoted an unnamed "friend" of Stein's, Mabel Dodge, who attempted to explain the writer's style and purpose. She is "tired of the limitations of literature," Mabel declared, "and she wants to create a new field . . . the reading of this literature demands an entirely new point of view." Just what that "entirely new point of view" was neither Mabel nor Van Vechten could quite articulate. But the significance of the article was not in its navigation of Stein's style and philosophy, a task that keeps dozens of academics in heroic full-time employment to this day. Rather, Van Vechten had introduced the name and legend of Gertrude Stein to the pages of the nation's most widely read newspaper. Without having ever met him, Gertrude Stein had an enthusiastic new cheerleader.

Just a few days earlier, on February 17, 1913, the International Exhibition of Modern Art, or the Armory Show, as it is more commonly known, opened in New York. The Armory Show that year displayed the best of American modern art, as well as Europe's cubists, fauvists, and futurists. Cézanne, Kandinsky, Gauguin, and Picasso all were displayed, though the work that became synonymous with the event was Marcel Duchamp's *Nude Descending a Staircase*, an abstracted depiction of a body in sequential stages of motion that signaled a bold departure from the realist tradition that most Americans considered art. Van Vechten excitedly attended the exhibition with his friend Henry McBride, an art critic and a fellow Stein worshipper who had just begun a new job at the *Sun* newspaper. "Everybody went and everybody talked about it," Van Vechten remembered with pleasure of the Armory Show. "Street-car conductors asked for your opinion of the Nude Descending the Staircase, as they asked you for your nickel."

The enthusiasm Van Vechten describes was not universally shared. With only rare exceptions, the prominent art critics in the United States ridiculed the Armory Show. It was all overly intellectual

European nonsense, they raged, accessible only to metropolitan cliques. Van Vechten's employers at the *Times* allowed the famous critic Kenyon Cox two pages to castigate the Armory artists and organizers as cynical charlatans who "seized upon the modern engine of publicity and are making insanity pay." *The Chicago Daily Tribune* went in even harder with its headline ART SHOW OPEN TO FREAKS.

As the historian Patricia Bradley points out, critics like Kenyon Cox were born before the United States' dislocating industrial revolution took hold. Their cultural world was shaped not by the roar of motorcars and the flash of electric lights but by a memory of a savage civil war that had brought the American project to the precipice. Like the box holders at the Metropolitan Opera House who threw up their hands in disgust at *Salome*, these critics believed the point of art was to unify and soothe, to create order from chaos, and to play a purposeful role in national life. To them modern art's violent abstractions, sexual overtones, and reordering of the physical universe were not only unpleasant but un-American and an affront to the traditional values that held the nation together. Van Vechten, however, had come of age in the first years of the twentieth century, when the function of art was very often not to create consensus but to question and explore the powerful forces that were propelling the United States into the next chapter of its astonishing journey. In his promiscuity and unconventional love affairs and his fascination with African-Americans and their culture, Van Vechten experienced those forces as the essence of modern life.

His delight at discovering Mabel Dodge, Gertrude Stein, and the Armory Show within the space of a few months made it painfully obvious that his ideas about art and American life were increasingly out of step with the preoccupations of mainstream critics and especially of his employers at *The New York Times*. Six years into his career at the paper he was treading water, still playing second fiddle to Richard Aldrich and still writing without a byline credit. When in May 1913 he was offered the job of drama critic at a rival paper, the *New York Press*, he leaped at the opportunity, hoping to make a name for himself with the public. He was to begin the job as soon as he arrived back from a forthcoming trip to Europe, where he was planning to meet Gertrude Stein and stay with Mabel at the now legendary Villa Curonia. He wrote Marinoff, who was away working on a play in New Haven, that an exciting future lay ahead for them both.

Armed with letters of invitation from Mabel Dodge, Van Vechten arrived in Liverpool on May 27. By the twenty-ninth he was in Paris, spending the evening at the Folies Bérgère with his friend, and sometime lover, John Pitts Sanborn, an arts critic, with whom he had sailed from New York. Inside the club Van Vechten went backstage to see his old friend the actress Polaire, who, by a freak coincidence, happened to be entertaining Anna Snyder at that very moment. It was an awkward encounter for them both, and Van Vechten's judgment on his ex-wife was far from kind. In his eyes she was haggard, overweight, and "altogether disgusting," he told Marinoff. This was his first time in Paris since the divorce, and he had hoped to experience it afresh, free of the memories of his ill-fated marriage. It was an unfortunate start.

Two evenings later he pushed Anna Snyder from his mind, put on his favorite shirt, a fancy white number decorated all over with tiny pleats, and walked across town to have dinner with Gertrude Stein and her partner, Alice Toklas, at their home in the Sixth Arrondissement. As he crossed the courtyard of 27 rue de Fleurus to the front door, his heart began to beat a little faster beneath his breast pocket. It was not like Van Vechten to be nervous, but on this occasion he could not help it. Over the last year the figure of Gertrude Stein had acquired mythical status in his mind: an avant-garde prophet who existed on a plain high above the common or garden artists of Greenwich Village. Even her address was legend, thanks to the amazing collection of art that she and her brother Leo had accrued. Van Vechten was expecting no ordinary home but a museum of wild curiosities, the Armory Show crammed between writing desks and dining tables.

When the front doors swung open and he was led inside, Van Vechten was astonished to discover that all he had heard was true: 27 rue de Fleurus was a veritable trove of modernist treasures. He told Marinoff about the remarkable Picasso paintings and sketches that met the eye at every turn, many of which featured "erect Tom-Tom's [*sic*] much bigger than mine." At the center of it all sat Gertrude Stein in a high-backed armchair. A portrait of her by Picasso, the jewel of her collection, hung close by on the wall. It showed her leaning forward into the viewer's gaze, hands on thighs in a solid, masculine pose, her face shining out iridescently from the dark, shapeless form of her body. The message was clear: this was Gertrude Stein's domain, and everyone who stepped inside was subject to her burning scrutiny.

Over dinner Van Vechten's nerves dissipated slightly, and the conversation began to flow. Intoxicated by her company, he believed there was no topic that Stein could not talk about at length: "a wonderful personality," he swooned to Marinoff. He loved her deep belly laughs, her inquiring eyes, and her supreme self-confidence; she was happy to greet the world in baggy brown corduroy skirts and carpet slippers. Van Vechten would not be the first or last young man to feel the force of her unconventional powers of seduction, not explicitly sexual but certainly sensual. Like a pilgrim in the presence of a holy relic, he was so eager to confirm Stein's otherworldly qualities that he allowed himself to ignore the machinating, manipulating part of her character that displayed itself that evening, as Stein dropped several unsubtle references to his adulteries and divorce into the conversation. Van Vechten was bewildered and embarrassed but did not question where Stein had received her information or why she had chosen to behave so cruelly. Years later Stein wrote in *The Autobiography of Alice B. Toklas* that Anna Snyder had been a dinner guest earlier that year and had spent much of the evening recounting intimate details of her marital difficulties. When Stein realized that Carl was the "villain of Mrs. Van Vechten's tragic tale," she could not help herself from having a little fun, she said. There was more to it than that. The teasing was a test of whether or not Van Vechten could be trusted as a friend and supporter. After all, he had been referred to her by Mabel Dodge, who Stein believed had exploited their friendship as a means of boosting her own profile. It was a favored tactic of Stein's. The writer Bravig Imbs likened his first meeting with her to an audience with "a Roman emperor, taking a deep malicious pleasure in the all but mortal combat she encouraged among her guests."

Being teased was a new experience for Van Vechten. He was usually the one who poked fun and made others blush for his amusement, pursuing his targets to the point of cruelty. If anyone tried to reverse the roles, he would react angrily and cut him off. In Stein's presence his usual self-assurance abandoned him, and he reverted to the impressionable youth spellbound by a compelling older woman that he had been with Mahala Dutton and Mrs. Sublett. Evidently his willingness to submit to the teasing earned Stein's approval. It set the tone for their relationship for the next twenty years: he was to be a faithful and unquestioning supplicant at the majestic court of Empress Stein.

Two days later, by either design or pure coincidence, Van Vechten and Stein were reunited, when they shared a box at the Théâtre des Champs-Élysées for the second performance of *Le Sacre du Printemps* by the Ballets Russes. Van Vechten had hoped to be in attendance for the premiere four nights earlier, but when he and Sanborn arrived at the theater a couple of hours before the curtain, they learned it had long ago sold out. That first performance hit Paris like a thunderbolt. With its subjects of paganism and ritual human sacrifice, this was a very different kind of ballet from any that had gone before, even for the progressive Ballets Russes. Almost as soon as the curtain came down, stories began to spread, mainly about the astonishing behavior of the audience. In one camp, it was said, jewel-laden defenders of the elegant traditions of classical culture hissed and booed and shrieked in horror from the opening bars. In the other, long-haired, shabbily dressed bohemians applauded the subversion while bellowing insults at the Philistine snobs. Punches were thrown, and duel challenges were issued by affronted gentlemen for the following morning.

Van Vechten's expectations for the second night were enormously high. He was not disappointed. In a letter to Marinoff he hailed it as the most remarkable theatrical event he had ever witnessed, even outstripping *Salome*. The dancing and the music he described as being of "an originality appalling," and the whole event, including the unruly behavior of the audience, was "wildly beautiful." Stravinsky's score on its own, dissonant and wailing and hammered out in complex, brutal rhythms, would have been enough to cause a stir. Allied with Nijinsky's impudent choreography, its every thrust and twist replete with a violent, primeval carnality, *Le Sacre du Printemps* was genuinely revolutionary. Van Vechten could have counted himself immensely lucky to have seen one of the first incendiary performances, but the fact that he had not made it to the premiere rankled him. Upon his return to the United States he decided to rewrite history by claiming he had been one of those privileged few who attended the infamous first night. The lie was a deliberate strategy to bolster his reputation as the United States' leading dance critic. Yet May 29, 1913, was not simply the premiere of a modish new ballet; it was the point at which, to quote Modris Eksteins, art became "provocation and event." Van Vechten grasped this immediately. He believed the opening night symbolized a crucial division between those who wanted to cling to the old values of the nineteenth century and those who wanted to embrace the new ones of the twentieth. In 1915 he published an account of what he claimed to be his experience of the debut performance, leaving nobody in any doubt where his sympathies lay:

> A certain part of the audience, thrilled by what it considered a blasphemous attempt to destroy music as an art, and swept away with wrath, began very soon after the rise of the curtain to whistle, to make cat-calls, and to offer audible suggestions as to how the performance should proceed. Others of us, who liked the music and felt that the principles of free speech were at stake, bellowed defiance. It was war over art for the rest of the evening.

His account reached truly absurd proportions, worthy of his most lurid efforts for the *American*, when he claimed that a man who was seated behind him was so intoxicated by the music, the dancing, and the atmosphere that in keeping with the primitive theme of the ballet, he began "to beat rhythmically on the top of my head with his fists. My emotion was so great that I did not feel the blows for some time . . . When I did, I turned around. His apology was sincere. We had both been carried beyond ourselves."

Van Vechten never intended to write accurate eyewitness testimony, although for decades many writers took his recollections at face value. In playing so freely with fact and fiction he was employing a favorite modernist technique, eliding the distinction between art and reality and using the mythology of *Le Sacre du Printemps* to furnish his own. After Stein read the piece, she wrote Van Vechten to query a minor detail of his recollection—but surprisingly not the date. Amused that she had not picked up on the fabrication, Van Vechten reminded Stein that it was the second night of the ballet that they had attended but assured her that the precise facts were of little importance, and that "one must only be accurate about such details in a work of fiction." Stein presumably felt similarly when she later claimed to have anonymously encountered Van Vechten at the ballet for the very first time and was so struck by his dandyish appearance that she went home and wrote the poem "One Carl Van Vechten" all about her brief encounter with this mysterious stranger. For both Stein and Van Vechten, the event of *Le Sacre du Printemps* was too perfect a moment to be sullied by the straightforward truth.

In June, with her new lover, the twenty-five-year-old socialist poet John Reed, a darling of the Greenwich Village radicals, Mabel Dodge arrived in France from New York, where she had just staged a remarkable pageant at Madison Square Garden in support of striking silk workers in Paterson, New Jersey. Along with Robert Edmond Jones, the future theatrical visionary, Van Vechten, Mabel, and Reed set off for Florence and the Villa Curonia. With Mabel and Reed's attentions firmly devoted to each other, Van Vechten provided most of his own entertainment en route, flirting suggestively with Jones and scaring the shy young man half to death in the process. He baffled the inhabitants of a number of medieval French towns as they motored through, standing on the backseat, lifting his hat, bowing, and shouting, *"Au revoir et merci."*

The Villa Curonia was even more marvelous than Van Vechten

had hoped. Suspended among the Apennine Mountains, the villa was surrounded by dense groupings of cypresses, gardenias, and bushes of sweet-smelling jasmine; peacocks strutted about the lawns as nightingales swooped and sang from the trees above. On the terrace where Van Vechten had his morning coffee, the soft contours of Florence clustered in the distance, the Duomo and Giotto's famous tower stretching high above them. The rooms inside were beautiful too: modern comforts draped in a fluid patchwork of silks, antiques, and tapestries. This was Mabel's Fifth Avenue apartment if decorated by the Medici. The cornerstone of the Italianate fantasy was Mabel's own bedroom, in which she had a velvet ladder affixed to the ceiling above her four-poster bed and from which John Reed descended each night before they made love. Gertrude Stein had been invited that summer but declined. No matter, the other guests provided stimulating company. Paul and Muriel Draper, who ran a celebrated musical salon in London, were there along with the celebrated pianist Arthur Rubinstein, though Van Vechten thought his playing greatly overrated and was annoyed by the attention it drew from the others.

As was customary at the Villa Curonia, the days and nights were taken up with arguments about art. Van Vechten took to the task well, spouting a stream of trenchant opinions in a manner that irritated Muriel Draper, who heard more bluster than considered opinion in his conversation. John Reed, however, found something striking about Van Vechten's swagger, a quality that was absent from any of his journalism, and urged him to adapt his writing to allow more of his personality to shine through. If he did, Reed felt, Van Vechten might find an authentic voice, certainly one that would separate him from the herd of bland American arts critics. At the end of a blissful summer it was a thought that Van Vechten took back with him to New York, Marinoff, and his new position at the *Press*.

With editorial control for the first time in his career, Van Vechten stayed true to the concerns he had spent the summer immersed in, those of the new, the sensational, and the primitive. All three of those encapsulated his review of *My Friend from Kentucky*, an African-

American musical written by J. Leubrie Hill and performed by the Darktown Follies at the Lafayette Theatre, a newly desegregated venue, the first of its type in New York. The show embodied all the things he believed to be authentically black, the thread that bound together the best of the African-American entertainment that he had seen in Cedar Rapids, Chicago, and New York. He praised its exuberant physicality and its "spontaneity" and noted the "semi-hysterical state of enjoyment" it produced in the audience, all of who, apart from Van Vechten, were black: "They rock back and forth with low croons; they scream with delight; they giggle inter-mittently; they wave their hands; they shriek." The visceral responses of the audience at *Le Sacre du Printemps* had sounded the arrival of a modernist revolt against tradition. Van Vechten was keen to point out that such reactions in the black theater were just a regular part of the evening's entertainment. It was a sign, he thought, that the primitive emotions with which Stravinsky, Nijinsky, Picasso, and many other modern artists were attempting to reconnect lay, like the epidermis, just beneath the surface of black skin. It was the first time Van Vechten had expressed in print the nub of an unwieldy idea that would slowly develop and consume his private and professional lives: in its essential primitivism, blackness contains the essence of modern art. In the United States the phenomenon of primitivism—the urge among artists to turn from the traditions of white Western culture and look to the supposedly more primitive traditions of nonwhite communities—is generally associated with the 1920s, after the devastating shock of the First World War had taken its toll and the Jazz Age was in full flow. Yet even before the war broke out in Europe, Van Vechten was promoting black culture in the popular white press. He urged audiences and producers to open their minds to the brilliance of New York's nonestablishment arts. "One thing is certain," he concluded his review. "There are few musical enter-tainments on Broadway that compare with this one."

Further notices about black theater followed, including a warm review of Bert Williams's comeback show at the Palace Theatre and an effusive editorial about *Granny Maumee*, a play starring an African-American cast, which Van Vechten praised not just for its humaniz-ing depiction of black people but because it "is not an imitation of a

French play or an English play or a German play. It is an American tragedy which sprang from the soil." He advocated that *Granny Maumee* should provide the template for a new phase in American theater, "using the negro or the Indian or something which really belongs to us," an extraordinary notion in 1913. He went so far as to investigate the possibility of establishing a black theater company to perform serious dramatic work by and about African-Americans, a venture aborted only because he failed to find black playwrights who wrote of the "essentially Negro character" that he felt needed to be expressed—that is, stories about black people told from what he considered a purely black perspective.

Away from the *Press* he continued to promote Gertrude Stein, one of dozens of artistic causes that he took it upon himself to champion over the next half century. His efforts for Stein were unpaid, but from the beginning it was clear that he saw his own public profile bound up with hers. One evening, in the Brevoort Hotel with Marinoff and Avery Hopwood, he decided to educate the entire dining room by reading aloud passages from *Portrait of Mabel Dodge at the Villa Curonia*. Nobody had asked him to, of course, and Marinoff was mortified at his showing off. Hopwood, however, approved; he was so intoxicated, Van Vechten said, that he even claimed to have deciphered its meaning. In a more sober moment, Van Vechten found Stein her first publisher, Donald Evans, who agreed to take Stein's *Tender Buttons* for his publishing company, Claire Marie. Evans had befriended Van Vechten a couple of years earlier, when working as a copyreader at the *Times*. Although demure and conventional on the surface, Evans was a deeply unusual character, like Van Vechten a devotee of Wilde and the decadents, and committed to living his life in accordance with his artistic principles. Also like Van Vechten, Evans believed himself special, a member of a natural aristocracy of artists. When *Tender Buttons* was published in June 1914, Evans wrote that "there are in America seven hundred civilized people only" and that the book was for them alone. In her very first published work in the United States Stein was depicted by Evans and Van Vechten as a complex author comprehensible only to a sophisticated minority. It was the opposite strategy to that of the

Armory Show, which publicized modern art as if it were a circus coming to town with posters and buttons and merchandising of all kinds. In the future Van Vechten's work as a promoter would employ a little of that same brashness to spread the popularity of various underappreciated artistic figures. For now he was content to carve himself a niche at the very heart of Stein's following, proving to himself and the fashionable crowd around him that he was one of a select band of radicals who would shake things up in the United States as others had done in Europe.

The same attitude is evident in a lengthy piece he wrote for the arts magazine *The Trend* in August 1914, entitled "How to Read Gertrude Stein," with which he established himself as Stein's greatest American champion. Van Vechten's essay was an attempt to demystify Stein as many recent articles, books, and public lectures had tried to do for other modernist causes. Frederick James Gregg, for example, published *For and Against*, which accessibly engaged with both sides of the debate surrounding the Armory Show, and Charles Caffin wrote *How to Study the Modern Painters*. What Van Vechten really did was reinforce the notion, still common today, that Gertrude Stein is a difficult author, explicable only when one has been guided through her work by an expert insider, and even then the mission may be fruitless; special writers require special readers, runs the notion.

He name-drops his way through the essay, allowing the reader to know that they are reading the opinions of a man who has surmounted the disorientating climes of modern art and is on friendly terms with not only Stein but her brother Leo, Henri Matisse, John Reed, and Mabel Dodge. Van Vechten wanted the world to appreciate Stein's genius but was equally eager that it should be through him that its appreciation would flow. When it comes to grappling with Stein's work, Van Vechten lets on that it is all a matter of technique. Only by reading it aloud, he says, can its innate musicality be felt. "Miss Stein drops repeated words upon your brain with the effect of Chopin's B Minor Prelude," he says, reaching for his favored musical metaphors. For readers hoping that Van Vechten might decipher for them the meaning of Stein's writing, he has bad news: he has no more clue than they do. Even his special, direct access to Stein has not helped him. "I have often questioned her," he writes, exaggerating the depth of their relationship at this point, "but I have met with no satisfaction." However, the truly sophisticated will cherish her inscrutability. "Her vagueness is innate and one of her most positive qualities," he declares in a statement as frustratingly vague as anything Gertrude Stein herself could have composed. It might sound like an elegant way of covering up his ignorance, but really this sums up his fascination with Stein—her strangeness and her indefinability. "How to Read Gertrude Stein" has a double meaning, referring to the work of the writer as well as to the personality of the woman. Both are apparently laden with mystery. In Van Vechten's sketch Stein is a literary magician with an elusive yet spellbinding charisma who has alchemically "turned language into music." There is nobody who can compare with her. "She lives and dies alone," he says, "a unique example of a strange art." Van Vechten sent Stein a copy of the piece upon its publication. She gave a measured, imperious response to let him know he had passed another test: "I am very pleased with your article about me."

Gaining Stein's approval was easier for Van Vechten than making a success of his new job at the *Press*. He had started with great energy and the best intentions, expanding the scope of the review section to include productions usually ignored by newspapers, and enlisted exciting new talent such as Djuna Barnes—his "favorite genius"—to write and illustrate reviews. Unfortunately for Van Vechten, the editors of the *Press* saw no signs of genius on his watch. The attention he lavished on black theater they could tolerate, but they became irritated by his refusal to tend to the paper's commercial concerns, especially by repeatedly failing to give review space to those theaters that provided regular advertising revenue. Following several reprimands, he was eventually fired in May 1914. It was obvious that Van Vechten's passions could no longer be accommodated within the narrow parameters of the daily press. He needed a new arena in which to work, but having spent the last decade on newspapers, he had little idea of where to turn next.

•

A few weeks later he was able to put the disappointment aside as he set off for Europe once more, the Villa Curonia being the ultimate destination, and before that, Paris with Marinoff. Among a crowded itinerary, the pair made a pilgrimage to Oscar Wilde's tomb at the Père Lachaise Cemetery, the solemnity of the occasion undercut by the outbreak of one of their spontaneous livid rows, though the following day neither could remember what it had been about. Their evenings were split between the opera and ballet and the sweaty backstreet bars in which ordinary Parisians drank and danced frenetically on tiny dance floors to mazurkas played on accordions, men and women of various ethnicities pressed together in intimate proximity. In between Van Vechten took Marinoff to meet Gertrude Stein and was delighted to find Stein unchanged—the same "intellectual Jewess, the same brown corduroy skirt with a non-descript shirtwaist—and breasts dropping low over her belt—and carpet slippers." It was obvious that Van Vechten was now firmly in Stein's good books: she could not have been more engaging, talking for hours about Spanish dancers, *Tender Buttons*, Donald Evans, Abraham Lincoln's Jewish ancestry, and Mabel's chaotic love life. Most pleasingly of all, she and Marinoff got along famously.

After visits to Venice and London, Marinoff returned to the United States for work at the end of July. Van Vechten soon wished he had left with her. Upon his arrival at the Villa Curonia on the morning of Friday, July 31, he discovered the place enveloped in a strange atmosphere. Neith Boyce had been haunted by the villa's resident ghost and had moved to an even more remote spot, a mountain retreat in Vallombrosa. As a result, Mabel had fallen into a gloomy mood. She had grown weary of the villa and was going to transport the entire household to Vallombrosa on Monday. In the meantime, other guests arrived: the English painter and writer Mina Loy, a zealous convert to futurism and mistress of its figurehead, Filippo Marinetti; Leo Stein, Gertrude's now estranged brother, and his current lover, the artists' model Nina de Montparnasse, a Frenchwoman of great charisma and physical beauty. In the evening Van Vechten found himself alone with Nina—who is perhaps better known today by her real name, Eugénie Auzias—and the two fell into a graphic conversation about their sexual peccadilloes, Nina recommending the thrills of exhibitionism. She also revealed that she knew Hener Skene, a Hungarian musician who claimed to have had an affair with Anna Snyder in the summer of 1911, a revelation that appeared to intrigue the voyeur within Van Vechten rather than cause him upset.

The following morning grave news came. Germany had declared war on Russia. The talk of war in Europe throughout the summer had not bothered Van Vechten much, and it took time for the seriousness of this new development to register in his mind. Greenwich Village and Mabel's salon had been suffused in ideological argument and political activism for the last three years, but Van Vechten never showed the slightest interest in any of it. Even when Marinoff participated in benefit performances for striking workers, he could not rouse himself to take an interest in the substantive underlying issues. As an old man in the 1960s, having lived through two world wars, the Depression, and many stages of the civil rights struggle, he admitted he had neither the knowledge nor the vocabulary to join in conversations about politics. When it came to elections, he cast his vote only if a particularly charismatic candidate was standing. For that reason he supported Franklin Roosevelt and John Kennedy, even though he thought the nation did best under "stupid republican [*sic*] presidents."

On the day that war broke out his diary entry mentions the conflict only in connection with what he regarded as a much more significant event: his decision to abandon journalism for a more artistic calling. He envisioned a swirling work of prose that would combine futurism and the war with Neith Boyce's visitation from a ghost and the bewitching character of Nina de Montparnasse. The disparate elements of the story would be pulled together in the half-fact, half-fiction format of George Moore's that he so admired. Rapidly, however, the gravity of the situation in Europe sank in, though Van Vechten claimed that only Mabel foresaw that this war would have further-reaching consequences than any before. "I've done it all," he had Mabel say in an account he wrote of the episode, "sixteenth, and seventeenth, and eighteenth century art. I've made a perfect place of this and now I'm ready for whatever will come after the war. I am through with all property, as every one else will have to be." Frantic with worry about the war and yearning for the absent John Reed, Mabel recalled in her memoirs how she descended into a foul mood. Van Vechten's flippant humor and his liberal consumption of red wine enraged her; his very presence made her seethe, but she refused to explain the cause of her temper. She screamed at him inside her head while remaining silent and withdrawn on the outside, wearing "a mask of quiescent boredom" that confused and unsettled the others.

For the next several days gloom and panic filled Vallombrosa. Communications with the United States were patchy at best, money was running worryingly low, Italy was descending into chaos, and opportunities to leave the country were few. Eventually Van Vechten and Neith Boyce decided to take their chances and bought themselves spots on a rickety ship back to New York. Mabel was incandescent. She had wanted to remain in Italy with her son long enough to meet John Reed before attempting to find a way home together. Boyce had children to look after, so her early return was understandable. But Mabel saw Van Vechten's departure as an inexcusable act of cowardice, leaving a woman and her child vulnerable to invading troops and the pandemonium of war. As he sailed back to New York at the end of August, Mabel mentally cut him adrift. They would not see each other again for nearly a decade. In reconstructing those final fraught days in print, however, it was to Mabel that Van Vechten gave the gift of prophecy. "Just think," he had her say as war commenced, "the world will never be the same again."

SIX

In Defense of Bad Taste

....

Almost as soon as Van Vechten arrived back from Europe, he was approached by John Pitts Sanborn to take over the editorship of *The Trend*, the magazine in which his article about Gertrude Stein had recently appeared. Despite having concerns about the magazine's finances—the last editor had resigned in a fury about the nonpayment of money owed to him by the publishers—Van Vechten agreed to step into the fold. Without his having to worry about the pressures of appeasing advertisers or writing copy that reflected the views of his superiors on a daily newspaper, this was his chance to develop his writing in the way John Reed had urged him to do. More prosaically, he was mighty relieved to have regular work again—especially now that he was a married man for a second time. The trauma of his separation from Marinoff made the couple realize that they could not live without each other, and in early October they married in a small, unfussy ceremony in Connecticut.

The experience of editing *The Trend* proved to be stressful yet satisfying. As editor he was able to shape the magazine in his own image, an image inspired by the milieu of Mabel Dodge's salon and 27 rue de Fleurus, the Armory Show and *Le Sacre du Printemps*, the Villa Curonia and the European war. Van Vechten's first editorial pledged to "exclude stupidity, banality, sentimentality, cant, clap-trap morality, Robert W. Chambersism, sensationalism for its own sake and ineffectuality of any kind." *The Trend* was to be the intellectual space of his fantasies, "an arena in which fiction writers,

Fania Marinoff and Carl Van Vechten, c. 1925

politicians and poets may find themselves face to face with wild beasts."

In the three issues he edited at the end of 1914, Van Vechten devoted much space to emerging—mostly American—talents who had something vital and new to express. He published illustrations by Djuna Barnes, an essay by Mabel Dodge, polemic prose by Louis Sherwin, and poetry by Mina Loy, Donald Evans, and Wallace Stevens. Perhaps the most remarkable contribution came from the editor himself. Appearing in the November issue, "War Is Not Hell" was unlike anything Van Vechten had previously written, a solemn disquisition on the meaning of the European war for American civilization, a bold step on the road to becoming the new type of writer he had resolved to become at the Villa Curonia. In the vein of so many of the idealistic young artists of Europe, he explained that the true purpose of the war was to "destroy dilettantism and the spirit of imitation, to destroy smugness; to destroy the sense of ownership; property rights, and rights in general; to destroy laws, customs, traditions; to destroy religions; to destroy the domination of *Things*; to destroy system; to destroy formulae . . . to destroy the army; to destroy the bench; perhaps to destroy marriage." Some of these opinions seem far too ideological to have been his own, borrowed instead from the Greenwich Village set or Mina Loy, who, under the spell of Marinetti, wrote excited letters from Italy about the cleansing properties of war and how her masculine spirit craved the heat of battle. However, the zeal for rebellion and the challenge issued to cultural orthodoxies were authentically Van Vechten's. War was not hell, he stated, because hell meant the stasis of eternal pain and drudgery. War, on the other hand, entailed not just conflict but creativity, climactic ends in concert with exciting beginnings. The vicious reality of war, the deaths and the misery that inevitably attend any conflict, was of secondary importance to him. As *Le Sacre du Printemps* had dared suggest, through violence and death, beauty and youth emerge anew. "That is what the war is for, he declared, "to recapture the word 'spontaneous,' to make people realize the meaning of life." It was a callous, idiotic statement, one that expressed nothing about the brutality of war, which of course he had been desperate to escape, but plenty about how he felt the last few months had liberated him.

Days after the article was published Van Vechten went to see a musical revue at the Winter Garden Theatre on Broadway, the venue at which Al Jolson had soared to national stardom over the last three years. Jolson, it turned out, had read the latest issue of *The Trend*, presumably because it included another piece by Van Vechten, which described Jolson as "gifted with the most magnetic and compelling personality upon the American stage today." Jolson sought Van Vechten out to tell him how much he had enjoyed reading the magazine and in particular "War Is Not Hell." Usually, he said, he did not go in for high-minded stuff, preferring to leaf through popular magazines like *Pearson's Magazine* instead. But "War Is Not Hell" had really grabbed him. Van Vechten was overjoyed; it confirmed his suspicion that a new path was beckoning. If such a mainstream Broadway star, a legend of vaudeville and blackface whose repertoire was studded with the songs of Jerome Kern and Stephen Foster, was intrigued by the stirrings of a new cultural moment, Van Vechten was sure that the United States was ready for a leap into modernity in its fullest sense, and if it was afraid to jump, then he would happily give it a push.

The trail to the cliff edge, however, was by no means straight and smooth. Shortly after that encounter with Jolson, Van Vechten's association with *The Trend* came to a sudden end. Having gone weeks without a paycheck, Van Vechten resigned his position after the December issue had been edited, unfortunately before he had been able to publish any new work by Gertrude Stein, as had been his intention. Without a regular income he was in real financial trouble. Marinoff's career was going well, but her earnings could scarcely cover their living expenses; they were particularly cash strapped because for the first year of their marriage they kept separate apartments, a bohemian arrangement that suited their independent lifestyles but bemused Charles Van Vechten, who thought it the latest example of his son's infuriatingly weak grip on the practical demands of the real world. Van Vechten even stopped making his alimony payments to Anna Snyder, who, on March 9, 1915, applied to the courts for back payments of $738. Furious, Van Vechten declared himself both unable and unwilling to pay.

When the alimony payments were first ordered back in 1912, Carl had written to both his brother and father, whining about the injustice of it all, even claiming he was prepared to martyr himself with a prison sentence for nonpayment. Because Snyder had a job of her own and the support of her family, Van Vechten thought it grossly unfair that he should have to contribute to her upkeep out of his modest income. Neither Charles nor Ralph was at all sympathetic. Ralph bluntly told his little brother it was about time he faced up to his responsibilities. "While the alimony seems like a great injustice," he conceded, "the best thing for you to do is buck up and pay it like a man. Your talk of going to jail is all bosh. You simply make yourself ridiculous and would disgrace your family . . . There is nothing like being a man when you are under the dog." Three years later, on Ralph's discovering that Carl had amassed several hundred dollars of arrears, his stance was barely more charitable, though he did provide him with an attorney, albeit one Van Vechten considered incompetent. Charles, ever the dutiful father, tried to soothe and reassure, but he told Van Vechten that he must find a dignified solution. The family's masculine honor was at stake. "Don't fear anything," he wrote Carl. "Do the best you can and stand up like a man," the implication being that thus far his behavior had been anything but manly.

Van Vechten repeatedly stated that he could not afford to settle the debt, yet Snyder refused to reduce her demands. She told the courts that her ex-husband had plenty of money sloshing about, but that he chose to spend it on expensive dinners, drinking sessions, and a wardrobe of fancy clothes, including numerous pairs of silk underpants. On April 5 Van Vechten was sentenced to the Ludlow Street Jail until the issue was resolved. Given the likely trigger of their separation—Van Vechten's roving eye and his homosexual dalliances—Snyder's decision to pursue him so vigorously for the alimony payments may have resulted from the hurt and confusion she felt now that he had a glamorous new wife with whom he was apparently besotted. Of course, if the reports are true, she may still have been grieving over the child they put up for adoption and been dismayed that Van Vechten was capable of putting the past behind him so effortlessly.

The sexual dimensions of the split from Snyder lurking unspoken in the background were not lost on Van Vechten, who wrote a comic verse while behind bars titled "The Ballad of Ludlow Street Jail," an allusion to Oscar Wilde's "The Ballad of Reading Gaol." His period of incarceration was, however, infinitely happier than Wilde's and far less injurious to his reputation. Ludlow Street was a relatively relaxed institution, housing many civil rather than criminal offenders, and numerous small luxuries could be acquired for a fee. Van Vechten boasted that he decorated his cell with a Matisse etching, courtesy of the art collector Walter Arensberg, and always maintained that he rather enjoyed his stay. Greenwich Village friends who visited him thought being locked up with an exotic array of ne'er-do-wells was just the sort of scandalous thing they had come to expect of "Carlo," as they all called him. "It was fearfully exciting going to meet you today," wrote Louise Bryant, the far-left journalist. "I terribly envy you . . . Do become well acquainted with the Blue Beard of the many wives and concubines. He is very like my first abortion doctor." From Florence, Mina Loy expressed similar envy: "The only place for a writer is prison." Back in Cedar Rapids the situation caused pain and humiliation. Van Vechten's father was only thankful that the editor of the local paper pledged to hush up the story out of respect for the family. Eventually Van Vechten was released on April 28 on the agreement that Snyder would receive a one-off lump sum of $2250, paid out of Van Vechten family money.

Over the years, Van Vechten embellished the tale of his imprisonment into something more befitting his self-image. He reveled in the notoriety, and with repeated telling his stories grew increasingly elaborate. He claimed to have had a piano in his cell—as was not the case—and his three-week sentence eventually became an ordeal of four months, a fabrication that possibly ended up supplanting the truth in his own mind. Following his release, he continued to write freelance, managing to get provocative articles published in various fashionable organs, including a fictionalized account of a visit to a Parisian brothel that was based on a Mina Loy painting, *Love Among the Ladies*, and heavily inspired in its form and style by George Moore. Entitled "An Interrupted Conversation," the piece appeared in *Rogue*, a new magazine founded and run by Louise and Allen Norton. The Nortons were committed to publishing anything that seemed likely to outrage conservative sensibilities, and their magazine's slogan "The cigarette of literature" neatly described a publication intended to be an illicit but sophisticated indulgence. Alongside his own work, Van Vechten convinced the Nortons to place pieces by Loy and Stein, to both of whom he was acting as agent-cum-cheerleader. Though Stein had numerous advocates and possessed the uncommon assurance of a self-proclaimed genius, Loy was far from certain that she had any talent for writing at all. Not only did Van Vechten's enthusiasm bolster her confidence, but his promotion turned her into one of the most talked-about literary figures in Manhattan; her visceral, erotic poetry both extolled and excoriated the New Woman's sexual awakening.

As an essayist, controversialist, and publicist Van Vechten's reputation was growing fast. But fomenting American modernism was not exactly a lucrative career choice. *Rogue*, for example, rarely paid contributors, so he received no remuneration for his own writing, let alone that of the third parties he helped publish in its pages. Not that Van Vechten ever promoted other artists in hope of financial reward. His primary goal was cultural capital. It excited him to feel as though he had an influence on developing tastes and fashions, and publicizing unusual and emerging talents was a means of promoting himself as a man of foresight and sophistication. To be admired in that way was something money could not buy.

By the fall of 1915 Van Vechten had been forced to attempt to live within his means, and his and Marinoff's separate domiciles were traded in for a single marital home, a three-room apartment at 151 East Nineteenth Street. They might conceivably have afforded a larger place elsewhere, but this was an achingly fashionable address. Tucked between Irving Place and Third Avenue and a stone's throw from Gramercy Park, this is what the journalist Harriet Gillespie, in an article in *American Homes and Gardens* in 1914, had famously christened the Block Beautiful, many of the buildings customized and decorated with eclectic designs that made it one of the most attractive neighborhoods in the city, inhabited by dozens of celebrated people. Residents of the Block Beautiful included the muckraker Ida Tarbell and Robert Winthrop Chanler, the aristocratic bad boy of American painting and one of New York's best-loved party hosts. Chanler's parties were held on the top floor of his characterful house, recognizable to many New Yorkers today by the intertwined giraffes bordering the front door, and Van Vechten claimed he was all but forced to attend his raucous parties, "for his unrestrained guests kept me awake if I didn't," though it is difficult to imagine he was anything but a willing and voluble guest. This was the Van Vechtens' kind of neighborhood, a perfect base for them to cultivate their profile as one of Manhattan's most stylish couples: Fania, a left-field star of Broadway and the movies; Carl, a prophet of the United States' emancipation into a new age of speed and sensuality.

In September Van Vechten accompanied Marinoff to New Providence in the Bahamas, where she was to have a starring role in a new movie titled *Nedra*. Even though Van Vechten had a tiny cameo in the production, he passed up the chance to write about the experience of making a movie on location and instead directed his voyeurism toward the island's native population. During the days he strolled the beaches of Hog Island, studying the local youths bathing naked in the sea, admiring their sleek dark skins as they swam and then let their bodies dry in the arid heat of the afternoon. "Wonderful in their lithe nudity, these Negroes," he reminisced in one of the two articles the trip produced, "gleaming in their bronze perfection." He was both erotically and intellectually stimulated. To his eyes, the Bahamians shared the same uninhibited character as many of the African-Americans he had encountered in Chicago and New York, the "essentially Negro character" that he found in *Granny Maumee*. In fact, the Bahamians' innate blackness seemed even closer to the surface of their being, unobstructed by the presence of white Western civilization. One evening a group of young local men and women agreed to entertain Van Vechten with a dance—in exchange for a small sum of money. Van Vechten sat transfixed as the dancers threw out their limbs and swayed their hips, their bodies illuminated in the flickering firelight, all the while accompanied by drumming and singing, a "primitive jingle," as he described it, which was "in its inception, symbolic of manifestations of sex." The Ballets Russes sprang to mind. The primitive feeling of *Le Sacre du Printemps* seemed spontaneously abundant in the folk culture of the Bahamians, their "wild leaps, whirls, contortions of the body, girandoles, occasionally suggesting the barbaric Polovtsian dances in *Prince Igor.*"

Another encounter on the island, this time with a charismatic evangelical sect known as the Holy Jumpers, encouraged him to draw even firmer parallels between blackness and the raw, rebellious spirit that surged within the new breed of radical artists. It was at a local tour guide's suggestion that Van Vechten ventured out of town to a rickety little building, a tiny church made of timber posts and palm leaves. Dozens of parishioners were tightly packed on the church floor, "strewn with dried palm branches," with even more worshippers spilling outside. On a platform at one end of the church, a preacher began an unrestrained performance, which Van Vechten thought resembled "a Mozart overture; there were descents into adagio and pianissimo, rapid crescendos and fortissimos; slowly, slowly, slowly the assemblage was worked upon and with the progression of the exhortation the emotion increased; the preacher was frequently interrupted by shrill distorted cries." As the sermon continued, Van Vechten described the congregation's losing control. His report soon skipped to improbable heights of melodrama as he likened the worshipers' communion with God to a moment of pulsating orgasm:

A young negress rose and whirled up the aisle, tossing her arms in the air. "Oh God, take me!" she screamed as she fell in a heap at the foot of the platform. There she lay, shrieking, her face hideous, her body contorted and writhing in convulsive shudders. [. . .] Her eyes rolled with excitement; supreme pleasure was in her voice. The crisis approached. It seemed as if the girl lying prone was in a frenzy of delight. Every muscle twitched; her nerves were exposed; her fists clenched and unclenched. Uncontrollable and strange cries, unformed words struggled from her lips . . . and then a dull moaning, and she lay still.

Aside from the narrow and, inadvertently, patronizing idealizations of black people, the Bahamian articles exhibit Van Vechten's cultural worldview. With an insouciance that failed to disguise a calculated provocation, he proposed that at root Americans and Europeans were in pursuit of the same visceral experience displayed in the "ecstasy of a Negro's sanctity," striving to access raw, truthful emotion buried beneath the patina of manners and social conditioning. "Americans are easily thrilled at a base-ball game; at best they seek a prize fight." It was the guiding force of the age, he argued, the thread that connected the bloodshed of Ypres with Keystone Kops. "Everywhere there is evidence of the search for the thrill, by the masses, by individuals: revolution, fast motoring, war, feminism, Jew baiting, Alfred [*sic*] Casella, aeroplaning, the Russian Ballet," as well as lynching and public executions.

In an article titled "In Defence of Bad Taste," written in September 1915 around the time of his trip to the Bahamas, he urged his compatriots to honestly engage with their instincts when he playfully mocked wealthy Americans who relied on interior decorators to tell them how a home should be properly furnished, for fear of straying from the herd and exhibiting "bad taste." The reticence of creating a home to reflect one's own identity, he argued, pointed to a greater truth about Americans' relationships with art and culture. "Americans have little aptitude for self-expression," he claimed. "They prefer to huddle, like cattle, under unspeakable whips when matters of art are under discussion." The Bahamians exhibited their willingness to abandon themselves to the power of their instincts, as did the Ballets Russes and its fans. Until Americans learned to do the same, he said, they would remain desperately unfulfilled. In what reads like a metaphor for his refusal to deny his sexual proclivities as well as his artistic ones, he avowed it pure folly to live by the rules of others and deny the irresistible force of one's true identity: "it is preferable to be comfortable in red and green velvet upholstery than to be beautiful and unhappy in a household decorator's gilded cage." It was the first time that Van Vechten crystallized on the page what was essentially his guiding philosophy: the objective of existence was to sate one's innate desires rather than to conquer them through the intellect; to thrill, excite, and challenge the senses rather than to explicate or dull them. His encounters with black people in Chicago, New York, and now the Bahamas convinced him that they had an instinctive understanding of this, and access to a fount of primitive feeling that was out of reach of the many white Americans tethered to a prudish and reactionary culture.

The leaden shackle of "good taste" was the ultimate target of Van Vechten's main venture of 1915, *Music After the Great War*, a collection of essays about the current and future states of music. The project had floated around his mind ever since that transformative trip to Europe in 1913. He was keen on the subject, not only because of his passion for and knowledge of new music but also because it was relatively open territory. For years James Huneker had occupied the position of the United States' most radical voice in music criticism, championing Wagner, Debussy, and Strauss with a devilish erudition. But as lively and novel as his criticism had always been, Huneker, now approaching sixty, had little feel for the sounds of ragtime that delighted the general populace and were influencing classical composers at home and abroad. In this respect, Huneker was regarded as a fusty Victorian, a very different figure from the jousting maverick he had been just a decade before. Van Vechten's reputation could barely have been more dissimilar. In 1912, while still at the *Times*, he had written an article about why ragtime was fundamentally different from other recent popular music fads, such as the Viennese waltz. Having interviewed the composer of the hit ragtime tune "The Gaby Glide," Louis A. Hirsch, about its unique qualities of syncopation, Van Vechten suggested that ragtime "is really distinctively American" and more sophisticated than the popular music of any other nation. It was a gentle burst of heterodoxy, but still an opinion that any critic of Huneker's generation would have choked on.

Handled by one of Huneker's old publishers, G. Schirmer Inc., *Music After the Great War* was an audacious first book. Over the course of seven essays it told the American public that music was on the precipice of revolution: the exalted canon of German romanticism "has had its day"; the tradition of Brahms, Bach, and Beethoven was to be incinerated in the flames of war, clearing the way for an uncompromising movement, led by the Russians. Ridiculing the banality of American and English classical composers, he declared the brutality of Stravinsky and the twisting ambiguity of Schoenberg to be the future of music. With a typically breezy flourish he prophesied "beyond doubt that music after the Great War will be 'newer' (I mean, of course, more primitive) than it was in the last days of July, 1914." The war would produce a "splendidly barbaric" new order in which the syncopations of Negro music, vulgar to the ears of most established critics, would thrive. The genteel tradition, he told his readers, was as good as dead.

Many reviewers, even those who praised the "clever" author for the robustness of his arguments, found the book so crammed with dissenting opinions that they found it difficult to believe it was meant to be taken seriously. A reviewer for *The Republican* in Springfield, Massachusetts, summed up the sense of incredulity by concluding that the book contained "considerable enjoyment but less sound sense." To some the book's very title was a loathsome impertinence. The war that was supposed to have been over by Christmas 1914 was entering a phase of bloody attrition that nobody had foreseen. To consider how marvelous its effects would be on something as frivolous as music was irreverent in the extreme.

Naturally, the bombast was calculated. Van Vechten was sincere in his desire to shake the United States from its artistic conservatism, and he believed what he said about the arrival of new musical sensibilities. Even so, a film of self-aggrandizing superiority sticks to the profanations of *Music After the Great War*. It was here that Van Vechten first published his lie about attending the premiere of *Le Sacre du Printemps*, clinging to the coattails of some of the greatest artistic innovators of his generation to gain notoriety by association and embroidering a personal mythology that he hoped might put the name Van Vechten in the same category as Duncan or Dodge or Stein. Modern music in America, after all, had no Armory Show moment as painting and sculpture had, so it was with this book that Van Vechten hoped to insinuate himself as a leader of the cultural rebellion. The preening did not go unnoticed. Not for the last time Van Vechten was dismissed by certain critics as a bohemian fraud. "His revolt," one otherwise complimentary reviewer snorted, "goes so far in mad, mad daring that one hears in it the gurgle of the vin rouge of Greenwich Village." Another said the book exhibited nothing more than that its author "has been in Paris, which seems to him to be a precious and exclusive privilege enjoyed by few, and that he has heard Russian music and seen Russian dancers, which are now about to bring glorification unto our poor souls."

Music After the Great War was published at a pivotal moment for the arts in the United States. In 1915 the author Van Wyck Brooks called for Americans to create a vibrant new culture, a "genial middle ground" between the highbrow of "academic pedantry" and the lowbrow of "pavement slang." Throughout the war years the shoots of this new culture burst through the soil. The plays of Eugene O'Neill debuted, thanks to the Provincetown Players. Mabel Dodge had moved away from Manhattan shortly after returning from Europe in 1914, but Van Vechten's friends Ettie, Carrie, and Florine Stettheimer opened their Upper West Side home to artists including Charles Demuth and Marcel Duchamp. Radical magazines, including *Others*, *The New Republic*, and *The Seven Arts*, among them published Robert Frost, Khalil Gibran, Ezra Pound, William Carlos Williams, T. S. Eliot, and Sherwood Anderson.

But more than any other person it was Carl Van Vechten who embodied Brooks's notion of the "genial middle ground." Embracing Stein and Stravinsky in one arm, ragtime and black musicals in the other, he elided the conventional distinctions between highbrow and lowbrow on and off the page. New York was the perfect—perhaps the *only*—place for such an existence. With Paris and London stymied by war with Germany, New York gained a prominent global standing. European avant-gardists such as Duchamp and Albert Gleizes thought the city more conducive to the creation of new art than anywhere in the Old World, not only because of the turmoil that war wrought in Europe but because New York was itself a work of art. Leon Trotsky, one of the many European radicals who sought asylum in the city, believed New York to be "the fullest expression of our modern age . . . a city of prose and fantasy, of capitalist automatism, its streets a triumph of cubism."

Integral to New York's character was the growth of industries to harness the city's creative talents. Publishing, in particular, boomed in the war years with dozens of ambitious new firms being established to promote and sell American literature. In 1916 Van Vechten signed a deal for his next book with perhaps the most exciting of all these outfits, Alfred A. Knopf, run by a twenty-three-year-old sharp-eyed whiz of the same name and his equally brilliant twenty-two-year-old wife, Blanche. Van Vechten was only the third author to join Knopf's stable, the other two being the novelist Joseph Hergesheimer and H. L. Mencken, the essayist and coeditor of *The Smart Set*, who had a compulsion for speaking his mind and tearing into hypocrisy and intellectual laziness wherever he encountered them. On the surface, Mencken and Van Vechten were conspicuously different animals: Mencken, an irascible ball of impatient machismo who saw softheaded idiocy at every turn; Van Vechten a glib, effeminate dilettante with no interest in philosophy, politics, or anything that did not have a direct bearing on the arts. Yet the two formed an instant bond, sharing a sharp, cynical wit and an aversion to abstemious Victorians, who they believed still tyrannized the United States, a type that Mencken characterized as "boobus americanus." They saw themselves as part of an elite order of outstanding citizens whose calling in life was to offer inspiration and guidance to the rest of the nation on all matters of sophistication and substance.

Van Vechten's first book for Knopf, *Music and Bad Manners*, was an exhibition of this cultural leadership, another collection of heretical essays about the musical arts that added an extra coat of varnish to his self-portrait. He furthered his reputation as the United States' lead combatant for contemporary music by taking the fight to its detractors, including his old boss Richard Aldrich, whom he described as "the enemy." Even more than in *Music After the Great War*, this book positioned Van Vechten at the cutting edge, boasting that "even the extreme modern music evidently protrudes no great perplexity into my ears. They accept it all, a good deal of it with avidity, some with the real tribute of astonishment which goes only to genius." He told his readers that they too could become up-to-the-minute connoisseurs, if only they discarded their irrational attachment to the past. Arguing about whether this newfangled music will catch on, he said, is as pointless as debating whether industrialization is here to stay. "Music *has* changed; of that there can be no doubt. Don't go to a concert and expect to hear what you might have heard fifty years ago; don't expect *anything* and don't hate yourself if you happen to like what you hear."

The collection set the template for the next four books of Van Vechten's music and arts criticism that Knopf was to publish by the end of 1920. It unveiled obscure artistic geniuses and elevated things traditionally regarded by the cultural establishment as lowbrow, vulgar, or indecent to the status of high art, using the churning metropolis of New York as its backdrop. In "Music for the Movies" Van Vechten wondered aloud how peculiar it was that as of that moment no serious composer had written a score for a motion picture, pointing out that because the movies represented the most pioneering and demotic form of storytelling, they offered thrilling new opportunities for music, which could in turn transform the art of moviemaking. In other chapters he dealt with Spanish and African-American folk music and Stravinsky's love of ragtime and music hall. The collection ends with a profile of Leo Ornstein, the Russian-American pianist from the Lower East Side, whose body of experimental compositions, Van Vechten said, "vibrates with the unrest of the period which produced the great war."

Two years after he had fled Italy, Van Vechten was still writing about the war as if it were a beneficent force, a catalyst that had delivered the world from artistic sterility. In 1914 and 1915 it was a stance that could be easily maintained and was in fact in keeping with the fashionable attitudes of many radical artists across Europe. But after the United States entered the conflict in April 1917, all such opinions acquired a new piquancy. When conscription was introduced in June that year, a number of Van Vechten's friends willingly filled out their cards. But not all did so in order to thrash the Boche. Donald Evans signed up straightaway and told Van Vechten he had done so "not to make the world safe for democracy, but for the aristocracy of thought. To make life comfortable once more for the decadent, the iconoclast, the pessimist." Having escaped the war once, Van Vechten certainly had no intention of getting caught up in it a

Blanche and Alfred Knopf, c. 1932, photograph by Carl Van Vechten

H. L. Mencken, c. 1913

second time. A letter sent from John Pitts Sanborn to Van Vechten in Iowa confirmed that Sanborn had just signed himself up but that he had also inquired of the conscription official "narrowly about your case." Eager to avoid any possibility of being called into service, Van Vechten appears to have temporarily removed himself from New York. "He says as the law stands if you left before the eleventh," Sanborn continued, "and return only after registration is over you do not have to register."

While an artistic generation, including John Dos Passos, Ernest Hemingway, and E. E. Cummings, left America to discover Europe from behind the steering wheel of an ambulance, Van Vechten stayed home, where he found the charged atmosphere thoroughly stimulating. The day before the United States officially entered the War, he wrote to Gertrude Stein to tell her how Isadora Duncan was whipping the theatergoers of New York into paroxysms of patriotism during her latest performances, which she conducted draped in the American flag, to her audience's roaring delight. "It is very exciting," he assured Stein, "to see American patriotism thoroughly awakened—I tell you, she drives 'em mad; the recruiting stations are full of her converts."

That the energy of the times had grabbed even Isadora Duncan, a fairly unlikely flag waver, demonstrated New York's excitation. Indeed, according to Van Vechten, Duncan was so overwhelmed by her sudden love for Uncle Sam that she seduced a sailor on the sidewalk one evening and spent a good while in the throes of passion with him in the gutter.

The fever of cultural nationalism found its way into Van Vechten's own work too, albeit in his inimitable style. In *Interpreters and Interpretations*, a book of highly subjective pieces about his favorite performers and the art of performance, Van Vechten argued, with extraordinary prescience, that ragtime was the foundation stone of future American music, and named "Lewis F. Muir, Irving Berlin, and Louis Hirsch, the true grandfathers of the Great American composer of the year 2001." To be sure, the United States' "serious" composers, such as Edward McDowell, wrote pleasing enough melodies and harmonies, he conceded, but it was only the syncopated rhythms of ragtime songwriters that managed to capture the "complicated

vigor of American life." Van Vechten explained that the nation's inability to recognize the artistic worth of its own culture was an inevitable consequence of the distinction that had been drawn between
art and entertainment, a distinction that seemed increasingly false
to him. "Americans are inclined to look everywhere but under their
noses for art," he explained. "It never occurs to them that any object which has any relation to their everyday life has anything to do
with beauty. Probably the Athenians were much the same." To his
mind, refusing to acknowledge the worth of ragtime was folly not
only because it denied the validity of American culture but also because it ignored the fact that no great art was ever created through
imitation. Producing facsimiles of European art was sheer futility.
"It is no more use to imitate French or German music than it is to
imitate French or German culture," he wrote. "The sooner we realize this the better for all of us."

Mencken applauded his friend for recognizing that "a vast body
of genuine American music has sprung up out of the depths of popular song, wholly national in idiom, as unmistakably of the soil as
baseball." More than any other writer, in his opinion, Van Vechten
demonstrated that "a man may be an American and still give his
thought to a civilized and noble art, and find an audience within
America." Others were less sure. Some critics accused Van Vechten
of simply being Van Vechten, tossing out an outrageous idea for
the delight of provoking an annoyed reaction rather than espousing
a sincerely held belief. "He likes what is new," sighed one writer,
"because it is new or else because to say he likes a certain thing will
shock a sufficient number of people to make him commanding in
the solitude of his appreciation." And in fairness, Van Vechten did
nothing to discredit such a theory with the public image he projected.
Still a relatively peripheral cultural figure writing esoteric books that
sold to a small, discerning readership, Van Vechten was as well
known for his exotic personality as for his writing. The character he
had been developing for the last decade—that of the sophisticated
dandy always ready with an acerbic put-down and a controversial bon
mot—had now become a professional persona. When interviewed
by *The Morning Telegraph* for a large feature on him in January
1918, he fed the interviewer a stream of quotable lines, some witty,

some insightful, others pretentious, and others still just plain silly. "It would be much better for everybody," ran one of his pronouncements, "if a law were passed consigning all creative work to the flames ten years after it saw the light. Then we would have novelty . . . it must have been thrilling to have lived in Alexandria at the time the library was burned." When asked for his prescriptions for strengthening the health of the arts in New York, he said only constant invention would do, and of the sort that brought together the poles of American culture in the way that Van Wyck Brooks urged, splicing the salons of Greenwich Village with the Broadway stage. "I would ask Gertrude Stein and Irving Berlin to collaborate," Van Vechten said, "or Avery Hopwood and Leo Ornstein."

Although his rhetorical gambits were clearly Wildean, Van Vechten had become nothing less than the archetypal American modernist. His experiences in Europe, combined with lessons he had learned about the arts of mythmaking and promotion from the Everleigh Sisters in Chicago, Oscar Hammerstein, Mabel Dodge, and Gertrude Stein, taught him that being a great artist was far from the only contribution to be made in the war on convention. It was more important to Van Vechten to be on the scene, connected to every new and exciting thing that was going on. He was a one-man publicity machine for American modernism; the Armory Show on two legs, a self-styled tastemaker who embraced taboo and sprayed camphor on moth-eaten ideas of good taste in everything he did.

Back in Iowa, the Van Vechten clan struggled to see the utility in Carl's radical work. As the war hauled itself into 1918 and the Allies inched closer to decisive victory, Charles Van Vechten urged his son to take some constructive part in the wartime displays of virile patriotism. Van Vechten Shaffer, Carl's nephew, became the pride of the family by fighting bravely in France, apparently relishing the opportunity to uphold American ideals against the barbarous Germans. Charles was pleased by Carl's success as an author, but he could not banish the distaste he experienced that his son, at the age of thirty-eight, should still be drawing on his wife's income for financial support and devoting his energies to something as niche and unprofitable

Carl Van Vechten, c. 1925

as music criticism. In ways subtle and unsubtle, Charles never let him forget that artistic fulfillment was no match for financial success. Upon the publication of *Music After the Great War*, Charles said that Van Vechten might become the more illustrious of his sons—but only if he sold enough books to become rich and famous, a reminder of what was expected of the Van Vechten men. The days when Carl was afforded special treatment for being the baby of the family were gone. When his next book, *Music and Bad Manners*, was published, Charles similarly sent sincere congratulations on its quality but again stated the need for Van Vechten to earn money, to take care of his wife and perform his male duty. Another book "for musical people" will "have necessarily a very limited sale," he griped, adding, "I should gladly like to have you write a book that would sell to a million people." The war, he suggested, could be Carl's making, an opportunity to become the steely, self-reliant man he wanted him to be. "Really it looks to us as though your time had come to enter the service of Uncle Sam," he wrote Carl in August 1918. "If you have the spirit which I suppose you must have you will wish to be 'over there' with the others . . . I only wish I was young and strong enough."

Charles's hopes for his son were simply unrealistic: there was no chance that Van Vechten could be dragged away from New York, not for the rush and push of war or even the bright lights of another metropolis. More than ever New York was filled with contradictory forces to shorten the breath and quicken the blood. In recent months Van Vechten had acquired a familiarity with the city's vibrant Yiddish theatrical and literary culture through Marinoff, and his enthusiasm for the entertainments of African-Americans grew all the time. In addition to the plays and musicals that he had raved about in *The Trend* and the *New York Press*, he was enjoying the current surge in cabaret clubs and hotel bars run by and primarily for black New Yorkers, mostly concentrated around the Tenderloin. Marshall's Hotel on West Fifty-third Street was the social hub for New York's most prominent black citizens—chiefly musicians, performers, writers, and theater producers—and was to them what the Algonquin was to be to the celebrated whites of the 1920s: a place to eat, drink, swap stories, show off, make contacts, hatch plans, and be entertained. Marshall's also attracted a coterie of liberal-minded whites,

and Van Vechten was an eye-catching patron of its basement cabaret
in the late teens, his presence there immortalized by Charles Demuth's painting *Cabaret Interior.*

Multiethnic, polyglot New York was the only place he wanted to
be, but the old routine of orchestral concerts and operas was beginning to grate, and in both his personal and professional lives, his
attention drifted toward more exotic territory. In four essays written
between October 1918 and May 1919 and eventually published together in a diverse book of themes entitled *In the Garret* in 1920, Van
Vechten painted a picture of New York as a place of infinite variety,
excitement, and pleasure by introducing his readers to the treasures
buried within unfashionable parts of town populated by black, Italian, and Jewish communities. In this other New York Van Vechten
depicted himself as an urban explorer. "Come with me on a Saturday
or a Sunday night" begins one description of a trip to an Italian theater, as if he were placing the reader's hand in his. "We are in one of
the delightful old Bowery theatres with its sweeping horseshoe balcony and its orchestra sloping gracefully up to the orchestra circle, a
charming old theatre of a kind in which it was possible for the audience to be as brilliant as the play." A million miles from the conventional theaters that his readership frequented, his penetrating gaze
locked on to the scrum of humanity inside and absorbed every sensory detail:

> working men in their shirt sleeves . . . women with black hair
> parted over their oval olive faces suckling their babies, or with
> half nude infants lying over their knees. Boys in white coats,
> with baskets of multi-colored pop and other forms of soda . . .
> mothers and children, young girls with their young men, grey-
> haired grandmothers tightly bound in thick black shawls in
> spite of the heat, sipping the red and pink and yellow pop
> through long straws . . . In a box a corpulent gentleman fin-
> gers his watch chain stretched across his ample paunch. All
> this observed in the smoky half-light of the darkened theatre.

At another Italian theater, this time uptown in Harlem, he found
a similar scene at a performance of Wilde's *Salome.* "No hysteria or

shuddering repugnance informed this mob," he said, in contrast with the outrage that had greeted the American premiere of *Salome*, the opera, at the Metropolitan in 1907. "Young mothers were there with their babes; they suckled them, if nature so demanded. Young girls were there, with lovely black hair and gold earrings; children were there and grandmothers. They had come to see a play . . . it was just a play."

Van Vechten was far from the first to write about the city's ethnic diversity. A number of his friends, including Ida Tarbell, Lincoln Steffens, and Hutchins Hapgood, were among the writers and campaigners who had pulled back the curtains to reveal the lives of the millions of migrants and immigrants who constituted early-twentieth-century New York, but most had done so as part of a mission to expose squalor, inequality, and injustice. Van Vechten's take was different. It was in its mixture of subterranean delights that he located the promise of New York, not its flaws. In February 1919 he wrote a panegyric to the city, rejoicing in its multifarious attractions. In his exhaustive lists of its different languages, communities, cuisines, and architectures, he intended to show that all humanity seemed to live within Manhattan's borders, a place where any appetite could be sated and any sight experienced. By the end of the twentieth century this would have become a common perception of New York, one that New Yorkers would proudly use to define themselves. At the time, in the midst of widespread fears about the latest huge surge of immigrants into the city as Europe tore itself apart, Van Vechten's unqualified celebration of difference was novel and bold. Soaring clear of the Progressive Era's rancorous political debates about immigration, assimilation, and the American "melting pot," he extolled New York's extravagant variety as the secret of its creative genius. This was no mere city, but a fantasy made real. "New York," he said, "is the only city over which airships may float without appearing to fly in the face of tradition. I might safely say, I think, that if a blue hippopotamus took to laying eggs on the corner of Forty-seventh Street and Broadway every day at noon, after a week the rite would pass unobserved."

SEVEN

What One Is Forced by Nature to Do

· ·

When carnage on the Western Front gave way to a shell-shocked peace in November 1918, the Old World rocked on its haunches, its vaunted civilization dreadfully tarnished. Across the Atlantic, the United States entered a decade of unprecedented self-confidence. Mass-production industries from textiles to automobiles fueled a consumerist boom, banishing the unpleasant memories of wartime and providing a renewed sense of national mission. In the cities, New York in particular, there emerged a youthful culture of instant gratification in which American fashions, technologies, music, and movies were preferred to those of Europe. "It was an age of miracles, it was an age of art, it was an age of excess," wrote F. Scott Fitzgerald, summing up the sense of liberation that swept through his generation. "We were the most powerful nation. Who could tell us any longer what was fashionable and what was fun?"

Not that all young Americans were seduced. To some, this was no emancipation, merely enslavement to old conventions concealed beneath garish distractions. Considering themselves outcasts within their homeland, a small cohort of literary tyros—a "lost generation," according to Gertrude Stein—headed to Europe in search of solemn purpose. "A young man had no future in this country of hypocrisy and repression" is how Malcolm Cowley recalled the sentiment that drove him and his clique to the Left Bank and beyond during the twenties. "He should take ship for Europe where people know how to live," where art and intellectual freedom were prized. As a middle-aged man who had long ago experienced his European rites of passage, and for whom the war, in which he had not fought, had precipitated the most creatively satisfying years of his life to date, Van Vechten did not share the disaffection of many of the clever young men who had come of age against the backdrop of industrialized slaughter. Certainly, he despaired at the provincialism and puritanism he still detected at the heart of the nation's culture, but as the 1920s began, he could not have agreed with Cowley's idea that Americans simply did not know "how to live." With every passing year New York's cosmopolitan luster seemed to shine more radiantly; living had never been such fun for Carl.

Into this life of gaiety and promise arrived a new companion who encapsulated the youthful giddiness of the moment. Blessed with soft, conventional good looks—full, plum lips and innocent doe eyes—Donald Angus arrived at the Block Beautiful one afternoon in 1919. The excitable nineteen-year-old fop of a boy was eager to meet the man whose writings on the opera and the ballet had charmed him with their arch wit. Van Vechten was keen to meet Angus too. Their introduction had been facilitated by Philip Bartholomae, a successful playwright, Broadway producer, and irrepressible gadabout with whom Angus had briefly been romantically involved. Such introductions were a key means by which Van Vechten met potential new lovers, safer than cruising and less irksome than going through the elaborate pickup rituals. When Van Vechten answered the door to Angus that afternoon, it was probably in his mind that this meeting would lead to more than a conversation about books.

Many decades later Angus still clearly remembered his first time inside the Van Vechtens' apartment. His eyes were drawn to the clutter of oriental trinkets and the rich scarlet paper studded with gold dots that covered the walls, most striking in such a small apartment. Following his own advice about eschewing interior decorators and their notions of good taste, Van Vechten had hung that wallpaper during one of Marinoff's working absences. On numerous occasions throughout their marriage she returned from a trip away to find the furniture rearranged, sometimes new curtains in place and whole rooms redecorated. This time his impatience to transform the living room meant he had decided to paper around the furniture rather than go to the effort of moving tables and chairs. Slapdash though the decoration may have been, to Angus the interior of 151 East Nineteenth Street matched the bohemian elegance of its celebrated residents. For at least part of the afternoon Marinoff was also there, and even though Angus was hardly an innocent, the couple was wonderfully glamorous to him. Van Vechten found Angus instantly attractive, the kind of sunny, high-spirited, and effeminate boy that he liked best. As they talked and drank, Angus felt Van Vechten's gaze crawling across him, sizing him up with a penetrating stare, at once both warmly playful and coldly scrutinizing. For women, and for some men he knew to be gay, Van Vechten had an intense greeting ritual. For several unsmiling seconds he looked steadily into their eyes, often gripping one of their hands between both of his, the way a charismatic preacher might with a member of his congregation. It made some people understandably uncomfortable. Angus was one of those who loved being the sole focus of Van Vechten's attention, feeling as though nothing in the world mattered more in those few seconds than the connection between him and the remarkable man opposite.

When Marinoff left the apartment for a theater engagement, Van Vechten took Angus to one of his favorite Village hangouts for dinner and drinks. Almost immediately after that first encounter a physically and emotionally intimate affair began; it lasted for one intense year before drifting into a more casual arrangement for the remainder of the twenties. It was an important relationship for them both. Approaching forty, "Carlo" was no longer able to play the neophyte in search of a knowing teacher, as he had with Gertrude Stein, Mabel Dodge, and various others. Instead he would give to Angus what they had given him, an education in how to live, lending him books to read, playing him phonograph records, and even arranging jobs for him with publishers and theater producers. In return Angus offered youth, beauty, and an outlet for Van Vechten's need to instruct, lead, and be admired.

It is difficult to know precisely what Marinoff thought of her husband's new relationship, which was his most involved with another man since they had met. Letters between Carl and Fania from this period betray the same affectionate mutual dependency they

Donald Angus, aged nineteen, c. 1919

had always done, though the sexual passion of their early correspondence had evaporated, as it had in their domestic life. There were no more descriptions of the physical yearnings each experienced in the other's absence, only their unwavering love and their need for companionship. Van Vechten still called Marinoff his baby, but he no longer told her how he wanted to cover her naked body in kisses, and Tom-Tom was never mentioned at all. Bruce Kellner, the same friend of Van Vechten's who suggested in his memoirs that Anna Snyder may have given up a baby for adoption in 1907, speculates that the cause of this change in the Van Vechtens' marriage may have been that Marinoff had also fallen pregnant and given the baby up for adoption during the last year or so. Central to Kellner's speculation is one strange postscript in a letter Marinoff wrote Van Vechten in September 1918 that makes pointed reference to "Baby Van Vechten."

Was Marinoff referring to a child or simply using "Baby" to address Van Vechten as she often did? In an echo of the circumstantial evidence that exists for the possible adoption of Anna Snyder's baby, a person close to Van Vechten's family—Ralph's wife's sister—adopted an infant in hazy circumstances at some point between 1918 and 1920. Perhaps, Kellner ventures, the child was Van Vechten and Marinoff's. The evidence is intriguing but not remotely concrete. It is true that around this time letters indicate that Marinoff was out of town for lengthy periods, perhaps a sign that she was attempting to conceal the pregnancy. However, her extended absences from New York for professional and personal reasons were a constant feature of the Van Vechtens' half-century relationship and should not necessarily be seen as evidence of something untoward. It is more likely that Van Vechten embarked on such an intimate affair with Donald Angus because after seven years with Marinoff the heat of their early passion had cooled, and he felt the need for involved homosexual relationships to be so great that he could no longer ignore it. What is certain is that Marinoff knew about Van Vechten's relationship with Angus from the start. If she harbored any jealousies or objections, she did not express them. In fact, she and Angus quickly became close friends, testament to the unusual but resilient arrangement that was the Van Vechtens' marriage.

•

Several months into his affair with Angus, in January 1920, Van Vechten received his first letter from Mabel Dodge in five years. In it, she made no reference to the events in Italy in 1914 but asked for news of Fania and details of his latest work and told him about the mystical properties of a Native American ring she was forwarding, "for the good of your soul." True to her word, she had long ago abandoned the Medici and Florence, as well as the grunt and grind of New York, to live among the indigenous peoples of New Mexico, and, free from the suffocating embrace of Western civilization, re-connect with nature. Writing just days after the Volstead Act brought Prohibition into effect, she may have thought this the perfect time to offer salvation to the pleasure seekers of Manhattan she had left be-hind. The ring she sent Van Vechten "has very strong (molecular!) vibrations," she assured him, "and if you wear it you will see the effects from it in your everyday life," though quite what they might be she did not relate, and Van Vechten decided it easier not to ask.

Within a month the two were corresponding as freely as if the recent years of silent hostility had never passed. Van Vechten was delighted to have her back in his life. Every time he received one of Mabel's letters, he told her, his brain and muscles raced as they would had he snorted a line of cocaine. She confessed that he excited her every bit as much, though she was always wary of his caustic wit. "Your enhancing appreciation ought to be eagerly claimed and craved by all kinds of personalities of your time," she said of his book *Interpreters and Interpretations*, a volume of essays on his fa-vorite performers. "I would crave it for my own perpetuity did I not fear it more than I desire it! For there is a terror lurking in your pages though I don't know exactly where in it lies. Maybe your wit is a little horrific at times—maybe your smile is full of little dag-gers." Little did she know that at that very moment Van Vechten was securing her "perpetuity" as one of a cast of characters in his first novel.

As he approached his fortieth birthday, Van Vechten had decided to attempt writing a novel because he feared he was a spent force as a critic. He "held the firm belief that after forty the cells hardened and that prejudices were formed which precluded the possibility of welcoming novelty." Less quixotically, he was irritated that his brilliance had earned him eminence and prestige but not fame and fortune. Writing novels, he said, "not only brings one money, it also brings one readers." Primarily, *Peter Whiffle: His Life and Works* is a fictional biography of a would-be writer who spends his life preparing to write a great work of literary genius but never commits a single word to paper because of what he describes as an "orphic wall of my indecision." Van Vechten narrates the story as himself, the conceit being that Whiffle's dying wish was for his friend to write the tale of his life, which Van Vechten agrees to do as "a free fantasia in the manner of a Liszt Rhapsody." Whiffle, who is essentially a composite of Van Vechten and Avery Hopwood, flits from one crowd to another in constant search of new sensations through art, illicit love affairs, alcohol, drugs, and the occult. His experiences mirror many of Van Vechten's memories of his own early adulthood: he plays piano in a Chicago brothel, quaffs champagne in Paris, luxuriates in the riches of the Uffizi. Yet each event is like a fairy-tale reimagining of the truth in which senses are overstimulated, logic dissipates, and people from the real world are bent into curious new forms as in a Coney Island hall of mirrors. Even though he fails spectacularly as a writer, Whiffle eventually realizes that he has turned living into an art form of the highest kind, the type of project that Van Vechten himself was engaged in. "I have done too much, and that is why, perhaps, I have done nothing," Whiffle says to Van Vechten the final time they meet. "I wanted to write a new Comédie Humaine. Instead, I have lived it." The novel's moral is delivered in a maxim that is unmistakably Van Vechten's own: "It is necessary to do only what one must, what one is forced by nature to do."

The novel was published in 1922, a literary year best remembered for two towering masterpieces of high modernism, *Ulysses* and *The Waste Land*, as well as early novels by a couple of future colossi of American letters, *The Beautiful and Damned*, by F. Scott Fitzgerald, and *The Enormous Room*, by E. E. Cummings, both of which crackled with the rebellious energy of the young postwar generation. That same year Sinclair Lewis gave capitalist America a swift poke in the ribs with *Babbitt*. It was a remarkable crop for one year, and at first glance the brittle decadence of *Peter Whiffle* seems glaringly out of place in that milieu. Yet the novel was not quite the florid misfit it now appears. Van Vechten was one of a number of successful but now mostly obscure novelists from the twenties loosely bound together by an appreciation of frivolity and fantasy, whom the literary critic Alfred Kazin aptly dubbed the Exquisites. All were united by an obsession with aesthetics, imagining themselves to be Oscar Wilde or J-K Huysmans with an American accent in an ambitious age of automobiles, airplanes, and moving pictures. The notional figurehead of this group was James Branch Cabell, whose novel *Jurgen* caused a scandal upon its publication in 1919. Though set in some indeterminate past, the novel deals with a thoroughly twentieth-century concept—sexuality—and is full of Freudian imagery, phallic symbolism, and very obvious double entendres. Van Vechten was a huge admirer of *Jurgen*, and its spirit of salacious adventure resounds throughout his own fiction.

Peter Whiffle also makes more sense when placed into Van Vechten's bespoke canon of American fiction, which he publicized in magazine articles in the late teens and early twenties, one populated by unusual and long-forgotten writers, most of whom discarded realism for fantasy and scabrous pleasures of the flesh. At the center was the great lost American genius Herman Melville. Van Vechten's tart, mannered sketches of life among New York aesthetes could scarcely be more dissimilar to Melville's sprawling tales of travel and adventure. Yet in Melville's voracious appetite for life, his taste for subversion, and the threads of sexual ambiguity that run through his work, Van Vechten detected a kindred spirit, one he thought should be recognized as a giant of the nation's artistic heritage. Since the publication of his last novel, *The Confidence-Man* in 1857, Melville's reputation had dwindled rapidly. By the time of the First World War his name was unknown to all but a tiny literary elite. The Melville revival began in earnest in 1921, when Carl Van Doren devoted an entire chapter in his book *The American Novel* to Melville's work. In a smaller way Van Vechten joined the fray later that year with a piece about the character of the American novel in a Yiddish newspaper edited by Jacob Marinoff, Fania's brother, in which he suggested that Melville was one of the foundation stones of the nation's literature. A month later the first biography of Melville was published: *Herman Melville: Mariner and Mystic*, by Raymond Weaver, which Van Vechten reviewed positively in the pages of *The Evening Post* on New Year's Eve 1921. The following January he issued the most strident claim made by any agent of the Melville revival, comparing *Moby-Dick* to *Hamlet* and *The Divine Comedy* in both the majesty of its construction and its importance to a national literary tradition. It is, he said, "Melville's greatest book, assuredly one of the great books of the world," the sort of opinion that is entirely commonplace in the early twenty-first century but seemed conspicuously eccentric at the time, if not willfully perverse.

In *Moby-Dick*, *Mardi*, and *Pierre*, Van Vechten identified Melville as someone more than a writer: he was an intrepid adventurer whose epic imagination was matched only by his unflinching bravery. Here was a true "cosmopolitan, a sly humorist," Van Vechten said, "[a] man who ballyhooed for a drunkard's heaven, flaunted his dallyings with South Sea cuties, proclaimed that there was no such thing as truth, coupled 'Russian serfs and Republican slaves' and intimated that a thief in jail was as honourable as General George Washington." It was the sort of description that could have been written of Peter Whiffle and surely one that Van Vechten hoped might one day be written of his creator.

When Mabel Dodge received her copy of *Peter Whiffle*, she was delighted that Van Vechten had captured so perfectly the emancipated spirit of their society. "Why don't you decide to be a kind of chronicler of your time & do dozens?" she suggested. "Times change— it would be an amusing record. Like Saint Simon & S. Pepys." In her curiously shamanic way, she had unknowingly suggested a type of project that he had already begun. In February 1922 Van Vechten started a diary to capture the events and atmosphere of the times, beginning just weeks before *Peter Whiffle* was published and ending amid the Depression in 1930. Like the minute scrawls of his college diaries, this was not a confessional journal through which he mediated his demons, but rather what he called his daybooks: lists of the people, places, and objects that whirled in and out of his life, his instincts as a writer overruled by the compulsions of a collector. Perfunctory though many of the entries are, they amount to a striking document of 1920s' Manhattan, full of the fights, flings, petty jealousies, and indiscretions of the canonical names of the decade—and, of course, a fast-flowing stream of revelations about his own life.

"The Twenties were famous for parties," he wrote in a recollection of the decade in the 1950s; "everybody gave and went to them; there was always plenty to eat and drink, lots of talk and certainly a good deal of lewd behavior." For once Van Vechten was guilty of understatement. In the unexpurgated, private pages of his daybooks the fevered excess of what he called "the splendid drunken twenties" fills every page, the entries themselves often scribbled through the fog of a hangover. His social calendar was crowded and wildly diverse. During a typical three-week period in late April and early May 1922, his engagements included a recital by the composer George Antheil, a tea party at the Stettheimer sisters' with Marcel Duchamp, an after-show party with Eugene O'Neill at the Provincetown Playhouse, a performance of the vaudeville revue *Make It Snappy,* starring Eddie Cantor, and Geraldine Farrar's farewell appearance at the Metropolitan Opera House, all dotted around the ubiquitous cocktail parties.

The reek of bootleg gin hung permanently in the air like background radiation. The Van Vechten family table in Iowa had always been dry, but neither Carl nor Ralph followed their father's abstemiousness, and both were enthusiastic drinkers their whole adult lives. Prohibition did nothing to curb either's habits, and in Carl's case it only increased its attraction, turning what had previously been a largely benign indulgence into another marker of bohemian sophistication, another medium of rebellion. He had two regular bootleggers: Jack Harper, who with his wife, Lucile, also ran a trendy speakeasy, and Beach Cooke, one of New York's most successful hooch merchants. He and Marinoff were never without a sizable stash of champagne, gin, and whiskey, and out-of-town friends knew that the Van Vechtens could always fix them up with good-quality liquor. Easy access to alcohol was as important to Van Vechten's public image as a Manhattan trendsetter as was his acquaintance with Gertrude

Stein. When Ralph came to visit New York in the summer of 1922, Carl took him for a night out at Leone's, a highly fashionable speakeasy, where Ralph proceeded to embarrass his little brother by bungling Prohibition etiquette. Impressed by his surroundings, Ralph had inquired about getting a membership card, but to protect his reputation as a respected banker, he assumed an obviously false identity to do so. Ralph "makes a provincial ass of himself" was Van Vechten's exasperated judgment in his daybook.

"Provincial" rather than "ass" was the insult here, about the worst thing Van Vechten could imagine being said about anyone. Florine Stettheimer completed a portrait of him around this time that perfectly captures his self-image as the embodiment of contemporary chic and so pleased him that he sent photographs of it to friends far and wide, including Gertrude Stein in France. In it he sits with his legs crossed in a black suit in the middle of his red and gold apartment, as sleek and slim as the cigarette balanced between his clawlike fingers, though in reality the onset of middle-aged spread was expanding his frame quite rapidly. Surrounding him are his cherished possessions: his erudite books and prowling cats, his objets d'art and piano. And in the corner is a fairground sign lit up by electric lights suspended above a miniature merry-go-round, a reference to the title of one of his volumes of essays, but also a metaphor for the life that he led, a brightly colored whirl of amusement.

The only thing missing from Stettheimer's canvas was Van Vechten's coterie of friends, of both sexes, young enough to be his children. They all were either beautiful or talented, or both. The hyperactive silent movie star Tallulah Bankhead became a particular favorite. She could often be found making an exhibition of herself at the Algonquin Hotel, where Van Vechten spent oceans of time either in the dining room or upstairs, taking illicit cocktails in the private quarters of Frank and Bertha Case, the couple who ran and later owned the hotel. Bankhead's loud extroversion annoyed many of the Algonquin's more serious-minded patrons, but Van Vechten found her antics hilarious. At one of his parties she provided a star turn when she "stood on her head, disrobed, gave imitations & was amusing generally." For more sedate reasons, he also found the company of the not-yet-famous George Gershwin, an "egotist" of "con-

Tallulah Bankhead, c. 1934, photograph by Carl Van Vechten

siderable charm," to be a welcome addition to any social occasion as
he filled the room with the strains of his early compositions
"Swanee," and "I'll Build a Stairway to Paradise." Van Vechten
himself had been playing the piano at a party in April 1922 when he
met another dazzling young talent, F. Scott Fitzgerald, for the first
time, the same night that the publisher Horace Liveright, in a drunken
moment of horseplay threw Van Vechten off the piano stool and
broke his shoulder.

The youthful friends and lovers, the parties and the constant
drinking: they all were ways of trying to repudiate the passing of
his own youth. Van Vechten regarded himself as a late starter who
had wasted the first sixteen years of adulthood and had only begun
to fulfill his potential after the life-changing events of 1914. He was
determined to make up for lost time and did so by turning the city
into his playground. This frivolous, self-indulgent atmosphere formed
the backdrop for his next book, *The Blind Bow-Boy*, a whip-smart,
funny, and deceptively insightful novel about a group of New York
sybarites. It is Van Vechten's best piece of fiction and one of the
great forgotten American novels of the 1920s. The story, which has
a far more conventional structure than *Peter Whiffle*, is essentially an
off-kilter retelling of *A Rake's Progress* in which Harold Prewett, a
timid, straightlaced college graduate, is sent to Manhattan by his
wealthy father to be educated in the ways of the world by Paul
Moody, a socialite and louche gentleman of leisure. On the surface,
Moody is a younger Van Vechten; he got the job as Harold's "guide
to fast life" because he is "of good character but no moral sense"
and had once been sentenced to the Ludlow Street Jail for refusing
to pay his ex-wife alimony. However, it is Moody's beguiling female
friend Campaspe Lorillard who expresses Van Vechten's interior
world, his core personality and opinions on life. It is she who lives
on the Block Beautiful, who rhapsodizes about Manhattan and
reads widely and voraciously, casting her eye over her circles of friends
while musing on the curiousness of "the manly American" and the
hidden desires that lurk within us all.

Between them, Moody and Lorillard introduce poor innocent
Prewett to avant-garde composers, fairground snake charmers, speak-

easies, casual sex, fine dining, and all the other sensual pleasures of 1920s Manhattan. It is a story of Harold Prewett's loss of innocence and self-discovery that cleverly doubles as a coming-of-age tale for the United States. When Prewett, a representative of Van Vechten's puritanical and conservative America, is taken on his first trip to Coney Island, he is assaulted by the spectacle of modern consumerism: "Ferris wheels, airplane swings, merry-go-rounds, tinsel and marabou, hula dolls, trap-drummers, giant coasters, gyroplanes, dodge 'ems." Prewett is overwhelmed; Lorillard, ecstatic. "It's superb," she gushes. "It's all of life and most of death: sordid splendour with a touch of immortality and middle-class ecstasy . . . It is both home and the house of prostitution. It is . . . complete experience. It is your education."

The one marvel of modern New York that Van Vechten could not write about overtly was homosexuality, though the subject is woven right through the story, using the language of codes and symbols that were a vital part of gay life in the real world. The effeminate clothing, vocabulary, and mannerisms of certain characters mark them out as homosexual without any categorical identification. The most obvious example is an English aristocrat by the name of the Duke of Middlebottom, a double entendre that seems to have eluded most readers at the time, whose motto is "A thing of beauty is a boy forever." Some of the codes were censored when the novel was published in Britain, but in the United States the book was left untouched. Either the references went unnoticed, or in the "anything goes" atmosphere of the Jazz Age, a little leeway was considered acceptable.

The Blind Bow-Boy is a masterpiece of camp, written decades before the term and concept came into existence, and it sealed Van Vechten's hero status to a small but discerning group of gay, literary-minded cosmopolitan men. Van Vechten was one of the first cultural figures to draw New York's gay subculture into mainstream visibility, leading ultimately to the so-called pansy craze of the early 1930s and the huge success of overtly homosexual cabaret performers such as Gene Malin. As the historian George Chauncey explains, the revolt against Prohibition that created the speakeasy culture fostered

other types of cultural rebellion, including the increasing prominence of homosexuals in public life. A year after *The Blind Bow-Boy*
was published the magazine *Broadway Brevities* complained about
the "impudent sissies that clutter Times Square." There had been
other American writers to include veiled themes of homosexuality
in their novels, but few had done it with such verve or indelicacy as
Van Vechten. His novels spoke to a gay audience with an urgency
that many heterosexual readers, even those who admired his work,
did not experience. One reader wrote Van Vechten to thank him for
portraying his sexually unconventional characters not as freaks but
rather as people in search of happiness because "that is what any so-
called pervert wants although he risks jail everytime he reaches for
that happiness." Another young fan who picked up on the subtexts
and codes was Max Ewing, a midwestern boy studying at the University of Michigan. Ewing, homosexual and a talented writer,
began corresponding with Van Vechten in 1922 for a profile in a
student newspaper. Their correspondence made no explicit reference
to anything sexual, but there can be no doubt that by the time that
Ewing visited Van Vechten in New York for the first time in October 1923 both knew of their shared orientation. The evening Ewing
arrived in town, Van Vechten took him to a party in honor of *The
Blind Bow-Boy*, thrown by Lewis Baer, a member of what Van Vechten had begun to call the *jeunes gens assortis*, the group of young,
handsome gay men whom he collected around him and who, like
Donald Angus, received the benefits of his educating influence. The
term had originally been coined by Jacques-Émile Blanche to describe Mabel Dodge's coterie of young men, but when Van Vechten
appropriated it—admittedly with tongue in cheek—it acquired an
extra layer of significance.

Seen from a distance of eighty or ninety years, the 1920s often
seem a time of striking sexual liberation but usually of a distinctly
heterosexual nature. Images of flappers in thick lipstick and high
hemlines being pursued by girl-crazy men, as in Anita Loos's *Gentlemen Prefer Blondes*, and the love stories of glamour couples, such
as Mary Pickford and Douglas Fairbank, have created a popular notion of a time in which men were men and women were women.
Many of the emblematic writers of the era who have been laid to rest

Max Ewing, c. 1932

in the mausoleum of Great American Novelists are also of a priapic and unambiguously heterosexual sort. Van Vechten wrote novels that offer a glimpse of the pansexual currents of the moment. In a pre-Stonewall world homosexuality was not openly expressed and embraced, but it was there all the same; you just had to know how to decipher its symbols. And with Van Vechten, those symbols were far from Delphic. Long after Van Vechten's death—and some years after the Stonewall revolution—one of his young male admirers said it best: "He knew everyone knew, but he wasn't going to carry a placard down Christopher Street on Gay Day."

The Blind Bow-Boy hurled its author to new heights of popularity. That summer of 1923 Carl Van Vechten was celebrated as a literary sensation. Sinclair Lewis wrote a letter of congratulation that delighted him because it got closest to identifying what he had attempted to express. "It is impertinent, subversive, resolutely and completely wicked," Lewis raved. "You prove that New York is as sophisticated as any foreign capital." The influential Chicago critic Fanny Butcher lauded him as one of the most essential novelists of the moment, and *The Blind Bow-Boy* was probably the sole Van Vechten novel that Scott Fitzgerald genuinely admired. A new friend, the *Vanity Fair* artist Ralph Barton, thought Van Vechten worthy of one of his caricatures, considered an unofficial sign that one was a star in the 1920s. Universal Pictures even entertained the idea of adapting *The Blind Bow-Boy* into a movie. After a lengthy period of consideration Van Vechten's contact at the studio, Winnifred Reeve, eventually got in touch to say that it was going to pass up the opportunity to buy the rights to the picture but forwarded the reader's report as way of explanation and for his amusement. The reader summarized the novel as a tremendously fun tale revolving around a "sissy hero" who is given "a liberal education in matters of sex." The book would be of great interest to the "neurotic cognoscenti," the report concluded, "but not for the radio or motion pictures." Van Vechten noted each letter of congratulation and each word of praise in his daybooks. All the attention came as a relief, confirmation that he really was the special talent that he had believed himself to be for so many years.

Van Vechten's new glitterati status was of no interest to the members of his family, who were shocked and embarrassed by the contents of his latest book. When *Peter Whiffle* was published, Charles Van Vechten had ordered copies for friends and relations and beamed with pride when people around town asked him questions about his boy, the novelist. While the book may have been a little racy at times, it all was handled in a civilized, intelligent manner. *The Blind Bow-Boy*, however, was smut from start to finish. "The new book is a very well written picture of depravity," wrote an exasperated Charles after reading the offending volume. "Not a decent character in the book. It will shock and disgust many readers. While apparently written to amuse it isn't amusing at all." He still intended to order copies for various friends who were fans of *Peter Whiffle*, but "what they may think of it, I don't know." Just before Christmas Charles wrote again to say that though the book was a Cedar Rapids bestseller, nobody ever dared discuss it with him. Uncle Charlie offered praise of what he thought was a "very clever" novel, which was "here and there brilliant," but teased Van Vechten that other members of the family took a dimmer view: "Aunt Mary says that it is a dirty book and that you ought to be ashamed of yourself."

Van Vechten was anything but that. Success as a novelist brought notoriety, influence, and wealth. "Very suddenly, out of the clear sky," he remembered of 1923, "I began to make a great deal of money." When his brother, Ralph, came to New York on business in December, Van Vechten took him, Avery Hopwood, and their friend Ernest Boyd for a slap-up meal at the Algonquin. The occasion was recorded in his daybook with the information that he, rather than Ralph, paid. At the age of forty-three Van Vechten could finally afford to pick up the check. It was a far more important milestone than he would like to have admitted. In the Van Vechten family making money was the mark of a successful man, and the need to make his writing pay had been a constant refrain from his father for the last twenty years. Ralph had been no less attentive on the matter in recent times. After one rebuke from his brother in February 1919 about the parlous state of his finances, Carl had replied with a lofty defense of his art. "The kind of writing I do requires time for reflection," he said, as well as all manner of expenses. "It is one thing or the other for me, either to settle down for a career of a mediocre journalist or to strive for something better." He had finally managed to achieve what had thus far been illusive: fulfillment of his creative ambitions combined with the financial success that his family valued.

Making a point to the folks in Cedar Rapids was at the heart of Van Vechten's intentions for his next novel, *The Tattooed Countess.* Concerning the teenage rebellion of an ambitious and artistic boy named Gareth Johns against the dull rectitude of a midwestern town in the summer of 1897, the story is an obvious retelling of Van Vechten's own adolescence. Van Vechten's escape route from Cedar Rapids had been college life in Chicago. Johns finds his way out of Maple Valley in the embrace of Countess Ella Nattatorini, a woman who left town many years ago to seek a life of refined indulgence in Europe, marrying an Italian aristocrat along the way before his death left her a wealthy widow, free to travel, live, and love as she saw fit. Recently turned fifty and jilted by a caddish French lover, she returns to her hometown to visit her kindhearted but prudish sister and scandalizes the local gossips by smoking cigarettes, wearing makeup, and having a French phrase tattooed on her wrist, "Que sais-je?," an apparent reference to the ironic skepticism of Michel de Montaigne. Bored rigid by the people of Maple Valley and their narrow universe, she eventually embarks on a passionate affair with the seventeen-year-old Johns, the one person in town in whom she detects a spark of life.

Nobody emerges from *The Tattooed Countess* particularly well. With few exceptions, Maple Valley's residents are portrayed as benign but comically small-minded, while the countess, for all her sophistication, "alert intelligence," and "abounding vitality," is presented as the proverbial mutton dressed as lamb, "at that dangerous and fascinating age just before decay sets in." Rarely was Van Vechten crueler in print than in ridiculing this creation of his, a middle-aged woman who still had the temerity to think herself attractive to younger men. For that sin, Van Vechten thought, she deserved to be pitied and scorned. To his friend Hugh Walpole, to whom the novel was dedicated, he derided the countess as "a worldly, sex-beset moron," who was taken for a ride, in every sense of the term, by a "ruthless youth" of "imaginative sophistication." To the poet Arthur Davison Ficke, with whom Van Vechten enjoyed swapping sexual gossip, he suggested *The Tattooed Countess* had a double meaning as "the Countess was certainly full of pricks." The ironic similarities between her predicament and his own—a middle-aged man of expanding waistline and receding hairline, still yearning for the attentions of brilliant boys—does not appear to have struck him. Of all the characters, Gareth Johns, the "ruthless youth" in possession of "imaginative sophistication," fairs best. Although his yearning for a life of excitement makes him cynical and calculating beyond his years, he takes control of his situation and ultimately gets what he wants when the countess whisks him off to Europe. There was never any ambiguity about who was the model for Johns, and Van Vechten's sister, Emma, believed he had got his teenage self down to a T. There are even veiled hints that Johns, like the adolescent Van Vechten, struggles with his sexuality. Despite being slavishly adored by the Countess, his beguiling English teacher, and a pretty female schoolmate, Johns never feels a spark of passion for any of them. He simply exploits their affections and discards them when their purposes have been served.

Cynicism and irony abound in *The Tattooed Countess,* slyly subtitled "A Romantic Novel with a Happy Ending." The joke there was that the "happy ending" was in fact the novel itself. As the real-life Gareth Johns, Van Vechten had come back to haunt and taunt the Midwest of the nineteenth century and in so doing created his bestselling work to date; the book sold in excess of twenty thousand copies in its first month on the shelves. Baiting provincial America was not in itself tremendously noteworthy; it was a favored sport of many writers and intellectuals in the 1920s. Since the end of the war, both Sinclair Lewis and Sherwood Anderson had written acclaimed fiction that lampooned the manners and mentalities of the Midwest, and various state-of-the-nation works such as *Civilization in the United States* expressed the fashionable opinion that the United States of eastern intellectuals was weighed down by the country's old-fashioned, reactionary heartland. Van Vechten was faithfully following the trend, posing, as other writers had done before him, as the chic prodigal son returning home, holding in one hand a color-tipped cigarette and wielding a hatchet in the other, guffawing at the yokels as he hacked away.

The novel was published in August 1924. In October he visited Cedar Rapids and smirked at how accurate his derision of the place had been. William Shirer, later the acclaimed chronicler of the early years of Nazi Germany, was then a twenty-year-old college student who lived with his parents a few doors from the Van Vechtens. He recalled meeting Carl, whom he described as "a sort of invisible force, especially for the young and rebellious in our town" and talking to him about literature and life in New York. Van Vechten's advice to him, "off the record," was to "get the hell out of Cedar Rapids as quickly as possible." Yet disdainful as he was of its charms, Van Vechten could never quite abandon his hometown. During his visit that fall, he wrote Marinoff that the whole place was talking about his book and described his glee at being reviled and feted all at once. He happily gave interviews for two local newspapers, smiling wryly as he protested that the novel was a work of pure imagination. Being liked by the townsfolk or gaining their approval was not important to him, but having their attention was. Tellingly, in the voluminous scrapbooks of press clippings through which he charted the progress of his public reputation over the decades, the judgments of reviewers from Cedar Rapids are always reserved a spot alongside Franklin Pierce Adams, Alexander Woollcott, and the other metropolitan writers. The Iowan critics were usually rather kind, even with *The Tattooed Countess*, proud that the son of a local family was among Manhattan's brightest stars. Van Vechten never decided which he should cherish more, their praise or their opprobrium, but he kept tabs on both all the same.

The spread of Van Vechten's fame from New York to the Midwest and beyond did not dull his efforts as a promoter of causes. Far from it; the boost to his celebrity only gave him more opportunity to put his stamp on the nation's culture and extend his reputation as a tastemaker. It was almost a compulsion; there was nothing that made him feel more vital.

As *Peter Whiffle, The Blind Bow-Boy,* and *The Tattooed Countess* flew off the shelves, Van Vechten used his contacts and influence to further the careers of numerous American writers. He convinced Knopf to publish *Harmonium* by Wallace Stevens and came close to pulling off the same feat for Gertrude Stein's *The Making of Americans.* Elinor Wylie felt so indebted to his public support of her novel *Jennifer Lorn* she gave him a copy inscribed, "Carl Van Vechten . . . But for whom this book would never have been read." In cheering on American talent Van Vechten was following the postwar trend of boosting previously underappreciated American culture, from Herman Melville to Native American folk art. Indeed, it was a trend that he had been instrumental in starting with his advocacy of art as diverse as Leo Ornstein, African-American theater, and Gertrude Stein.

However, his advocacy was by no means restricted to Americans. In the early twenties one of Van Vechten's great successes was an eccentric Englishman by the name of Ronald Firbank, whose hammy comic novels made Van Vechten's look like sober tracts of social realism. His introduction to Firbank's writing came in February 1922, when James Branch Cabell's editor, Stuart Rose, recommended Firbank's novel *Valmouth,* a frothy comedy of manners set in an English spa town, with a barely concealed subtext about interracial and homosexual sex carried out between characters with names such as Dick Thoroughfare and Jack Whorwood. Van Vechten saw Firbank as a fellow rebel against propriety and a man who, like him, found it impossible to dilute his true inner self. Sensing the opportunity to claim him as his latest cause, he immediately wrote Firbank to announce himself as his unofficial American publicist, revealing that he had already produced an article about him for the April issue of *The Double Dealer*—Firbank's first notice in the United States— and more would follow. Firbank was bashful in his reply but also clearly excited by Van Vechten's enthusiasm, and the two began a long-distance friendship through correspondence. Though they had never met—and indeed never did meet; Firbank died suddenly in 1926—they established a close bond, their shared homosexuality at its core, always bubbling beneath the surface of their warm and humorous letters but never overtly mentioned.

Over the summer of 1923 the two swapped gifts via airmail. Van Vechten sent Firbank a copy of the record that the United States was crazy about, "Yes, We Have No Bananas," a song so wonderfully mindless and vulgar, Van Vechten said, it was the anthem of the national mood. In return, Firbank sent a photograph of himself that Van Vechten hung in his bathroom, in a space between a couple of his favorite divas, Mary Garden and Gaby Deslys. More important, he sent his latest novel, *Sorrow in Sunlight*. Set in the West Indies, the story is a fish-out-of-water tale about a black family from the country who go to the city to find their fortune and shin their way up the social ladder. Bouncing along with all the social comedy, frivolity, and innuendo that he so admired in Firbank's writing, *Sorrow in Sunlight* delighted Van Vechten, who took it into his own hands to find the book an American publisher. On September 19 he wrote to Firbank to say that Brentano's was keen on publishing it, as well as all his previous novels, for the American market. With extreme presumptuousness, Van Vechten also mentioned that he would of course write the preface for *Sorrow in Sunlight* should this happen. On October 30, he contacted Firbank again to explain that he had been thinking the matter over and had decided that *Sorrow in Sunlight* was a dreary title. A particular phrase from the novel would be much better: *Prancing Nigger*. With this title, he assured Firbank, audiences would know immediately that the book was exotic, naughty, and fun, and sales would increase enormously. Brentano's agreed: he had already told the editors, and they were set on it. The final decision was Firbank's, but Van Vechten let him know that rejecting the new title would be foolhardy. "Beyond a doubt," he said, "the new title would sell at least a thousand copies more."

Firbank agreed to rename the book—the "title is delicious," he told Van Vechten in November—and arrangements were made for publication in the spring of 1924. He was sincerely thankful for, and flattered by, Van Vechten's interest in him but startled that Van Vechten had been discussing publication deals for his books without telling him first. Van Vechten had championed causes with great enthusiasm before, but this was something else. *The Blind Bow-Boy* had been published just months earlier, and his ego was surging. Never before had he been so sure of the correctness of his opinions. The notion that Firbank might have objected to his interference never entered his thinking. Over the coming years this proprietorial attitude became a recurring feature of his promoting, dispensing orders and grave words of advice in a voice strangely reminiscent of the one both his father and his brother used when lecturing him on financial matters. A close friend once remarked that Van Vechten had "an autocratic way of taking possession of things he wanted." That was especially the case when the thing he wanted could bolster his reputation. When *Prancing Nigger,* complete with Van Vechten's preface, was published later in 1924, the American public knew that Firbank was Van Vechten's discovery. Firbank apologized if some of the outraged reviews the book received from conservative critics harmed Van Vechten by association. "My books are quite unconventional," he wrote, "and shock a lot of people (even in England) and you were brave to champion them." Van Vechten assured him that apologies were unnecessary; riling the critics and attracting controversy were all part of the fun.

The following year Van Vechten's certainty in his tastes spilled over into hubris when he wrote the introduction to *Red*, a collection of essays that was his swansong to music criticism. "I seemed always to be about ten years ahead of most of the other critics," he wrote, immodestly but accurately, in 1925, looking back over his career as a critic. In 1915 he had published his prediction that the primal rage of Stravinsky would conquer America; in 1924 *Le Sacre du Printemps* finally made its New York debut. And now, he assured his readers, he was about to be proved right about African-American music too.

He may have sounded insufferably arrogant, but there is no question that he was correct. Two years earlier, in November 1923, jazz reached an important crossover moment when, accompanied by George Gershwin, the mezzo-soprano Eva Gauthier dedicated the second half of her "Recital of Ancient and Modern Music for Voice" at Aeolian Hall to ragtime and jazz tunes, an unprecedented move

that Van Vechten claimed was originally his idea. There is no definitive proof of that, but it does sound strongly plausible. Nowadays
Gershwin and Gauthier do not seem like such a strange pairing. In
1923 it was the sort of perverse scheme that only someone like Van
Vechten would have dreamed up, like his suggestion to *The Morning Telegraph* in 1918 that Irving Berlin should collaborate with
Gertrude Stein. In the weeks following Gauthier's recital, American
newspapers and magazines earnestly debated the question of whether
ragtime and its offshoots should be taken seriously as great American art—approximately eight years after Van Vechten had caused
irritation and disbelief for suggesting they most definitely should
and more than a decade after he had written an apologia for ragtime
in *The New York Times*.

One evening the following January Van Vechten stopped in at
the sumptuous West Fifty-fourth Street home of the arts patron
Lucie Rosen, where he and a select group of other guests enjoyed
a repeat performance of Gauthier's and Gershwin's unique double
act. After they were through, Gershwin hung around at the piano
and gave a sneak preview of a brand-new piece he had written for
another upcoming concert at Aeolian Hall, "An Experiment in
Modern Music," curated by the orchestral director Paul Whiteman.
It was Gershwin's first long-form concert piece, and he had a title
for it that encapsulated its fusion of African-American and classical
traditions, *Rhapsody in Blue*. Though it was only a fragment, Van
Vechten was rapt by what he heard. A week before the concert he
spent an afternoon in the stalls at Aeolian Hall, listening to Gershwin play the whole of *Rhapsody in Blue* twice. The concert on
February 12, which Van Vechten attended with his friend Rebecca
West, proved crucial in establishing Gershwin's credentials as a composer and the reputation of jazz as a "serious" musical form. It was
also the moment that convinced Van Vechten that his predictions
about the art form were coming true.

So ardent was Van Vechten's belief in the potential of jazz he seriously considered an intriguing proposition from Gershwin a few
months after the Whiteman concert, a collaboration on a jazz opera
about black America, for which Van Vechten would write the libretto and Gershwin the score. "He [Gershwin] has an excellent

George Gershwin, c. March 1937, photograph by Carl Van Vechten

idea," Van Vechten told Hugh Walpole in October '24, "a serious jazz opera, without spoken dialogue, all for Nègres!" Despite his excitement, the project never got off the ground, though Gershwin persevered with the idea and of course eventually wrote *Porgy and Bess* with his brother, Ira, and DuBose Heyward. Of the respected, established music critics of the day, Van Vechten was unusual in his zeal for jazz. Even Paul Rosenfeld, the man who took on Van Vechten's mantle as America's leading advocate of modern music, obstinately rejected the notion that jazz could be considered great art and cited its influence on Aaron Copland as that composer's greatest flaw. By the time he came to make his valedictory comments in *Red*, published in 1925, Van Vechten's mind was certain on the matter. "Jazz may not be the last hope of American music," he conceded, "nor yet the best hope, but at present, I am convinced, it is its only hope."

EIGHT

An Entirely New Kind of Negro

● ●

In May 1924 Van Vechten—out of debt and on the bestseller lists—moved with Marinoff into a new midtown address more befitting their means and celebrity. In Apartment 7D, 150 West Fifty-fifth Street, they found a large, elegant space complete with a dining room, a drawing room, and an entrance hall in which to entertain. Every square inch was adorned by some beautiful object, and visitors were overwhelmed by a bounty of artifacts the moment they stepped through the doorway: antique chairs, towering bookcases crammed with precious first editions, a gilded carriage clock, oriental rugs, oil paintings, and vases of lilies, carnations, and roses all competing for attention. Van Vechten decorated these rooms in the same way he filled his scrapbooks, every last blank space obliterated by color and curiosities. The luxury extended to separate living quarters, Van Vechten and Marinoff each having a bedroom and bathroom of their own. To their wider circle, this was an emphatic expression of the Van Vechtens' unconventional companionate marriage. A small number of closer friends knew it was necessitated by creeping marital tensions. The sexual element of their relationship had fizzled out sometime ago, and Carl's hard-drinking, hard-partying lifestyle was igniting the bickering that had always been one of their favored forms of communication into fearsome rows. Add to this Marinoff's persistent insomnia, and it is clear that the separate rooms were places of refuge for both of them.

The new apartment's mixture of material comforts and emotional volatility made it a fitting venue in which to compose *Firecrackers*, Van Vechten's most abstruse novel to date. *Firecrackers* was another present-day tale featuring Campaspe Lorillard and Paul Moody as they continued their search for meaning and fulfillment amid the carnival madness of Jazz Age New York. The action begins with Moody reading a novel about the Tattooed Countess's relationship with Gareth Johns in Paris, though his attention is not held for long: "It was Paul felt, rather than thought, too much like life to be altogether agreeable." That moment of self-referential humor sets the tone for the rest of the novel, which reads like one long inside joke about modish Manhattan circa 1924. Psychoanalysis, self-improvement philosophies, the cult of youth, pansexual desire, excessive drinking, and an obsession with athleticism and physical perfection all contribute to make *Firecrackers* as "of the moment" as *The Great Gatsby*, a book published that same year. Van Vechten had particular fun sending up the present craze among Manhattan socialites and intellectuals for the teachings of George Gurdjieff, the Armenian spiritualist who claimed that his repertoire of ancient dances held the key to complete spiritual enlightenment. Van Vechten's skepticism inured him to Gurdjieff's charms, and his methods are ridiculed in *Firecrackers* as specious opportunism.

At the end of the novel's madcap, frolicking narrative one is unsure whether to laugh at the gaiety of the pageant or sneer at its shallowness. The author himself no longer knew. Both in his daybooks and in letters to friends Van Vechten admitted that he could not quite articulate what this latest opera buffa was really about. His low-boredom threshold was partly to blame; there were only so many tales of fashionable excess that could be written before the novelty wore off. Mabel Dodge pointed out something more pertinent: that Van Vechten's life was wedged in a familiar groove, endlessly repeating the luxuriant lunacy of his fiction. After visiting New York for a few days during the summer, she wrote him a series of stern rebukes for clinging to a lifestyle that appeared to her to be faintly pathetic, like a prolonged adolescence. "You're too evolved really to be amused by the facts of crude sex in any of its inter relations—rape or whoredom—or bed athletics of whatever kind," she said, referring to the smutty conversations he'd had with Avery

Hopwood in her presence. "You make me sorry for you when I hear you still trying to raise the wind over any of these old and over-worked manifestations." Following Van Vechten's protestations against these derisive remarks, Mabel put her case as plainly as possible in a subsequent letter: "who sleeps with who isn't funny anymore." Clearly she felt he needed some new external stimulus to lift his mind to higher matters. When it arrived, it came from a source that surprised them both.

On June 19 Van Vechten finished redrafting the eighth chapter of *Firecrackers* and settled down to read a book passed to him by George Oppenheimer, an editor and publicist at Alfred A. Knopf. What he found between its pages dazzled him: "a great negro novel." *Fire in the Flint*, was an impassioned protest against segregation, written by an African-American writer named Walter White. This was White's first novel, inspired by his experiences of investigating racial violence on behalf of the National Association for the Advancement of Colored People (NAACP), an organization for which he was then the assistant secretary and was to go on to successfully lead between 1931 and 1955. Consequently, his novels had a fiercely polemical edge, the sort of thing Van Vechten usually dismissed as propaganda rather than literature. Not so *Fire in the Flint*; Van Vechten was enthralled by the ferocity of its rage against a cruel white society and given a new insight into a type of American life far removed from his own.

"I had no idea that you would be so interested in a novel such as mine," wrote White on learning of Van Vechten's appreciation, clearly astonished that the Wildean chronicler of Manhattan sophisticates should be concerning himself with the serious business of southern race relations. Intrigued by his new fan and acutely aware of the commercial implications of having a well-connected trend-setter behind his novel, White was only too happy to accept the invitation to pay him a visit. The two men met at the Van Vechtens' apartment on August 26 and hit it off immediately. White told stories about how his light complexion allowed him to cheat segregation; Van Vechten enthused about *Fire in the Flint* and advised on

Walter White, c. March 1942

how it might be adapted into a stage play. Even after several hours, when Avery Hopwood arrived with his boyfriend John Floyd, both steaming drunk and wanting to party, Van Vechten could not be tempted away from his latest discovery and shooed them off.

That August afternoon was a revelation for Van Vechten. For years he had sought out African-American culture in places most white people would never have dreamed of venturing. But until he read *Fire in the Flint*, his idea of blackness was a caricature centered largely on physical performance. Mrs. Sublett's prayer rituals, the "Negro Evening" at Mabel's salon, the display of the Holy Jumpers in the Bahamas, Bert Williams's genius on the stage, even a growing interest in prizefighting: all suggested to Van Vechten that black people could captivate audiences with their voices, faces, hands, and feet, but not with the written word. In his 1920 essay "The Negro Theatre," Van Vechten said that while "most Negroes have a talent for acting," he had yet to encounter an accomplished black playwright who could capture the experience of being a Negro in the way that the best black actors could. J. Leubrie Hill's 1913 show *My Friend from Kentucky*, which Van Vechten had reviewed in the *New York Press*, was still his benchmark of black creativity, sensual and unrestrained. "How the darkies danced, sang, and cavorted," he exulted in "The Negro Theatre." "Real nigger stuff, this, done with spontaneity and joy in the doing. A ballet in ebony and ivory and rose. Nine out of ten of those delightful niggers, those inexhaustible Ethiopians, those husky lanky blacks, those bronze bucks and yellow girls would have liked to have danced and sung like that every night of their lives."

This was Van Vechten's essential idea of the black artist. Walter White therefore was an unknown quantity: a high-minded black man who used his brain rather than his body for creative expression yet managed to maintain, as Van Vechten saw it, an authentic black identity in his writing. He wrote an excited letter to Mabel trumpeting his new discovery and urged her to tell everyone she knew about him. "He speaks French and talks about Debussy and Marcel Proust," he told Edna Kenton. "An entirely new kind of Negro to me." He could have been describing a precocious child rather than a thirty-one-year-old graduate of Atlanta University and the assistant secretary of the NAACP. Making an intellectual connection with a black novelist genuinely excited Van Vechten, but in the presence of white friends like Kenton he felt compelled to show off, talking of White as his latest novelty. He told Kenton that White was apparently not a one-off: there was an entire community of other literary Negroes. He told her that he hoped to learn more about these "cultured circles."

And indeed he did. Van Vechten could not have picked a better guide to lead him into black Manhattan society had he advertised for one in *The New York Times*. As Van Vechten described him, Walter White "was a hustler." He shared Van Vechten's tendency to value people in terms of their usefulness to him, and though their friendship in these early days was warm, each eyed the other up as a potential asset, White recognizing the benefits Van Vechten's influence could bring to his career and to the African-American cause; Van Vechten seeing White as a fast track to the "cultured circles" in black society. Van Vechten admitted that their relationship was opportunistic in 1960, around five years after White's death. "I was never completely sold on Walter," he said. Explaining how they had grown apart over the years, he said that as time passed, "I was no particular use to him and he was less use to me." From that casual remark one would never guess that Van Vechten was talking about an old friend who had actually named his son Carl in his honor. The best he could muster in White's memory was that "he served his purpose."

White ushered Van Vechten into the center of Harlem, the uptown Manhattan neighborhood that absorbed the majority of the vast flow of black people into New York City in the early twentieth century, some as immigrants from the African and Caribbean colonies of declining European empires, others as migrants from the racially divided South. Harlem was the crucible for a self-confident black identity attuned to modern America, the New Negro, as it became known. Celebrated examples of this postwar urban blackness were as diverse as they were numerous. Madam C. J. Walker, whose parents had been born into slavery, became the United States' first female self-made millionaire producing and selling beauty products specifically for black women. Her daughter, A'Lelia, dressed in silk robes, turbans, diamonds, and furs, was the queen of the Harlem social scene, hosting legendary parties at her properties on Edgecombe Avenue and 136th Street. W.E.B. DuBois, black America's leading intellectual, edited *The Crisis*, the official publication of the NAACP, which dedicated itself to issuing "uplift" propaganda designed to galvanize "the talented tenth" of African-American writers and thinkers. Marcus Garvey led thousands in parades through Harlem's streets under the flag of the Universal Negro Improvement Association. There was even a black Lindbergh, Hubert Julian, who attempted a transatlantic flight from New York to Liberia. These people were just a few members of the varied groups of black artists, activists, and entrepreneurs responsible for what is now called the Harlem Renaissance, one of the most vibrant and important American cultural moments of the twentieth century, which helped push black culture into the national mainstream as never before. In the words of one of its most celebrated citizens, the writer and diplomat James Weldon Johnson, Harlem "was a miracle straight out of the skies."

Van Vechten's initial reaction to mixing in black company that encompassed showgirls, vaudevillians, polemicists, and poets was one of enchanted disbelief; it was the type of thing that only New York could offer, one that not even Campaspe Lorillard had experienced. In November, as keen as ever to show off to his idol, he told Gertrude Stein that his latest diversions were "Negro poets and Jazz pianists." His lightness of tone made it sound as though he expected his Negrophilia to go as suddenly as it came. But unlike birds' eggs, the music of Richard Strauss, Italian theater, and his many other fancies, this was to prove no passing whim.

Over the ensuing months Van Vechten became, in his words, "violently interested in Negroes. I would say violently, because it was almost an addiction." With trademark speed he worked his way through the great texts of an American literary tradition hitherto unknown to him. He mined DuBois's seminal *The Souls of Black Folk* and the novels of Charles Chesnutt. He also discovered a bold and ambitious younger generation of writers who constituted the creative heart of the Harlem Renaissance, expressing the reality of what life was like for young, urban blacks in the new century. He

James Weldon Johnson, c. 1920

especially admired Jean Toomer's radical modernist novel *Cane*; the poems of Countee Cullen, some of which H. L. Mencken published in *The American Mercury*; and the urgent short stories of Rudolph Fisher sent to him by Walter White. The work that affected him most was *The Autobiography of an Ex-Colored Man*, a pained but beautiful novel by James Weldon Johnson. The novel centered on the experiences of a black man passing as white, a subject that fascinated Van Vechten. Johnson was the national secretary of the NAACP, and after being introduced by Walter White, he and Van Vechten became firm friends. For the length of their friendship Van Vechten was astonished by the range of Johnson's talents: he was a gifted musician, an accomplished writer, a skilled diplomat, a shrewd politician, and one of the few black lawyers to be admitted to the Florida bar. It seemed there was nothing he could not do. In awe of his talents, Van Vechten held Johnson up as one of the great living Americans, black or white, as flawless in his eyes as Gertrude Stein.

Schooling himself in African-American cultural history by day, by night Van Vechten developed an obsession with the physical experience of Harlem, "the great black walled city," as he described it. Of course Van Vechten's encounters with the Tenderloin and Chicago's Black Belt meant he was no stranger to African-American neighborhoods after dark. Harlem itself was not entirely unknown to him. In recent years he had occasionally visited theaters in the area and browsed the numerous bookstores that peppered 125th Street. But under Walter White's guidance Van Vechten became acquainted with black people from all backgrounds, from straitlaced social workers to brash artists with smart mouths, sharp minds, and a thirst for hard liquor to rival his own. Very quickly Harlem ceased to be simply another of New York's many exotic diversions that kept Van Vechten amused; it became his all-consuming passion, the absolute center of his social universe.

In 1924, if white people had any familiarity with Harlem's nightlife, it generally came in the racially segregated venues whose names are still known around the world today. The Cotton Club, on 142nd Street and Lenox Avenue, was a temple of primitivism: African drums, African sculpture, and a sprinkling of wild vegetation allowed white patrons to feel as though they had stumbled upon

tribal rites in a jungle clearing. The only black people allowed in
were the dancers and jazz musicians hired to entertain the white
customers and a select band of celebrities to provide a veneer of exotic glamour. Similarly, the Plantation Club on 126th Street between Lenox and Fifth Avenue, catered to a farcical antebellum fairy
tale. Log cabins and picket fences dotted the club's interior while
African-American women in the role of dutiful, chuckling mam-
mies tossed waffles and flapjacks on demand for hungry white customers. When the club was smashed to pieces by a gang in the
employ of a rival speakeasy owner in January 1930, *The Afro American* newspaper reported that "Harlem is laughing—long and loud.
It refuses to be segregated in its own home." These clubs were in
Harlem but clearly not of it.

By and large Van Vechten avoided those places, dedicating
himself to what he considered the *real* Harlem, where black people
could be encountered as drinking pals and not merely as entertainers. Small's Paradise, at 2294 Seventh Avenue, was one of his preferred haunts and arguably the pivotal social venue of the Harlem
Renaissance: an upmarket—"dicty"—"black and tan" club, deliberately catering to whites but welcoming blacks. Small's main attraction was its cadre of lithe waiters, who Charlestoned their way from
table to table, spinning on the balls of their feet, knees darting inward, trays of drinks and plates of Chinese food held high above
their heads. The tables on which they waited enveloped a tiny dance
floor that was always packed. Patrons of all colors pressed up close
against one another, the air between them thick with perspiration,
as they ground their bodies to the gutbucket, the long, meandering
jam sessions performed by the club's resident jazz band.

Small's was the hip joint, the place to be seen, a little like the
uptown Algonquin. Van Vechten could not resist that, but what
excited him most were the low-down venues that the Harlemite
Claude McKay described as "bright, crowded with drinking men
jammed tight around the bars, treating one another and telling the
incidents of the day. Longshoremen in overalls with hooks, Pullman
porters holding their bags, waiters, elevator boys. Liquor-rich laughter, banana-ripe laughter." The Nest fitted the bill perfectly: a scruffy,
smoke-filled, after-hours den in the basement of a brownstone house

on 134th Street. Its clientele was almost exclusively black, including many performers from more salubrious spots who came there to unwind after long sets. Nora Holt was among them: an unconventional and gifted cabaret singer who captivated Van Vechten from their first meeting. Describing Holt to Gertrude Stein, he expressed her charms as exotic, outrageously funny, "adorable, rich, chic," and plenty else besides. Born in Kansas City in 1885, Holt was christened Lena Douglas but changed her name after each of her five brief and turbulent marriages, the first of which she entered at the age of just fifteen. In 1918 she became the first black woman to receive a master's degree from the Chicago Musical College, and she worked for many years as a teacher, composer, and music critic, during which time she founded the National Association of Negro Musicians. But like Van Vechten, she also claimed to have performed at the Everleigh Club brothel in Chicago, and she gained terrific notoriety for her extramarital affairs and her penchant for stripping off and dancing naked at parties.

Perhaps more than any other Harlemite he encountered, Holt expressed within one body what Van Vechten regarded as the ideal elements of black identity: the urbane and thoughtful "entirely new type of Negro" that Walter White had astounded him with as well as the physically expressive and sexually charismatic type that he had romanticized since childhood. Harlem had the curious effect of both dismantling and reinforcing his stereotypes of black people. Despite introducing him to a group of educated African-Americans whom he had previously never given any thought to, Harlem was also Van Vechten's place of escapism, a land of freedom and abandon where fantasies came to life. The Committee of Fourteen and New York City's other powerful moral guardians who had asserted themselves during the Progressive Era were not nearly as interested in monitoring vice and criminality in Harlem as they were in predominantly white areas of New York, just as they had steered a wide berth of the Tenderloin in years gone by.

Harlem's permissiveness manifested itself in numerous ways. Nightclubs in the neighborhood had a rampant drug culture, even at high-profile venues like Small's Paradise, where Avery Hopwood, among others, went for an opium fix; Van Vechten, never a big drug

Nora Holt, c. 1930

user, likely contented himself with the odd joint and line of cocaine. To the annoyance and revulsion of the community's churches and social conservatives, Harlem also offered greater sexual freedoms than most other New York locales, especially to white homosexuals. To echo Henry Louis Gates, Jr.'s famous declaration, the Harlem Renaissance "was surely as gay as it was black." The male writers Van Vechten socialized with in Harlem's nightclubs included Countee Cullen, Eric Walrond, Alain Locke, Wallace Thurman, and Richard Bruce Nugent, all pivotal figures of the renaissance, all gay, and, with the exception of Cullen, more open about their sexuality than the majority of homosexual men of the era.

Richard Bruce Nugent was so frank about his homosexuality he made Van Vechten seem like a sheltered bumpkin from *The Tattooed Countess*. In his extraordinary short story "Smoke, Lilies and Jade," Nugent appears as Alex, a young man who picks up a stranger at four in the morning and brings him back to his apartment. As "they undressed by the blue dawn," Nugent wrote, "Alex knew he had never seen a more perfect being . . . his body was all symmetry and music . . . and Alex called him Beauty." It is worth noting that Nugent once wrote Van Vechten to express his admiration of *Peter Whiffle*—unsurprising considering that Whiffle's declaration to do "what one is forced by nature to do" mirrored Nugent's own philosophy for living. "Harlem was very much like the Village," Nugent recalled decades after the Harlem Renaissance had passed. "People did what they wanted to do with whom they wanted to do it. You didn't get on the rooftops and shout, 'I fucked my wife last night.' So why would you get on the roof and say, 'I loved prick'? You didn't. You just did what you wanted to do. Nobody was in the closet. There was no closet."

Nugent was surely overstating his case in that instance. But there was unquestionably an atmosphere of liberation in Harlem at night that outstripped most of the city's other neighborhoods. Van Vechten was a regular and enthusiastic guest at A'Leila Walker's extravagant parties, infamous for their same-sex and interracial exhibitionism, and he befriended Walker's circle of rent boys and pimps. In one of his first turns as tour guide of Harlem for white outsiders, Van Vechten took the English writer Somerset Maugham to a Harlem institution at the other end of the social spectrum, a buffet flat. There were dozens of these venues in Harlem, modest apartments in which various rooms were rented out for gambling, sex shows, and orgies. In small, dimly lit rooms heaving with bodies, soft cushions, and throws scattered on the floor, this was where the fantasies of white tourists like Van Vechten came vividly to life. Any combination of people—black, white, male, female—enjoyed anonymous sexual encounters as the sound of hot jazz tunes rippled out from a phonograph or an upright piano. "All around the den"—Claude McKay described the atmosphere in one Harlem establishment—"luxuriating under little colored lights, the dark dandies were loving up their pansies. Feet tickling feet under tables, tantalizing liquor-rich giggling, hands busy above." In a Harlem buffet flat, there was no curb on the sexual possibilities. The former *Vanity Fair* editor Helen Lawrenson described in her memoirs one notorious place that reputedly listed Cole Porter among its return clientele and featured a "young black entertainer named Joey, who played piano and sang but whose *specialité* was to remove his clothes and extinguish a lighted candle by sitting on it until it disappeared."

The ethical dimensions of sex tourism never entered Van Vechten's mind. He was too enamored by the atmosphere of transgression and fantasy to be bothered about the fact that buffet flats and rent parties existed mainly as imaginative—or desperate—ways for people to pay their bills. However, it was not the use and abuse of his wealth and status that Van Vechten found arousing. Harlem was sexually attractive to him mainly because it was a point of fusion among his homosexuality, his fascination with blackness, and his natural voyeurism. Neither was Harlem, in any of its guises, the exclusive focus of Van Vechten's sexual interests. He was part of the select crowd at Bob Chanler's House of Fantasy, where heterosexual porn movies were projected, and he badgered Arthur Davison Ficke to obtain Japanese pornographic art on his behalf. One night at his friend Ralph Barton's midtown apartment in September 1925 Van Vechten watched Barton and his wife "give a remarkable performance. Ralph goes down on Carlotta. She masturbates and expires in ecstasy. They do 69, etc." "Performance" here is the operative word. In moments of sexual encounter more often than not Van

Vechten reverted to type: the sharp-sighted critic reveling in the spectacle.

At home sexual exhibitionism was substituted for something less scandalous yet still with the power to shock, as Van Vechten brought Harlem down into the fashionable circles south of Central Park. From the first weeks of 1925 he and Marinoff routinely invited black people into their home—not as servants or novelty entertainers but as guests, a practice almost unheard of in white New York.

The entire block knew when it was the night of a Van Vechten party. Taxicabs and chauffeur-driven limousines lined up along West Fifty-fifth Street, decanting illustrious passengers into the lobby of 150, the doorman escorting them to the elevator. They were millionaire bankers dressed in jet-black tuxedos and stiff white collars and Hollywood movie stars in mink coats and strings of iridescent pearls, Harlem jazz musicians, and chorus girls rushing from Broadway shows, the smell of greasepaint still faintly detectable beneath their perfume. Van Vechten welcomed each guest at the apartment door like an old and cherished friend, no matter how recently they had become acquainted. Within seconds they had a drink in their hand, a cocktail made from Jack Harper's premium bootleg liquor mixed by Van Vechten himself. Entertainment was usually provided by some combination of the remarkable talents on the guest list: a recital by Marguerite d'Alvarez in her clipped, powerful contralto; a reading by James Weldon Johnson, his voice deep and sonorous. George Gershwin was virtually the resident pianist. "He was extraordinary. It was impossible to get him off of [*sic*] the piano stool after he settled there," Van Vechten recalled. "He used to play all night without ever repeating anything."

Inside 7D Van Vechten replicated all he had learned from Mabel's Evenings with one key twist. At his salon the byzantine rules of racial division that existed beyond his front door were suspended. Here white society magnates and struggling black artists drank and laughed and danced the Charleston together, as equals. He knew the damage that could be done to racial prejudice through the simple act of socializing because he had experienced it firsthand. One night he came home from Harlem and told Fania "in great glee" that he had just met a black person he had not taken to. "I'd found one I hated," he recollected to an interviewer. "And I felt that was my complete emancipation, because now I could select my friends and not have to know them all." He continued, "Up to that time, I had considered them all as one." There is something perverse about that statement; usually one would expect to have one's racial prejudices challenged by making friends with those from other ethnic communities. However, this was not Van Vechten indulging in a Wildean inversion of conventional logic; he meant what he said. Since his college days he had idealized black people and inadvertently reduced them to generic character types rather than real people. This moment of epiphany reinforced his conviction that to humanize one race in the eyes of the other, there was no better method, he felt, than shutting them in a room, plying them with drink, and letting nature take its course.

Tales about what went on at the Van Vechten's interracial parties became part of Manhattan lore in the 1920s and 1930s. Most repeated was the story of the night that Bessie Smith came to perform in December 1928. The account that Smith herself was fond of telling has it that upon her arrival Van Vechten flounced up to her and offered "a lovely, lovely dry Martini." Smith, who was already drunk, apparently screwed her face up and said she had never had a martini, dry, wet, or any other kind, and wanted nothing but straight-up whiskey. Recoiling from Van Vechten's fussing, she downed the first whiskey shot, then a second, and a third. Fortified by liquor, she launched into a short but mesmerizing set of blues standards in the style that Van Vechten described as "full of shouting and moaning and praying and suffering, a wild, rough, Ethiopian voice, harsh and volcanic, but seductive and sensuous too." When it came time for Smith to leave, Marinoff, full of her usual theatricality, flung her arms around the singer and attempted to give her a kiss goodbye. Smith apparently threw Marinoff to the floor, yelling, "Get the fuck away from me! . . . I ain't never *heard* such shit," and stormed out, leaving Van Vechten to scoop his wife up from the hallway rug while horrified guests stared on.

Across the years the story has been told and retold, used either to convey Smith's uncompromising character or to ridicule Van Vechten's obsession with African-American culture, mocking him as a wealthy white aesthete trying to insinuate himself with the black working class. It is worth noting that the anecdote is based entirely on Smith's recollection, which, considering how intoxicated she was, may not have been 100 percent clear. Van Vechten does not appear to have written any account of the incident to friends, and his daybook records only that Smith arrived drunk and sang three numbers. Nevertheless, at a time when intimate social interaction between blacks and whites was conspicuously unusual the anecdote soon did the rounds because it sounded plausible: to those who spread the story, discord and confrontation seemed the inevitable outcome when white high society mixed with black blues singers late at night, everybody soused.

The night of Smith's appearance might have produced the most gossip, but Van Vechten's most important party occurred on January 17, 1925, when he welcomed Paul Robeson and his wife, Eslanda—Essie to friends—into his home for the first time. A few days earlier Van Vechten had heard Paul singing spirituals at Walter White's home and was keen to have him repeat the performance at 150. In front of some of the most influential figures in New York, including Alfred and Blanche Knopf and the investment banker and chairman of the board of the Metropolitan Opera House, Otto Kahn, Robeson performed arrangements by his musical partner Lawrence Brown. Though he had taken up acting only within the last two years, Robeson was an emerging celebrity, having earned excellent reviews in 1924 for his performances in the Eugene O'Neill plays *The Emperor Jones* and *All God's Chillun Got Wings*. Even so, he and Essie realized that performing at a Van Vechten party in the presence of so many opinion formers and wealthy patrons was an opportunity to showcase his singing talent and accelerate his career. Robeson's short set caused a sensation among Van Vechten's guests. Van Vechten wrote his friend Scott Cunningham to tell him how marvelous the party had been, thanks to Gershwin's piano playing and Adele Astaire's dancing. But the highlight, he said, had been the "really thrilling experience" of hearing Paul Robeson sing spirituals in a way only he could.

Van Vechten believed spirituals to be the purest expression of African-American experience and that "the unpretentious sincerity that inspires them makes them the peer of any folk music the world has yet known." He was sure that Robeson—handsome, charismatic, and gifted with an incomparably beautiful voice—was the man to convince white audiences that spirituals were an American cultural treasure. In collaboration with Walter White and Essie Robeson, Van Vechten set about organizing and publicizing Robeson's first solo concert at the Greenwich Village Theatre on April 19, even managing to persuade his friend Heywood Broun, an influential critic and journalist, to dedicate his column on the day before the concert to Robeson. The event was a resounding success: the house sold out, and hundreds had to be turned away at the door; Robeson performed sixteen encores to rapturous ovations from the almost exclusively white audience. Reviews in the newspapers were equally effusive, heralding Robeson as "the new American Caruso." To Gertrude Stein, Van Vechten likened Robeson to Fyodor Chaliapin, which, considering his hero-worship of the Russian singer, was high praise indeed.

In public Van Vechten embodied the carefree spirit of excess and experimentation that defined Manhattan's Jazz Age adventure. In private the frenetic lifestyle was taking its toll. Every wild night brought hangovers, exhaustion, and physical discomfort, a grim confluence that he often attempted to break with yet more cocktails. The fractures previously apparent in his marriage were forced open. More than once, drunk and angry, he was "rough" with Marinoff, in the euphemism of his own diary, forcing her to stay the night with friends while he calmed down and sobered up. On occasion she removed herself from New York entirely with trips to Atlantic City and farther afield. Their periods of separation frequently caused them more upset and annoyance than the fraught time they spent together. When Marinoff set off for a trip to London in April 1925, Van Vechten, pained at the prospect of their temporary separation, accompanied her to the docks. During her trip each wrote to the other of how unhappy they felt at being apart. Van Vechten's letters

Paul Robeson, c. 1933, photograph by Carl Van Vechten

were particularly lachrymose. Life was pathetic and worthless without her, he wailed, and he grumbled that her declarations of love were less frequent and heartfelt than his. Yet he made no effort to curb the behavior that was causing Marinoff such upset. The evening after she left New York he joined Angus and friends for a rip-roaring night out at a gay-friendly speakeasy named Philadelphia Jimmie's and other Harlem nightspots, returning as the sun came up at dawn. It was a sign of his essential immaturity. Composing grand romantic gestures for a loved one far out of reach had become something of a specialty of his; changing his selfish behavior to demonstrate the undying love he professed was something he had not mastered. Anna Snyder had spotted the tendency twenty years earlier, when she accused him of caring more for "symbols than reality" in the love letters they shared. Two decades on, little had changed. Responsibility still bored him; it was a loathsome distraction from the festival of self-indulgence that he wanted life to be.

Marinoff would have been approximately two-thirds of her way across the Atlantic that spring when Van Vechten accompanied the Harlem writer Eric Walrond and the white actress Rita Romilly to the inaugural awards dinner of the monthly black publication *Opportunity*, the journal of the civil rights organization the National Urban League. *Opportunity*'s subtitle, "A Journal of Negro Life," gives a good indication of its purpose: to exhibit the full continuum of African-American experience and opinion. Its editor, the sociologist Charles S. Johnson, belonged to a different era from that of W.E.B. DuBois, who used his editorship of the NAACP's magazine *The Crisis* as propaganda for the political cause of racial uplift, committed to always presenting black people in their proverbial Sunday best. Johnson wanted *Opportunity* to be a debating chamber rather than a propaganda sheet and opened its pages to a lively mix of up-to-the-minute social research and the brightest talents of an emerging generation of black writers who explored and exposed black life in the round, street gambling, buffet flats, and nightclubs included.

The most exciting and important of those talents was Langston Hughes, an unknown twenty-three-year-old college student from Washington, D.C, who was creating a lot of excitement with his sonorous blues poetry. At the awards that night Hughes won first prize and read aloud some of his work to the assembled guests in their finery.

> Droning a drowsy syncopated tune
> Rockin back and forth to a mellow croon

As Hughes recited those opening lines to "The Weary Blues," his poem about a Harlemite "who sang the blues all night and then went to bed and slept like a rock," Van Vechten sat listening, bewitched. Hughes's poetry was intelligent, stylish, and modern but also fun-loving and steeped in his racial identity, what he himself described as a "heritage of rhythm and warmth." The blues was a natural source for his work because it contained not only the historical experience of black America but also everyday life as lived by "the low-down folks" who "hold their own individuality in the face of American standardizations." If DuBois and his followers always wanted to present African-Americans to the outside world scrubbed and groomed, Langston Hughes was happy to have the white folks take them as they found them, as "people who have their hip of gin on Saturday nights" and are happy "to watch the lazy world go by." It was an entirely new type of poetry to Van Vechten: colloquial and sensual in a way that captured the raw emotion of the blues. To his ears it was both unmistakably black and distinctively American.

At some point that evening Van Vechten asked Hughes if he might be permitted to show the Knopfs some of his poems. Hughes said yes without hesitation. For a young, penniless black poet unknown outside literary Harlem, the prospect of having his work placed with the most fashionable publishing house in New York was the stuff of dreams. At five o'clock the following afternoon Hughes arrived at Van Vechten's front door with his manuscript. Van Vechten had been out drinking until 7:30 a.m., had barely slept and was not in an ideal state to study poetry. Still, he was eager to read Hughes's work and promised to do so right away. When Hughes dropped in again the following day, on his way back home to Washington, Van Vechten gave him a list of instructions about which poems should be excised and which edited in order to turn his mass of unfettered creativity into a commercially viable edition of poetry.

Van Vechten had a title for this revised manuscript too: *The Weary Blues*, the title of Hughes's prizewinning poem. With everything in place he handed the manuscript over to the Knopfs, urging Alfred and Blanche not to let some other publishing house snap the boy up. Two weeks later Hughes received a letter from Van Vechten to say that all was arranged: Alfred A. Knopf was to publish the book. "I shall write the introduction and the cover design will be by [Miguel] Covarrubias," he announced, referring to the Mexican artist. Hughes was astonished. "You're my good angel," he gushed. "I'll have to walk sideways to keep from flying!"

Hughes's obvious delight was qualified by a nagging doubt about how his association with Van Vechten might look to other black people. He worried that being plucked from obscurity by an attention-seeking dandy from downtown would only give further fuel to those older, more established literary figures in Harlem who thought his poems pandered to white stereotypes of black life, focusing too much on jazz, whiskey, and sex. His fears were prescient. Over the years—and especially after the publication of Van Vechten's hugely controversial novel *Nigger Heaven* in 1926—the impression that Van Vechten somehow exploited or led Hughes astray has persisted. In reality, Van Vechten's input into *The Weary Blues* was little more than it had been with Firbank's *Prancing Nigger* a year earlier. He haughtily assumed control of the project by shaping it into a publishable book and made sure that everyone knew of his connection to Hughes by writing the book's introduction, but the themes, subjects, and style of Hughes's work were never significantly affected by Van Vechten. Despite their differences in age and social status, they were friends, not patron and client or even mentor and protégé. And contrary to the rumors that have floated down the decades, neither were they lovers. Whether or not Hughes was sexually attracted to men is difficult to discern. The same cannot be said of Van Vechten, whose flirtatious correspondence with the men he had affairs with was full of homosexual coding and innuendo. His letters to Hughes feature none of that and disclose nothing but warm, jovial friendship and honest exchanges of opinions.

"The influence, if one exists," Van Vechten said of their relationship, "flows from the other side." In his very first letter to Hughes, written while arranging a publishing deal for *The Weary Blues* with Knopf, it was Van Vechten who was seeking instruction, asking for information about raunchy southern ballads and recommendations for books about Haiti. Soon after, he also elicited Hughes's help in writing an article about the blues for *Vanity Fair* and quoted him at length in doing so. Van Vechten was in awe of Hughes's talent. It had taken him until his mid-thirties to find his writing voice; Hughes had discovered his while still in college, and crafting his lyrical jewels seemed to come as naturally to him as breathing. Even if Van Vechten had wanted to, Hughes was far too talented and self-confident to allow Van Vechten to manipulate or control him. Around the same time he met Van Vechten at the *Opportunity* awards, Hughes encountered the successful poet Vachel Lindsay, who gave him a marvelous piece of advice: "Do not let any lionizers stampede you." Hughes never did. When he declined Van Vechten's words of advice or ignored lengthy criticisms of some latest work, Van Vechten's bottom lip might jut out a little, but their friendship was never seriously affected. Hughes's innate emotional intelligence enabled him to intuitively realize what many others failed to: that despite his proprietorial tendencies, Van Vechten could reconcile himself with not being in control of a particular situation, so long as he was made to feel brilliant, unique, and admired. As Richard Bruce Nugent remarked, all Van Vechten really wanted was to have his head patted and to be told he was "a nice boy."

The same was essentially true of Van Vechten's relationship with Paul Robeson. As Robeson's career entered the stratosphere in the months after those first concerts, Van Vechten was a constant and key adviser and played a pivotal part in convincing Otto Kahn to lend the Robesons five thousand dollars to clear off a mounting pile of debt. Early in their acquaintance, perhaps wary that he did not appear too proprietorial over Paul's professional activities, he joked with Essie that he was "beginning to sound like a grandpa, always offering advice. Remember that it is the advice of a friend. Reject it when it does not meet your approval. The friendship will remain." And so it did—at least until Robeson infuriated Van Vechten by not paying him sufficient attention during the late 1930s. Van Vechten could stomach having his advice rejected, but his ego would not

Langston Hughes working as a busboy at the Wardman Park Hotel, Washington, D.C.

tolerate being ignored altogether. Nearly three years after his performance at Van Vechten's party Robeson wrote Van Vechten to thank him for what he had done for his career. No matter where in the world he was performing, Robeson said, he would always think of Van Vechten because "it was you who made me sing."

Van Vechten's work as a publicist and dealmaker was one of the furnaces that fueled the Harlem Renaissance. His reputation as a white impresario of black art even allowed him to influence the success of African-American performers abroad. When the theater producer Caroline Dudley wanted to export to Paris the sort of black stage entertainment that was all the rage in New York, it was to Van Vechten she turned for advice. He acted as a creative consultant on *La Revue Nègre*, Dudley's cabaret show at the Théâtre des Champs-Élysées that launched the career of Josephine Baker in 1925. In the grand spectacle that Dudley arranged, Van Vechten's flamboyant aesthetic sensibilities and his ideas about blackness were vibrantly evident. Twenty-five singers, the Charleston Steppers dancing troupe, and the seven-piece Charleston Jazz Band provided energetic backing to the show's real stars, who included a nineteen-year-old Josephine Baker. Dudley's intentions for the show echo Van Vechten's beliefs in keeping black theater "authentically" black. *La Revue Nègre* would exhibit the core of blackness, she told a French magazine, "their independence and their savagery, and also that glorious sensual exuberance that certain critics call indecency." That pronouncement could have fallen straight from Van Vechten's lips. By neat coincidence, in the same month that *La Revue Nègre* opened in Paris, Van Vechten published his article "Prescription for the Negro Theatre" in *Vanity Fair*. The most important thing, he said on how to construct the perfect Negro revue, is to ensure that the chorus girls are nice and dark, and certainly no lighter than "strong coffee before the cream is poured in." With his dark-skinned cast in place, he then speculated on the type of scenes they should act out, skipping off into the sort of primitivist fantasy that would mark passages of *Nigger Heaven*, published in 1926, and dictated the look and feel of *La Revue Nègre*. He daydreamed about "a wild pantomimic drama set in an African forest with the men and women nearly as nude as the law allows." Against this backdrop he imagined a cast of spear-carrying warriors and "lithe-limbed, brown doxies, meagerly tricked out in multihued feathers" performing a "fantastic, choreographic comedy of passion."

Despite his successes in raising the profile of black artists at home and abroad, some Harlemites were highly suspicious of his motives. To judge from his early novels, in which black people appear as only mute servants to a cabal of white decadents, Carl Van Vechten seemed the least likely man in New York to act as the downtown envoy to Lenox Avenue. The poet Countee Cullen, for one, did not buy it. From the time of their first meeting in late 1924, Cullen was more than happy to socialize with Van Vechten; he found him unwaveringly good company and even offered to teach him how to Charleston. But he never fully trusted him and suspected Van Vechten was interested in black people for sex and song—and a chance to bolster his own profile. When a Van Vechten article about African-American culture appeared in *Vanity Fair*, Cullen confided to one of their mutual friends that he had not bothered to read it because he simply thought Carl was "coining money out of niggers."

That was an unfair judgment. Van Vechten's interest in black people and their culture was complex, long-standing, and continually deepening, and his work on behalf of Hughes and Robeson brought him no financial gain. The article Cullen referred to was one of a series that Van Vechten published in *Vanity Fair* in 1925 and 1926 on different aspects of African-American arts. If Cullen really never read these pieces, he missed a landmark in American critical writing. It is not Van Vechten's prose that makes these essays so remarkable—at times he strays into the melodramatic mode characterizing his earlier writings about black people that tends to fetishize rather than demystify his subject. Rather, it is his approach that is so arresting. In each essay he presented a mainstream white audience with a serious examination of subjects—black theater, spirituals, and the blues—most had never previously encountered and, if they had, would never have considered them art. Yet Van Vechten wrote about them in the same terms he had once written about the opera and ballet. On describing the blues singer Clara Smith, he wrote that her "voice, choking with moaning quarter tones, clutched the heart. Her expressive and economic gestures are full of meaning. What an artist!" He stressed how the inherent racial gifts of black people for improvising and harmonizing had allowed them to create a folk culture whose quality and beauty could not be matched by any the world over. "The music of the Blues," he wrote, "has a peculiar language of its own, wreathed in melancholy ornament. It wails, this music, and limps languidly: the rhythm is angular, like the sporadic skidding of an automobile on a wet asphalt pavement"; the poetry that accompanies this music is "eloquent with rich idioms, metaphoric phrases, and striking word combinations." Nobody, certainly no white man, had written about black folk culture quite like this before: not just as worthy and beguiling but as genuine, authentic American art of the highest quality.

However, some Harlemites saw in Van Vechten's mania for blackness a ghostly shadow of the blackface tradition, a white man who thought African-American culture was a costume that could be slipped on and off for the entertainment of white audiences who sat gawping, astonished that a white man could perform the trick of imitation so thoroughly that he seemed to be inhabiting a Negro soul. Certain black observers publicly expressed their hostility to Van Vechten's cheerleading for Harlem's artists. In 1927, at the premiere of *Africana*, a Broadway revue starring his close friend Ethel Waters, Van Vechten's exhibitionist display of whooping and cheering and shouting out requests between songs became a feature of the ensuing reviews. "Mr. Van Vechten did everything to prove that Miss Waters is his favorite colored girl and no fooling," wrote the reviewer for the *New York Amsterdam News*, clearly of the belief that there was something sinister about Van Vechten's motivations. "There was the passion of possession in Mr. Van Vechten's claps and cheers."

In a way the reviewer had it just right. Van Vechten adored Waters and wanted to flaunt their connection publicly. He even splashed out on a bust of her by Antonio Salemme, the African-American artist, just as he bought a bust of Paul Robeson by the British sculptor Jacob Epstein. After all these years he was as mesmerized by fame as ever and desperate to warm himself in its glow. At times the strength of his desire to connect himself to his favorite stars made him appear desperate, like a celebrity hanger-on forever pushing his way into the back of paparazzi photographs. He once wrote James Weldon Johnson praising his friend as one of the greatest writers in the history of the English language—a peer of Daniel Defoe's, no less—and said it was an honor for him to be able to call such a man a personal friend. The only thing that irritated him, Van Vechten said, was that he could claim no part in having discovered Johnson for the world to enjoy. Van Vechten, intending this to be the highest compliment, was unaware that it risked making him sound patronizing, possessive, or self-obsessed. To black observers like Countee Cullen this behavior may have appeared unsettling, as if Van Vechten were attempting to own black performers in some way. Yet the crucial point is that Van Vechten behaved in a proprietorial, self-publicizing fashion with all the artists he supported; race had nothing to do with it.

If some blacks were irritated or angered by his self-appointed role as Harlem's one-man publicity machine, many whites found it absurd and teased him for it. According to a report in *Zit's Weekly*, a leading theatrical trade paper, he was reported to have been a victim of a hoax along these lines during a visit to Hollywood in 1928. Egged on by the movie director Dudley Murphy, apparently the actress Madeline Hurlock introduced herself to Van Vechten as Pansy Clemens—note the pseudonym: a gibe at Van Vechten's sexuality—a light-skinned black woman who wanted to make it big on Broadway. The story runs that Van Vechten fixed her with his usual stare and promised her all sorts of introductions to big-shot producers. When the ruse was revealed a little while later, Van Vechten supposedly hid his embarrassment and insisted that the joke was on Hurlock: he, "an expert on things Ethiopian," as the reporter described him, could tell that Hurlock really was of Negro heritage, even if she claimed otherwise. Enraged, Hurlock threatened to sue Van Vechten should he try to spread the rumor that she had even a drop of African blood. The story has the strong odor of gossip column embellishment about it, but even if apocryphal, it reflects how his association with black New York society had come to define his public image.

Van Vechten took no mind of the teasing. As he saw it, he was doing vital work, creating a bridge between the racially divided worlds of New York. With pride and seriousness he assumed the role of expert on the New Negro, the man to call upon to explain the mysteries of blackness to curious, or ignorant, whites. By 1927 his favorite party trick was sitting in the dining room of the Ritz, or some other fashionable downtown spot, and pointing out to incredulous friends the patrons who were passing as white. With the *Chicago Defender* he shared his eccentric pet theory that within a few decades passing would be obsolete; miscegenation would simply absorb all Negroes into the white population. At the end of the decade Andy Razaf, the composer of 1920s' hits such as "Ain't Misbehavin,'" dropped Van Vechten's name into his song "Go Harlem." "Like Van Vechten, start inspectin,'" ran the line, a clear sign of how closely he had been linked to the neighborhood in the public's mind by that point.

Van Vechten's presence in Harlem as a white patron and publicist for black artists was conspicuous—he was temperamentally incapable of being anything else—but it was not unique. The very institutions that provided the organizational thrust of black America's reinvention, the NAACP and the National Urban League, had been founded by white philanthropists. In March 1925 the white-owned *Survey Graphic* produced what is still regarded as the Harlem Renaissance bible, entitled "Harlem: Mecca of the New Negro" and soon after published as *The New Negro* anthology. The Spingarn Medal, given annually by the NAACP to the person who had done most to promote the cause of African-Americans that year, was the gift of the white Spingarn family and the most sought-after prize in Harlem. Without the patronage of these whites—the "Negrotarians," as the writer Zora Neale Hurston referred to them—the Harlem Renaissance could not have happened.

Inevitably, though, the patronage of whites was wrought with complications. Charlotte Mason was a fabulously wealthy woman with a mansion on Fifth Avenue overflowing with African art, who created around her a circle of black writers dependent on her spectacular but sinister largess. Mason made three basic demands of her stable of black protégés: they call her Godmother, they keep her identity a secret, and they gain her approval for all their writing projects, thus ensuring they stayed true to her idea of their core racial identity. Langston Hughes was one of the godchildren for several years, though it was another of Van Vechten's close friends, Zora Neale Hurston, who was Mason's favorite. Hurston believed as fervently as Mason in the ideal of the unpolluted, primitive African soul. Van Vechten believed in that too, of course, but he was no Charlotte Mason, who patronized, hectored, and manipulated the black writers in her orbit to the most outrageous degree. Under the terms of their agreement, Mason paid Hurston two hundred dollars per month and obliged her to collect a great store of material about black folklore, none of which Hurston could use without Mason's explicit permission. Hurston appeared to have no problem with this. Indeed she thought a cosmic link bound her and Mason together and wrote her letters that express the uncomfortable inequality that defined their relationship. "I have taken form from the breath of your mouth," reads one. "From the vapor of your soul am I made to be." In another she described Mason as "the guard-mother who sits in the twelfth heaven and shapes the destiny of the primitives" and signed off, "Your Pickaninny, Zora."

She never sent letters like that to Van Vechten, who over the years helped many struggling black writers and artists get work and publicity and occasionally gifted them money too. Over two decades Hurston and Van Vechten maintained a friendship of intense warmth, as evinced by their lengthy correspondence, interrupted by silences only when Hurston disappeared on some adventure, through letters that could be flirty and boastful simultaneously but always funny and always passionate, as they swapped stories about Mae West, Lead Belly, or some surprising new discovery—a gospel choir, perhaps, or the Caribbean islands. Van Vechten adored Hurston for the same reason he adored anyone, black or white: he thought she was an extraordinary individual, a beautiful, charismatic talent whose entire being resonated with a life-affirming energy. Ultimately that may have been the crucial distinction between

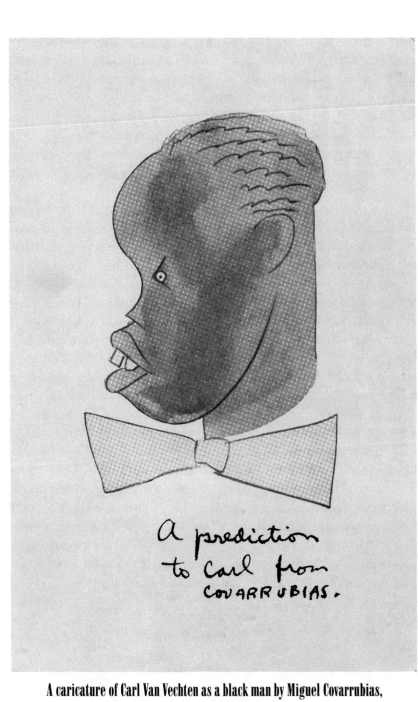

A caricature of Carl Van Vechten as a black man by Miguel Covarrubias,
entitled *A Prediction*

him and Godmother Mason. Both believed in the singularity of the black soul, but Van Vechten wanted to be a friend and peer of the black people who interested him rather than some omnipotent overlord always sitting in stern judgment.

That positive distinction had a crucial effect on his relationships with Harlemites. Behind his back there were some teasing words and eyes lifted to heaven when he tried too hard to appear at home in the company of black people or display his knowledge of their culture, but it was that very same attitude of unself-conscious enthusiasm that endeared him to many. He thought the differences between blacks and whites were self-evident but no reason to keep the races apart. They were in fact an exhilarating life force, what the historian Emily Bernard has aptly termed his belief in "the importance—and insignificance—of racial difference." Harold Jackman, a black teacher and writer who was a linchpin of Harlem society, circled Van Vechten with gawping curiosity when the two first met in February 1925. Jackman said he had never before felt comfortable in the company of white people, but in Van Vechten's presence racial differences seemed to dissolve. "You are just like a colored man!" he exclaimed. "I don't know if you will consider this a compliment or not." To Van Vechten, who prided himself on his ability to effortlessly befriend exceptional people in almost any environment, it would have surely been the highest compliment possible. However, considering Van Vechten thought he had been able to pass as black in Chicago two decades earlier, Jackman's praise would not have come as a surprise to him. When the artist Miguel Covarrubias drew a caricature of Van Vechten as a black man entitled *A Prediction* in 1926, Van Vechten had special copies printed to keep for posterity and send to friends. Being black, he was beginning to believe, was just another of his exquisite talents.

NINE

Exotic Material

· ·

By the midpoint of the 1920s there were few aspects of contemporary life in New York that had not been penetrated by the nation's crop of exciting young literary talents. In particular, the city's fashionable and flighty spirits—the sorts of characters that filled Van Vechten's books—had been thoroughly documented, celebrated, ridiculed, and pitied as the epitome of the Jazz Age. Yet no writer, black or white, had published a novel about the New Negroes of Harlem, the community that had set the Jazz Age in motion. The first one to successfully do so could secure canonical status. The idea of attempting a novel about Harlem occurred to Van Vechten as early as the fall of 1924, a few weeks into his friendship with Walter White. On October 23 he told Marinoff that should his proposed opera collaboration with Gershwin come to nothing he would try his hand at "a Negro novel." As the Gershwin project drifted away, and his immersion into Harlem society deepened, the idea of writing a novel about its inhabitants gradually turned into an obsession.

But Van Vechten was nervous about such an undertaking from the very start. His tremendous self-confidence usually allowed him to write with an air of absolute authority on any number of subjects regardless of how new to him they were, including many aspects of African-American culture. Since meeting Walter White, however, his relationship with black people had changed profoundly: he had come to know them as individuals rather than mere character types.

Finding a black person he did not like had been his "emancipation" on a social level, allowing him to see the individual personality beneath the skin color. From the point of view of a novelist hoping to capture the entire experience of the three hundred thousand citizens of Harlem, the knowledge that black society was every bit as complicated as white society was vexing. He confided to Langston Hughes that prior to his immersion in Harlem it would have been "comparatively easy for me to write" a novel about the place, but his recent experiences had simply underlined how much more complex black society was than he had hitherto realized. In the same letter he expressed his enormous admiration for Hughes's ability to crystallize what he saw as the essence of black experience within his poems. "You have caught the jazz spirit and the jazz rhythm amazingly," he gushed; "some of them ought to be recited in stop-time!" Achieving similar deftness in a full-length exposition of black New York was not a task that even Van Vechten would take lightly. The following month he told Gertrude Stein of his planned novel, though he still had no plot in mind, only its setting. "It will be about NEGROES as they live now in the new city of Harlem," he said, informing her that the neighborhood contained aspects of black American life never before explored in a novel, and which hardly any white people knew about. With unintended irony Stein breezily replied that she could not wait to read "the nigger book."

The breakthrough came in August 1925, on the day that *Firecrackers* was published. That evening Van Vechten went to *The Crisis* awards at the Renaissance Casino and on his return noted in his daybook: "Title of 'Nigger Heaven' comes to me today." Although he was still not able to sit down and start writing the book for three months, stumbling upon the title was a catalyst. Two days later he told one friend that he had "found so good a title" for the new book that "it should be very easy to write." To his mind, he had come upon not just an arresting title but a scheme for the novel. The term "nigger heaven" was a common colloquial expression for the balcony seating area in segregated theaters, high up in the gods, reserved for black audience members. Both shocking and tartly satirical, it suited Van Vechten's desire to write an overtly serious novel—his first and only—without straying into polemical earnestness. Most important, framing Harlem as "Nigger Heaven" helped create a suitably epic atmosphere for a novel that would encompass the grand sweep of black experience.

Van Vechten eventually managed to begin his novel on the morning of November 3. By lunch he had finished the first chapter. Before Christmas he had an entire first draft. What he produced was a strange and sensationalist exposition of his ideas about what it meant to be black, set against a backdrop of the different Harlems that had so absorbed him over the last year: the nocturnal scene of jazz, drink, and casual sex; A'Lelia Walker's expensively debauched high society parties; and the literary cliques, or "cultured circles," as he had once described them to Edna Kenton. The plot is carried by the doomed love affair of two well-educated young Harlemites, Byron Kasson and Mary Love. Both are presented as having allowed white cultural influence to dilute their essential blackness, their "primitive birthright," as Van Vechten puts it, which enables all black people to "revel in colour and noise and rhythm and physical emotion." Mary is a bookish librarian with an interest in European history who can—somewhat unfeasibly—recite gigantic passages from "Melanctha," Gertrude Stein's story about a black woman from the South but cannot experience the ferocity of emotions that Melanctha feels. Byron is a writer who struggles to write, but not, like Peter Whiffle, because of indecision; instead he eschews race literature and attempts to imitate the white authors he read at college. This was a perennial bugbear of Van Vechten's. When he attempted to find black playwrights to promote in 1913, he was frustrated that none seemed prepared to tackle subjects that he felt were "essentially Negro." In the novel a magazine editor, clearly based on H. L. Mencken, tells Byron straight out that black writers who do not write about black subjects are being artistically dishonest.

Shut out of white New York because of his color and ridiculed by black society for having the fancy airs of a white man, Byron grows angry and despondent. Mary's emotional and sexual frigidity renders her incapable of consoling her man, and Byron is soon seduced by the attentions of Lasca Sartoris, a cabaret star and professional man-eater modeled on Nora Holt, who draws him into her wild existence. This is Van Vechten's other Harlem, his hell-raiser's

paradise of nightclubs, hustlers, pimps, and whores, where black people have no trouble acting on the primal instincts that supposedly
flow through their veins. In this Harlem of the night, the threat of
violence and the promise of casual sex are ever present. Van Vechten's relish in describing it all is palpable, at points nauseatingly so.
In one scene inside a nightclub he describes "men and women with
weary faces tired of passion and pleasure" who resemble "dead prostitutes and murderers," listening to "shrieking, tortured music from
the depths of hell," while a sixteen-year-old girl, "pure black, with
savage African features, thick nose, thick lips, bushy hair," and "eyes
rolled back so far that only the whites were visible," emerges naked
in the center of the dance floor, brandishing a dagger, primed to
perform "evil rites" as the scene ends. It brings to mind Van Vechten's similarly overblown account of the Holy Jumpers' religious
ceremony in the Bahamas a decade earlier. His core idea of the black
soul had barely changed in all that time.

When Sartoris tires of Byron, she discards him for another man.
Driven by bitterness and wounded pride, Byron grabs a gun and
heads for the Black Venus nightclub, planning to kill Sartoris and
her new lover. But inside the club his immersion in white civilization proves to be his undoing: his calculating mind prevents him
from committing a crime of passion. At that moment Sartoris's
lover is shot dead by another aggrieved rival, who has arrived deus
ex machina. The book ends with the white hands of a policeman
apprehending Byron for a crime he did not and, more important,
could not commit.

Nigger Heaven is from start to finish a work of pure melodrama,
peppered with Van Vechten's usual adornments of lists, mentions of
obscure artistic figures, and digressions into esoteric topics. There
are also numerous set pieces that do nothing to propel the narrative
and are included only to unveil aspects of African-American existence about which most white people were entirely ignorant. In one
scene characters talk about passing as white; another explains the
different types of parties to be found in Harlem. Van Vechten was
demonstrating not only the breadth of Harlem society but also the
depth of his expert knowledge.

One of the many things he had learned over the past year or so

in Harlem was the power of language. From 1925 onward the abrasive racial epithets that he had routinely used to describe black people entirely disappeared from his writing, even in his diaries and
notebooks. His new friendships with black men and women had
taught him the hurt that such words can cause. The only term
he now used to refer to black people was "Negro"—the *n* always
capitalized—the accepted, respectful designation of the day. When
reviewing his old notebooks in the 1940s prior to committing them
to academic archives, he even crossed out some uses of "nigger" and
wrote "Negro" over the top, embarrassed that he had once used the
word so indiscriminately. He knew therefore that he risked causing
offense with his title, but its dark, lacerating irony seemed too perfect to abandon, as did the prospect of flirting with another taboo.
Its dangerousness made it irresistible. Commercial reasons probably
came into his thinking too. As recently as the fall of 1923 he had of
course urged Ronald Firbank to introduce himself to American
audiences by changing the title of his novel *Sorrow in Sunlight* to
Prancing Nigger in order to boost sales of the book. A shrewd promoter and an ambitious author, Van Vechten was attached to his
title partly because he knew that it would get people talking—and
spending.

Three weeks into writing, he revealed the title to his most trusted
black friends. Grace Nail Johnson, James Weldon Johnson's wife,
warned him to expect a venomous response should he stick with it,
though Walter White judged it a wonderful title and wished he had
thought of it himself. Countee Cullen, on the other hand, was incensed that Van Vechten would even consider such a thing. As is
often the way with those who are quick to offer it, Van Vechten had
little capacity for taking criticism. It was not really Cullen's opinion
he sought but a rubber stamp. He wanted Harlem's men and women
of letters to sanction the title, thereby ridding him of any moral
qualms about using it. Not gaining that from Cullen infuriated
him. Van Vechten dismissed Cullen as oversensitive and incapable of
understanding irony, failings he identified as common to most black
people. Thirty-five years later his stance had not changed. When an
interviewer asked him whether he had used "nigger" in the title of
his book because the word had had fewer "unpleasant connotations"

in 1925 than in 1960, Van Vechten was bullish: "It had more, I'd say . . . But emancipated people like [the African-American writer George] Schuyler and James Weldon Johnson understood the way it was used. It was used ironically, of course, and irony is not anything that most Negroes understand."

That one barb lays bare the tension within Van Vechten's personality that made his involvement with African-American culture so contentious: the conflict between his fierce individualism and his firm belief in immanent racial identities. He prided himself on being able to value black people as individuals yet repeatedly spoke of "Negroes" as a monolithic bloc, bound together by a common blackness inside and out. When it came to others' judging him, he balked at the idea that he should be seen as anything other than a unique individual whose racial identity as a white man was of no consequence. In the novel Byron is portrayed as foolish and inauthentic for writing about issues that are not explicitly linked to his race. Van Vechten never considered imposing such parameters on his own work, as the very existence of *Nigger Heaven* demonstrates. In his mind he was free of all the constraints that bound others. The first chapter of *Nigger Heaven* includes a footnote that says as much, explaining that while the word nigger "is freely used by Negroes among themselves, not only as a term of opprobrium, but also actually as a term of endearment, its employment by a white person is fiercely resented." The implication is clear: in the mouths of ordinary whites, with their lack of understanding and experience of the Negro, the n-word is a lethal weapon, but for Van Vechten the rules did not apply. Consequently, when some black people reacted negatively to his use of an inflammatory word, he lashed out with petty insults.

Perhaps the criticism that hurt the most came not from Harlem but from Cedar Rapids. When he wrote his father about his latest work, Van Vechten probably expected to receive words of congratulation for following the family tradition of challenging the rigidity of the color line. Instead Charles delivered his son a stern lecture. "Your 'Nigger Heaven' is a title I don't like," he said bluntly. "I have myself never spoken of a colored man as a 'nigger.' If you are trying to help the race as I am assured you are, I think every word you write should be a respectful one towards the blacks." Insisting on using this horrid title was pure folly, he maintained, the behavior of an overindulged child who has never fully grown up. "You are accustomed to 'get away' with what you undertake to do," he warned, "but you do not always succeed, and my belief is that this will be a failure if you persist in your 'I shall use it nevertheless.' Whatever you may be compelled to say in the book your present title will not be understood and I feel certain that you should change it." Again Van Vechten dismissed the criticism. His father, after all, was an elderly midwestern businessman whose ideas about black-white relations had been shaped in the Civil War. What did he know of Harlem and the New Negro of the twentieth century? Although he recognized his father's sensitivity was born of good intentions, he thought it as prissy and reactionary as Cullen's. The matter was dropped, unresolved, over the Christmas of 1925. On January 4, Charles died of a sudden illness. It was a horrendous start to a long year of emotional strife, probably the most turbulent of Van Vechten's life thus far.

Charles was buried on January 7 in a service attended by the great and good of Cedar Rapids, many wearing the distinctive sashes of the Masonic order to which he had belonged. On the ninth, Van Vechten was on a train heading back to New York, where he sat alone, drank a bottle of bourbon, and slipped effortlessly back into the old routine of self-destructive indulgence. Throughout January and February the evenings he stayed sober were so noteworthy that he recorded them in his daybook alongside the names of guests at the parties he attended. Naturally, the heavy drinking combined with his sudden grief was having a deleterious impact on his health. His letters to distant friends, which usually avoided any suggestion that his life in New York was anything other than the glorious fizz of one of his Manhattan novels, showed signs of strain. He told Hugh Walpole that this book was ruining him, exaggerating hugely that he had been working twelve hours a day for six months. He vowed that when it was all over, he would never write again. *Nigger Heaven* actually went to the printers two weeks after that letter, on March 18, fractionally more than four months from his writing the opening sentence of the first draft. Those years of churning out copy in Hearst's Madhouse and dashing off reviews late at night for the morning edition of the *Times* had paid off; even under the most unpleasant circumstances, he could summon the powers of concentration and self-discipline to write, and write quickly.

If nothing else, the novel seemed to be well timed. In February *Lulu Belle* opened at the Belasco Theatre. The play was David Belasco's take on Harlem street life, infused with all the striking realism for which the star producer had become renowned—save for the fact that the leading roles were taken by white actors in blackface. The play bore certain striking similarities to *Nigger Heaven*, especially in its melodramatic exposition of the characters' inner blackness. *Lulu Belle* presented Harlem as the wild place of white American fantasies, in which the checks and balances of American civilization are no restraint on the inborn passions of its black population. The title character, a treacherous black prostitute played by the white actress Lenore Ulric, breaks hearts and marriages as she pursues a string of men before being murdered by one of her conquests. Audiences and reviewers alike were smitten. Among white New Yorkers it marked the moment when Harlem went from being the obsession of a small clique of artists and socialites to a bona fide mainstream craze. Even if black performers were not always as prominent as they should have been, Van Vechten was excited about the breakthrough of African-American entertainments on the mainstream stage. On March 4 he wrote Gertrude Stein that "the race is getting more popular every day."

Within Harlem not everyone was so thrilled at how the community was being presented to the white population. A number of prominent literary and intellectual figures, most notably W.E.B. DuBois, were expressing serious concerns that the younger generation of Harlem writers was encouraging a portrayal of black people as drinkers, gamblers, and fornicators. A matter of weeks before *Nigger Heaven* was published Van Vechten dipped his toe into the debate, knowing that the rest of him would be submerged before long. In a provocative piece for DuBois at *The Crisis* he encouraged African-Americans to write about the underbelly of black society, as Langston Hughes and Rudolph Fisher did. "The squalor of Negro life," he believed, provided wonderful material for artists, and he posed what he felt was the vital question facing Harlem's creative community: "Are Negro writers going to write about this exotic material while it is still fresh or will they continue to make a free gift of it to white authors who will exploit it until not a drop of vitality remains?" It could be argued that the phrasing of that question was intended more as a rhetorical flourish to nudge black writers into action than an admission that he had "exploited" Harlemites or African-American culture. After all, it had been his contention for many years that Americans should engage with taboos as a way of producing distinctive and stimulating art. However, Van Vechten knew that in writing *Nigger Heaven,* he was joining an already lengthy roll call of white artists who had attained great success by absorbing or purloining black culture. It had started of course with minstrelsy almost a century earlier and was to carry on throughout the twentieth century, touching everyone from Elvis to Eminem via Norman Mailer and Jack Kerouac, developing into a central but problematic motif of American identity. In Van Vechten's time both Al Jolson and George Gershwin belonged to that tradition in their different ways, and even Van Vechten's paradigm of black theater, *Granny Maumee,* had been written by a white playwright, Ridgley Torrence. Frequently Van Vechten expressed unease with this phenomenon. After seeing *Granny Maumee,* of course, he attempted to find a generation of black playwrights to express the African-American experience on the stage because relying on white writers to do so felt inauthentic. He was also of the firm belief that white singers should be kept away from the blues and spirituals because they did not have it within their racial gift to perform them as evocatively as black singers could. His words of warning in *The Crisis* about the risks of allowing white authors to write books about black street life emanated from similar concerns. Yet stunningly, he did not consider himself one of those whites who threatened to "exploit" black culture or bleed it of its "vitality." There was no doubt in his mind that most white people could not be trusted with such a jewel, but he, Van Vechten told himself, was different. As with the use of "nigger," he assumed he had special dispensation to uncover the "squalor and vice" of Harlem because he was at one with its people.

•

In the weeks leading up to publication, Van Vechten felt his affinity with black America strengthen. One afternoon Zora Neale Hurston took him to a sanctified church on West 137th Street located in the offices of a real estate agent, one of the many tiny charismatic sects that sprang up in Harlem out of nowhere only to disappear as quickly as they had emerged. He said the place rocked with "shoutin', moanin', yelling" for "hours on end to the music of a cornet & a guitar & jumping and dancing. Exactly like the jungle." A similar feeling of awe struck him when the Johnsons took him to New Jersey to visit the Bordentown Manual Training and Industrial School, known as the Tuskegee of the North, and heard the young pupils sing spirituals in perfect pitch. It seemed there was nowhere in the black world of the North that Van Vechten felt out of place. During a trip to Virginia, however, he wrote Marinoff of his frustration that although he encountered black people at every turn, the strictures of southern society made him unable to communicate with *his* people in the same easy manner in which he could in Harlem.

In June any illusions he may have had about being an honorary black man were burst as it became clear that "his" people might not embrace *Nigger Heaven* as the compliment it was intended to be. Two months ahead of publication a number of black newspapers revealed they would not allow the novel to be advertised within their pages. Walter White spoke out in Van Vechten's defense in *The Pittsburgh Courier*, one of the most influential African-American newspapers in the country. "There is seldom much prejudice of any sort, among those who are intelligent enough to do a bit of thinking and investigating for themselves," White wrote tartly, comparing Van Vechten's inquiring spirit with what he condemned as the knee-jerk reaction of certain blacks, chiming Van Vechten's own belief in the oversensitivity of the race.

By this stage Van Vechten was anxious about the book's reception and, very often, obnoxiously drunk. For Marinoff the stress had become too much. When he returned from the New World speakeasy in Harlem at four o'clock one morning, he lashed out, either verbally or physically, and quite possibly both, his daybooks give only elliptical details of his behavior, and Marinoff made her escape. He went to bed still drunk and rose at ten, expecting Marinoff to come back before lunch, as she always did in these situations. Not this time. Unable to find her, Van Vechten asked Donald Angus to intervene. Over the telephone Angus tracked Marinoff down at the Algonquin. When Van Vechten came on the line, he was stunned. "She says she is through forever. If she is, what is there in life left for me?"

His disbelief is hard to fathom; surely he must have seen this coming. The only surprise was that Marinoff had not left sooner. In October 1925, she even told the *Brooklyn Eagle* newspaper that she felt neglected by her husband, although she made no mention of the physical and verbal violence he subjected her to. Reminiscing about their first year of marriage, when she and Van Vechten kept separate apartments, she told a reporter: "I was having an affair with my husband. Living in sin, you know. Oh, I quite miss that." Since Van Vechten had become a celebrity, however, she had to share him with the whole of New York and its never-ending parties, which made her feel lonely and unloved. On returning to New York from her recent trip to Europe she had been bursting to see Van Vechten, who had sent her numerous letters and telegrams communicating his misery at their separation. But on the first night back after three months she discovered that they were not to spend the evening alone; instead Carlo had invited some new friends to the apartment for a party. "Oh, yes, there were my friends there too, and the party was fine. It was thoughtful of him, but—." She trailed off, not needing to finish the thought aloud.

Remarkably, with his marriage falling apart around him, Van Vechten considered a dinner party at Rudolph Fisher's that evening too important to cancel, though he did not enjoy himself or provide the other guests with much entertainment. Upon his return to the apartment he discovered that Marinoff had come back during his absence, but only to pack her bags. The next morning he got wind that she had taken shelter at her sister's house in New Jersey. When he arrived around lunchtime, he was lucky to find her in a conciliatory mood. She agreed to give him another chance, and they talked things over while walking and picking flowers in the surrounding countryside. In the immediate aftermath a chastened Carl was on his best behavior. Early the next week he treated Marinoff to a romantic evening for two, dining together before catching Mae West in her outrageous new show, *Sex*, and then returning to the apartment to distill two gallons of homemade brandy, an unusual method of spousal reconciliation, perhaps, but somehow entirely fitting.

After months of nerves and drama, *Nigger Heaven* was finally unleashed on the American public on August 20, 1926. Alfred A. Knopf's publicity campaign promised readers a genuine publishing landmark, a thrilling new type of American novel that would transport whites into a secret existence within their midst. An advertisement in *Publishers Weekly* advised bookstores that "between the covers of this unusual novel you will be selling your customers a new world." Consciously or not, Knopf's marketing blurbs described the novel in terms similar to those of the muckraking exposés of the early 1900s that had guided wealthy, respectable New Yorkers into the tenements of the Lower East Side, titillating, fascinating, and enraging them all at once. The feverishly positive critical responses from the white press took up the same line. Walter Yust, a leading literary critic of the 1920s, wrote admiringly in *The Evening Post* of Van Vechten's "careful observations" of "the tortured ecstasies of Harlem," a place populated by "a melodramatic people" of "unashamed passion" as if Van Vechten's tale were a sober compilation of empirical facts. In a similar vein, the *New York Times Book Review* praised the novel's "understanding and insight." An effusive notice in the *New York Evening Graphic* stressed the authenticity of *Nigger Heaven* and made much of the fact that Van Vechten had "lived among the colored people" for nearly two years. "Read *Nigger Heaven*," the reviewer exhorted. "Read it and think."

From across the Atlantic D. H. Lawrence rolled his eyes and dismissed the book as "a second-hand dish barely warmed up," and suggested that Van Vechten's idea of blackness was a myth: "It is absolutely impossible to discover that the nigger is any blacker inside than we are." His compatriot M. P. Shiel was more complimentary about Van Vechten's writing, yet he too thought the book curious. He found the issue of the color line fascinating, he said, because it revolves around the strange notion of "purity of race." It felt to Shiel as if he were eavesdropping on an American conversation that was engrossing yet thoroughly peculiar. He was right too. Although *Nigger Heaven* found great favor with foreign readers the world over and chimed with Europe's own explosion of interest in nonwhite culture after the First World War, this was a distinctly American novel. To the fashionable white crowd of Jazz Age New York, *Nigger Heaven* was a revelation. Sinclair Lewis and H. L. Mencken thought it Van Vechten's best work by far; F. Scott Fitzgerald wrote to say he had read it in one night before pushing it into Zelda's hands; Franklin Pierce Adams described it as "one of the most enthralling books we have ever read," a "fine, exciting, heart-breaking, tragic tale of life in Harlem." Arthur Davison Ficke asked what "the Race" thought of this grand work. "Probably enormously flattered, aren't they?"

The short answer was no. Hostility toward the book from African-American communities came loud and early. The Van Vechtens' housekeeper, Meda Frye, depressed her employer when she came into the apartment one morning with a pile of furious reviews from the black press. They savaged Van Vechten for a prurient obsession with the underbelly of Harlem nightlife and for his dialogue, which many thought a ludicrous mangling of African-American dialect. Some critiques of the book failed to get beyond the title. One of the stinging pieces that Van Vechten masochistically cut out and pasted in his scrapbooks focused less on the novel and more on its impression of the author, whom it described as one of New York's effete voyeurs who, "with their noses arched, twirling their canes, and peeping over their eyelids," go to Harlem simply to satisfy their voyeuristic impulses, before heading back down to Greenwich Village to swap stories about the outrageous things they have seen.

Soon all manner of stories began to circulate: an elderly white man had been verbally and physically attacked in the 135th Street branch of the public library when mistakenly identified as the author of *Nigger Heaven*; a preacher had burned copies of the book as part of a protest against southern lynchings; Van Vechten had been barred and disowned by establishments all across Harlem and hanged in effigy on St. Nicholas Avenue. Some of these tales were accurate; others, apocryphal. But all conveyed the outrage that as many black people saw it, a wealthy white man from downtown had come up to tear around Harlem and then taunted its inhabitants with a book portraying black life as dripping in sex and drugs and violence, capping it off with the most offensive word possible. *The Afro American* of Baltimore summed up the incredulity when it reported a conversation about *Nigger Heaven* supposedly overheard in a Harlem beauty parlor: "You mean to say a man went to people's houses and accepted their hospitality and then called 'em nigger?"

For a brief moment Van Vechten feared that the community for which he had such affection was about to cut him off. Over the previous year Van Vechten had become friendly with W. C. Handy, the great blues pioneer. Handy was one of the most respected figures in Harlem, and a birthday party to which Van Vechten had been invited was due to be thrown for him at Small's. Three days before the event, however, Van Vechten's friend Lewis Baer contacted him to say that his presence at the party would not be tolerated by the management of Small's, with which he had previously enjoyed good relations. "We don't care when we get written about, but not when we get exaggerated about" was the line given to Baer. For a man who put so much stock in being "on the scene," the prospect was humiliating, unthinkable; to be banished from the hub of Harlem nightlife would be banishment from Harlem itself. The more strident of his black friends rallied around and convinced him that he should attend the party regardless; if the management of Small's decided to throw him out, the club would lose the patronage of Van Vechten's supporters too. Accompanied by Zora Neale Hurston, a formidable character for any nightclub bouncer to deal with, Van Vechten arrived at Small's for Handy's party, and to his immense relief, the evening went without incident. It was ironic that Van Vechten, who was happy to end friendships over sins as trivial as tardiness or bad table manners, and who boasted that if "somebody does something to offend me, I can stop a relationship immediately," could be so shaken when he feared that certain acquaintances might do the same. Again Van Vechten was shocked to discover that he could not always play by his own rules.

Nora Holt had guessed Van Vechten would receive this sort of response. From France she wrote to say that although she thought

Zora Neale Hurston, c. 1938, photograph by Carl Van Vechten

Van Vechten had presented certain aspects of black life with unerring accuracy, she was certain the book would cause a stink. "The cries of protest from the Harlemites reach me even in Paris." The loudest cries of protest came from two of the most influential African-American voices of the day: Hubert Harrison and W.E.B. DuBois. Both men delivered astonishing attacks on the novel and its author, accusing Van Vechten of being a crude, exploitative racist. Harrison's lengthy invective characterized *Nigger Heaven* as a "breach of the peace" typical of "blase [*sic*] neurotics whose Caucasian culture has petered out and who come to this corner of Manhattan for pungent doses of unreality." Deploying barely concealed homophobia to counter perceived racism, Harrison said the only good thing about the book was Van Vechten's ability to "describe furniture and its accessories, female clothes and fripperies with all the ecstatic abandon of maiden lady at a wedding and the self-satisfaction of a man-milliner toying with a pink powder-puff. In that domain, I think, he hasn't his equal—among men."

DuBois's review was even more excoriating. Ignoring the book's genteel, well-educated characters, DuBois lambasted Van Vechten for writing about the seedier side of Harlem, its nightclubs, prostitutes, gamblers, and street violence. It was evidence, he said, of Van Vechten's shallow, inhuman nature: "It is the surface mud he slops about in. His women's bodies have no souls; no children palpitate upon his hands; he has never looked upon his dead with bitter tears. Life to him is just one orgy after another, with hate, hurt, gin and sadism."

Harrison, DuBois, the incident at Small's, the accusations of exploiting the community he longed to be admired by: it all hurt dreadfully. Van Vechten's pattern of broken, drunken sleep became haunted by strange dreams that reflected his feelings of persecution and rejection. Shortly after the first bad reviews were published he experienced a vivid recurring nightmare in which he had turned into a black man and was being chased through the streets by an angry, rioting mob.

The criticism was intense, but Van Vechten had certainly not been abandoned. Most of those Harlemites closest to him said both privately and publicly that *Nigger Heaven* was a powerful novel that portrayed black people and their place within the urban United States honestly and empathetically. Alain Locke, Eric Walrond, and Paul Robeson all wrote to congratulate him for having written a fine book, though Locke privately held mixed feelings about it. Charles Johnson, in his capacity as a friend and the editor of *Opportunity*, told Van Vechten that although some part of him wanted him to "make a stir about your title and be a good 'race man,' " he thought *Nigger Heaven* very fine, a view of African-American lives that was neither hostile nor dripping with "patronizing sympathy." Johnson subsequently published a glowing review of the book by James Weldon Johnson, who praised Van Vechten for paying "colored people the rare tribute of writing about them as people rather than as puppets." With a dash of pride Van Vechten recounted to Johnson a scene at a popular Harlem restaurant when Langston Hughes tore a strip off some hostile critics, suggesting they might like to read the book before criticizing it. Moreover, when Van Vechten was pursued for breach of copyright for failing to gain clearance for song lyrics peppered throughout *Nigger Heaven*, it was Hughes who worked through the night at the Van Vechtens' apartment, writing new verses to replace the copyrighted ones.

The resoluteness of his black defenders bears testament to the genuine friendships he had forged in Harlem. But it is also true that Van Vechten was frequently the catalyst for outrage and argument rather than its object. *Nigger Heaven* and its depiction of nightclubs, promiscuous women, and murderous men were the perfect totem around which Harlem's opposing camps aligned: DuBois's bourgeois crowd and the rebellious youth committed to freedom of expression. Van Vechten's black critics repeatedly accused him of insulting those Harlemites who had shown him hospitality. But equally criticized were the Harlemites who had supported and encouraged him in the first place. Hubert Harrison's review, for instance, appeared under the title "Homo Africanus Harlemi," a reference to a well-known article by L. M. Hussey that described how black Americans adopted shifting roles and personalities in order to navigate their way through white society. In converting Hussey's title for his review, Harrison was speaking not to Van Vechten but to Van Vechten's black friends, whom he mocked as

"Harlem's new and nocturnal aristocracy of 'brains' and booze,'" chasing "salvation by publicity" and indulging the rank prejudices of white voyeurs. Harrison hated the book—and Van Vechten—but his criticism of it was part of a broader agenda against the way certain black youths chose to present their communities to the white world. On the other side of the argument, when Wallace Thurman predicted that a statue of Carl Van Vechten would one day be erected on the corner of 135th Street and Seventh Avenue, he did so not because he thought Van Vechten a great man, or even a good writer, but because he wanted to rile the old guard, which deplored Van Vechten's interest in a side of black life they wanted to keep hidden. Consequently, Wallace, Hughes, and the others who viewed art as a means of expression rather than propaganda saw attacks on Van Vechten as attacks on their own creative freedom.

Despite, or perhaps because of, the rumpus, *Nigger Heaven* was read voraciously in Harlem, becoming one of the most requested books of the 1920s at the 135th Street Library. In her column in the October 1926 edition of *Opportunity*, Gwendolyn Bennett remarked that "the vogue for *Nigger Heaven* has set its tentacles upon Negro readers. I have seen its pale blue jacket with its discreet white printing in more brown arms than I have ever seen any other book." By the very next edition, Bennett reported, the book had caught the imagination of the city to such an extent that it had spawned a brand-new verb. "Sightseers, visitors and other strangers that might find themselves within the limits of Harlem . . . are said to be 'van-vechtening' around." She also pointed out that by including his name in the book, Van Vechten had created a new wave of interest in the works of Charles W. Chesnutt, an overlooked elder statesman of African-American literature whose work Van Vechten greatly admired. In fact, librarians and rare book dealers were now contacting Van Vechten directly to find out where to get copies of Chesnutt's work, and Chesnutt himself wrote to Van Vechten to thank him for the kind things he had said about his books. This delivers us to a crucial point about Van Vechten's intention for *Nigger Heaven* and its legacy: though the novel had been about black Americans, it was most definitely not written for them. In the space of a single novel Van Vechten wanted to introduce white Americans to all the spectacles, challenges, joys, and frustrations that defined daily life for the diverse community of black people squeezed into a cramped quadrant of the modern world's most exciting city. In that respect, at least, he had succeeded.

In the months and years following its publication Van Vechten received letters from readers across America amazed at what *Nigger Heaven* taught them about black people. Almost all were dumbfounded by Mary and Byron. From Iowa, a hospital superintendent wrote to express her astonishment at his cultured black characters, who read Gertrude Stein, take trips to Europe, and hold elegant dinner parties. "Can it be possible that there are any like those of yours? And if so do they have a culture so like to our own sophisticated upper classes?" A student from New Haven wondered whether Van Vechten had done his research properly because although "all the other characters are vividly negro, with vivid negro traits," Mary "is too fine" to be black. Most remarkable was a letter from a onetime New Yorker. She questioned whether the book had been written after close research because the wealthy and sophisticated characters bore no relation to any black people she had ever encountered. And could it really be true, she wondered, that there are white people in New York "who go to Negro homes or receive them in their own homes as social equals?" This, more than any other facet of the novel, she found wholly implausible. At the end of her letter, the correspondent revealed herself to be a white woman married to a Chinese man. As she herself could confirm, interracial marriages as mentioned in Van Vechten's book can work perfectly well, though she suspected the problems between blacks and whites may prove intractable.

A letter also arrived from Arthur Reis, a successful clothing manufacturer from New York. Recommended *Nigger Heaven* by their mutual friend Lawrence Langner, Reis found the novel so revelatory that he offered Van Vechten seventy-five dollars to give a talk to him and a group of other prominent Jewish businessmen about the realities of life in Harlem and the struggles of its people. Always strangely shy of public speaking, Van Vechten arranged for Walter White to address the group instead. Throughout the evening White explained that yes, just as in *Nigger Heaven*, there were indeed educated black people living in New York City who read books and ran their own businesses, all of which, apparently, came as a complete surprise to the white millionaires sat before him. Afterward White took the opportunity to write DuBois and let him know the impact Van Vechten's work was having on white America: "The things that I said are commonplace to those of us who, being Negroes, know about them but to this group it was of amazing newness." At the end of the event, two of the audience approached White to tell him that the greatest obstacle in eradicating the color line is that "the average white person knows nothing about the things which you have said here tonight which are set forth in 'Nigger Heaven.'"

Regardless of the energetic defenses that his black allies proffered on his behalf, the image of Van Vechten as a sinister white man whose interest in Harlem was driven by a desire to exploit back people lingered throughout the 1920s, among certain black critics at least. Langston Hughes's second anthology, *Fine Clothes to the Jew*, was published to accusations that Van Vechten had "misdirected a genuine poet," as Allison Davis put it in his damning appraisal of the book, which he thought vulgar, profane, and harmful to the Negro cause. Hughes responded by pointing out that he had written many of the poems in his collection before he and Van Vechten had even met and that Van Vechten had been critical of a good number of them. Claude McKay's 1928 novel *Home to Harlem* was similarly identified by those who disliked its frank descriptions of working-class black life as having been inspired by Van Vechten. Really, the novel's depiction of Harlem street life bares only superficial resemblances to *Nigger Heaven*, and McKay had been writing in that style even before Van Vechten's obsession with the New Negro had begun. Van Vechten provided extensive editorial and business help to the novelist Nella Larsen in the late 1920s, but even she was arguably a greater influence on Van Vechten than the other way around. Born to a white Danish mother and a black father, who abandoned her as a child, Larsen struggled with her racial identity and served as one of the models for Mary Love, the awkward heroine of *Nigger Heaven*. The ambiguities and ironies of race provided the spine of her own novels too: *Quicksand*, in 1928, and *Passing*, the following year, both of which Van Vechten adored and found fascinating.

What Van Vechten did best for these young African-American writers was to provide commercial opportunities for them by stimulating white readers' interest in the lives of ordinary black people. His influence was always more on white receptivity than black creativity. Those writers he directly influenced were not the likes of Hughes, McKay, Thurman, or Larsen but white authors, such as Gilmore Millen. In 1930 Millen published *Sweet Man*, a novel about African-American life in California, essentially the Los Angeles version of *Nigger Heaven*. The novel was largely dismissed by black critics as predictable melodrama, though Van Vechten thought it "powerful . . . daring and even sensational."

Looking at *Nigger Heaven* from the vantage point of the early twenty-first century, one is struck by both the strangeness of the book and the familiarity of the arguments it provoked. To most modern readers Van Vechten's attempt to distill the distinctive character of the black soul seems deeply odd, perhaps overtly racist. Yet the furor caused by the book's title is entirely understandable to any reader. The arguments about who, if anyone, should be allowed to use "that" word are running as indefatigably as ever. The book is also one of many chapters in the long and meandering postemancipation story of white artists absorbing and repackaging black culture for white audiences. In the nation's collective understanding of this still unfolding narrative, the moments from the 1920s that exert the tightest grip are Gershwin's experimentations with African-American music and the white craze for Harlem-style cabaret. But upon its publication *Nigger Heaven* was as significant as either of those, and for the many thousands of Americans who read it, black and white, it posed urgent questions about the state of race relations that few other artistic works of the era seriously tackled. Perhaps more important, the clash within Harlem between Van Vechten's supporters and his detractors over his portrayal of blackness publicly posed a question that twisted itself through twentieth-century American culture: Is positing the notion of racial difference in itself fundamentally racist, or is it a greater act of intolerance to reduce the uniqueness of racial groups by suggesting they all are essentially the same? To Van Vechten the answer was axiomatic. He not only believed in racial difference as a self-evident fact but thought it a blessing, part of the rich diversity that made urban life in the United States such a thrilling experience.

Van Vechten's love of black culture—and many black people— was genuine, and he sincerely intended his work in *Nigger Heaven* to challenge attitudes of racial prejudice among his fellow whites. To this extent he deserves to be remembered as a pioneer, an artist who attempted to remove the barriers of ignorance and hatred that kept Americans apart. His failing, as so often, was his haughty disregard of complexity. He was so desperate to be the first novelist to encapsulate black New York society that he shrugged off warnings about the book's title and similarly brushed aside concerns that he as a successful white writer was exploiting African-Americans for his own ends. He had set his mind on writing the first novel about the New Negro and Harlem, complete with all its "squalor and vice," and nothing would dissuade him. "I pay no attention to rules if I want to do something," he once explained, bluntly. "The main difficulty you get into is that sometimes you hurt other people by doing what you want to do." Simply, he concluded, "often it's better to pay no attention to their opinion."

If Van Vechten had been less visible in Harlem, less proprietorial in his interest in black culture, and less keen to attach his name to the great African-American artists of the day, perhaps *Nigger Heaven* would not have attracted quite so much splenetic criticism. But that was not an option: Van Vechten without his bulldozing was not Van Vechten at all. His zeal for Harlem and his need to be publicly associated with it were the very things that drove him to promote black artists in *Vanity Fair* and to encourage his white friends and colleagues to share his appreciation. What was truly remarkable about his adoption of black culture was that he attempted to immerse himself in the everyday lives of black people in a way that few other white artists ever had, socializing with them in their homes, entertaining them in his. It says so much about his contrary, self-centered nature that he was willing to risk the friendships he had made with one sensationalistic novel entitled with a word he knew he should not use.

As 1926 drew to a close, Van Vechten, exhausted by the whole affair, rocked on his haunches while the volleys whistled over his head. Marinoff was desperate for him to escape, to expel Harlem's air from his lungs as if the neighborhood were some fetid miasma that had infected him. He agreed that a period of self-exile was called for, but not this time in the capitals of Europe. America had alluring new playgrounds of its own way out west that he was eager to explore.

TEN

Cruel Sophistication

· ·

On New Year's Eve 1926 New York prepared for the biggest parties of the year. The Marx Brothers, Eddie Cantor, Sophie Tucker, Al Jolson, Jack Benny, and other stars of vaudeville were gathering at Essex House for an evening of music and dancing, which doubled as an opportunity to perform material too risqué to use on the circuit. At the Algonquin various members of the Round Table dropped in for dinner and an illicit swig or three in the Cases' quarters, while a few blocks north, at Alfred and Blanche Knopf's, sidecars and mint juleps were being mixed in anticipation of a long night ahead.

For the first time in years Carl Van Vechten would not be at any of the celebrations. Staring out of a train window at "long, lone, uninspired Kansas," he was heading west, tired and fretting. Two days ago he had left New York, showering Marinoff with the usual syrupy apologies for his most recent outburst of drunken boorishness. He had not heard from her since. Why had she not telegrammed the train to let him know she was thinking of him? He was *always* thinking of her. Six months ago she had packed her bags and headed for her sister's house in New Jersey, threatening to leave him; he feared his absence now might give her the opportunity to follow through with the threat. He desperately needed to shed his Manhattan skin for a while but felt naked and vulnerable without it. And without his baby, his "nerves"—brief flurries of anxiety aggravated by too much drink and not enough sleep—always returned. After long, uncomfortable hours of travel, the first morning of 1927 finally arrived, and with it a world far removed from New York: "Stars everywhere, and at 7 in the morning a pale new moon over my right shoulder. We are now in New Mexico."

Ever since they had reestablished contact in 1920, Mabel Dodge had tried to entice Van Vechten into visiting her at her new home in Taos. While postwar New York got in touch with its inner primitive self through Freudian psychoanalysis, jazz, and Harlem, Mabel found hers in the opposite corner of the United States among the indigenous people of New Mexico. Over the last few years she had hoped that Native Americans might become Van Vechten's latest obsession too and that he would do for them what he had done for Russian composers, Herman Melville, and now, of course, the American Negro. She had written to ask whether Van Vechten might encourage *Vanity Fair* to publish an article about the Native American cause; for pointers on how to get a recording contract for them from Columbia or Victrola; and to suggest that he make the natives of New Mexico the subject of his next book. In vivid prose she described the local art to him as "naïve—yet blood stained— always sad—disheartened—sadistic—and childlike. Blood streams from brows and breasts." She insisted there was all around her limitless material out of which he could fashion something truly remarkable, if only he would make the effort of leaving New York. "How *can* you like cities so much when you could vampire the country so much more[?]" she asked. Not many people could have accused Van Vechten of vampirism without his taking umbrage. Their friendship depended on those barbed little comments, praise wrapped up in criticism, and vice versa, that kept the spirit of competition between them crackling. To draw him west, she even appealed to his baser instincts, describing handsome young Native American men in fantastical costumes, one of whom, "tall and slight," once danced in "an emerald green satin shirt with a magenta yoke" for the prim, elderly painter Mary Foote, "as she examined him sympathetically thro' her pince nez." Until the *Nigger Heaven* controversy none of it worked; the prospect of hauling himself away from the buzz and thrum of New York to spend weeks without nightclubs, blues records, parties, and theaters seemed almost sacrilegious. However, after the bruising friction of the past months, a temporary detachment from civilization was deeply alluring.

In 1917 Mabel had herself withdrawn from urban society after she married her third husband, Maurice Sterne, an artist inspired by the untrammeled beauty of the American West. Though the marriage was doomed from the start—a combination of her possessiveness and his unfaithfulness—Sterne changed Mabel's life when he introduced her to the Puebloan people of New Mexico. Captivated by their religious rites, their art, and what she regarded as their spiritual purity, Mabel wanted her husband to enshrine them in his painting. The only difficulty was that Native Americans could not be easily accessed from the comfort of a New York drawing room. As she often did, Mabel assumed her wealth could square the circle. From her home in Croton-on-Hudson, Westchester County, she suggested to Sterne something approaching a human zoo: "Couldn't you pick out a family of Indians & put them to live in the cottage in Croton? . . . You could hire them for 6 months & you could get infinite riches out of them."

The plan, unsurprisingly, did not come to fruition. Mabel and Sterne instead moved to New Mexico permanently, settling in Taos, a small town a little north of Santa Fe and close to a large Native American pueblo of the same name. Since the late nineteenth century white artists had been coming to Taos because of the natural beauty of the surrounding area as well as the opportunities it offered to interact with Native American communities. When Mabel and Sterne arrived, the flow of outsiders increased sharply as the couple fostered a colony of European and American artists. Mabel thought that her colony could serve a mighty purpose: harnessing native traditions to establish an American artistic culture that was untainted by the ideologies and wars of Western civilization. To complement a new type of life, Mabel acquired a new type of husband. Tony Lujan, an imposing Native American from the Taos Pueblo, wooed Mabel with his drumming and singing and instructed her in his people's traditional way of life. Through his guidance Mabel felt reborn. She had "finally overcome all the conditioning of the years gone by," she wrote in her memoirs, "and all

Mabel Dodge Luhan, c. 1934, photograph by Carl Van Vechten

the crystallizations of heredity and environment." They married in April 1923, much to the consternation of his community. While Mabel believed their union was ordering her life into a radical simplicity, the pueblo feared that exactly the opposite was happening to Tony, as he moved into Mabel's enormous new home, acquiring expensive leather boots and the keys to his wife's roaring Cadillac.

Arriving in Taos on New Year's Day 1927, Van Vechten shared Mabel's initial sense of awe. He found New Mexico in winter eerily beautiful, "like the dawn of the world," as Mabel put it, the arid russet landscape vibrant beneath brilliant sunshine and a crystalline blue sky. To help him strip off the layers of the metropolis, Mabel gave him a pile of clothes more in keeping with his western surroundings. Whether he gladly swapped his silk shirts for ponchos is highly unlikely, but he seemed happy with the change of environment at least. His letters to Marinoff raved about the balance Mabel had achieved between child-of-the-earth simplicity and East Coast comfort, creating yet another sumptuous environment after the Villa Curonia and 23 Fifth Avenue. He was also glad to be in the company of the others at Mabel's house, who included the cubist painter Andrew Dasburg, the actress Ida Rauh, and Dorothy Brett, the deaf English artist who had served as D. H. Lawrence's secretary when he stayed at the colony a few years earlier.

Despite Mabel's disapproval, with Van Vechten around her guests were keen to re-create just a little of the Jazz Age spirit in somnolent New Mexico. A steady stream of visitors appeared at Van Vechten's door, seeking access to the alcohol stored in the cellar beneath his room, which he was only too glad to grant, so long as they poured some for him too. On his first Friday night there he and the others dived into the stash and partied in his room, before dining and then heading to the studio of another local artist, Kenneth Adams, for more drinking. "I got *very* drunk," Van Vechten confided to his daybook, "& Loren [Mozley, the painter] again begins to scream. In bed at 3." Their antics incensed Mabel. She retold the tale of Van Vechten's stay in an unpublished short story entitled "Twelfth Night," in which Van Vechten appears as Louis Van der Comp, a foulmouthed drunk who pollutes the purity of his surroundings with smutty jokes and coarse behavior. "His face was

red and swollen . . . he had a mock of obedient submission in his
lowered eyes and drooping lips. He was full of malice and moonshine." She had never liked Carl's vulgar streak, his preoccupation
with sex, alcohol, and double entendre but had accepted that in
New York such uncouthness—"cruel sophistication," she called it—
was inevitable. In the pristine wilderness, however, his drunkenness
and shrieking laughter were revolting, demonic even. She particularly resented the way in which he and Andrew Dasburg acted
like "two overgrown schoolboys" around Dorothy Brett, exploiting
her deafness and her sweet-natured naivety in order to make her the
butt of their teasing and innuendo. Furious, Mabel descended into
sullenness, locking herself away in her room for long periods, avoid-
ing everyone, just as she had often done at the Villa Curonia in 1914.

   Aside from artists Taos attracted a peculiar cast of drifters and
eccentrics. In one of her more sanguine moments, Mabel took Van
Vechten to the house of Arthur Manby, an Englishman who, convinced that she and her ex-husband Sterne were German spies, had
a habit of climbing onto Mabel's roof and putting his head down
the chimney to earwig her conversations. Van Vechten developed a
fondness for some of Taos's oddballs: he was very taken with
Dr. Martin, a physician who had lived in New Mexico for nearly
forty years, knew all his patients' secrets and peccadilloes, and, with
scant regard for the Hippocratic oath, regaled Van Vechten with
tales of a nearby whiskey priest who possessed two mistresses and
a well-stocked wine cellar. Van Vechten wrote Marinoff to say that
Dr. Martin had arranged for him to meet the priest later that week.
A further letter, however, suggests there was a change of plan, and
Van Vechten passed the evening in a bar that reminded him of
something out of a cowboy movie, full of mustachioed gunslingers
downing fortified liquor as the town sheriff looked on. He had been
in New Mexico two weeks, had not once looked at a New York
newspaper, and could not be happier about it, he told Marinoff. The
only thing he was missing about home was his beloved baby, Fania.

   When not enjoying himself with the local misfits, Van Vechten
experienced the Pueblo culture up close, the main reason that Mabel had been so keen for him to visit. One evening he and Tony were
preparing to leave for a wedding feast when, unannounced, a group

of young men and boys arrived on horseback to entertain him with a dance. After two hours of preparation—they stripped naked and daubed themselves in intricate painted designs before dressing again in feathers, beads, and colored cloth—the men danced energetically to the accompaniment of Tony's drumming and singing. Van Vechten found the whole performance enchanting, in particular the men's careful attention to decorating their bodies. He even wrote Marinoff asking if she might be able to fetch a batch of large feathers from Bloomingdale's to be distributed among the dancers by way of thanks. It was very rare that he could find nothing of interest in a dance performance, no matter from which culture it originated, and Mabel noted his appreciation in "Twelfth Night." "Not even Louis could find anything louche in the dances," she wrote of Van Vechten's fictional incarnation. "It was like a respite from evil thinking."

Even so, the real Van Vechten could not help comparing the Pueblo culture, unfavorably, with the singing and dancing of African-Americans. As decorative as the Pueblo rites were, suffused with what to him appeared a beguiling innocence and authenticity, he found them nowhere near as thrilling as black folk culture. The "Indians" of Taos, he told Marinoff, lacked the vivaciousness of Harlem's Negroes, who lived their lives with a relentless emotional honesty—joy, despair, sexual ecstasy, and religious fervor always at the surface. After only five days in Taos Van Vechten told Marinoff how pleased he had been to have met the only black person in town, a woman named Lulu Williams, who worked as a cook at the local inn. Her warmth lifted his mood and made a very welcome change from what he considered the emotional coldness of the Pueblo natives. Despite all the negativity surrounding *Nigger Heaven*, Van Vechten still found the company of black people life-affirming.

A little more than two weeks into his stay, Van Vechten decided it was time to move on, not least because of the increasing fractiousness between him and Mabel. After so many years of being badgered to visit he was confused and deeply irritated that she should subject him to one of her prolonged bouts of silent hostility. A couple of days before moving on he wrote in his daybook: "Mabel sends for me to tell me that she is going through a change of life.

Possibly this is true, but it sounds like a Tenth Day explanation of her moodiness." He was right. She was livid that he had corrupted her tranquil paradise with New York dissipation and felt the bite of public humiliation when Van Vechten gave his opinion on Native American culture to a local newspaper. In a piece about his visit a reporter noted that "Mr. Van Vechten was disappointed in the Taos deer dance, given the sixth of January, not finding in it the emotional excitement which he feels is so great a force in the dances of Harlem." For Mabel, a self-appointed authority and guardian of Pueblo culture, this was intolerable impudence; she cut the article out and attached it to the end of her "Twelfth Night" story. Once, as Van Vechten's mentor, she had held the upper hand in their friendship, teaching him the true meaning of sophistication. Now the balance of power had shifted. Her former protégé was lauded, by other whites at least, as the nation's unrivaled expert on the Negro, the man who had unveiled to the world the remarkable truth about the United States' hidden artistic genius. But Mabel had fully expected her guest, invited to her home in the artistic colony over which she presided, to bend his knee and fawn over her own collection of primitive marvels. Instead he had the temerity to insult her prized possession, which also happened to be her husband's native culture, though that, to Mabel, was a secondary issue. Furthermore, he magnified the insult by taking the opportunity to advertise his own cause yet again. Vast and sparsely populated though it was, the state of New Mexico was clearly only big enough for one proprietorial champion of ethnic Americans. When Van Vechten left, Mabel felt the whole of Taos had been disinfected. Her story "Twelfth Night" ends: "The air was all clear again and likely enough that night she would hear the stars singing."

After such a disastrous visit, aghast at the prospect that Van Vechten might write a book about the "Indians," she wrote him a letter suggesting he steer clear of the subject altogether because he had failed to find the true spiritual worth of the Pueblo culture during his stay. She need not have worried; Van Vechten had never seriously considered writing about Native Americans at any length. The trip to Taos had been a welcome break and an introduction to a fascinating community. But it was only ever intended as a stop on the way to observe the tribes of a much more exciting destination: Hollywood.

Like Harlem, Hollywood in 1927 was still a relatively new presence in the American imagination. Originally, and ironically, founded by socially conservative Christians seeking a haven from the over-crowded and licentious cities farther east, by the early 1920s the town of Hollywood had become the focus of the nation's film industry and synonymous with all that entailed. It was the soft-focus image of the American dream, a symbol of the United States' mania for fame and spectacle where those with talent and a work ethic could find their fortune. In Hollywood, a confident new culture forged by technology, capitalism, and youthful liberation found its boldest form. But the celluloid glamour of Hollywood also pos-sessed a dark photonegative. In 1921 Fatty Arbuckle had stood trial for allegedly raping and murdering a young actress in a hotel suite. A stream of lurid tales about the deviancy, corruption, and exploi-tation that governed Hollywood swiftly followed. The Hollywood sign, erected as a real estate advertisement in 1923 and only just becoming recognized as a national landmark, was seen as a warning and an invitation, a siren beckoning impressionable dreamers onto the rocks of a place that was materially rich but morally bankrupt.

Van Vechten's limited experience of the movie industry con-vinced him that Hollywood was neither as dangerous nor as excit-ing as Manhattan, but probably an awful lot sillier. His novel *The Tattooed Countess* had been adapted and retitled *A Woman of the World* for a 1925 movie starring Pola Negri. At the time Negri was one of the most celebrated stars in the business, but she is probably best known today as Rudolph Valentino's lover, the young woman who repeatedly fainted at his funeral in 1926. Van Vechten liked Negri very much but hated the film, saw it only once, and suggested to his friend Max Ewing that it was, in its own peculiar way, a sort of masterpiece—so bad it was almost good. He echoed the senti-ments of the critic who wondered aloud why the studio responsible had bothered to buy the rights to the novel when the plot bore so little resemblance to Van Vechten's original story and even the title had been completely changed. Despite that episode, which he considered the nadir of his artistic life, he had heard all sorts of outlandish tales of Hollywood's excesses and was keen to give the place a closer look.

Upon his arrival in Los Angeles Van Vechten was astonished by its sheer size. Manhattan was just beginning its ascent into the skies; plans for the Chrysler Building were being sketched at that very moment. In Los Angeles it was the horizontal scale rather than the vertical that dominated. For a man who usually crossed the Hudson only under extreme duress, these wandering Californian miles were extraordinary. Nothing better reflected the hubris and rapacity of the modern United States than the vast expanse of this playground of the rich, famous, and nakedly ambitious. Some weeks later, in a short series of articles about his trip that he produced for *Vanity Fair*, Van Vechten said that the geographical expanse of Hollywood was a metaphor for all of its other excesses. Hollywood, he said, possessed "more money, more sunlight . . . more work, more poverty and bad luck, more automobiles, more flowers . . . more beautiful gals . . . and more dissatisfaction" than any place he had ever been, New York included.

In the land of excessive consumption there was plenty to sate Van Vechten's ravenous appetites. Even his hotel, the Ambassador, was of immense proportions. Set far back from Wilshire Boulevard, the Ambassador's grounds were swathed in palm and bamboo trees, and a huge verdant lawn separated the hotel's reception from a community of well-appointed bungalows, where its wealthy guests stayed. The Ambassador was famed not only for its A-list clientele but also for its nightclub, the Cocoanut Grove, Hollywood's most fashionable and exclusive hangout, where California's best jazz bands performed. Van Vechten worried that he might need a tour guide to navigate his way around the hotel, never mind the city. Much to his delight, within minutes of his checking in, Scott and Zelda Fitzgerald appeared at his door. Scott had come to Hollywood to write a screenplay for *Lipstick*, Constance Talmadge's next movie, and as chance would have it, they had taken the next-door bungalow. The caliber of neighbors was very much to Van Vechten's approval. Aside from the Fitzgeralds, Pola Negri and the actress

Carmel Myers were nearby, and John Barrymore was staying in the suite directly above. Van Vechten unpacked, dressed, and joined the Fitzgeralds for a drink. Any hopes any of them had of a quiet, abstemious stay were in that moment definitively dashed. Although Scott was under pressure to finish his script and did his best to avoid temptation, Van Vechten admitted that he was frequently guilty of interrupting Scott's labors by knocking on his door, "often late in the afternoon, often late at night."

It was not unusual that these two East Coast novelists should find themselves neighbors in Hollywood. Recently several of Van Vechten's peers, including Theodore Dreiser and Joseph Hergesheimer, had come west to write scenarios for the big studios. It was a sign that Hollywood was in a moment of transition, making great efforts to infuse the movie business with a degree of class, turning mass entertainment into art. Louis B. Mayer, the head of MGM, was at this instant attempting to confirm the transformation by establishing the Academy of Motion Picture Arts and Sciences. Movies were beginning to capture and create the zeitgeist. The big titles of 1927 were *The Jazz Singer*—Al Jolson's groundbreaking talkie that dealt with themes of race, class, and religion—and *It*, in which Clara Bow delivered one of the definitive models of the flapper. This was the reason that Van Vechten was intrigued by Hollywood. He wanted to mix in the circles of wealthy, talented, and influential people who were turning this town into such a gigantic cultural force. Movies were actually something of a blind spot of his. It was not until the sound era of the 1930s that he developed a passion for the medium that approached his love of live performance. He was being honest when he assured journalists upon his arrival that he was in Hollywood only to satisfy his sense of curiosity. "Say that I am one author who came to Los Angeles not to make money," he instructed an interviewer, "or to write for the movies, or to get color for a story. Say that I just came out, to look around."

Within a matter of days that all changed. On his second night in town Van Vechten experienced a Hollywood premiere for the first time, the debut screening of *An American Tragedy*, adapted from a Theodore Dreiser novel. The movie itself was forgettable. It was the spectacle of the occasion that left him gasping: "an astonishing sight," he said, "Kleig lights & megaphones, announcing the arrivals and taking their pictures. I see a great many people I know & meet [the silent movie stars] Pauline Starke & Patsy Miller." Afterward he was invited to a party at the home of the writer Edwin Justus Mayer, a villa with glorious panoramic views, high up in the hills. The very next morning the actor—and future Academy Award winner—Joseph Schildkraut drove him out to the set of his new movie, the biblical epic *The King of Kings*, directed by Cecil B. DeMille, where Van Vechten watched in awe the filming of the earthquake at the end of the movie, great mounds of rock and soil shaking and churning at the director's command. The excesses of the movie world had Van Vechten rapt. Before the week was out, he was seized by the idea of writing a definitive Hollywood novel. He warned Marinoff that such a venture would necessitate "as much intensive study as Harlem," at least two months of total immersion. "There is nothing else like it on Earth," he told her.

His mention of Harlem was apt. Although the two places were starkly different, they were united in Van Vechten's mind as exotic locations of extremes and complexities that few outsiders were capable of penetrating and understanding. A key motivation for writing *Nigger Heaven* was that no other writer had already successfully written about Harlem, and he believed the same was true about Hollywood. Here he could cement his status as "a chronicler of our times," as Mabel had once described him, the writer who captured the twin pillars of the new American culture—New York and Hollywood—at their most exhilarating moments.

For the time being only he and Marinoff knew that his vacation had turned into a research trip; he wanted to see Hollywood as it really was, not preening to be put in its best light. Over the next four weeks Van Vechten trawled the party circuit and the studio lots, seemingly meeting every significant person in Hollywood, from the starlets Lillian Gish and Joan Crawford to B. P. Schulberg, the legendary producer at Paramount Pictures, to the Hollywood power couple Mary Pickford and Douglas Fairbanks. The latter Van Vechten particularly approved of because he was an enthusiastic practitioner of goosing, an art that Van Vechten had worked hard to master.

Fairbanks and Pickford also gave Van Vechten a taste of genuine

Carl Van Vechten at the Famous Players–Lasky studio, Los Angeles, January 30, 1927. From left to right: Frank Case, Van Vechten, Flora Zabelle, Emil Jannings, Bertha Case, Jesse Lasky

superstardom when they took him as their guest to the premiere of *Old Ironsides*, a maritime epic directed by James Cruze, at Sid Grauman's Egyptian Theatre. For *Vanity Fair* Van Vechten described his excitement at being sat with Fairbanks and Pickford in the back of their car as they drove slowly toward the venue. A good two miles from the theater crowds filled the street; countless men, women, and children craned their necks or ran up to the car windows in hope of catching a glimpse of their idols. "Mary Pickford was cheered," he noted with astonishment and delight, "not faintly, not half-heartedly, but lustily, even hysterically. Having made it out the car in front of the theater, Van Vechten was bowled over by the spectacle that confronted him: "Searchlights streamed in all directions. A battalion of policemen vainly attempted to push back the seething hordes of gaping humanity." They were now forty-five minutes late, and Van Vechten was astonished to find that the screening of the movie, in which neither Pickford nor Fairbanks had the slightest involvement, had been delayed just so the reigning royal couple of Hollywood could see it in its entirety. As the three of them entered the auditorium, Van Vechten recalled, the entire audience sprang to its feet and gave them a rousing ovation. The approbation was obviously for the two pinups by his side, not for Van Vechten, but the vicarious thrill he got from it is tangible in that breathless description. Only in his days of reporting on the New York opera had he felt so energized and excited by being in the presence of celebrity.

In his observation, Fairbanks and Pickford possessed almost superhuman powers. These deities of the flesh, he pointed out, not only received more adulation than any royal figure he could think of, but they possessed an uncommon and invaluable gift: "the power of satisfying wishes." That sense of autonomy and influence was immensely attractive to Van Vechten; the ability to transform one's environment at will was an abiding fascination of his. For a successful and imaginative Hollywood star every possible fancy was apparently indulged. If the whim should take them, Hollywood stars could probably arrange to have exotic animals paraded up and down their street, Van Vechten joked, "accompanied by nude Nubians with torches." The movie stars he met, half of whom he had never seen in any film, absorbed him so fully because their extravagant lives represented the sort of existence that he had tried so hard for so long to make reality but could never entirely achieve, one created and controlled according to his lusts and whims and in which he bore no responsibility to anyone else. The fundamental business of Hollywood, the motion pictures, was of virtually no interest to him. In his daybooks, his letters to Fania, and his four *Vanity Fair* articles his sole focus was the power of celebrity. "I am swimming among movie stars," he boasted to Marinoff in one of his daily missives home. Like a tourist rushing through a sightseeing itinerary with guidebook in hand, he admitted that he carried around a list of the town's most famous people; each time he encountered a new celebrity he checked their name off the roll call. He was less interested in the people he met than the fame attached to them, the surface glamour rather than the substance—or lack of it—beneath.

Yet his seduction was never entirely complete. As a man who lived under the shelter of his own towering fantasies, he understood intuitively that Hollywood was make-believe. The entire town was a movie set, its inhabitants continually acting. "Never before," he believed, "have I heard virtues and talents, domestic and professional, extolled as whole-heartedly as they are at Hollywood." He knew this was simply part of the Hollywood hustle. Unlike in New York, where scabrous insults flew from the mouths of writers and artists with nonchalant ease, in Hollywood terrified that some careless insult could cost him or her the next role, everyone claimed to think that everyone else was a marvel. At one party four sparkling young stars—Constance Talmadge, Louella Parsons, Betty Compson, and Bebe Daniels—collected around him and, according to Van Vechten, spent an hour talking exclusively about his books. It was, he said, an experience "which may have been something of a strain for them, but which was extremely agreeable as far as I was concerned." After the critical scolding he had received at the end of the previous year, even disingenuous praise was welcome.

Not all the attention was insincere. As a bestselling novelist Van Vechten had genuine currency. Clara Bow and Lois Moran, two of the hottest young actresses of the day, told him how much they would love to star as the snake charmer Zimbule O'Grady in a screen adaptation of his *The Blind Bow-Boy*, and he had meetings with the two great directors of the decade, Cecil B. DeMille and King Vidor, about the possibility of turning *Nigger Heaven* into a movie. As he told Marinoff, if he only had a story in his head, he could get a movie into production tomorrow. The talk of parties and movie stars worried Marinoff. The point of this trip had been to ease off the drinking, she reminded him, to get the Harlem nightclubs out of his system and escape a brutal New York winter, so he could return to her sober, fit, and free of nerves. Equally disturbing was the regular appearance of Scott Fitzgerald in his letters. Like a mother chiding a son led astray by an unruly classmate, she told Carl bluntly that Fitzgerald was a bad influence and she did not approve of the two of them spending so much time together. She received reassurances that Hollywood people were so professional and hardworking that the parties were nowhere near as debauched as in New York, and as for Scott his work commitments meant he was practically teetotal.

In fact, it was Zelda who had reason to worry about Van Vechten's effect on *her* husband. Not only did Van Vechten distract Scott from his script, but he also introduced the actress Lois Moran into his life. On their first meeting at the Mayfair Ball Van Vechten veritably swooned when the delicate, beautiful Moran asked him to dance. Only seventeen and accompanied by her mother wherever she went, Moran was a prodigy whose uncommon wit and intellect matched her talent in front of the camera. Van Vechten knew she was a rising star and was therefore excited to be in her presence, although he admitted to Marinoff that he had not actually seen any of the girl's movies. The two quickly became great friends, and along with Mrs. Moran, they spent hours together, frequenting Hollywood's most fashionable places, including Madame Helene's tearoom opposite the Famous Players-Lasky lot, often packed with movie stars taking a break from filming. When Van Vechten heard that Moran's next picture was desperately in need of a leading man, he suggested Scott Fitzgerald. Everyone involved in the movie, Moran most especially, thought it an inspired suggestion. When Van Vechten put it to Fitzgerald, however, the idea was not met with the same enthusiasm, Fitzgerald wary no doubt of tarnishing his reputation as a literary heavyweight. But when he met Moran at Pickfair (the estate belonging to Mary Pickford and Douglas Fair-

Lois Moran, c. 1932, photograph by Carl Van Vechten

banks), Fitzgerald's camera shyness seemed to dissipate. From that very first encounter he was smitten and allowed himself to be screen-tested. The movie never materialized, but over the following months and years Fitzgerald's infatuation intensified. Moran eventually became the model for the movie star Rosemary Hoyt in *Tender Is the Night*, and her appearances at the Fitzgerald home caused serious ruptures in an already unsettled marriage.

After a monthlong stay, Van Vechten returned from Hollywood feeling refreshed and inspired, the events of 1926 seemingly put behind him. He may have been the only man in history to have gone to Hollywood to "get away from it all" and succeeded. Hollywood had revealed itself to have been "incredible, fantastic, colossal," he enthused in his *Vanity Fair* articles. He wrote about the parties and the movie lots, the nightclubs and restaurants, the demands of starry actors and the luxury of the Ambassador all with an amused detachment. It was Van Vechten at his best: cheeky and breezy while skillfully managing to guide the reader into a barely believable alien environment. The Hollywood he depicted was the one he experienced, in which oversize appetites were constantly indulged, and outlandish ambitions were just as frequently destroyed. In his last article of the series, he wryly observed that the "walls of the Hollywood houses are constructed of plaster with wire netting between so that it would be quite possible to kick a hole through the average domicile. A good deal of the Hollywood attitude is equally hollow." The town was simultaneously formidable and flimsy, but who was Carl Van Vechten to complain about that?

Fun though it was, Hollywood was never going to be Van Vechten's home away from home any more than Taos was. With an earnest sobriety, Mabel's vision of the United States repudiated the thrills of modernity, while Hollywood's valorized them to an absurdly dishonest degree. Back in New York, the place with the bravery to steer the honest course in between, Van Vechten set himself the task of encapsulating Hollywood into a book that would do to Los Angeles what his previous novels had done to Manhattan.

ELEVEN

A Quite Gay, but Empty, Bubble That Dazzles One in Bursting

. . . .

Marinoff was looking forward to having her husband home. For the last two years she had felt Van Vechten slipping away from her, his obsession with Harlem and his heavy drinking pushing them ever farther apart. She took Charleston lessons and read the books by African-American authors that Van Vechten piled around their home as a means of staying close to him, but too often all she got in return was a raised hand and a nasty insult when he had taken too many drinks. Having read his letters over the past month, she honestly believed that the Southwest had cleansed him and that he would come back the man she had first married. Within twenty-four hours of his return her hopes were dashed as he drank and caroused with a renewed intensity, as if making up for lost time. When Marinoff left for England at the end of March in search of work on the London stage, she sent letters home that laid things out plainly. There could be no more broken promises; unless sanity was restored, their marriage was over. The party must come to an end.

In response to Marinoff's pleas Van Vechten bombarded her with his usual overblown profusions of unique and undying love, while never actually addressing any of the important issues she raised. If anything, the unpleasantness that Marinoff was so sick of appeared to increase during her stay in London, as a new sense of menace enveloped Vechten's social scene. Self-indulgence gave way to addiction, and formerly high-spirited parties were now turning violent, including on a couple of occasions at Bob Chanler's, where the host himself grappled and traded blows with a paralytic E. E. Cummings. In the early years of Prohibition Manhattan's smart set believed the cocktail glass to be the ultimate symbol of rebellion against the antiquated morality of a tired old order. It was learning the hard way that nobody ever drank himself to liberation. Ill, nervous, and hardly ever sober, Van Vechten boozed his way through party after party under the grip of dependency and a grim sense of duty to the myth of carefree Manhattan that he had done as much as anybody to create.

In Fania's absence, he dashed off his four Hollywood articles for *Vanity Fair*, but there was no sign of the planned novel, and although the movie producer Arthur Hornblow approached him to write a scenario for Gilda Gray's next picture, he never did, largely because he was unable to think of a story. In years gone by he had managed to juggle the demands of writing and his hectic social schedule with impressive ease. His ability to compartmentalize the various spheres of his life had enabled him to work through the hangovers, shutting out all distraction to secure a few productive hours of creative endeavor each day. The majority of *Nigger Heaven* was written in precisely that fashion, in spells of intense concentration on weekday mornings. It was a skill he first honed in his early twenties, rushing to beat deadlines amid the cacophony of the Madhouse at the *Chicago American*. Now, in his mid-forties with a serious drinking problem and still somewhat bruised from the critical lashing *Nigger Heaven* had received in the black press, he was simply too addled to write with the discipline and vigor of old. Mabel Dodge had once accused him of "vampiring" New York. It might have been that the reverse was true: the parties and the hedonism that appeared to be the city's life force had finally drained Van Vechten of his creativity.

In an attempt to get him working, Marinoff appealed to his vanity, reminding him that since the publication of *Nigger Heaven* the world was eager to see what he would do next. That only made things worse, piling the pressure of expectation upon an impenetrable creative block. Plenty of those around him were suffering from similar problems, including Scott Fitzgerald, whose time in Hollywood proved to be a washout. According to one biographer, although

Fitzgerald had the best intentions when he arrived in Los Angeles, as soon as Van Vechten, John Barrymore, and Lois Moran arrived in town, he "embarked on a party that lasted three months." The script he produced was deemed so bad that United Artists refused to pay the eighty-five hundred dollars that was promised him on completion. He and Zelda served their retribution by gathering every stick of furniture in their bungalow at the Ambassador, piling it artfully in the center of the living room, and leaving their unpaid bill at its summit.

In May Van Vechten accompanied Lois and Gladys Moran for a weekend at Ellerslie, a mansion the Fitzgeralds were renting in Delaware. On the first night almost all of them drank until they threw up or passed out, the hosts included, Zelda descending into screaming hysterics before doing so. Van Vechten ended his diary entry for the day with an unexpected but apposite comment on events happening in the world outside this tiny bubble of self-destruction. "Charles Lindbergh arrives in Paris today in 33 hours from N.Y. in his aircraft," he noted, as if conscious that the two events were in a perverse way linked: the light and shadow of American modernity, the Fitzgeralds' dissolution the inverse of Lindbergh's straight-backed heroism. The following week he received an extraordinary letter from Zelda, begging forgiveness for her behavior at the party: "From the depths of my polluted soul, I am sorry that the weekend was such a mess. Do forgive my iniquities and my putrid drunkenness."

With deliberately black irony, Van Vechten responded by sending her a new cocktail shaker in thanks for her hospitality. The gift was gratefully received, though Zelda pointed out that they were well stocked on these now, so in the future "a gas range and a rug for the dining room" would be appreciated. In his dotage Van Vechten attempted to distance himself from the Fitzgeralds' spiral of excess, characterizing their infamous bad behavior as of an order entirely different from his own habits. To the interviewer William Ingersoll he disingenuously claimed that Scott's "way of life didn't appeal to me." To another writer he said: "they both drank a lot—we all did, but they were excessive." As Marinoff would have pointed out, by any sane measure Van Vechten's drinking fitted that description

F. Scott Fitzgerald, c. 1937, photograph by Carl Van Vechten

too. It was only embarrassment or self-delusion that prevented him from admitting it.

A few friends outside Manhattan's alcoholic fug recognized that this lifestyle was damaging both his health and his ability to create. Hugh Walpole, perhaps at Marinoff's urging, invited Van Vechten to recuperate at his home in the English Lake District. "You need a change physically," Walpole noted, "and everyone in England will be simply delighted to see you." But it was in Chicago, not England, that he ended up when, a few weeks later, news came that Ralph was fighting for his life. He had been ill for some time, ailing from an aggressive cancer. His condition had now deteriorated to such an extent that his doctors gave him just weeks, if not days, to live. The sight of his dying brother floored Van Vechten. In his prime Ralph was a formidable man, nearly three hundred pounds and six and a half feet tall. He was now gaunt and pitifully weak, though in his mind he was still an indomitable Van Vechten, capable of laughing at his little brother's recent escapades. Carl spent the next week in Chicago, fretting over Ralph during the day and then going out at night to see Nora Holt perform at the Sunset nightclub and to drink with friends at the Café de Paris until dawn. For a man watching his brother slip away into death it was unusual behavior, callous even. There was something deeply clinical within Van Vechten's character that allowed him to coldly sort life into neat sections when he needed to, pushing one set of emotions aside in order to access another. And in a strange way, carousing was now something of a necessity, the closest thing he had to a routine to keep him steady in a time of crisis.

Ralph passed away in the late morning on June 28. The funeral was held on the thirtieth, after which Van Vechten returned immediately to New York. Four days later Marinoff arrived back from Europe to discover a husband grieving, exhausted, and worryingly ill, with unpleasant bladder problems resulting from an enlarged prostate and phlebitis in his leg, both conditions likely worsened by his drinking. Her presence was just the tonic Van Vechten needed. "I *adore* having Marinoff back," he admitted to his daybook. "She is the only satisfactory person alive." It was as close as he ever got to committing to paper any sign of remorse for his abysmal treatment of her over recent times.

Work eventually began on the new novel and carried on throughout the rest of the year. Writing the book was a slow-going, uninspired ordeal attended by the pain and sleeplessness of ill health, further exacerbated by a recurrence of his long-standing dental problems. In the small, quiet spaces between parties in Harlem and bedridden agony at home, Ralph's death gave him cause for reflection about his future, as his mother's had done twenty-two years earlier. After a few days in the Berkshires at his friend Bill Bullitt's home, Van Vechten fell in love with a neighboring farm that he was told was up for sale. He wrote Mabel that he and Marinoff were thinking of following her lead and turning their backs on Manhattan to start a new life of bucolic tranquillity. They never bought the farm, of course. More than a few days away from New York City, and they felt bored and trapped in the countryside with only Mother Nature for company and no distractions to diffuse their livid arguments. As the end of the year approached, Van Vechten made a fresh effort to kick some of his bad habits by going cold turkey for a while in Atlantic City, which partially worked: he did not stop drinking, but he never touched a cigarette again. He found it a depressing experience and wondered whether a permanent move to Hollywood was the answer to his problems. That idea was almost as implausible as his and Marinoff's becoming New England farmers. Their fidgeting whimsicality could be accommodated only in a city as variegated as New York. If they were to work themselves out of their rut, they would have to do so with Manhattan as their backdrop.

In the early weeks of 1928 the next book was finally complete. *Spider Boy* was the most uncomplicated and conventional of all of Van Vechten's novels. Returning to his trusted theme of the innocent abroad, the story concerns Ambrose Deacon, a shy and taciturn playwright from the Midwest of meager talents who unintentionally, and against his wishes, becomes the toast of Hollywood. The novel was a lightweight response to the faddishness of the 1920s, with moments of slapstick humor as broad as anything the Keystone Kops ever committed to celluloid. As a follow-up to *Nigger Heaven* it was anticlimactic and certainly a smaller, safer effort than the definitive satire of the movie industry that he had initially planned. Both the novel and its depiction of Hollywood were neatly summed up by the headline of a review in the *Brooklyn Eagle*: VAN VECHTEN FOLLYWOOD A QUITE GAY, BUT EMPTY, BUBBLE THAT DAZZLES ONE IN BURSTING. On reading that headline, Van Vechten might have thought that it summed up much of his life at that point too. He had always enjoyed the process of publishing a book much more than the experience of writing it; the excitement of the publicity campaign was what he liked, seeing his name in print, hearing his work discussed by fashionable cliques, feeling part of the cultural moment. When the reviews were good, he noted them in his daybook, clipped them for his scrapbooks, and quoted them at length in letters to friends on both sides of the Atlantic. When they were bad, he fumed and turned to drink. With this book he seemed remarkably uninterested in how it was received. *Spider Boy* gave him little pleasure of any sort. The writing had been painful, and the end result distinctly mediocre. Being a novelist had never been so underwhelming.

Shortly after the novel was finished, Ralph's widow, Fannie, died. When Van Vechten went to Chicago for the funeral, it emerged that he was to inherit a sixth of his brother's multimillion-dollar estate, meaning he and Marinoff now had a large secured income for life. Apparently exhausted by the stress of a third family funeral in a little more than two years, he decided to head west for a vacation. Santa Fe was first on the itinerary before moving on to Hollywood, though he could stand it for only a few days. The superficialities that had so amused him a year earlier now struck him as contemptuously shallow. "My revulsion towards the picture world & all it connotes is complete," he wrote in his daybook. The highlight of the trip was when he met Aimee McPherson, the famous Pentecostal preacher. In an interview with Gilmore Millen of the *Los Angeles Herald* Van Vechten said he had heard McPherson preach on the radio in his hotel room the previous night and her soulfulness and passion had had the most extraordinary effect on him. "I listened for two hours," he said, "and I was enchanted. When she finished, I was almost on my knees." Considering McPherson's favorite targets for damnation were the heathens of Broadway and Hollywood, that was no slight achievement. Four days later, on March 1, he managed to get himself invited to a dinner with McPherson, or Sister, as she insisted people call her, and a few other Hollywood figures. After dinner they went to hear Sister perform baptisms at the Angelus Temple, a vast space packed with five thousand worshippers that reminded Van Vechten more of Carnegie Hall than any church he knew. The service was spectacular in every sense and prompted a tremendous outpouring of emotion from the congregation. Van Vechten wrote to both Marinoff and H. L. Mencken about how wonderful the experience had been—so wonderful that Mencken wondered whether Van Vechten had managed to behave himself properly: "I only hope that you didn't attempt her person. Christian women are usually disappointing. It takes a lot of high-pressure work to convince them that God really doesn't care a damn."

It was not the first time that Van Vechten had been awestruck in the presence of religious preachers. The Holy Jumpers service he witnessed in the Bahamas and the evangelical churches that he visited in Harlem had excited him because he viewed them as performances of undiluted blackness, a little like seeing Bert Williams or Nora Holt onstage. McPherson, however, was white, and the extreme reaction that Van Vechten had to her sermons is a sign of a tiny chink in his emotional armor presenting itself to the outside world. Usually he expressed feelings of self-doubt or weakness only to those closest to him—Marinoff, Avery Hopwood, or Donald Angus. Of course there is no chance that Van Vechten considered joining McPherson's congregation, but after the bereavements, his illnesses, the rickety state of his marriage, and his dissatisfaction with his writing, McPherson's offer of spiritual nourishment fell on receptive ears.

Those stirrings of vulnerability evident in the spring consumed him just a few months later. On July 1, after an evening of cocktails and absinthe with some of the jeunes gens assortis, a reporter from *The New York Times* called Van Vechten at home to get his reaction to some terrible news: Avery Hopwood was dead. The story at first was that Hopwood had got into difficulties while swimming in the Mediterranean and drowned. Within three weeks Somerset Maugham wrote to say that in fact, a heart attack had been the culprit, the

culmination of an epic binge. Maugham explained that Hopwood
had arrived in Juan les Pins one evening after four days of heavy
drinking in Nice. Already drunk, he helped himself to several more
drinks before sitting down to dinner. "Immediately after dinner he
insisted on going in to the water," Maugham said, implying the
outcome was inevitable. Hopwood's death hit Van Vechten as hard
as any of the recent family deaths, perhaps more so. Van Vechten's
experience of New York had been entwined with his relationship
with Hopwood, who was one of the few close friends during the last
two decades with whom he had never fallen out, as well as having
been his lover, albeit briefly. Marinoff, away on another of her re-
storative breaks, wrote him a tender letter of sympathy but also im-
plored him to learn from Hopwood's demise. The issue was no
longer merely the survival of their marriage, she said, but their very
lives. "You just can't beat that sort of game darling," She said, referring to the recklessness with which Hollywood had faced life. "It
gets everyone sooner or later." She was terrified that Van Vechten's
turn was next.

For the first time in their marriage Van Vechten paid serious attention to Marinoff's supplications. On September 5 he boarded
the SS *Mauretania* to join her in Europe, his first trip abroad since
1915. Perhaps there was a little of his essential selfishness in that
decision. After all, he was reaching out to Marinoff at a moment
when he most needed her support, after years of making little effort
to atone for his atrocious behavior. Even so, the time they spent in
each other's company traveling through England, France, Germany,
Austria, Hungary, Czechoslovakia, and Italy was physically and
emotionally the closest they had been for many years, perhaps a full
decade since Van Vechten had begun his affair with Donald Angus
and certainly since his immersion in Harlem. The central problems
of their marriage—Van Vechten's chronic self-obsession and his alcohol dependency—were not obviated by the trip, but Van Vechten's decision to leave New York and devote himself to Marinoff
for a few weeks was a sign to her that he thought their relationship
worth saving. Until now that had seemed very far from obvious.

•

The vacation afforded Van Vechten a vital moment of respite. Several thousand miles away from Manhattan he had the opportunity to break the rhythms of his usual existence, dedicate more attention to his relationship with Marinoff, and take stock of his life and career. That he was attempting to view the world from a fresh perspective that fall is evident from the journal he kept, in which he observed his European surroundings with a reflective, analytical calmness, a tone that he had not been using much of late.

On his first visit to Europe, in 1907, Van Vechten had been among the many Americans who scampered there in search of enlightenment. When he had returned, in 1913 and 1914, his motivation was essentially the same, and his direct exposure to European modernism had set his life on a new course. Fourteen years later he found the United States' relationship with Europe drastically changed. His nation was a genuine cultural force in the Old World; its newness and brashness, once reviled, were now widely envied. As he and Marinoff journeyed through Western and Central Europe, Van Vechten scribbled in his notebook his surprise at how thoroughly Europe had been seduced by the fashions of New York and Hollywood. He thought the new urban Germany of the Weimar Republic at night could almost be Manhattan: jazz bands played in New York–style cabaret venues, and assertive young women walked the streets in their modern finery, no doubt influenced by the emancipated flappers they had seen in American movies. In shops in Prague, American names jumped out from the shelves in translations of novels about urban America, such as *Manhattan Transfer* by John Dos Passos, and any number of books by Upton Sinclair. The streets may have been lined with bicycles rather than motorcars, and Czech women had not caught the smoking habit yet, but American shadows were cast at every turn.

He noted all this with a combination of patriotic pride and a little amusement, a gentle disbelief that the cultural interests of the United States should have snaked their way not only across the Atlantic but down the full length of the Danube. It was with genuine excitement that he discovered the extent to which black America had made the journey too. Aside from the blare of jazz filling the streets, Van Vechten discovered photographs of Josephine Baker and other black American entertainers gazing out from magazine stands in numerous cities. The point of this trip was to cut the cord to Manhattan and heal the wounds he had inflicted upon his marriage. But try as he might, Van Vechten could not dislodge Harlem from his mind, and he pined for the company of the black people who inhabited his life in New York. A few days after spotting a black man in the center of Prague, Van Vechten was still rebuking himself for not having engaged him in conversation, as this man turned out to be the only person of color he saw in his whole time in Czechoslovakia. He was a snappily dressed fellow too, Van Vechten thought, who would have surely been wonderful company.

In noting Europe's pockets of blackness, Van Vechten was also measuring his success as the publicist in chief of the New Negro. *Nigger Heaven* was proving a great success in Europe, selling well in Britain and France and translated into several European languages; when he met Greta Garbo in Hollywood earlier that year, he cabled Marinoff to send Garbo one of the Swedish versions immediately. Even before the book was published, he was acting as tour guide to Harlem for inquisitive outsiders, many of whom were visiting European artists, writers, and journalists, such as Paul Morand, Beverley Nichols, Rebecca West, and Somerset Maugham, who returned home with tales of black New York that fascinated their compatriots. Van Vechten was a crucial influence in spreading knowledge of African-American culture among not just white Americans but white Europeans, an achievement of which he was immensely proud. "That was almost my fate for ten years at least: taking people to Harlem," he recalled. "You'll find little Harlems everywhere you go," Langston Hughes wrote him regarding his travel plans; "you were a mighty big part starting it all."

When Van Vechten and Marinoff arrived in Paris in the fall of 1928, they encountered what the French called *le tumulte noir*, a craze for African-American art that swept all social classes right across the city. Van Vechten had played a small but significant role in this through his contribution as creative consultant to the producer Caroline Dudley on her *La Revue Nègre* show at the Théâtre des Champs-Élysées. Marinoff's desire to insulate Van Vechten from the hedonistic patterns of his life in New York was frustrated in

Paris, where Carl's old drinking pals, including Scott Fitzgerald and Ralph Barton, turned up everywhere. However, his nights out on the town were curbed by illness, exhaustion, and another flare-up of the phlebitis in his leg, a sure sign to Marinoff that Van Vechten's lifestyle during these last few years threatened to drag him into dark territory from which he would never return.

After a tour of the European mainland they decamped in November to London, where their social diary was full but less frenetic than in New York. Their arrival coincided with Paul Robeson's highly praised reprisal of his role in *Show Boat* at the Drury Lane Theatre. Of all of Van Vechten's causes Robeson was at this stage the most conspicuously successful, and when he wrote friends back home about how Robeson was stunning the English critics, he did so in the satisfied tones of someone who believed a good share of the credit was his. Showing off to Gertrude Stein, Van Vechten told her all about a party that the Robesons' threw in his honor at their upscale house in Swiss Cottage. "It was their first party & a great success," he began before providing a detailed breakdown of the guest list. "All the distinguished Negroes in London were there," he said, along with many others, including Hugh Walpole, the politician and newspaper tycoon Lord Beaverbrook, the singer Alberta Hunter, and Fred Astaire. The British establishment mingling with a multiracial group of America's pop culture icons: this was an eclectic guest list to rival one of Van Vechten's own and had been an unthinkable proposition when he was last in London fourteen years earlier. Van Vechten took great pride in being the guest of honor at this extraordinary event, a sign that he held some exalted position among this remarkable company, the reason they all had been brought together. Before he left England, Van Vechten purchased a portrait bust of Robeson sculpted by Jacob Epstein to be displayed in the hallway of his apartment. It was a monument in stone of his link to Robeson's celebrity and a reminder to all who entered his home that it was in this very space that Van Vechten had set the world's most famous black man on his path to stardom.

Van Vechten and Marinoff returned to New York laden with expensive gifts for themselves and others shortly before Christmas. If Marinoff had hoped the break would act as some sort of purification

ritual from which her husband would emerge cleansed and re-
formed, she would have been disappointed. The anxieties of the last
eighteen months had certainly eased, but Van Vechten still had a
long way to go to shake off the grip that alcohol had taken on him.
Over the next year he made repeated attempts to cut down on his
drinking and told various friends that he was getting on the wagon
for good. As often as not a declaration like that was quickly followed by a relapse, but he was earnest in his intentions of reining in
the excess for fear of going the same way as Hopwood.

In the summer of 1929 Van Vechten accompanied Marinoff
back to Europe. Most of their time was spent in Spain and France,
where Van Vechten passed several long nights in Paris in the bars of
the rue de Lappe, picking up Arab soldiers and rent boys. Even if
they did not discuss explicit details, Marinoff must have had a pretty
good inkling of the sorts of things that Van Vechten was doing
when he chose to stay up late after kissing her goodnight. Here they
were on a joint vacation as part of an effort to strengthen their
marriage, and Van Vechten was taking the opportunity to engage in
sexual adventures without any apparent objections from his wife.
Nothing better expresses the Van Vechtens' peculiar arrangement.
Marinoff was apparently content to let Van Vechten satisfy his sexual
needs however he saw fit, so long as she did not feel neglected or
taken for granted. In New York, where Van Vechten's coterie of young
men was always buzzing around him, she often felt as if she had to
wait in line for an audience with her husband. Here she knew that
Van Vechten was all hers until the moment she retired for the evening. In any case, his nighttime assignations were only fleeting; soon
they would be leaving for some other destination, just the two of
them. To Van Vechten the situation was even more straightforward:
he was devoted husband by day, sex tourist by night, another bit of
pragmatic compartmentalizing that allowed him to avoid compro-
mising any of his varied desires.

They returned to New York at the end of August. In October
the stock market crashed. Manhattan's gaudy carousel screeched to a
sudden stop. Even with his unerring ability to disregard the realities
of the outside world Van Vechten, who was relatively unaffected by
the crash and barely mentioned it in his daybooks or in his letters to

others, appreciated that the time had come to survey the devastation and count the bodies.

Written over the early months of 1930, *Parties* was the final installment of Van Vechten's Manhattan chronicle, a brutal send-up of the alcohol-induced insanity of the last few years. David and Rilda Westlake, based not too loosely on the Fitzgeralds, take center stage as the fulcrum of a community of dyspeptic party animals, who spend their time fighting, sleeping around, taking drugs, gossiping, dancing, and, most of all, drinking—until the debauchery and sexual jealousy result in a murder. It is in many ways Van Vechten's most effective novel, a vivid evocation of a remarkable moment in American history, told with humor and insight, but it is also an exhausting read. As frenetically silly as any of his previous efforts, *Parties* contains a menace and viciousness entirely absent from other Van Vechten novels, a legacy of the bereavements that he had suffered in the last two years. The death of Avery Hopwood, who had treated life with the same reckless abandon that defines many of the characters in the novel, seems to have had a particular impact on *Parties*'s bitter atmosphere. Knopf's advertisements announced it as a state-of-the-nation address told through a sly, caustic smile: "Exhausted by wars and peace conferences, worn out by prohibition and other dishonest devices of unscrupulous politicians, the younger generation, born and bred to respect nothing, make a valiant and heart-breaking attempt to enjoy themselves."

Weaving around the high-octane self-destruction is a valedictory salute to New York City. More sharply than in any of Van Vechten's other books, the sensory experience of the city appears as a character in its own right. Its unmistakable landmarks, such as the Brooklyn Bridge, are name-checked, as are its smells—"hot asphalt, a distinct smell of chop suey and occasionally even of cooking opium on Broadway and the adjacent streets"—and its sounds, "most of which," Van Vechten points out as if barely unable to believe it himself, "did not exist twenty years ago." The novel unambiguously reiterates his long-standing belief that "what is *new* in New York is always more beautiful than what is old." This is the strange ambiguity at the heart of *Parties*: that although New York is a mad, violent, exhausting city, it is the greatest place on earth for precisely those reasons. As detestable as the New Yorkers in the book are Van Vechten can never bring himself to condemn them because they represent much of what he thought best about the United States, a nation now imitated across the world. In publicity interviews he mentioned how his trips abroad had shown him "that interest in America is increasing rapidly in Europe." Almost every European he encountered, he said, wanted to know about New York and Hollywood. In *Parties* he expressed this through the character of an elderly German aristocrat, the Gräfin Adele von Pulmernl und Stilzernl, who swaps the stuffy grandeur of her usual existence for the kinetic energy of New York. Among the first English words she learns are "bootlegger, speakeasy, buffet-flat, racketeer, stinko and ginny," and she is enthralled of course by Harlem. In a scene that signifies a passing of the modernist torch from Europe to the United States, the *Gräfin* watches men and women dance the lindy hop, a new dance, which Van Vechten describes in detail as the greatest of all African-American dances, the one that "most nearly approaches the sensation of religious ecstasy." The Gräfin looks on astonished at "the expression of electricity and living movement." There was nowhere on earth quite like New York. The Gräfin speaks the novel's telling final lines: "It is so funny, David, so very funny, and I love your country."

The reviews were mixed. Some admired its ingenuity; others found its satire too cynical and its characters loathsome. " 'Parties' scared me to death," wrote Mabel Dodge. "I think it must be well done since it is so upsetting." A "strange" and "disquieting" work, was Joseph Hergesheimer's verdict. Marinoff was less diplomatic and told Van Vechten she hated it, probably because it was a little too close to home. A perceptive reviewer noted that the novel was published in the same week as Sigmund Freud's *Civilization and Its Discontents*, which also deals with the alienation and unhappiness wrought by modernity, and that "they have so much in common that 'Parties' might be a case book for Freud."

It would not have taken a man of Freud's deductive powers to fathom that Van Vechten had grown weary of the atmosphere that *Parties* evokes. In time he came to see the novel as his greatest literary achievement, a biting satire that delivered a sharper verdict on the decade's follies than any other writer of the time achieved. In 1930 he found it difficult to judge its merits; he was just pleased to have finished it. For readers familiar with the hidden messages and in jokes of a Van Vechten novel, there was a transparent admission that the 1920s were over, even for the heartiest partygoer of them all, who had been forced to recognize his mortality by the turbulent events of the last two years. "He was getting on," Van Vechten wrote of his character Hamish Wilding; "a career of drinking and drifting must stop at some date, he supposed: probably when he was fifty." In August 1930, when the book was published, Van Vechten had just hit his half century.

At the moment *Parties* was published, Van Vechten ensured he was out of New York. As with *Spider Boy*, the writing process had been a protracted struggle, and once it was finished he was not sure whether he even liked the book, so could muster little enthusiasm for reading the reviews when they came out. For a third year in a row he and Marinoff sailed for a lengthy vacation in Europe.

In addition to the old favorites London and Paris, there was a new stop on the itinerary: Berlin. Although in the early 1930s Berlin existed as a complex tessellation of extraordinary issues, Van Vechten's interest was not caught by the rise of nazism or the films of Fritz Lang. To paraphrase Christopher Isherwood, who had discovered the city for himself the previous year, for Carlo, Berlin meant boys. On August 22 he visited its renowned gay bars for the first time, as a new acquaintance chaperoned him to four different venues, all of them at the mainstream end of the spectrum catering to those in search of champagne and jazz as much as the company of gay men or lesbians. The Eldorado was one of those four: a luxurious establishment famed for its transvestite clientele and drag competitions where the man judged to be wearing the most beautiful outfit was customarily awarded a live monkey, while the runner-up received a parrot. Also on the schedule that night was the Silhouette, a favorite nightspot of Berlin's artists and performers, including Marlene Dietrich, who was wont to turn up dressed in her trademark suits and ties. For the rest of the week the pattern was fixed, much as it had been when Van Vechten went cruising in the rue de Lappe the previous year: after dinner and a couple of drinks he kissed Marinoff goodnight as she retired to her hotel room, leaving him to explore until the early hours of the morning. Sometimes his destination was a ritzy venue with a top-class cabaret and a sophisticated crowd; other times he slummed it in rough trade joints, cruising for working-class locals. He enjoyed both equally. When the time came to leave Berlin, he did so reluctantly. "I am very sad," he confessed to himself. "I adore the place."

Back in New York, with no project to occupy him, he toyed with the idea of writing a novel about Reno after gambling was legalized there in March 1931. Quickie divorces, casinos, drink, and drugs in a city of bright lights adrift in the desert: the setting was so perfect for a Van Vechten novel that the book would have almost written itself. That was the problem. *Parties* had given the twenties' culture of frivolity and excess such an almighty kick in the guts that Van Vechten could not fathom what else he could say about it. Even if a new angle could be found, he feared he would no longer have an audience to share it with. The tone of American cultural life had changed so radically since the crash that the public Van Vechten and the rest of the Exquisites had once merrily indulged no longer seemed to exist. Hergesheimer and Cabell, who had been remarkably successful ever since the late teens, saw their careers implode in the early thirties, their novels without appeal to a nation that had swapped Warren Harding for FDR and looked to John Steinbeck and Nathanael West for literary evocations of its times. Now that he was financially secure it seemed crazy to go through the struggle of writing a book that stood a good chance of being ignored, a fate Van Vechten could not bear to contemplate. On May 18 he told Marinoff that he had scrapped plans to go to Reno for research. He would have to think this one out again.

Two days later his friend Eddie Wasserman rang with some dreadful news. Ralph Barton, insane with jealousy over his ex-wife Carlotta Monterrey's marriage to Eugene O'Neill, had killed himself with a single bullet shot straight through his temple. Barton had clearly been in a highly disturbed state for some time, his private life and mental health torn to shreds by his alcoholism. One might presume that Van Vechten, of all people, could sympathize with that. Instead his reaction to the news of Barton's suicide was brutally unfeeling. The next day he wrote Marinoff complaining about Barton's "rotten act," a display of craven selfishness, he thought. According to Van Vechten, Barton had taken his own life because he was jealous and angry that his ex-wife had married O'Neill, a man whose celebrity far outstripped his own. Firing a bullet through his skull was simply Barton's way of kicking up a fuss, so Van Vechten reasoned, making an old friend's suicide sound like the naughty outburst of a stroppy child. Two days later Van Vechten read Barton's obituary in the *Times* and coldly noted that Barton was "already forgotten: nobody called to see him; there were no flowers."

Van Vechten's pitiless response to Barton's passing was indicative of his chilling ability to remove people from his life without emotional residue. But it also had a deeper symbolism. Barton had been instrumental in both creating and satirizing 1920s celebrity culture, his caricatures of the rich and famous being a staple of *Vanity Fair*'s coverage of the goings-on in New York and Hollywood. His short film *Camille* assembled a huge number of those celebrities in its cast, featuring bona fide movie stars such as Lois Moran, Charlie Chaplin, Dorothy Gish, and Paul Robeson, alongside Sinclair Lewis, H. L. Mencken, Sherwood Anderson, Alfred Knopf, and three dozen other seminal names. Louis Mayer himself could not have compiled such a line-up; even the sultan of Morocco was given a role. When Barton died, it delivered a final, brutal blow to Van Vechten's "splendid drunken twenties"; by discarding Barton's memory so ruthlessly, Van Vechten was distancing himself from that milieu. Bob Chanler had died a few months earlier, and later that summer the party hostess A'Lelia Walker succumbed to a brain hemorrhage, a moment many cite as the symbolic end of the Harlem Renaissance. Van Vechten's link to the atmosphere of the previous decade was decisively severed, and with it his career as a novelist.

TWELVE

Papa Woojums

• •

For more than a decade alcohol and parties had been Van Vechten's means of escape from the mundane realities of life. It seemed to him, surrounded by youth and gaiety, and with a belly full of booze, as if he need never grow up or grow old but forever remain the wide-eyed adventurer he had been when he arrived in New York in 1906. With the convergence of illness, bereavement, economic crisis, and the passing of his literary career, the pretense became impossible to maintain. To stay fresh, young, and vital, he would have to reinvent himself as he had done so many times before.

The initial phase of his latest transformation took place in the seat of an airplane in the fall of 1931. Van Vechten had long harbored an ambition to fly. Air travel was bound to be of interest to him: a cutting-edge adventure accessible to only a special few. He gasped at the exploits of the great early aviators, especially Charles Lindbergh, whose bravery as much as his celebrity fascinated him. Van Vechten took his first plane trip in October of 1931, when he flew to Richmond, Virginia, and found the experience exhilarating. In flight he was able to perform feats he had previously managed only in a metaphorical sense: racing at remarkable speed high above the humdrum lives of the earthbound; risking life and limb in search of a new thrill. The moment he landed he telegrammed Marinoff about it and wrote excitedly to friends to tell them that he had now joined the ranks of the airborne. In an interview she gave to a New York newspaper a few months later, Marinoff confirmed that her husband "tinkers with planes, flies in them to every-where, and all the time," adding that this new passion of his was infinitely preferable to his last. "I have tasted all the drinks in all the speakeasies . . . and I am tired of them. I have memories of hundreds of parties in apartments, in nightclubs, in Harlem, in the Village. It was a phase in the life of this generation. It was very hollow. I never liked it," she said, the last utterance perhaps a trifle disingenuous.

Aside from experiencing the thrill of his maiden flight, there had been another motivation for traveling to Richmond that fall. In July his friend Hunter Stagg had put him in touch with Mark Lutz, an idealistic thirty-year-old journalist on *The Richmond News Leader* who added a refreshing, youthful presence to the town's aging lit-erary scene. Lutz had been on vacation in New York that summer and was hopeful of meeting Van Vechten, a man he had heard much about yet never encountered in the flesh. Van Vechten too was intent on getting acquainted, for Lutz was one of the young men about whom Stagg wrote gossipy letters during long, hot Virginian afternoons when he should have been working. As early as 1926 Stagg men-tioned Lutz in response to Van Vechten's teasing that Richmond lacked any attractive young men. "Taylor Crump is good-looking," Stagg protested, "and Berkley Williams, and in a way, Mark Lutz. So there." When they first spoke, Van Vechten suggested Lutz come to a gathering he was hosting at his apartment. Already having plans for the evening, Lutz attempted to politely decline the invitation, but Van Vechten was insistent: whatever other engagements he had could be arranged for another time; a party at the Van Vechtens' was not something anybody in Manhattan could afford to miss. Lutz had no choice but to relent, his diffident southern manners no match for Van Vechten's Manhattan high-handedness.

Just as Donald Angus had been, Lutz was attracted to Van Vech-ten for his worldliness, his self-confidence, and his sophistication. Van Vechten was never interested in anyone who played hard to get, and in some measure he surely took to Lutz because the young man was fascinated by him. Yet Lutz was not the frolicsome gadfly that Angus had been when they met, and he was certainly no debauchee. He was a more sedate companion for a less frenzied period of Van

Vechten's life. In one of his notebooks Van Vechten pondered the things that made Lutz interesting. Most unlike his own profligate ways, Lutz was cautious, parsimonious even, and a nonsmoking teetotaler. He was also highly superstitious, believed himself to have psychic powers, and followed peculiar rules, such as never swatting flies in airplanes, an act that seemed to him a tiny perversion of the laws of nature. What they did have in common was an interest in the plight of African-Americans and their culture. As a liberal-minded journalist from Virginia, Lutz was always seeking out examples of the brutalities of segregation and worked to expose them in his work if and when he could. At the time of their first meeting, in July 1931, the infamous Scottsboro Boys trial, in which eight young black men were sentenced to death for the alleged rapes of two white women in Alabama, had just concluded, and Lutz fiercely backed the campaign to get the convictions overturned. Pressure groups and organized campaigns were not Van Vechten's thing, but he did put Lutz in touch with Langston Hughes, who was heavily involved in the matter and had spoken out publicly about the injustice of the trial.

By the start of 1932 Van Vechten and Lutz were engaged in a love affair of the deepest intimacy. When they were not together as, because of the great distances that often separated them, was frequently, they sent each other letters, postcards, and clippings from newspapers and magazines almost every day for the next three decades. In his will Lutz requested that Van Vechten's letters to him, perhaps as many as ten thousand, be destroyed after his death, but Van Vechten seemingly kept every piece of mail he had received from Lutz. In them all subjects are raised: from family bereavements, to international diplomacy, to rows with work colleagues, to race relations, reflecting the extent to which each was involved in the other's life. "It was disappointing to have NO word from you in the mail of yesterday," Lutz wrote on one of the rare occasions he found his mailbox empty one morning. More than a decade into their relationship he spelled out exactly how important Van Vechten had been to him from their first meeting in 1931. Before then, he said, he had played the field, but meeting Van Vechten had changed him: "I settled down to ONE . . . and would not change it for a MILLUN."

At almost exactly the same moment that he found a new lover Van Vechten discovered the artistic calling he had been seeking. His friend Miguel Covarrubias had recently returned from Europe with a marvelous gadget, a new Leica camera that was lightweight and portable, yet capable of taking exceptionally crisp pictures. Photography was not new to Van Vechten. His relationship with the art laced its way through his life, usually in close concert with his valorization of the famous. As a child he lived among his stage idols through their cigarette card photographs and placed friends in dramatic poses before the family's box camera. At the *Times* he recorded his association with opera stars through photographs. Being photographed himself by Nickolas Muray, one of New York's most fashionable photographers during the 1920s, was an important moment to him, confirmation of his celebrity status. Photography to Van Vechten was a quintessential modern art, combining technology, spectacle, and glamour, though the cost of equipment and the time commitment involved in perfecting a technique had never permitted him to be anything other than an occasional practitioner. As Covarrubias demonstrated, the Leica allowed the amateur a freedom and a degree of precision previously unimagined. Always an early adopter of technology, and eager to test himself in a new element, Van Vechten soon bought one for himself. He turned unused space in the apartment into a makeshift darkroom and studio, and by January 1932 the new hobby was becoming a full-time obsession. Van Vechten roped in Mark Lutz to help him in his early shoots. Lutz set up lights and posed in front of the lens, allowing Van Vechten to experiment and learn from his mistakes. When Lutz was unavailable, other members of the jeunes gens assortis were employed to lend a hand, notably Donald Angus, and the artist Prentiss Taylor, who on "bright winter Saturdays" accompanied him on shoots in Harlem as well as a trip to Copenhagen in upstate New York to photograph the gravestones of Van Vechten antecedents long since dead.

Despite the amateur setup, Van Vechten was convinced from the

Carl Van Vechten, self-portrait, c. 1934

start that the gift of taking a good photograph, and in particular a good portrait, was his. "Great photographers are born, not educated," he believed, and if not great quite yet, he suspected it was only a matter of time. As early as February 1932 he boasted to Gertrude Stein that Stieglitz had pledged to hold an exhibition of his work and told Max Ewing that he was struggling to decide whether his first show would be photographs of Harlem or portraits of the great and good. Stieglitz never hosted a Van Vechten exhibition and almost certainly would not have offered one to such a novice. Probably Van Vechten's bulletproof ego decided that he *deserved* an exhibition mounted by the godfather of American photography, and that was what counted. The facts, again, were irrelevant to his sense of truth. By June he was even comparing his capabilities, favorably, to those of Stieglitz's when he sent Mabel Dodge some examples of his work, including a self-portrait. These, he declared, were just a taste of his considerable talent.

In truth, the photographs he took in the early 1930s were of wildly varying quality. Many were enchanting, but many others poorly lit, peculiarly composed, or spoiled by fussy backgrounds that seem more a reflection of the photographer's taste than the sitter's personality. It is the number and range of his sitters that are extraordinary. "My first subject was Anna May Wong," he often claimed, "and my second was Eugene O'Neill." Though that was not strictly so, it was a trademark Van Vechten embellishment in that it articulates a general truth, in this case the volume of celebrated people who sat in front of his camera. In addition to Wong and O'Neill, Bill Robinson, Langston Hughes, Bennett Cerf, Frida Kahlo and Diego Rivera, Henri Matisse, Gladys Bentley, George Gershwin, Lois Moran, Georgia O'Keeffe, and Charles Demuth, to name but a few, all were shot within roughly the first year of his photographic career. Scattered among the artists and impresarios were various interesting people outside the public eye. Over the years Marinoff posed endless times, of course, and usually in some extravagant costume: a belle epoque society lady; a flamenco dancer; resplendent in an Indian sari. Numerous other relatives were captured, as were favored domestic servants, window cleaners, doormen, and Sarah Victor, the pastry chef at the Algonquin Hotel.

Anna May Wong, c. 1932, photograph by Carl Van Vechten

Even Harry Glyn, a bootlegger and pimp whose services Van Vechten had used on occasion over the years, was summoned for a shoot.

The discipline of portrait photography was tailor-made for Van Vechten. It indulged not only his voyeurism but also his fascination with exceptional people and the immense pleasure he took in being in their company. It was no coincidence, either, that photography seized him at a point in his life when change was taking place all around him and outside his control: the deaths of friends and loved ones, the economic situation that transformed New York's social world, and the end of his writing career. With photography the holder of the camera had complete power; moments in time could be frozen forever. Van Vechten discovered that he was able to dictate the entire process of producing a photograph from beginning to end. The one variable was the attitude of his subjects, but he soon found that he was able to rely on his ebullient charm to get from them exactly what he wanted.

At Apartment 7D his shooting space was small and quickly became hot under the studio lights. In coming years he moved to larger premises, but in all his studios there was a closeness, an atmosphere of emotional intimacy. All around lay the clutter of Van Vechten's props and backdrops—crumpled sheets of colored cellophane, posters, rugs, African sculptures, floral wallpaper. To the sitters who arrived this was clearly neither an artist's workroom nor the studio of a commercial artist but the den of an obsessive hobbyist. Observing him at work at close quarters for many years, Mark Lutz believed Van Vechten's greatest attribute as a photographer had nothing to do with technical expertise or artistic flair but rather with his ability to put people at their ease, that silky charisma he had first used to get stories and photographs as a Chicago journalist. An arm placed lightly across the shoulder and some rich encomiums would do the trick for most. Even when a high-profile movie star came for a session, Van Vechten was unfazed: "a few glasses of champagne and he or she would pose contently and without self-consciousness," Lutz recalled. Once things felt suitably loose, Van Vechten would position his subject and photograph quickly "in about a twentieth of a second" before self-consciousness arrived to spoil the moment. Occasionally, it would take considerably more effort. When Billie Holiday came for a shoot in 1949, Van Vechten struggled for two hours to break through her contrary, sullen exterior. It was only when he retrieved some shots he had taken of Bessie Smith, Holiday's great heroine, that she let her guard down. "She began to cry, and I took photographs of her crying, which nobody else had done," he remembered; "later I took pictures of her laughing." Holiday ended up staying until five in the morning, telling Van Vechten and Marinoff her life story, and Van Vechten thought it one of his finest moments, a devastating combination of his charm and artistic skill used to capture an American icon. "There are no good photographs of Holiday except the ones I took of her," he said a year after her death.

Financially secure, Van Vechten had the freedom to pick and choose his subjects and never had to compromise for the sake of meeting a commission or appealing to a particular audience. He refused to sell his work too and only ever gave away prints or permitted them to be reproduced as a personal favor. That degree of autonomy allowed him to produce an enormous portfolio of work strikingly different from any other major American photographer of the era. The 1930s marked the start of a golden age of photojournalism in the United States, with magazines such as *Life* and *Sports Illustrated* giving photographers the opportunity to share their work with millions, bridging the gap between the artistic tradition of Stieglitz and Steichen and the functional mass-market photography that appeared in popular newspapers. The New Deal also freed up millions of dollars for government bodies such as the Farm Security Administration to fund the work of Dorothea Lange, Walker Evans, Louise Rosskam, and other social documentarian photographers whose work fell somewhere between art and journalism as they captured an ailing rural and small-town United States colliding with the forces of modernization. Van Vechten existed entirely outside the social documentarian tradition, yet he used much of the same vocabulary to describe his work, insisting that the purpose of his photography was also "documentary." He saw it as his mission to document a different America, one of modernity and sophistication that he had seen develop over the last three decades, inhabited not by the average folks of the nation's heartland but by a cosmopolitan breed iridescent with talent and personal magnetism. In the fantasia of his studio the outside world evaporated; the Depression, the New Deal, and all the other facts of 1930s America ceased to exist. Nothing remained but the individual and the act of self-expression.

In that sense Van Vechten's photographs were a fluid continuation of his novels. His gaze through the camera was that of an elitist; his concern was to immortalize outstanding individuals, the brilliant and the beautiful. His rigid individualism kicked against the trend he discerned among many young artists of the 1930s for politicizing their work with leftist dogma. When Langston Hughes sent him *Good Morning, Revolution*, a collection of his latest poems that was as staunchly ideological as the title suggests, Van Vechten was dismayed. "The revolutionary poems seem very weak to me," he wrote Hughes, who at that point was traveling the Soviet Union. "I mean very weak on the lyric side. I think in ten years, whatever the social outcome, you will be ashamed of these." Of course Hughes's political views were his own concern, he said, but he worried that in servicing them in his poetry, he had sacrificed his individuality, the essence of his genius. He urged him to abandon this new direction and rediscover the warmth and personality of his earlier work. "Ask yourself . . . Have I written a poem or a revolutionary tract?" As if to underline his own commitment to the cause of individual expression, he concluded the letter by letting Hughes know that "I am still taking photographs: Better than ever."

As far as Van Vechten was concerned, politics, especially the politics of the left, could only corrupt or dilute individual character and was therefore antithetical to art. A half dozen years later he summed up his position when he wrote his friend Noël Sullivan about Paul Robeson's growing attraction to socialism, at which he was equally appalled. Politics in all systems and irrespective of ideological persuasion, he informed Sullivan, is nothing more than a game played by megalomaniacs. For those who want to change the world the best they can do is to lead by example and invest their energies in self-development, because ultimately "the only person one can improve is oneself." Even the rise of fascism in Europe could not rouse him to take an interest in politics. On March 7, 1934, Marinoff went with Lawrence Langner and Armina Marshall to join twenty thousand other spectators at Madison Square Garden, to watch a mock trial of Adolf Hitler put on by the American Jewish Congress. As a proud Jew herself Marinoff was eager to attend and acutely concerned about the situation in Germany. But Van Vechten chose to spend the evening indoors, exercising his Promethean powers in the darkroom, creating his own tiny universe populated by talented and fascinating souls, untouched by the complications of the real world.

It might be a stretch to say that Van Vechten was now living a quiet and healthy life, but it was certainly a world away from the self-destruction of the late twenties. His drinking was under control, and the constant business of taking and developing photographs provided a diversion from temptation. He also made frequent trips to a health resort at Briarcliff Lodge in Westchester County under the supervision of Dr. William Hay, a naturopath whose regimen of vegetarian diets and colonic irrigation was a popular fad with the Van Vechtens and many of their friends in the early thirties.

The bond with Marinoff remained intact but no less fraught. When they were together, they sniped and bickered constantly, and when apart, they pined for each other. Marinoff, now semiretired and with fewer grand projects than Van Vechten to keep her occupied, suffered bouts of tremendous loneliness and anxiety. She spent a good deal of time with Eugene and Carlotta O'Neill at their home in Georgia, silently studying their mutual dependency, at times envying the tranquillity and normality of their relationship compared with her own peculiar marriage. She was delighted that debauchery had finally relaxed its grip on Van Vechten, though she often felt excluded by his new obsessions with air travel and photography, activities he chose to practice in the company of the young and beautiful, as if their vitality would seep into his pictures. In the summer of 1933 Van Vechten left Marinoff behind and flew out for a grand tour of the West with Mark Lutz, photographing him at every new place they visited: at the Grand Canyon; in Chinatown, San Francisco; on the beach in Malibu; outside Mabel Dodge's home in Taos. Vacations in London, Paris, Amsterdam, Genoa, Barcelona,

Madrid, Valencia, Mallorca, Marrakech, and Casablanca all followed soon after, with Van Vechten rekindling acquaintances along the way and taking more pictures of new subjects, Joan Miró and Salvador Dali included. As was invariably the case with Van Vechten's closest male companions, Lutz quickly became a dear friend of Marinoff's. Their adoration of the same man gave them common ground on which to meet, but Marinoff also used the friendship as a means of maintaining a romantic closeness to her husband. In the past she had been able to accommodate Van Vechten's affairs with relative ease, perhaps because her busy and successful career as an actress had given her opportunities to express herself independently of Van Vechten. Now, without a career to invest in, she could not help feeling the time that Van Vechten devoted to his young men and his photographs was an act of rejection and abandonment. Van Vechten behaved as if oblivious that his new fixations were causing Marinoff upset. He was once again lost in self-interest; the fulfillment of his wishes took precedence over all else, including the health of his marriage. Even on December 31, 1935, when Marinoff hoped they might see out the year together by sharing lunch in their apartment, Van Vechten refused, saying he was too busy in the darkroom across the hallway to spare her an hour of his time.

His obsession with photography was total. Wherever he went he captured the world with his Leica. Even if he was walking ten blocks to meet a friend, the camera went with him in case he saw something enchanting in a department store window or was struck by the beautiful face of a waitress or a group of laughing children playing on a street corner. The old collecting instincts were channeled into a new medium, striving to capture and contain the gaiety of life in its innumerable tiny manifestations. It was another thread that connected Van Vechten the photographer to his previous iterations as novelist, essayist, critic, and reporter. A young Lincoln Kirstein joined the periphery of the jeunes gens assortis in the early 1930s and said Van Vechten's commitment to "elegance in the ordinary" provided vital inspiration for his own work with George Balanchine that led to the establishment of the School of American Ballet in Connecticut in 1934 and in time to the New York City Ballet. It was through Van Vechten, Kirstein said, that he "first saw an

American ballet had to have more to do with sport and jazz than czars and ballerinas."

Kirstein also impressed Van Vechten, who said Kirstein's work as a patron of the arts in New York was as important as the activities of the great Renaissance princes of Italy. Young, handsome, charismatic, wealthy, and gay, Kirstein was almost the Platonic ideal of a Van Vechten photographic subject, and Van Vechten took some excellent portraits of him that drew out much of Kirstein's ambition and intense complexity. The best of these were shot in 1933, by which time Van Vechten had already compiled an impressive gallery of America's key artistic figures. But at the center of Van Vechten's catalog of excellence there was one gaping hole: Gertrude Stein. Since the end of the 1931 he had sent Stein repeated evidence of his camera skills in the form of postcard prints, but by the fall of 1933 he had yet to shoot her. He was desperate to do so and to have Stein recognize his prowess as a portrait artist. In May 1933 he pleaded with her to come to the United States, where he would photograph both her and Alice Toklas, promising that she would be overjoyed at the results. "I do nothing but make photographs now and they are good." With Steinesque repetition he included passages virtually identical to those in letters to her throughout 1932 and 1933. His persistence was partially motivated by a nagging sense that in recent years his place in Stein's court had been diminished. In 1914, when he wrote "How to Read Gertrude Stein" for *The Trend* and secured the publication of *Tender Buttons*, he was unrivaled as Stein's leading American supporter. In the interim, others had moved her profile forward. In 1923 Jo Davidson enshrined her as Buddha in his famous statue, and Man Ray photographed her extensively throughout that decade. Robert McAlmon risked financial ruin in 1925 by publishing *Making of Americans*, a book that Van Vechten had failed to publish through Knopf, and most recently Edmund Wilson dedicated a whole chapter to Stein in his highly acclaimed book on American literature *Axel's Castle*. The encroachment of these figures on territory he had staked out during the First World War stirred his natural feelings of covetousness.

His friendship with Stein was never in jeopardy. Ernest Hemingway had it right when he said that Stein "only gave real loyalty to

people who were inferior to her." There is no question that Stein
thought Van Vechten fitted into that category, unthreatening and
biddable. Though they had corresponded avidly for twenty years,
Stein showed minimal interest in Van Vechten's writing, which she
thought entertaining but not true literature, especially not his bestselling novels. From any other friend Van Vechten would not have
tolerated such open indifference to his achievements. From Stein he
accepted it unquestioningly. He still regarded her as the brightest
star in his galaxy of brilliant people; being a member of her inner
circle was proof enough for him that she recognized his specialness.
What grated him was the prospect that the wider world might not
appreciate the closeness of their bond.

When Stein registered a literary hit in the United States during
the summer of 1933, Van Vechten felt both elated for her success
and bitterly jealous that he had played no direct part in it. The work
that catapulted Stein into the mainstream was *The Autobiography of
Alice B. Toklas*. The book, ostensibly the life story of Stein's partner,
was filled with juicy gossip about the European and American stars
of the Left Bank, giving an inside look at the years of artistic foment
before, during, and after the war. Written in a much more accessible
style than her previous efforts, it was such a critical and commercial
success that *Time* made Stein its cover star in September 1933, confirmation that she was at last a mainstream literary phenomenon. It
was a huge moment for Stein and her supporters, a vindication of
their persistent support. Van Vechten was bothered that the photograph used on the magazine's front cover was not taken by him, but
by the twenty-seven-year-old George Platt Lynes, Stein's new favorite boy. A few weeks after the *Time* cover, Van Vechten wrote Stein
pressing his credentials once again, hoping for some praise in return. Seeing other photographers' shots of her gave him "a tinge of
jealousy," he said, with an almost audible pout. "You've seen very
few pictures taken by me. When you do, I think you'll be very surprised." Physically unable to contain his desire to bind his name to
her success, when he wrote Stein about an introduction he had been
asked to write for a reprint of her book *Three Lives*, he referred to
it pointedly as *"OUR Three Lives."* Bursting to gain some public
recognition for Stein's sudden ascension, Van Vechten espied the

perfect opportunity when *Four Saints in Three Acts*, an opera with an all-black cast, written by Stein and the composer Virgil Thomson, made its premiere in Hartford, Connecticut, on February 7, 1934.

He arrived at the opening night in the mode of Stein's official representative. "I am getting very excited," Stein wrote him from Paris two days before the premiere, saying she was glad that Van Vechten would be acting as her eyes and ears. It was a role Van Vechten took with conspicuous seriousness. Before the curtains parted, he stalked up and down the aisles of the auditorium three times, surveying the scene as if conducting some vital task, making a mental list of all the celebrated people in attendance, and allowing his own presence to be known. Eventually he took his seat for one of the most extraordinary nights at the theater he had ever experienced.

The performance began with a near-empty stage and a drumroll. Slowly the saints made their entrance, and the scene was infused with color. Black men and women in tunics and robes of red, blue, purple, yellow, and green filled the stage, assembling themselves in shapes, fusing, then separating. The setting was supposed to be medieval Spain, but it was clear from the beginning that this was a world detached from geography and history, existing nowhere but in the imaginations of its creators. At one point seminaked angels dressed in loincloths danced the Charleston. Tinsel habits, golden halos, and cellophane roses drifted in and out of sight. The audience was baffled but transfixed. Every word of Stein's libretto was carefully enunciated—"pigeons on the grass alas"; "Leave later gaily the troubadour plays his guitar"—but its meaning floated off high over the heads of the those in the auditorium, as freely as helium balloons released into fresh air. When the curtain came down, there was rapturous applause.

To Van Vechten and many others in the audience this had been more than a gripping night at the theater: it was the fulfillment of a prophecy; a colloquial, multiethnic spectacle of color and unconventionality that could only have been produced in the United States and written by their great messianic figure. "I haven't seen a crowd more excited since Sacre du Printemps," Van Vechten wrote

Stein the following day. For twenty years he had been making allusions to the audience reaction at that historic production, but this
occasion merited the comparison more than any other. Henry-Russell
Hitchcock, for example, was apparently so overcome at the finale
that he ran up and down the aisle, tearing wildly at his fine-tailored
evening clothes, while others were left gasping in tears.

Within twenty-four hours Van Vechten had written an introduction for the libretto, which Random House would publish before the
month was out. In it he told the story of how *Four Saints in Three
Acts* came to be and found himself a place at the heart of the narrative. He let his readers know that it was at his apartment that Virgil
Thomson had given the opera its first American performance back
in 1929. More significantly, he also implied that it was his influence
that gave Thomson the idea to cast black actors because it was he
who had taken Thomson to a performance of *Run, Little Chillun*, a
choral play with an African-American cast, at the Lyric Theatre in
1933—though Thomson maintained his inspiration was derived
from elsewhere. When the opera opened on Broadway soon after,
Van Vechten similarly ensured that his name was associated with the
occasion, the point at which American high modernism punched
through to the mainstream. For the program he reprised his role as
a gatekeeper to Stein's work with an introductory article entitled
"How I Listen to *Four Saints in Three Acts*," echoing his first Stein
apologia, "How to Read Gertrude Stein," written twenty-one years
earlier.

The work that Van Vechten had done years ago in promoting
Stein as a musical artist whose prose should be valued for its sound
rather than its meaning was vindicated with *Four Saints in Three
Acts*. But now that she was a bestseller and a Broadway hit, his old
role of intermediary between Stein and a bewildered and hostile
American public seemed redundant. To remain relevant to her cult,
he had to adopt a new strategy. That summer he headed for France
to take Stein's picture for the first time. He photographed her as if
this would be his one and only chance to do so, shooting several
dozen frames in a range of poses and backgrounds at her home in
Bilignin: reclining on a deck chair; petting her dogs; sitting on
a garden wall with Toklas. The sheer volume of pictures he took

suggests he was here to imprison memories rather than make art, to "document," as he would say. None of the images were particularly satisfying and certainly no better than the ones taken by Man Ray and George Platt Lynes, the two photographers he was keen to displace as Stein's favorites. He was less technically skilled than either of them, and outside the tightly controlled environment of his studio Van Vechten's photography often appears generic and amateurish, the personality of his subjects diffusing into the ether. While at Bilignin, however, he did press his belief that the time was ripe for Stein to return to the United States. With her on his home turf he was sure he would be able to achieve something remarkable.

Stein arrived in New York on October 24 for a short lecture series, one that Van Vechten had helped arrange. Having worked so long for public recognition, Stein felt unusually vulnerable on this return from exile, frightened that audiences would be unsympathetic. As Van Vechten had suspected it would be, the tour was actually an immense success. What had originally been planned as a fleeting promotional visit turned into an epic seven-month homecoming parade. Without Van Vechten's assistance, it might have been very different. He nursed and encouraged Stein through her early lectures, building her confidence and dispelling her nerves. On her first night back in the country she dined at his apartment, where he delighted her with copies of the New York papers, her arrival splashed across them all. A few days later, to help her prepare for her first lecture, "Plays and What They Are," at the Museum of Modern Art, Van Vechten arranged for a test run in front of a small sympathetic audience in Manhattan, held at the apartment of Elizabeth Alexander, a friend of Prentiss Taylor's and the widow of the painter John W. Alexander. A week after that, on November 7, Stein and Toklas took their first airplane ride when they flew from New York to Chicago to see a performance of *Four Saints in Three Acts*. Van Vechten joined them, promising to hold their hands should they get scared.

He was once again working behind the scenes to secure success, as he had for Robeson, Hughes, Firbank, and so many others. And as always, he ensured that his name was tightly bound to the artist he was promoting. Before he escorted Stein and Toklas on their flight to Chicago, he alerted the press to the photo opportunity and posed proudly in the frame next to the couple as they climbed aboard. He also distributed one of the photographs that he had taken of Stein in France to promote her lectures. The scholar Tirza True Latimer perceptively notes that the picture he chose was a close re-creation of the George Platt Lynes photograph that *Time* had put on its cover—Stein's profile as she gazed across rural France—his way of blotting out the presence of a rival.

Naturally, Van Vechten photographed Stein obsessively, taking her portrait whenever he had the chance. In Virginia he photographed her before monuments and grand architectural forms, including the Jefferson Rotunda. Some of them could be mistaken for the sorts of holiday snaps habitually taken in front of the Eiffel Tower or Big Ben, but it seems there was an agreed plan between Stein and Van Vechten to use these photographs as a means of rooting her in American history, making her epic and durable. On receiving the Virginia photographs, Stein composed a letter of fulsome thanks in which she suggested they collaborate on a "pictorial history" of the United States. Stein would write the text, Van Vechten would supply the photographs, and "we will all be so happy."

Stein in fact was already happy. Not since Oscar Wilde's triumphant tour of 1882 had a writer generated such excitement by traveling the nation; no American literary figure other than Mark Twain had delivered so many enthusiastically received lectures. To recognize Van Vechten's prominent role in her triumphant return, Stein allowed their relationship to take on a new aspect, reflecting her gratitude for all the work he had done on her behalf. Among them, Van Vechten, Stein, and Toklas created a fictitious family unit called the Woojumses, the name adapted from a cocktail that Van Vechten had invented for *Parties*. Van Vechten became the organizing patriarch, Papa Woojums; Toklas, the nurturing Mama Woojums; Stein was Baby Woojums, the brilliant but vulnerable child who must be indulged, protected, and controlled in equal parts. He relished being Stein's paternal guardian and gatekeeper. A matter of weeks into the tour Van Vechten wrote to Mabel Dodge to warn her that the chances of Stein's being able to visit Taos were slim to none, so great were the demands on Gertrude's time. Mabel was cut to the quick

Gertrude Stein, January 4, 1935, photograph by Carl Van Vechten

by the snub; Van Vechten, more than a little gratified to have got
one over on his former mentor. When Stein slipped out of his grasp
and went to stay with a lesser acolyte, Thornton Wilder, in Chicago,
Van Vechten wrote her a letter of mock protest. "Thornton Wilder
has got me down with jealousy. Don't go and like him BETTER,
PLEASE!" The tone was jokey, but the feelings of jealousy were
entirely real.

Shortly before she left, Stein returned to Van Vechten's apartment for a final photo session. From the studio wall Van Vechten
hung a crumpled Stars and Stripes, looking at first glance as if bil-
lowing in a strong wind. In front of the flag he posed Stein and took
what is perhaps the definitive image of her. With her thick, solid
frame statuesque and her gaze strong and steady, she looks like a
female addition to Mount Rushmore. The symbolism was not remotely accidental. Gertrude Stein was no longer a figure of ridicule
but a national treasure, and the cultural forces she represented were
now recognized as integral to the American experience as were the
Model T and the Marx Brothers' movies. Stein liked the photograph so much that she chose it as the front cover of her book *Lectures in America*. "I always wanted to be historical, almost from a
baby on," Stein admitted shortly before her death. Thanks to Van
Vechten's portrait that ambition and sense of mission were immortalized, the image intricately bound up with the public perception
of Stein as an American great, a unique genius who set the United
States on a new path. It was exactly how Van Vechten thought of
her. He may not have been as technically slick as Lynes, Man Ray,
Cecil Beaton, or the other giants of photography who took Stein's
portrait, but he had an instinctive understanding of the medium's
power to exploit symbolism and communicate myth, the mightiest
weapons in the modernist arsenal. Stein was the first American
artist whose reputation he affected in this way, but there would
be many more to follow, from Scott Fitzgerald to Ella Fitzgerald.
When he died, he ensured that his photographs would continue to
embed themselves within public consciousness, bequeathing thousands of prints to institutions across the United States. On almost
all of them the words PHOTOGRAPH BY CARL VAN VECHTEN are

Carl Van Vechten and Gertrude Stein aboard the SS *Champlain* as Stein waves
farewell to the United States, May 4, 1935

clearly embossed on the bottom of the image, his name indivisible from the artist in shot.

On May 4, 1935, Van Vechten accompanied Stein and Toklas aboard the SS *Champlain*. Their tour at its end, the couple returned to France with heavy hearts, nervous that yet another hideous conflict was brewing in Europe and sad to leave behind a country that felt more like home than when they had lived there. On the gangplank, journalists bombarded Stein with questions about her final thoughts on America. "It is violent and gentle," she said. Despite all the casual brutality of the modern world, Americans had managed to preserve the kernel of innocence that had defined them in the days of her youth before skyscrapers and airplanes and nightclubs arrived. That "their gentleness has persisted while they have been becoming sophisticated," she declared, "shows that it is genuine." The front-page picture that accompanied Stein's farewell messages showed the lady smiling joyously, waving her famous cap in the air with her left hand. Standing next to her is Papa Woojums, his teeth deliberately hidden from the cameras with a tight-lipped half smile, while the little finger on his left hand hooked gently into Baby's coat pocket. It was a sign to those watching of his importance to the woman by his side, who was now a pillar of the establishment, but the gesture also displayed his enormous affection for a friend, a cause, and a fellow iconoclast. Moments later he said his goodbyes and disembarked, heading back into the embrace of the New York night, satisfied that no matter the distance between them, he and Stein would be forever entwined in their mutual legacies.

THIRTEEN

Yale May Not Think So,
but It'll Be Just Jolly

• •

Aged fifty-five and into a fifth career, Van Vechten was as excited as a schoolboy when his first photographic exhibition opened to the public in New York in November 1935. "Im [*sic*] in a big show at Radio City," he informed Langston Hughes, "and here is my first notice!" He had enclosed for Hughes's attention a short review of the exhibition by Henry McBride, whose kind words about Van Vechten's work may not have been entirely unbiased; he and Van Vechten had been friends for twenty years, and both were apostles of Gertrude Stein. Still, Van Vechten regarded public praise from McBride as confirmation of his inestimable talent. The exhibition displayed an eclectic mix of Van Vechten's most celebrated subjects, hinting at the outline of his experience of the century so far, from Theodore Dreiser, to Fania Marinoff, to Ethel Waters and Bricktop, the African-American woman who ran the most fashionable night-club in Paris during the 1920s. McBride's verdict was brief but unequivocal: "literature's loss is photography's gain."

Over the following years Van Vechten's stature as a portrait pho-tographer grew enormously, as did his skill. He gained the respect and admiration of many fellow photographers, including Man Ray, who was so pleased with shots that Van Vechten took of him and Salvador Dalí that he asked for permission to use them to promote his work. The praise that most pleased Van Vechten came from Alfred Stieglitz, who, along with his wife, Georgia O'Keeffe, sat for him on numerous occasions over seven years. "They are damn swell,

Bessie Smith, 1936, photograph by Carl Van Vechten

a joy," Stieglitz told him about one set of prints. "You are certainly a photographer. There are but few." More and more great names ascended to Apartment 7D at 150 West Fifty-fifth Street and, from the fall of 1936, to the Van Vechtens' two subsequent homes on Central Park West, to have their pictures taken. In February 1936, a year before her death, Bessie Smith returned to the scene of her infamous outburst eight years earlier to pose, this time on her best behavior, "cold sober and in a quiet reflective mood." "I got nearer her real personality than I ever had before, and the photographs, perhaps, are the only adequate record of her true appearance and manner that exist." Given that this was the only time that Van Vechten had met her while both were sober, quite how he would have known who the true Bessie Smith was is up for debate. However, his immodesty does nothing to alter that the portraits he took were among his best, and they immortalized in photographic form the same woman generations have discovered in Smith's recordings: an artist who is alive, bright, and playful in some; reflective, pained, and soulful in others.

Not long after, he photographed Scott Fitzgerald, though not at his studio. "I hadn't planned to meet Scott," he told a biographer of Zelda's when relaying how the two had accidentally met at the Algonquin one afternoon. Fitzgerald was at a table with the literary critic Edmund Wilson, but at first Van Vechten did not recognize Fitzgerald and stood waiting to be introduced. "It was a terrible moment; Scott was completely changed. He looked pale and haggard. I was awfully embarrassed." After lunch Van Vechten shepherded Fitzgerald outside to take his photo. "He posed for two or three," he explained, "and that was the last time I saw him." Those impromptu shots are among the definitive images of Fitzgerald. Had things turned out differently, had Fitzgerald flourished after the twenties, perhaps Van Vechten's photographs would not be known at all. As it is, Fitzgerald looks strangely uncomfortable before the lens, smiling but ever so slightly stooped and squinting in the sunlight and perfectly reflecting the faded glamour that he has come to symbolize.

Those close to him saw something different in the photographs. Some years later the Fitzgeralds' daughter, Scottie, wrote to thank

Van Vechten for sending her a print of one of the photographs, the best ever taken of her father, she thought, which captures "a nice sober, serious look . . . his hard-working side," which she remembered much more clearly than his hedonistic tendencies. Scottie would have dearly loved for Van Vechten to have captured her mother in that same way, but he never heard from Zelda again save for a couple of odd, rambling missives she sent after her mental health problems had overwhelmed her. Just eight days after Scott's death, in December 1940, she scribbled Carl a letter in pencil, betraying a fragile and distressed woman who bore no resemblance to the exuberant flapper Van Vechten had known in New York and Hollywood. She thanked Van Vechten for some kind words that he had written about Scott, and reflected on their shared experiences of the 1920s, "the glamour, and tragedy, of those courageous and dramatic lives so many years ago."

It was the sort of maudlin reflection with which he had become all too familiar. In June 1938 James Weldon Johnson was killed in a car accident. Van Vechten was heartbroken at the news, one of the rare occasions when the death of somebody he knew caused him genuine distress. During the fourteen years they had known each other, they had fostered not just a close friendship but an intellectual kinship that for both of them symbolized the hope of a new era in which black and white Americans would eliminate the divisions of racial difference through social contact, the two races uniting over a shared love of art and entertainment, socializing together in apartments and nightclubs, forging friendships over drinks and love affairs on the dance floor. The two men celebrated their shared birthday together every year along with Alfred Knopf, Jr., who had also been born on June 17. Langston Hughes remembered the last birthday party they had, in 1937, at Van Vechten's apartment. Presented to the three guests of honor were three cakes, "one red, one white, and one blue," as Hughes recalled, "the colors of our flag. They honored a Gentile, a Negro, and a Jew—friends and fellow Americans."

Sadly, Van Vechten realized that he and his great friend were never able to stand as equals in the eyes of wider society and that Johnson's talents had been smothered by racial prejudice. "I always said, if he had been white he would have been ambassador to St. James in London," Van Vechten stated. "He was a very tactful, diplomatic, extraordinary man, very delightful company, very amusing." When he tried to express his feelings for Johnson as a man and a totem for the African-American cause, the only fitting way he could do it was to compare him with Charles Van Vechten, his own father. Both men had gifts that Van Vechten admired immensely: kindness, generosity, and conviviality, but most especially an ability to be both "tolerant of unorthodox behavior in others" and "patriarchal in offering good advice." The comparison reveals that beneath his carefully managed image of the sophisticated iconoclast Van Vechten's moral exemplars were his parents, whose bold stand on race relations kick-started his interest in African-American culture. Of course his parents, like his brother, Ralph, and his dear friend Avery Hopwood were long dead. When Johnson joined them, Van Vechten felt the presence of his own mortality and decided that now was the time to shape a concrete legacy for himself and to honor Johnson's memory.

The first step Van Vechten took was to convene the James Weldon Johnson Memorial Committee. Featuring, among others, Walter White, W.E.B. DuBois, and Eleanor Roosevelt, for three years the committee attempted to create a public monument in tribute to Johnson: a bronze statue of a black man by the black sculptor Richmond Barthé placed at the entrance to Central Park on West 110th Street and Seventh Avenue. Barthé's design, enthusiastically supported by the committee, had the man, who was a representative figure, rather than a depiction of Johnson himself, naked and shackled to celebrate the efforts of African-American artists whose work projects the beauty and humanity of their race in the face of discrimination and oppression. The project never materialized, partly because of the timidity of the city authorities, who feared the proposed design could be incendiary, and partly because of Van Vechten's impatience with the politics of the situation and his refusal to sanitize the memorial by unshackling the statue or putting it in a pair of pants, as was requested. Van Vechten was frustrated with the processes of compromise and amelioration that committee work involved and equally vexed that there were those who seemed not to recognize that Johnson was a unique man who deserved a unique tribute. He guarded Johnson's memory with jealous fervor, as if it were his own possession. One of the reasons his opinion of Walter White soured so much in later life may have been that White had replaced Johnson as the national secretary of the NAACP in 1931 and ran the organization with tremendous success for twenty-four years, his presence in the national consciousness outstripping Johnson's, a fact Van Vechten seemed to resent. "Walter was never, in my mind, anything like as big a man as James Weldon Johnson was," he said in an interview after both men had died.

With the plan for the statue dead and buried by 1941, Van Vechten moved on to something less striking but equally radical. For nearly the past twenty years, the collecting passion that was first fired in his childhood had been focused primarily on African-American materials. In boxes, drawers, chests, and cabinets and crammed onto the floor-to-ceiling bookshelves that wrapped around his apartment he compiled a huge depository of books, records, music scores, and manuscripts by and about African-Americans as well as thousands of items of correspondence with black artists, writers, performers, educators, and public figures. This stockpile of materials was so large he fancied it would make an excellent founding contribution to an archival collection dedicated entirely to the culture of black Americans. Yale University accepted his proposal to house the collection and so became the first Ivy League institution to hold any resource of that kind. It was named the James Weldon Johnson Memorial Collection of Negro Arts and Letters, founded by Carl Van Vechten. Besides this being a fitting tribute to his friend, the name locked Johnson's memory to his for time immemorial. Van Vechten also openly admitted that the use of Johnson's name first and his second was "to induce others to make valuable additions to the collection." He knew that the words "Carl Van Vechten" still caused icy chills in some parts of black America, and he suspected that eliciting first editions, letters, and other precious materials from prominent black figures would be vastly easier if it were done in the name of an African-American pioneer rather than the white author of *Nigger Heaven*.

Van Vechten's plan for the collection was for it to be a vivid, living record of black culture. Throughout the 1940s, and for the rest of his life, he sought out valuable material wherever he could, entreating authors to gift draft manuscripts and inscribed first editions, along with letters that would shine a light on the intimate connections among and within black American communities. Langston Hughes joked that now he was to be absorbed into the august archives of an Ivy League college Van Vechten should expect his letters to acquire a new tone "and no doubt verge toward the grandiloquent." "Don't be selfconscious about Yale," Van Vechten replied. "Henry Miller puts more shits and fucks and cunts in than ever when I assure him his letters are destined for college halls." Beyond the joke there was a serious message. This was not to be an airbrushed record of the Negro edited by the white establishment; it was to be the unexpurgated story of a people in the words, sounds, and images of their highest achievers. To ensure that the great swath of African-American talent was represented, Van Vechten made it his mission to photograph every interesting and prominent black person he could entice to his studio and sent the results to Yale. As the years passed, the old guard of the Harlem Renaissance was joined on the rolls of Van Vechten's film by a younger generation, including the likes of Eartha Kitt, Harry Belafonte, and James Earl Jones. And though Sidney Poitier and a few others declined invitations to pose—probably the lingering association of *Nigger Heaven*'s putting them off—the opportunity to be immortalized in the James Weldon Johnson Collection was irresistible to most. Even W.E.B. DuBois agreed to put past hostilities to one side and submit to Van Vechten's lens, smiling warmly as he did so.

At the same time he was helping Yale amass its vast record of black culture, Van Vechten arranged for Fisk University, a small, historically African-American liberal arts college, to begin a collection detailing the history of American music, named the George Gershwin Memorial Collection of Music and Musical Literature, in honor of another recently departed veteran of the glory days, Gershwin having passed away in 1937. Again, the core collection was provided by Van Vechten himself from the piles of material that he had hoarded over the decades, all of which crowded the large, high-ceilinged rooms of his apartment. Having already donated the

African-American materials to an Ivy League college in New England, he carefully calculated the choice of a black college in Tennessee at a time when Jim Crow laws were still very much in force. While the Gershwin collection "was all white people's music for a Negro college," he recalled some years after both collections had been established, "if you want to study the Negro since 1900, you have to go to Yale . . . I thought this would interest people of the other race to go and look up things in their respective places." To his friend Arna Bontemps he admitted that the means were as important as the ends: "I am mad over the idea of breaking down segregation" by drawing white researchers into the archives of black universities.

Sitting on committees for grand civic projects and establishing formidable educational resources to strike a blow for racial equality, Van Vechten looked as though he had turned into his father. Certainly there were striking similarities, principally that both devoted themselves to projects that stressed the importance of individual self-improvement. But Carl's ambitions had an aesthetic dimension that Charles's never had. Creating beautiful surroundings was a passion of his that flowed irresistibly through his works as well as his private life. With the collections at Fisk and Yale he wanted to furnish environments of the mind through which scholars could have their imaginations stimulated and their prejudices challenged. Van Vechten once copied into a notebook a passage from the 1935 novel *The Last Puritan*, by George Santayana, that perfectly articulates his approach to his role of wealthy patron: "The use of riches isn't to disperse riches, but to cultivate the art of living, to produce beautiful homes, beautiful manners, beautiful speech, beautiful charities. You individually can't raise the lowest level of human life, but you can raise the highest level."

Noblesse oblige, one might call it, an aristocratic individualism conducive with his love of material splendor and his desire to be seen as an exceptional man of foresight and influence. In the catalog he wrote for the James Weldon Johnson Collection, he left no doubt about which beneficent benefactor had laid the foundations. The catalog, an exhaustive document of 658 pages that provides information about every item and major personality appearing in

Van Vechten's gift, is a thing of mesmeric scope, reflecting the depth and breadth of his passion for African-American culture. Obscure abolitionist novels are explained alongside even more obscure eugenicist tracts; Josephine Baker and Claude McKay rub shoulders with Booker T. Washington and Charles Chesnutt. But on every page is Van Vechten. The story of his life is found scattered in fragments, conspicuously written in the third person, among the larger, more complex stories of black America postemancipation. In the entry for a biography of Paul Robeson, Van Vechten notes that one chapter includes rich descriptions of his cocktail parties at 150 West Fifty-fifth Street; on detailing a book about the history of American boxing, he draws attention to his interest in the sport and to the black fighters he has photographed; when he comes to his copy of *Half-Caste*, Cedric Dover's evisceration of the pseudoscientific basis of white supremacy, he thinks it vital to note that there is a passing, unflattering reference to him on page 14. After reading a document in which Van Vechten parachutes himself into the black history of the United States at every possible moment, one might easily interpret his immense generosity in establishing the collection as lordly largess. The same often applied to his personal life. Once he had taken up photography full-time as a man of great private wealth who never need work again, certain friends felt uncomfortably beholden to his benevolence. He spent hours taking and developing photographs for them but refused to accept money or favors in return. Inevitably, this could cause frustration and resentment. After receiving some prints in the mail, Mahala Dutton—or Mahala Dutton Benedict Douglas, as she was now known—asked Van Vechten why he insisted on making people feel "so much in your debt" by refusing to accept payments for his photographs, and only ever issuing them as gifts. "I never seem able to do anything for you," she said in a letter that balanced gratitude and exasperation.

Imperiousness was a characteristic too deeply embedded to be changed now, however. And neither should it render his objectives unworthy. His egocentrism aside, the collections at Fisk and Yale reflect Van Vechten's glee at the vitality of American culture, a vitality created by its founding commitment to the genius of the individual. Coinciding with the outbreak of the Second World War, the act of establishing these archives of American brilliance might just have been the first and last overtly political act of his life. During the same period his revulsion for communism deepened, at a time when lots of his closest friends thought the Soviet Union Europe's greatest hope of defeating fascism. Many of his cohorts had enthusiastically supported communism's role in the Spanish Civil War and were attracted by its creed of class solidarity, which appeared to cut across the racial dividing lines that held the United States' culture of segregation in place. Van Vechten had no truck with any of this. "With great pleasure," he wrote his left-wing friend Dorothy Peterson in December 1939 a few days after the outbreak of the Winter War between the Soviet Union and Finland, "I spit on Russia and all the Russian sympathizers." Beyond the ruthless imperialism of the Red Army there was a bigger issue: he believed that leftist ideologies promoted the idea that sameness could be a virtue, and his individualist instincts could not tolerate that notion. His disdain even made its way into the James Weldon Johnson Collection catalog when he noted that C.L.R. James's adherence to Trotskyism fatally damaged his abilities as a writer.

When the United States entered the war with the Soviet Union as an ally, Van Vechten took the opportunity to express his fealty to his nation's individualistic ethic by spending Monday and Tuesday nights running the Stage Door Canteen, a venue where servicemen in New York could eat, drink, dance, and socialize while being waited on by celebrities from the entertainment world. It proved such a hit that it provided the basis of the 1943 propaganda film *Stage Door Canteen* starring, among many other Hollywood A-listers, Katharine Hepburn. Marinoff was actually first to volunteer her services at the canteen, but when Van Vechten decided to get involved, he swiftly bundled her aside and turned the venture to his own purposes. As well as being a site of respite for servicemen away from home in the Big Apple, the canteen became another venue for Van Vechten to challenge the authority of the color line. He wrote with pride to many friends about the racial mixing he was facilitating, as black soldiers danced with white girls and got to know white fellow servicemen in a way they would never have done elsewhere. It reaffirmed his belief that political campaigns, committees, and state-run projects were no match for the transforming power of direct social contact—especially when he was in charge. He told Dorothy Peterson that the success of the canteen was "proof" of his belief that if blacks only had "nerve enough" to enter white establishments, then racism, outside the South, "could be broken down in a week."

The naivety of that statement is breathtaking. Considering how often black friends of his had been turned away from restaurants, theaters, and nightclubs that he himself patronized, it seems bizarre that he believed the social timidity of the black community to be the biggest obstacle in defeating racism. It was the type of observation he made all the time. When the African-American academic Norman Holmes Pearson asked him to sign a petition in support of the Civil Rights Congress in 1948, Van Vechten declined the invitation, telling Pearson that he made it a rule never to add his name to petitions, before ostentatiously claiming that he had followed his own methods for opposing racial discrimination for half a century, "sometimes almost single-handed," and with tremendous effect. He added that he had been particularly successful in challenging the behavior of the many African-Americans who attempt to "Jim Crow other Negroes." Beyond the supercilious, self-regarding waffle, Van Vechten's response reveals that his fixation with individual transformation blinded him to the structural nature of racism, the deep-rooted social and political issues that kept black and white America divided. When a new, more organized and politicized phase of the civil rights struggle began after the Second World War, Van Vechten could not take to its petitions, marches, demonstrations, and rallies, which, to him, emphasized collective rights over individual experiences. The unwieldy complexities of politics had no place in his scheme to "cultivate the art of living," as George Santayana had put it in *The Last Puritan*. He clung to the idea that racism would be destroyed if whites and blacks were encouraged to lindy hop together on a Saturday night and that the world could be revolutionized one elegant cocktail party at a time. It was a fanciful, quixotic indulgence that could be enjoyed only by a rich white man to whom racial discrimination was an abstract problem rather than a vicious reality that blighted his daily life.

Still, there is something inspiring about Van Vechten's inexhaustible faith in the capacity of the individual to effect change, and before his eyes at the canteen he saw young lives set on a path of self-discovery. The unusually named George George, sensitive, awkward, and barely twenty, was drawn in almost immediately when he spent an evening at the canteen, shyly watching the other soldiers spin the pretty girls around the dance floor. Van Vechten could spot the truth about boys like George a mile off. He had, after all, been just like them once, a confused outsider dreaming of escape. The currents of longing and frustration that George thought were buried deep within him surged to the surface under Van Vechten's gaze. To George, Van Vechten was an exemplar of the life he dreamed of living. Though too self-conscious to speak at any length to him on the night, George struck up an extraordinary correspondence with Van Vechten, writing vivid and intense letters from Miami, Brazil, and all the other places he was stationed. In return Van Vechten sent him anecdotes of memorable times past and present and copies of his novels. George immediately identified with Gareth Johns, the frustrated youth at the center of *The Tattooed Countess*. Like Johns, George said, "I am understood by no one; liked by fewer." He apologized for the melodrama, blaming it on his feelings of vulnerability and confusion. George came to idealize Van Vechten and described him as one of the greats of the twentieth century, an artist of beauty, poise, style, and authenticity, for whom no exaltation was too grand. The canteen was a magnet for lonely and bored young servicemen far from home—just like George—and it provided Van Vechten the opportunity to swell the numbers of the jeunes gens assortis. As he entered his old age, this seemed more important than ever; inculcating these youngsters with his values, interests, and way of living was the surest means by which his influence would live on after his death.

In the last twenty years of his life securing a legacy became the focus of Van Vechten's work. As the forties bled into the fifties, his days were split among three principal activities: letter writing, photography, and boxing up material to be stored for posterity. He was helped in the latter two of these by Saul Mauriber, another much younger man who became the main object of Van Vechten's sexual and romantic attentions after his relationship with Mark Lutz had settled into warm friendship in the early forties. The materials they were arranging were not just for the James Weldon Johnson Collection at Yale or the archive in memory of Gershwin at Fisk. Van Vechten was donating reams of his correspondence and personal photographs to the New York Public Library and Yale's Collection of American Literature. Those grand institutions were only too glad to receive them. His relationships with H. L. Mencken, Gertrude Stein, the Fitzgeralds, and hundreds more are preserved in their letters to him and in their submission before his camera, providing a twisting paper trail of Van Vechten's life and his nation's cultural transformation.

These are the archives of a kind of cultural alchemy that took place in the United States from the start of the twentieth century, the curious tale of how the unseemly forces of modernism conquered the conventions of the past—but with a vignette depicting Van Vechten's involvement on every page. Among the thousands of photographs he donated, by far his most common subject is himself, either shots taken by others or the hundreds of vainglorious self-portraits. He bequeathed piles of receipts, tax returns, report cards, student essays, scraps of fabric, and even a box of dried flowers that belonged to him. In the margins of letters and on their envelopes he scribbled explanatory notes about the identities of his correspondents and the people, events, and places they discuss. He was talking to the future generations he imagined poring over his belongings, narrating for them the story of the times through which he had lived. By the mid-1940s Van Vechten's literary fame was a distant memory. His impish novels, so firmly fixed to the era in which they were written, aged poorly, and his essays on dance, music, and the theater faded almost entirely from view. In the meantime, many of his great causes had outstripped him: Stein, Hughes, Gershwin, and Robeson, for example, all were world-famous, and in 1949 Ethel Waters became only the second black woman in history to receive an Oscar nomination. Fabulously wealthy and well connected though he was, Van Vechten was frustrated by his slide from public prominence. He viewed these archives as his best chance of immortalizing himself, of leaving definitive proof of his uniqueness and the role he had played in helping the United States realize its artistic potential.

In the mountains of papers and objects he cataloged and sent away, Van Vechten exhibited his inner life in minute detail. When researchers looked through these materials in the years immediately before and after his death in 1964, they were overwhelmed by the volume of evidence that attested to those private relationships of his that hurdled the barriers of race and class. Signs of his varied sexual interests, however, were far less prominent—visible, certainly, but often obscured by codes, innuendos, and meanings that nestled between the lines. It was as if Van Vechten had excised that important part of his life from history. For myriad reasons such self-censorship would have been entirely understandable. Leading an openly homosexual life had of course never been an option for Van Vechten, but in the years during and immediately after the Second World War, the sexually playful atmosphere of the twenties, in which he had written about homosexuality with relative candor, seemed remarkably distant. J. Edgar Hoover began his grotesque campaign against homosexuality as early as 1937, ordering FBI agents to compile thousands of reports on homosexuals within the military, government, politics, and various other fields of public life. By 1947 Hoover was warning Congress that homosexuality was a key threat to national security, second only to communism, and urging President Truman to flush it out wherever it existed. His invective proved greatly persuasive. By the early fifties Senator Joseph McCarthy and numerous other prominent federal and state officials were joining in the witch-hunts, and between 1947 and 1955 twenty-one states and the District of Columbia introduced sexual psychopath laws that specifically targeted homosexuals. Life for many American gay men and lesbians was now more fearful and secretive than ever before.

In a direct sense, Van Vechten was relatively unaffected by these developments. He turned seventy in 1950, and his years of cruising in gay bars were behind him. All the same, the demonization of homosexuality enraged him, and he refused to be victimized. On his death he left instructions that certain documents, sealed in boxes, should be handed to Yale and the New York Public Library, only to be opened many years after his passing. His daybooks from the 1920s were sent to the New York Public Library, the perfect place for his shorthand chronicle of Manhattan's coming of age. To Yale he left very different materials: boxes of homoerotic photographs and eighteen scrapbooks recording an adult life of homosexual desire. The books are a jumble of newspaper clippings, erotic and pornographic photographs, sketches, and scraps of personal correspondence, the majority of which comes from the 1940s and the 1950s, though one newspaper story included came from as early as 1917. The article in question concerned the notorious playboy Harry K. Thaw, who was jailed for kidnapping and whipping a teenage boy named Frederick Gump in a violent sexual assault. There are many clippings like that dotted throughout the scrapbooks; stories of gay bashings, of persecution, and of men, fearful that some dark secret would emerge to destroy them, who had taken their own lives. These of course were the tragic realities for all too many Americans in a pre-Stonewall society—and, to a lesser extent, continue to blight the lives of some gay people today—yet without his inclusion of them here, it would be tempting to believe that such darkness did not encroach on Van Vechten's horizon. His treatment of homosexuality in his published writing in the 1920s was rarely anything other than exuberantly camp, some of his male characters conforming to the pansy stereotype of the day: effete, flamboyant, superficial, and unashamed of their sexual interests. His private correspondence, even with other gay men, gives little indication that he found anything troubling about his sexuality. When writing friends, often he signed off his letters with extravagant farewells that lavished imaginary gifts upon his correspondent, wonders such as exotic multicolored birds of prey, priceless jewelry, and a thousand tender kisses. When addressed to his closest gay male friends, these read like positive affirmations of a shared identity, especially when they mentioned flowers—pansies, lilies, violets, and carnations being particular favorites—as they frequently did. The tales of misery and torment in the scrapbooks show a different man, not one tor-

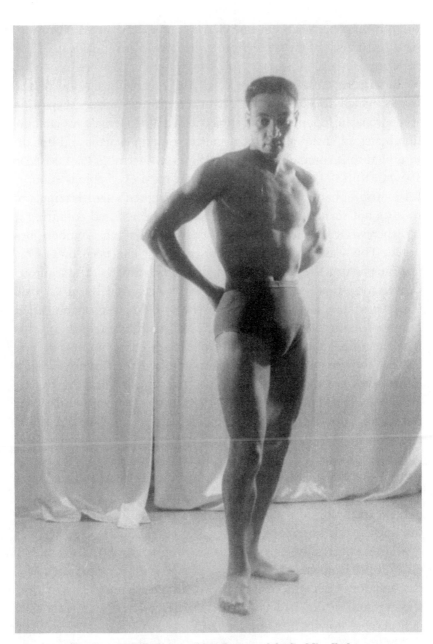

The dancer Al Bledger, c. 1938, photograph by Carl Van Vechten

tured by his sexual self but one clearly touched by the pain of those who were and angry at an intolerant world insensitive to their suffering.

Bitterness, however, is not at all the controlling mood of the books, which also document acts of astonishing bravery. Christine Jorgensen, the first publicized subject of a male to female sex change, dominates an entire page, for instance, looking elegant and defiant in a picture accompanying the headline DAD PRAISES COURAGE OF SON-TURNED-DAUGHTER. The inclusion of the press clippings, mournful or triumphant, are evidence of Van Vechten's scrutinizing eye rooting out sexual difference wherever it appeared and conjuring it up wherever it was absent, as the historian Jonathan Weinberg has noted. This was no recent habit, of course; it had been one of his favorite pasttimes for decades, and it informed much of the scabrous conversation that so infuriated Mabel Dodge. Had the great lady seen the contents of his scrapbooks, she would have probably pitied him for his arrested development that manifested itself in this inexhaustible—and sometimes exhausting—obsession with sex. Maybe, though, she would have also admired the inventiveness of his collages that constitute the most arresting part of the books. Frequently crass and juvenile, although just as frequently hilarious, the collages appear to have been constructed mainly in the 1950s and, probably unintentionally, display a certain ironic pop art sensibility, with faint echoes of the best-known work of Richard Hamilton. It is an irresistible image: a rich, venerable silver-haired gentleman in his seventies sat in his sumptuous apartment overlooking Central Park, rearranging newspaper cuttings to make dirty jokes that he can stick in his scrapbooks and pack off to the librarians at Yale, chuckling and hissing through his crooked teeth all the while. No other scene from his rich and varied life captures so perfectly the combination of instincts that drove his creativity: the attention seeking and love of bad taste on the surface and the current of a radical cause flowing urgently beneath.

Some of the pages feature sexually explicit photographs of young men, though judging from the sheer profusion of the images and from his long-standing glee at subverting convention, one senses that Van Vechten most enjoyed assembling the pages that fuse photographs of traditionally masculine men with headlines from entirely unrelated newspaper stories, mischievously turning the images into works of celebratory homoeroticism. In the sexual revolution of Van Vechten's collages, all sorts of famous American males, from Montgomery Clift and James Dean to President Eisenhower and Bobo Holloman, the pitcher for the St. Louis Browns, were out and proud. The obvious delight that Van Vechten took in projecting the world through a filter of homoeroticism unveils one of the paradoxes of his identity: at times he actively enjoyed the furtiveness that his attraction to men compelled him to pursue. Being unable to publicly express love and affection for other men without fear of reprisal was obviously loathsome, but still, he felt there was something to be said for the thrill of clandestine activities, forbidden pleasures, and the intense bonds forged among members of a community only permitted to exist subterraneously.

Those bonds are quietly eulogized in the scrapbooks too. Van Vechten had been an enthusiastic trader of pornography and dirty jokes for many decades. Into his seventies and eighties he was still sending Aileen Pringle, his friend of nearly forty years, letters that ended with gags about fornicating rabbis or the homosexual termite that only had eyes for woodpeckers. With the jeunes gens assortis and other friends he similarly maintained an exchange of sexual gossip, jokes, and pictures. Most of his closest friends knew that his collecting interests extended to sexual matters and were aware of his top shelf, a portion of his bookcases dedicated to erotic material as well as more serious scientific works about sex, by writers such as Havelock Ellis and René Guyon. The painter Elwyn "Wynn" Chamberlain clearly had his tongue in his cheek when he sent Van Vechten deliberately camp sketches of angels and cowboys, knowing that the old man's ribald sense of humor would be tickled by them. Other artists gave him much more explicit material. Thomas Handforth is best known for his elegant illustrations and etchings of China, but he drew for Van Vechten a side of the Far East that was never touched upon in his award-winning children's books: pornographic drawings of American sailors and Chinese gigolos that, unlike Chamberlain's gifts, were designed to arouse rather than amuse.

Considerable courage was required in exchanging those draw-

A sketch by Wynn Chamberlain at some point during the mid-1950s that Van Vechten put in his scrapbooks. Chamberlain identifies this as a preparatory sketch for *Doorway*, a painting that was subsequently bought by Lincoln Kirstein.

ings. During the Eisenhower years Postmaster General Arthur Summerfield crusaded against what he termed "pornography in the family mailbox" and gained extensive powers to censor any materials sent via the post that supposedly promoted homosexuality. Being caught sending or receiving homoerotic material could have ruinous consequences, including prosecution for acts of sexual deviancy. One clipping in the scrapbooks comes from *One*, a periodical launched in 1953 by a homophile group named the Mattachine Society, whose mission was to counteract the slew of vicious antigay propaganda, and promote the message of gay rights. The FBI infiltrated the Mattachine Society, and after *One* had run a story claiming that homosexuals "occupy key positions with oil companies and the FBI," agents outed the magazine's staffers to their employers. A retired millionaire whose wife and close friends all knew about his sexuality, Van Vechten had relatively little to lose by being similarly exposed, but still, if he was receiving *One* in the mail, he was knowingly opening himself up to unpleasant forces.

Until his suicide in 1934, Max Ewing had been one of the most prolific correspondents, and his presence is strongly felt in the scrapbooks too, especially because he had an eye for the more subtle allusions to homosexuality of the sort that Van Vechten himself was adept at spotting. "Dear Carl," he scribbled at the top of a poster mocked up to show the Marx Brothers in drag, "For one or another of your collections of AMATORY CURIOSA!" A story about plans in Italy to censor classical scenes on postcards on grounds of taste and decency also caught his attention; he forwarded the clipping to Van Vechten with a note suggesting "we should exchange a great many very soon before the movement gets under way here."

Ewing had picked up the photography bug around the same time as Van Vechten, and from 1932 he sent him many prints of his work, including those from his "Carnival of Venice" series, studio portraits taken in front of a Venetian backdrop. Largely thanks to Van Vechten, Ewing had befriended many of the leading lights of New York's art establishment, and Paul Robeson, Muriel Draper, and Lincoln Kirstein all posed for his camera before the painted gondolas and canals of a two-dimensional Venice. When Ewing wrote to inform Van Vechten about a winter exhibition of the Venice series, he said he hoped all his subjects would arrive in the costumes they posed in, though as "some of them have worn no costumes at all, it will be hard on them if the night is cold." The photos of the disrobed models made their way to Van Vechten, naturally. One featured two shirtless men: the tall and powerful Herbert Buch next to the Greenwich Village eccentric Joe Gould, half Buch's size, slight and fragile as a baby bird. "Note the influence of 'Freaks,'" Ewing pointed out, a reference to one of his and Van Vechten's shared enthusiasms, the 1932 movie about the lives of conjoined twins, hermaphrodites, bearded ladies, and other sideshow performers. The diversity of human forms that *Freaks* exhibits enthralled Van Vechten and it remained one of his favorite movies for the rest of his life. The fact that he was apparently unmoved by any suggestion that those in the film were exploited is perhaps a reflection of contemporary attitudes toward physical disability and certainly an insight into Van Vechten's fascination with individual difference and unordinary lives.

Gould and Buch were not pretty enough to make it onto the pages of Van Vechten's homoerotic scrapbooks, but Ewing's nude shot of the dancer Paul Meeres did, in addition to some of Van Vechten's own photographs of male dancers and naked male models. His earliest nudes were taken in the summer of 1933, but it was in the early 1940s that he shot a lengthy series of pictures with his two favorite models, Hugh Laing, a white dancer, and Allen Meadows, a black youth from Harlem. Often Van Vechten shot the two together, sometimes at his studio, other times in the lush grounds of Langner Lane Farm, the Connecticut home of his friends Lawrence and Armina Langner. Shared only with a select circle of friends during his lifetime, those photos are possibly the most explicit manifestation of Van Vechten's abiding artistic obsessions: race, sexuality, and performance. In a letter to Langston Hughes he described Meadows as "my African model," despite the fact that Meadows was American and lived on St. Nicholas Avenue in Harlem. Yet it was an accurate description, for within the gaze of his lens that is exactly what Meadows represented: Van Vechten's vision of the black African soul juxtaposed with the whiteness personified by Laing's pale skin. In some shots they stand side by side, looking

Allen Juante Meadows, c. 1940, photograph by Carl Van Vechten

Hugh Laing, c. 1940, photograph by Carl Van Vechten

passively into each other's eyes as if they are photonegatives; occasionally their hands, arms, and bodies interlock, two swirling halves of a single being. Almost always they are performing in highly stylized poses. Van Vechten might have Meadows hold an African mask in his hands or decorate him with African jewelry or a scanty piece of fabric, while Laing showed the power and elegance of his dancer's body by stretching into a balletic position. The combination of their nudity and their performance is intriguing. Beyond the obvious pleasure he took in looking at their bodies, Van Vechten was returning to that ruling tension of American lives: the need to live honestly and unapologetically as an individual, while adopting guises to pass between a multitude of collective identities. Stood naked in the same frame, both of them revealed their inescapable selves. In performing, they embellished those selves, hinting at their potential for transformation.

While his scrapbooks suggest that his collection of pornography was considerable, there is nothing close to a porn aesthetic in the photos he took of Laing and Meadows. They are erotic, undoubtedly, but they communicate a vulnerability that robs them of the ability to merely excite or titillate. Meadows, especially, with his sad eyes and the pimples of late adolescence still visible on his forehead, has an unavoidable fragility. It was something Van Vechten was aware of, and actively accentuated. One of his favorite themes for his nudes was that of St. Sebastian, the Christian martyr who was tied to a tree by the emperor Diocletian and tortured by arrows that punctured his flesh. Since the Renaissance, Sebastian—or at least his depiction on canvas—led a double life as a gay icon, his martyrdom in the name of God serving as a metaphor for the suffering of homosexual men. "Grace in suffering," declared Thomas Mann in reference to his novel *Death in Venice*, "that is the heroism symbolized by St. Sebastian." A little more than thirty years before, when Oscar Wilde entered self-exile after his release from prison, it was no coincidence that he chose Sebastian as his pseudonym. With Meadows, Laing, and other models Van Vechten repeatedly re-created the scene of Sebastian's torment. Each stood alone, bound and naked, pained and vulnerable; in need of protection and prone to seduction. Behind the camera and in control of the image, it was

Van Vechten who had the potential to do either or both. George George believed the photographs drove to the heart of Van Vechten's attitude toward young men in his later years, which was a mixture of caring paternalism and eroticized indulgence. George wrote a fellow Van Vechten acolyte that Carl's fascination with Sebastian, "drilled with poison-tipped arrows launched by an intolerant society," shows that he was sensitive to the vulnerability of youth—but he was equally enamored by Narcissus, the cocksure and conceited young man obsessed with his own beauty.

The scrapbooks and the photographs represent the one portion of Van Vechten's life that he could not parade in public, a defiantly irreverent avocation of his innate nature and a declaration that homosexuality is a form of love and not only a form of sex—although that could be tremendously good fun too. During the Second World War he told Arthur Davison Ficke that he planned to hold on to his collections of pornography and erotica until he died. He joked that the more graphic pictures would make "life more easy in a concentration camp." Of course that eventuality never came to pass, and instead he decided to leave them for what he hoped would be the study and enjoyment of a more enlightened generation decades after his own demise. Perhaps the choice of Yale as the recipient was influenced in part because that same institution housed a collection of the papers of Walt Whitman, that lodestone of American literature whose homosexuality also left an indelible mark on his work. Without doubt it appealed to Van Vechten's sense of humor to bequeath this celebration of homosexuality—ribald, explicit, delicate, scatological, thoughtful, and plain silly all at once—to such an auspicious seat of learning. The setup took a quarter of a century, but when the boxes were eagerly unpacked, it was discovered that through an inscription on one of the books Van Vechten had delivered the perfect punch line from beyond the grave: "Yale May Not Think So, but It'll Be Just Jolly."

Epilogue: The Attention That I Used to Get

After twenty-five years it felt as if history were repeating itself. In February 1951 the Avon publishing house reprinted *Nigger Heaven* in paperback, a quarter of a century after the book had first made such an impact on the American reading public. Months before its publication Avon prodded and cajoled Van Vechten, trying to persuade him to change the title, which it suspected might cause trouble. He would not budge. *Nigger Heaven* was the only possible title, he said, the only one that made sense, and without it the book could not be published.

His intransigence of course was not really about the title at all but about his freedom of expression. He would not be told what he could or could not say, especially when it came to a cause he knew as expertly as the American Negro. In his author's note in the Avon version, Van Vechten went on the defensive, dedicating the first three paragraphs to the support that James Weldon Johnson had given *Nigger Heaven* in his autobiography. Van Vechten quoted Johnson's belief that "most of the Negroes who condemned *Nigger Heaven* did not read it." But even the sainted Johnson could not insulate Van Vechten from a second backlash, albeit one that was nowhere near as ferocious as the first. After complaints from the general public about the title, Avon decided to withdraw the novel in November 1951. With it went Van Vechten's last significant appearance in public as a writer.

The irony was that this incident happened while the black establishment was celebrating Van Vechten's contributions more than ever. In 1949 Fisk University, acknowledged Van Vechten's role in persuading Georgia O'Keeffe to donate her collection of modern art to its institution by housing them in a room called the Carl Van Vechten Gallery. In further recognition of his foundation of the George Gershwin Memorial Collection and of his efforts to create an archive of African-American brilliance at Yale, Fisk also awarded him an honorary doctorate in 1955. When the time came for the ceremony, he took a couple of days off from his regimen of sifting through piles of old letters and developing photographs to attend the ceremony in Tennessee. Marinoff proudly took snaps of Dr. Van Vechten in his academic regalia, surely a sight that neither of them had ever anticipated. Amid the formality of the occasion, Van Vechten, now aged seventy-five, still found an opportunity to lower the tone by asking the Scottish academic seated next to him on the stage whether he was the type to leave himself exposed to the elements beneath his kilt.

Having ascended to new heights of respectability, Van Vechten was rewarded for his tremendous work in helping to bring African-American culture into the mainstream of white consciousness, an effort that only a few other Americans could claim to have matched. It was also a sign that his time as a dangerous voice was over, at least in the realm of race relations. Increasingly, his fixation with erasing the color line by throwing parties in which celebrated whites could meet celebrated blacks seemed antiquated. For his author's note in the Avon reprint of *Nigger Heaven* in 1951 he wrote that "segregation is being dealt severe blows from more vantage points than ever before," citing as evidence the success of a host of black celebrities such as Jackie Robinson and Marian Anderson and also noting that the "captain of the football team at Yale is a Negro." In an era when Rosa Parks, the Freedom Riders, and numerous other civil rights warriors demanded that the doctrine of separate but equal be sent to the furnace, the achievements—significant and impressive though they were—of a small group of conspicuously talented individuals felt more like light jabs than "severe blows" in the fight against segregation. The realization that he was gradually being consigned to

Carl Van Vechten, c. 1960

the past in an area of life where for so long he had considered himself the future, was painful. "My relations with the NAACP are not so personal as they were," he complained in 1960. "I usually don't get anywhere near the attention that I used to get."

In the final decade or so of his life he was as busy as ever, but far less visible, spending the majority of his time hunkered down in his apartment, creating his archives and memorializing the past. He certainly had plenty to keep him occupied. When Gertrude Stein died of cancer in 1946, Van Vechten discovered in the pages of *The New York Times* that she had named him her literary executor. He claimed to have been stunned, but the decision made sense. Their public identities were bound together, Van Vechten twisting and looping like creeping ivy around Stein's monumental frame, and of all her followers he was the only one who had never failed to do her bidding. The task he had been set was formidable: to get into print all of Stein's unpublished work, and Van Vechten's immediate reaction "was that Gertrude had bitten off more than I could easily chew." Nevertheless, his stewardship was a triumph, and by 1958 he had managed to publish every last word of Stein's enormous back catalog, testament to his gifts of perseverance and canniness.

Without the prominent public profile, he was unable to promote new talent as he had so effectively done in previous decades, but old age did not dim his passion for making new discoveries. He helped Chester Himes get a publishing deal with Alfred A. Knopf, and the early novels of James Baldwin and Philip Roth thrilled him with their frank portrayals of modern life. Both Himes and Baldwin were corralled into his studio to join his gallery of the exceptional, along with a galaxy of other bright young things, Marlon Brando, Truman Capote, Norman Mailer, and Gore Vidal among them. Brando even posed in his costume from *A Streetcar Named Desire*, staring out at the viewer with the top buttons of his pants undone, making Stanley Kowalski one of Van Vechten's homoerotic models. One name he never got was Marilyn Monroe, though he adored her. Aged seventy-eight, Van Vechten went to see *Some Like It Hot* a few days after its release in 1959 and laughed uproariously at the final scene in which the cross-dressing Jack Lemmon is sailed off into the sunset by an old man who has an eye for the boys. It was the sort of scabrous joke he had made thirty-six years earlier in *The Blind Bow-Boy*; he was glad to see that the younger generations were catching up.

His own collection of radiant youths grew and grew right up until his death, but with old age and gradual infirmity his sexual escapades lessened. In his final decade the adoring youngsters in his orbit—there were writers and dancers, sailors and seminarians—thought of him as a grandfather figure: wise, generous, loving, and with a wicked sense of humor. The artist Wynn Chamberlain was one of the many young men who fell under the spell of Van Vechten's charisma as the old man attempted to expand his cultural horizons, turning him on to Ronald Firbank, though the ballet proved a step too far. When Chamberlain, a fellow jazz devotee, visited Yale to take a look at the James Weldon Johnson Collection, he wrote Van Vechten to express his admiration. "Very few Americans have the right feeling about the culture of their country," he said. "Most feel that CULTURE floats just out of reach somewhere in capital letters and should be talked about never, hardly ever engaged in." Van Vechten, however, instinctively understood that the greatest aspects of contemporary American culture were not things to be passively received, but to be experienced, lived, and shared "between sensitive and creative people," Chamberlain said.

That, in the final analysis, was Van Vechten's greatest achievement. Far more lasting than his output of essays, books, and photographs was the example of the life he lived; no other man or woman before him embodied the vision of modern American culture as emphatically as Carl Van Vechten. His twentieth-century urban odyssey made a virtue of racial and sexual diversity and collapsed the nineteenth-century distinctions between edifying art and facile entertainment, constantly probing the boundaries of what was considered good and bad taste. At his core he was a gifted individual in pursuit of experience and self-gratification, obeying no authority other than instinct, doing *"what one is forced by nature to do."* These obsessions of Van Vechten's, which made him so conspicuously unusual throughout his life, are now regarded as the hallmarks of a vibrant and diverse American urban culture, one that has not only reshaped a nation but profoundly affected the experiences of the entire world. When Van Vechten, aged eighty-four, passed away in his sleep, on December 21, 1964, the United States was entering a new era, in which these key concerns of his public and private lives—race, sexuality, and freedom of expression—were pushed to the very front of the national consciousness. Van Vechten would have found the heavily politicized language of the late sixties' counterculture totally alien but would have recognized many of its causes as the outgrowth of his own rebellions, started fifty years earlier during the First World War.

Marinoff stayed by his side valiantly until his final breath, devoted but damaged, the very definition of the long-suffering wife. The city of New York too remained true to him over half a century of turbulence and triumphs, always unveiling something tantalizing and unexpected to amuse and enchant him. But the strongest, most fulfilling relationship Van Vechten ever built was with himself. To the last he was the consummate individualist, a preening egotist fascinated by his own specialness, the extraordinary things he did, and the élan with which he did them. Eighteen months before he died *The New Yorker* interviewed Van Vechten for a piece in the magazine's "Talk of the Town" section, reserved for whimsical stories about New York life. Van Vechten was a perfect fit, cast as "one of the city's most durable boosters," a curious, forgotten relic of modern New York's genesis. Infirm and hard of hearing, he was "still imposing at eighty-two, even ornately so," wearing "Italianate loafers and a dapper striped cardigan jacket" and taking his daily bourbon highball as the interview progressed. He tossed out anecdotes about his history as a mischief-maker, his dealings with the rich and famous, his brilliance as a photographer, and his central importance to black America. "I have photographed everybody from Matisse to Isamu Noguchi," he said, before boasting, "I still get about twenty-five letters a day from Negroes." Though the world outside was changing as quickly now as when he first arrived in New York, inside the sanctity of his own apartment Carl Van Vechten was still the only show in town.

Notes

· ·

ABBREVIATIONS

Berg=The Berg Collection of English and American Literature, The New York
   Public Library, Astor, Lenox, and Tilden Foundations
CCOHC=Columbia Center for Oral History Collection
CVV=Carl Van Vechten
FM=Fania Marinoff
NYPL=Manuscripts and Archives Division, The New York Public Library, Astor,
   Lenox, and Tilden Foundations
YCAL=Yale Collection of American Literature, Beinecke Rare Book & Manuscript
   Library, Yale University

PROLOGUE

5 *"I'm going to . . . Paris"*: The Reminiscences of Carl Van Vechten (March 3,
   1960), 21, CCOHC.
5 *"a serious menace to our civilization"*: Josiah Strong, *Our Country: Its Possible
   Future and Its Present Crisis* (New York: Baker & Taylor, 1885), 128.
6 *"For him Manhattan . . . world"*: Emily Clark, *Innocence Abroad* (1931; repr.,
   Westport, CT: Greenwood Press, 1975), 138.
6–7 *On February 16 . . . began*: CVV daybooks, February 16, 1927, Carl Van
   Vechten Papers, NYPL.
8 *"If people have . . . juice"*: The Reminiscences of Carl Van Vechten (May 25,
   1960), 355, CCOHC.
8 *"I can cut . . . me"*: Ibid., 354.

1. THE GILDED AGE: A TALE OF YESTERDAY

12 *In 1651 he . . . action*: A.J.F. Van Laer, ed. and trans., *Minutes of the Court of
   Rensselaerswyck, 1648–1652* (Albany: University of the State of New York,
   1922), 149–52.

12 *"His Excellency and . . . frisk"*: Gerald M. Carbone, *Nathanael Greene: A Biography of the American Revolution* (New York: Palgrave Macmillan, 2008), 120.

13 *The town boasted . . . Midwest*: Figures cited from a collation of U.S. Census Bureau data by the State Library of Iowa, State Data Center Program, http://data.iowadatacenter.org/datatables/PlacesAll/plpopulation18502000 .pdf.

13 *"churchy, Republican, wholesome"*: William L. Shirer, *The Start, 1904–1930*, vol. 1 of *20th Century Journey: A Memoir of the Life and the Times* (New York: Simon and Schuster, 1976), 171.

14 *"very surprised . . . stork"*: The Reminiscences of Carl Van Vechten (March 3, 1960), 5, CCOHC.

14 *"My little boy's . . . been"*: Ada Amanda Fitch Van Vechten, diary, June 17, 1882, Carl Van Vechten Papers, NYPL.

16 *"tear wildly at . . . way"*: Charles Lewis Fitch to CVV, December 22, 1889, Carl Van Vechten Papers, NYPL.

16 *"surrounded by great . . . lawn"*: CVV, *The Tattooed Countess: A Romantic Novel with a Happy Ending* (1924; repr., Iowa City: University of Iowa Press, 1987), 33.

17 *In its rolling . . . locations*: CVV, "The Folksongs of Iowa," *Sacred and Profane Memories* (London: Cassell & Company, 1932), 29–30.

17 *Van Vechten admitted . . . boy*: The Reminiscences of Carl Van Vechten (March 3, 1960), 45, CCOHC.

17 *"I hated interference . . . attention"*: CVV, "The Tin Trunk," *Sacred and Profane Memories*, 15.

17–18 *"my mother, picturing . . . nest"*: Ibid., 8.

18–19 *"Death, up to . . . about it"*: The Reminiscences of Carl Van Vechten (April 23, 1960), 144, CCOHC.

19 *"I'd begun to . . . not"*: Ibid., 145.

19 *"was not civilized . . . beauty"*: Susan Glaspell, *The Road to the Temple* (London: Ernest Benn, 1926), 60.

20 *"to be themselves . . . live for"*: CVV, *Tattooed Countess*, 224.

20 *"It was the day . . . bee"*: Louis Raymond Reid, "The Small Town," *Civilization in the United States: An Enquiry by Thirty Americans*, ed. Harold E. Stearns (London: Jonathan Cape, 1922), 288.

21–22 *To his embarrassment . . . tablecloth*: CVV, "Chapter Four," unpublished juvenilia, Carl Van Vechten Papers, NYPL.

24 *He proudly told . . . autodidactic*: CVV to Arthur Davison Ficke, August 19, 1937, Arthur Davison Ficke Papers, YCAL; CVV, *Letters of Carl Van Vechten*, ed. Bruce Kellner (New Haven, CT: Yale University Press, 1987), 156.

24 *"sophisticated enough to . . . existed"*: The Reminiscences of Carl Van Vechten (March 3, 1960), 41, CCOHC.

24 *In an unpublished . . . boys*: CVV, "Chapter One," unpublished juvenilia, Carl Van Vechten Papers, NYPL.

24 *"boys with imagination . . . suspicion"*: CVV, *Tattooed Countess*, 109.

24–25 *"They have some practical . . . 'Soap?'"*: Charles Lewis Fitch to CVV, December 22, 1894, Carl Van Vechten Papers, NYPL.

25 *"excelled in female . . . stardom"*: CVV, "Terpsichorean Souvenirs," *The Dance Writings of Carl Van Vechten*, ed. Paul Padgette (New York: Dance Horizons, 1980), 3.

26 *"Imagine two hundred . . . soup"*: "The Cherry Sisters Chestnut," *Cedar Rapids Gazette*, March 15, 1893, 4.

27 *"as 'homelike' as . . . children"*: B. F. Keith, "The Vogue of the Vaudeville," *American Vaudeville as Seen by Its Contemporaries*, ed. Charles W. Stein (New York: Alfred A. Knopf, 1984), 17.

27 *When the Marx Brothers . . . flag*: John E. DiMeglio, *Vaudeville U.S.A.* (Bowling Green, OH: Bowling Green University Popular Press, 1973), 185.

28 *Van Vechten documented . . .* men: CVV scrapbooks 4125 and 4126, Billy Rose Theatre Collection, The New York Public Library for the Performing Arts.

28 *As a teenager . . . rest*: The photographs CVV took in Cedar Rapids can be found in the Carl Van Vechten Papers, NYPL.

2. THE COSMOPOLITAN STANDARD OF VIRTUE

30–31 *He was repulsed . . . sight*: CVV to Ada Amanda Fitch Van Vechten, July 1892, Carl Van Vechten Papers, NYPL.

31 *"First in violence . . . none"*: Lincoln Steffens, *The Shame of the Cities* (New York: Peter Smith, 1948), 234.

32 *It has been suggested . . . Matisse*: Hilary Spurling, *The Unknown Matisse: The Life of Henri Matisse: The Early Years, 1869–1908* (Berkeley: University of California Press, 2001), 65.

32 *"until then I had . . . women"*: CVV, "The Tin Trunk," *Sacred and Profane Memories*, 18.

33 *"novel to most . . . delighted me"*: Ibid.

33 *"you will see . . . conceive"*: Lisa Krissoff Boehm, *Popular Culture and the Enduring Myth of Chicago, 1871–1968* (New York and London: Routledge, 2004), 61.

33 *In the first chapter . . . destiny*: CVV, "Chapter One," unpublished juvenilia, Carl Van Vechten Papers, NYPL.

34 *His own brother . . . emotions*: The Reminiscences of Carl Van Vechten (March 3, 1960), 40, CCOHC.

34 *"a frightfully stupid life"*: Mahala Dutton Benedict Douglas to CVV, August 8, 1927, Carl Van Vechten Papers, YCAL.

35 *"quite respectable enough"*: The Reminiscences of Carl Van Vechten (March 3, 1960), 40, CCOHC.

35 *Even thinking of females . . . might be*: CVV, "Chapter One," unpublished juvenilia, Carl Van Vechten Papers, NYPL.

35 *"high-spirited" girl . . . "further"*: Henry Seidel Canby, *The Age of Confidence* (New York: Farrar, Straus and Giroux, 1934), 37.

36 *"a brown derby hat . . . boots"*: CVV, *Tattooed Countess*, 24.

36 *In the 1950s . . . himself*: CVV to Peter David Marchant, April 25, 1956, Kellner, *Letters of Carl Van Vechten*, 260.

37 *"the cosmopolitan standard of virtue"*: Theodore Dreiser, *Sister Carrie* (New York: Bantam Books, 1958), 1.

37 *"In no other city . . . soul"*: CVV, "The Spanish Theatre," *In the Garret* (New York: Alfred A. Knopf, 1920), 336.

37–38 *When Van Vechten was taken . . . do so*: CVV to Ada Amanda Fitch Van Vechten, c. July 1892, Carl Van Vechten Papers, NYPL.

38 *"all that is gaudy . . . windows"*: Jane Addams, *The Spirit of Youth and the City Streets* (New York: Macmillan Company, 1909), 27.

39 *"If you do not like . . . yours"*: Lawrence W. Levine, *Highbrow/Lowbrow: The Emergence of Cultural Hierarchy in America* (Cambridge, MA: Harvard University Press, 1988), 189.

39 *In a creative writing . . . great art*: CVV, "Unfinished Symphony," Miscellaneous College Themes, Carl Van Vechten Papers, NYPL.

40 *"came from the leading . . . Chicago"*: Peter A. Gabauer et al., *Annals of Psi Upsilon, 1833–1941* (New York: Psi Upsilon Fraternity, 1941), 215.

40 *"drunken ruffians . . . men"*: George Ade, "The Fable of the Copper and the Jovial Undergrad," *The America of George Ade,* ed. Jean Shepherd (New York: G. P. Putnam's Sons, 1960), 81.

40–41 *In his perfunctory . . . assignation*: CVV diary, 1901–1902, Carl Van Vechten Papers, NYPL.

41 *He confessed to . . . acted upon*: CVV diary, August 13 and August 14, 1901, Carl Van Vechten Papers, NYPL.

41 *Two weeks after . . . only ask:* CVV diary, June 29, 1901, Carl Van Vechten Papers, NYPL.

41 *In some quiet . . . heart*: CVV diary, December 26–31, 1902, Carl Van Vechten Papers, NYPL.

42 *He claimed that . . . mother*: CVV, "Chapter One," unpublished juvenilia, Carl Van Vechten Papers, NYPL.

42 *"I picked it up fast"*: The Reminiscences of Carl Van Vechten (March 3, 1960), 55, CCOHC.

42 *In the Levee . . . path*: Karen Abbott, *Sin in the Second City; Madams, Ministers, Playboys and the Battle for America's Soul* (New York: Random House, 2007), 10–13.

42 *In a diary entry . . . morning*: CVV diary, December 1, 1901, Carl Van Vechten Papers, NYPL.

43 *"philandering spirit"*: Anna Elizabeth Snyder to CVV, undated, Carl Van Vechten Papers, NYPL.

44 *In the writer . . . Vanderpool*: See Abbott, *Sin in the Second City* for an absorbing account of the Everleigh sisters and their club. Also Charles Washburn, *Come into My Parlor: A Biography of the Aristocratic Everleigh Sisters of Chicago* (New York: National Library Press, 1936).

44 *When asked as an old man . . . begin with*: CVV to Bruce Kellner, September 27, 1957, Bruce Kellner Papers, YCAL.

45 *"one of the great memories . . . surpassed"*: CVV, "Terpsichorean Souvenirs," *Dance Writings of Carl Van Vechten*, 5.

45 *According to his own . . . party*: The Reminiscences of Carl Van Vechten (March 3, 1960), 15, CCOHC.

46 *Shortly after joining . . . Sublett*: In 1904 CVV wrote "The Inky Ones," a semifictionalized account of his relationship with Desdemona Sublett and

his experiences of African-American Chicago. Because of his use of various pseudonyms in the story, some writers have previously identified the story's character, Mrs. Manchester, as a woman named Aurelia Veta Clement. However, in a manuscript of "The Inky Ones," which constitutes the fourth chapter of his autobiographical novel, now held in the Carl Van Vechten Papers at the New York Public Library, CVV wrote in the margin that Mrs. Manchester is in fact Desdemona Sublett. In a subsequent essay he wrote in 1925 titled "A Note on Breakfasts," he also names his fraternity housekeeper as Mrs. Sublett, and the description of her resembles the sketch of Mrs. Manchester in "The Inky Ones." In 1922 Elizabeth Lindsay Davis wrote *The Story of the Illinois Federation of Colored Women's Clubs*, in which a photograph of Desdemona Sublett appears along with a description of her as "one of the pioneers in Illinois club work" and "an active member of the Civic League of Quinn Chapel." This matches CVV's description of Mrs. Manchester as a pious woman who worked tirelessly on behalf of Quinn Chapel.

46 *She was a hefty . . . faith*: CVV, "The Inky Ones," unpublished manuscript, Carl Van Vechten Papers, NYPL.

46 *Before long Van Vechten . . . attendance*: Ibid.; CVV, *Keep A-Inchin' Along: Selected Writings of Carl Van Vechten About Black Art and Letters*, ed. Bruce Kellner (Westport, CT: Greenwood Press, 1979), 4.

46 *"uncultured and uneducated . . . clever"*: Ibid., 5.

48 *"dusky matrons with ample bosoms"*: Ibid.

48 *"invariably taken for a coon"*: CVV, "Chapter One," unpublished manuscript, Carl Van Vechten Papers, NYPL.

3. THAT SHUDDER OF FASCINATION

49 *In a dingy . . . west*: Larry Lorenz, "The Whitechapel Club: Defining Chicago's Newspapermen in the 19th Century," *American Journalism* 15, no. 1 (Winter 1998): 83–102.

49 *"I cannot remember . . . write"*: CVV, "Notes for an Autobiography," *Sacred and Profane Memories*, 225.

50 *"the first novelist . . . account"*: Ibid.

50 *An entry from . . . face*: CVV diary, July 17, 1901, Carl Van Vechten Papers, NYPL.

51 *"the modern editor . . . facts"*: Wayne Klatt, *Chicago Journalism: A History* (Jefferson, NC: McFarland, 2009), 77.

51 *"to enlighten and . . . San Francisco"*: William Salisbury, *The Career of a Journalist* (New York: B. W. Dodge & Company, 1908), 146

51 *"never allow any . . . 'features'"*: Ibid., 166.

52 *"the most terrific din you ever heard"*: The Reminiscences of Carl Van Vechten (April 1, 1960), 72, CCOHC.

52 *As William Salisbury . . . existence*: Salisbury, *Career of a Journalist*, 153.

52 *"I was so successful" . . . unscathed*: Ibid., 60.

53 *He spent a bleak . . . withdrawal*: CVV, "Letter from Chicago," *Pulse* 4 (January 1904): 88, Carl Van Vechten Papers, NYPL.

53 *It turned out . . . exclusive*: For a lengthier account of Howey's unethical but ingenious espionage see Klatt, *Chicago Journalism*, 74–76.

53 *"on the sidewalk . . . smothered"*: The Reminiscences of Carl Van Vechten (April 1, 1960), 78, CCOHC.

54 *"chorus of opinion . . . Van Vechten"*: Jack Lait, "Should a Teacher Marry? Yes—and No!," *New York Journal*, September 15, 1934, CVV scrapbook 26, Carl Van Vechten Papers, NYPL.

54 *He wrote about a young woman . . . death*: "Sues Suitor, Cooled by Glass Eye," *Chicago American*, c. September; "Gossip of the Chicago Smart Set," *Chicago American*, July 18, 1905; "Find Hanish an Imposter; Two of Faithful Desert," *Chicago American*, March 21, 1905; "'High Priest' Forced to Flee from New York in Order to Avoid Arrest," *Chicago American*, c. March 1905. All in CVV scrapbook 27, Carl Van Vechten Papers, NYPL.

54–55 *With puckish delight . . . feet*: "A New Type of Chorus Girl," *Chicago American*, c. May 1905, in CVV scrapbook 27, Carl Van Vechten Papers, NYPL.

55 *"I have never seen . . . killed him"*: "Xmas Toys Boy's Death Messenger," *Chicago American*, December 26, 1904, CVV scrapbook 27, Carl Van Vechten Papers, NYPL.

55 *"creative rather than critical"*: CVV, *Red: Papers on Musical Subjects* (New York: Alfred A. Knopf, 1925), xvii, x.

56 *"That was some life . . . there"*: The Reminiscences of Carl Van Vechten (March 3, 1960), 58, CCOHC.

56 *"I learned to dislike [it] heartily"*: Ibid., 12.

56 *"there are lots of ways . . . eventually"*: Ibid., 13.

56 *"I didn't get over it . . . usually didn't"*: Ibid.

57 *"human or normal . . . call it"*: The Reminiscences of Carl Van Vechten (April 23, 1960), 130, CCOHC.

57 *"lowering the tone of the Hearst papers"*: CVV, "Theodore Dreiser as I Knew Him," *Fragments from an Unwritten Autobiography*, vol. 2 (New Haven, CT: Yale University Press, 1955), 3.

57 *"New York, my dear . . . restaurants"*: CVV to Leah Maynard, January 1907, Kellner, *Letters of Carl Van Vechten*, 3.

58 *On the Lower East Side . . . world*: In 1907 the journalist Barton W. Currie investigated the nickelodeons of New York City and estimated that they entertained around two hundred thousand customers a day. Barton W. Currie, "The Nickel Madness," *Movies and American Society*, ed. Steven J. Ross (Oxford: Blackwell Publishers, 2002), 32–37.

58 *"one's trousers full of maybugs"*: Richard Strauss, *Recollections and Reflections*, trans. L. J. Lawrence (London: Boosey & Hawkes, 1953), 152.

59 *It lacked the insight . . . opera*: CVV, "Salome: The Most Sensational Opera of the Age," *Broadway Magazine* 17 (January 1907), 381–91.

59 *He wrote Leah . . . match it*: CVV to Leah Maynard, January 1907, Kellner, *Letters of Carl Van Vechten*, 3.

60 *"tense with a sort . . . fascinating"*: Richard Aldrich, "Strauss's 'Salome' the First Time Here," *New York Times*, January 23, 1907.

60 *"Her entrance was . . . staircase"*: CVV, "Olive Fremstad," *Interpreters and Interpretations* (New York: Alfred A. Knopf, 1917), 34.

60 *"I cannot yet . . . passion"*: Ibid.

62 *"overpowering and dominating temperament"*: Ibid., 11.

62 *"Salome is the worst . . . nothing"*: "Take Off 'Salome' Say Opera House Directors," *New York Times*, January 27, 1907, CVV scrapbook 1, Carl Van Vechten Papers, NYPL.

62 *"We take issue . . . text"*: "'Salome' Withdrawn; Conried Fully Yields," *New York Times*, January 31, 1907, CVV scrapbook 1, Carl Van Vechten Papers, NYPL.

63 *"In defence [sic] of bad taste"*: CVV, "In Defence of Bad Taste," *The Merry-Go-Round* (New York: Alfred A. Knopf, 1918), 11–20.

63–64 *"Caruso's Mustache Off . . . without it?"*: "Caruso's Mustache Off," *New York Times*, December 8, 1906, CVV scrapbook 1, Carl Van Vechten Papers, NYPL.

64 *Luisa Tetrazzini took to . . . fame*: Luisa Tetrazzini, "The Story of My Operatic Career by Luisa Tetrazzini," *Cosmopolitan* (June 1908): 49–51; and Tetrazzini, *My Life of Song* (London: Cassell & Company, 1921). Tetrazzini's autobiography gives an entertaining insight into this charismatic and self-regarding woman, as well as a vivid snapshot of the "golden era" of New York opera.

64 *"exuberant," "like a great . . . football"*: CVV, "Feodor Chaliapine," *Interpreters and Interpretations*, 98–99.

64 *"I spik English . . . you!"*: Ibid., 98.

65 *"The effect in" . . . memory*: Ibid., 99.

65 *"gilded, but shabby . . . crowded"*: CVV, "Oscar Hammerstein: An Epitaph," *In the Garret*, 238.

65 *"check all children . . . this one"*: "Baby Checked at Opera," *New York Times*, February 15, 1907, CVV scrapbook 1, Carl Van Vechten Papers, NYPL.

66 *"some of the artists . . . any more"*: The Reminiscences of Carl Van Vechten (April 1, 1960), 130, CCOHC.

4. A CERTAIN SENSUOUS CHARM

67 *"You don't pick up . . . wanting to"*: The Reminiscences of Carl Van Vechten (March 3, 1960), 27, CCOHC.

67 *"burst out of . . . desires"*: Lewis A. Erenberg, *Steppin' Out: New York Nightlife and the Transformation of American Culture, 1890–1930* (Westport, CT, and London: Greenwood Press, 1981), 24.

69 *At clubs like . . . regulars*: Ray Argyle, *Scott Joplin and the Age of Ragtime* (Jefferson, NC: McFarland, 2009), 65–78.

69 *Van Vechten insisted . . . double act*: The Reminiscences of Carl Van Vechten (March 3, 1960), 19–20, CCOHC.

69 *In the ramshackle . . . encounters*: Kevin Mumford, *Interzones: Black/White Sex Districts in Chicago and New York in the Early Twentieth Century* (New York: Columbia University Press, 1997).

69–70 *At the Bowery's . . . drag shows*: See George Chauncey's riveting study of New York's gay subcultures in early-twentieth-century New York: George Chauncey, *Gay New York: The Making of the Gay Male World, 1890–1940* (London: Flamingo, 1995), 34–45.

70 *Van Vechten's fascination . . . too*: The diaries of CVV's friend Edna Kenton make several brief but telling mentions of his love of slumming and "bohemian" pastimes, both in Chicago and in New York. Kenton's diaries for the years 1906 to 1914 are held as part of the Yale Collection of American Literature at the Beinecke Rare Book & Manuscript Library, Yale University.

70 *A fleeting moment . . . taken further*: Chauncey, *Gay New York*, 188–89.

70 *The myth of Leda . . . mainstream*: Paul Cézanne was one of many late-nineteenth-century painters to depict this scene, but the most famous articulation of the sexually subversive subtext of the Leda and the swan myth is W. B. Yeats's poem "Leda and the Swan," first published in 1924. At the same time that CVV started to wear his intaglio ring, the English writer and occultist Montague Summers was strutting around Oxford with an image of Leda and the swan engraved on his silver-topped cane.

71 *"but not without . . . tie"*: CVV, *Firecrackers: A Realistic Novel* (Alfred A. Knopf; New York, 1925), 45.

71 *In the poses . . . sexuality*: For lengthier analysis of CVV's homoerotic photography, see James Smalls, *The Homoerotic Photography of Carl Van Vechten: Public Face, Private Thoughts* (Philadelphia: Temple University Press, 2006), and Jonathan Weinberg, "Boy Crazy: Carl Van Vechten's Queer Collection," *Yale Journal of Criticism* 7, no. 2 (1994): 25–49.

71 *"the air of . . . wolf"*: Linda Simon, *The Biography of Alice B. Toklas* (Lincoln: University of Nebraska Press, 1991), 208.

71 *"gay, irresponsible and brilliant"*: Alice B. Toklas, *What Is Remembered* (New York: Holt, Rinehart and Winston, 1963), 126.

73 *"dead sweet affectionateness"*: Mabel Dodge Luhan, *Movers and Shakers*, vol. 3, *Intimate Memories* (New York: Harcourt, Brace, 1936), 45.

73 *"Women, seemingly, have . . . men"*: The Reminiscences of Carl Van Vechten (April 23, 1960), 144, CCOHC.

73 *"I am determined to be . . . forgive me!"*: Anna Elizabeth Snyder to CVV, August 31, 1904, Carl Van Vechten Papers, NYPL.

74 *"I do care . . . ever"*: Anna Elizabeth Snyder to CVV, September 8, 1904, Carl Van Vechten Papers, NYPL.

74 *Comparing the "pure passion" . . . adoration*: Anna Elizabeth Snyder to CVV, December 1, 1906, Carl Van Vechten Papers, NYPL.

74 *"Do you remember . . . you again"*: Anna Elizabeth Snyder to CVV, c. 1904, Carl Van Vechten Papers, NYPL.

74 *"all the men . . . years"*: Anna Elizabeth Snyder to CVV, February 20, 1907, Carl Van Vechten Papers, NYPL.

74 *the defense used . . . history*: Neil McKenna, *The Secret Life of Oscar Wilde* (London: Random House, 2011), 527.

75 *"with all the joy . . . before him"*: Ibid.

75 *"This wouldn't be . . . one another"*: Neith Boyce, "Art and Woman," unpublished manuscript, Hapgood Family Papers, YCAL. For analysis of Boyce and Hapgood's personal lives and professional works, see E. K. Trimberger, *Intimate Warriors* (New York: Feminist Press at CUNY, 1991).

76 *"I could never . . . with me"*: The Reminiscences of Carl Van Vechten (May 14, 1960), 259, CCOHC.

76 *"I am not writing . . . realities?"*: Anna Elizabeth Snyder to CVV, c. January 1907, Carl Van Vechten Papers, NYPL.

76 *"It shall be a day . . . you"*: Charles Duane Van Vechten to CVV, June 28, 1907, Carl Van Vechten Papers, NYPL.

77 *"It would be difficult . . . head"*: CVV, *Peter Whiffle: His Life and Works* (New York: Alfred A. Knopf, 1922), 19.

77 *"the first night . . . of it"*: Ibid., 19–20.

77 *"your indecent and . . . world"*: Edna Kenton to CVV, February 15, 1909, Carl Van Vechten Papers, YCAL.

77 *"It wasn't formal . . . delightful"*: The Reminiscences of Carl Van Vechten (April 9, 1960), 121, CCOHC.

78 *"No American, with . . . behind you"*: CVV, "Some Literary Ladies I Have Known," *Fragments from an Unwritten Autobiography*, vol. 2, 53.

78 *"I don't think . . . wanted"*: The Reminiscences of Carl Van Vechten (April 9, 1960), 122, CCOHC.

78 *On his return . . . himself*: The historian Arthur Frank Wertheim expands on the importance of 1908 in New York as the genesis moment for modern American culture. Arthur Frank Wertheim, *The New York Little Renaissance* (New York: New York University Press, 1976).

79 *"ritual, pleasure, light-heartedness . . . need"*: Van Wyck Brooks, *The Wine of the Puritans: A Study of Present Day America* (London: Sisley's, 1909), 15.

79 *"the elements of . . . left out"*: Levine, *Highbrow/Lowbrow*, 214.

80 *"I was almost . . . dancing"*: CVV, "Terpsichorean Souvenirs," Padgette, *Dance Writings of Carl Van Vechten*, 6–7.

82 *"the corporeality of things"*: Charles Caffin, "Henri Matisse and Isadora Duncan," *Camera Work*, no. 25 (January 1909): 17–30.

82 *"life and gaiety . . . Samothrace"*: "Isadora Duncan Reappears," *New York Times*, November 10, 1909, CVV scrapbook 1, Carl Van Vechten Papers, NYPL; "Miss Duncan's Vivid Dances," *New York Times*, November 17, 1909, CVV scrapbook 1, Carl Van Vechten Papers, NYPL.

82 *"a sacrilege" her use . . . "dancing"*: Ibid.

82 *"an inartistic child"*: "Annual Fall Salon Exhibit of Freaks," *New York Times*, October 3, 1908, CVV scrapbook 2, Carl Van Vechten Papers, NYPL.

82 *"Like any other . . . to me"*: CVV, "The New Isadora," *Merry-Go-Round*, 314.

82–83 *"a more sensuous . . . emotion"*: "Loie Fuller Shows Her Dancing Girls," *New York Times*, December 1, 1909, CVV scrapbook 3, Carl Van Vechten Papers, NYPL.

83 *"there were no . . . applause"*: "Maud Allan as Salome," *New York Times*, January 30, 1910, CVV scrapbook 3, Carl Van Vechten Papers, NYPL.

83 *"grace, a picturesque . . . head"*: "Maud Allan in Greek Dances," *New York Times*, January 21, 1910, CVV scrapbook 3, Carl Van Vechten Papers, NYPL.

84 *"I not only . . . desire you"*: Anna Elizabeth Snyder to CVV, May 16, 1911, Carl Van Vechten Papers, NYPL.

84 *"suppress the tale . . . opinion"*: Elsie Stern Caskey to CVV, January 26, 1912, Carl Van Vechten Papers, NYPL.

84–85 *In his memoirs . . . graduation*: Bruce Kellner, "Carlo's Wife," *Kiss Me Again: An Invitation to a Group of Noble Dames* (New York: Turtle Point Press, 2002), 183.

85 *"the things you have not . . . written"*: Charles Lewis Fitch to CVV, February 19, 1912, Carl Van Vechten Papers, NYPL.

85 *"she influenced me . . . progress"*: The Reminiscences of Carl Van Vechten (April 9, 1960), 136, CCOHC.

86 *"I can stop . . . hard"*: The Reminiscences of Carl Van Vechten (May 25, 1960), 354, CCOHC.

86 *According to the accounts . . . stardom*: CVV, "Fania Marinoff's Memoirs," unpublished manuscript, Carl Van Vechten Papers, NYPL; Kellner, *Kiss Me Again*, 170–73.

86 *"a maid of . . . charm"*: The Reminiscences of Carl Van Vechten (April 9, 1960), 150, CCOHC.

86 *"If there was a door . . . through it"*: Reverend Peter Francis O'Brien, S.J., interview with author, October 2011. O'Brien paraphrased a line from "Waiting in the Wings," Noël Coward's play about a retirement home for actresses.

88 *"prompt responses for . . . automatic"*: Mabel Dodge Luhan, "Twelfth Night," unpublished manuscript, Mabel Dodge Luhan Papers, YCAL.

88 *"Darlingest Angel baby . . . sure"*: CVV to FM, May 19, 1913, Carl Van Vechten Papers, NYPL; Kellner, *Letters of Carl Van Vechten*, 4.

89 *"I must have kisses . . . over me"*: Charles Duane Van Vechten to Ada Fitch, April 9, 1861, and March 30, 1861, Carl Van Vechten Papers, NYPL.

89 *"the only one . . . satisfies me"*: CVV to Fania Marinoff, July 13, 1913, Carl Van Vechten Papers, NYPL; Kellner, *Letters of Carl Van Vechten*, 8.

90 *"Fania's native intelligence . . . worthless"*: The Reminiscences of Carl Van Vechten (April 23, 1960), 150a, CCOHC.

5. HOW TO READ GERTRUDE STEIN

91 *"Any one or two . . . first one"*: "Real Music and Art Rising out of a Sea of Fake," *New York Times*, March 9, 1913, CVV scrapbook 8, Carl Van Vechten Papers, NYPL.

91–92 *"We have left . . . ugly!"*: Mabel Dodge Luhan, *European Experiences*, vol. 2, *Intimate Memories* (New York: Harcourt, Brace, 1935), 453.

92 *"a repudiation of grimy New York"*: Dodge Luhan, *Movers and Shakers*, 5.

92 *According to Dodge . . . "malice"*: Ibid., 14–15.

92 *"affectionate fun . . . hope"*: Ibid., 15.

92–93 *"warm friendships for . . . rooms"*: Ibid., 16.

93 *"Curtis Cigarettes, poured . . . piano"*: CVV, *Peter Whiffle*, 145. In CVV's semiautobiographical novel *Peter Whiffle*, Mabel appears as a character named Edith Dale, a celebrated salon hostess. His descriptions of Dale's salon were based directly on CVV's experiences at 23 Fifth Avenue.

93 *"The groups separated . . . whisky"*: Ibid., 124.

95 *"women in low-necked . . . locks"*: Ross Wetzsteon, *Republic of Dreams: Greenwich Village: The American Bohemia, 1910–1960* (New York: Simon and Schuster, 2002), 23.

95 *"The man strummed . . . hands"*: Dodge Luhan, *Movers and Shakers*, 80.

96 *In the early nineteenth century . . . raised*: Eric Lott, *Blackface Minstrelsy and the American Working Class* (New York and Oxford: Oxford University Press, 1993), 49–55.

97 *"I think I owe . . . person"*: CVV, "Some Literary Ladies I Have Known," *Fragments from an Unwritten Autobiography*, vol. 2, 36.

97 *"The days are . . . pleasant"*: Gertrude Stein, *Portrait of Mabel Dodge at the Villa Curonia* (Ann Arbor, MI: University Microfilms International, 1994), 1.

98–99 *"cubist of letters . . . view"*: "Cubist of Letters Writes New Book," *New York Times*, February 24, 1913, CVV scrapbook 8, Carl Van Vechten Papers, NYPL.

99 *"Everybody went and . . . nickel"*: CVV, *Peter Whiffle*, 123.

100 *"seized upon the . . . pay"*: "Cubists and Futurists Are Making Insanity Pay," *New York Times*, March 16, 1913.

100 *"Art Show Open to Freaks"*: Patricia Bradley, *Making American Culture: A Social History, 1900–1920* (New York: Palgrave Macmillan, 2009), 128.

100 *As the historian Patricia Bradley . . . together*: Ibid., 117–34.

101 *He wrote Marinoff . . . both*: CVV to FM, May 19, 1913, Carl Van Vechten Papers, NYPL.

101 *"altogether disgusting"*: CVV to FM, May 19, 1913, Carl Van Vechten Papers, NYPL; Kellner, *Letters of Carl Van Vechten*, 5.

102 *"erect Tom-Tom's . . . mine"*: CVV to FM, May 19, 1913, Carl Van Vechten Papers, NYPL; Kellner, *Letters of Carl Van Vechten*, 5.

102 *"a wonderful personality"*: CVV to FM, June 2, 1913, Carl Van Vechten Papers, NYPL; Kellner, *Letters of Carl Van Vechten*, 6.

102 *"villain of Mrs. Van Vechten's tragic tale"*: Gertrude Stein, *The Autobiography of Alice B. Toklas* (London: John Lane, The Bodley Head, 1933), 149.

102–103 *"a Roman emperor . . . guests"*: Bravig Imbs, *Confessions of Another Young Man* (New York: Henkle-Yewdale House, 1936), 162.

103 *That first performance . . . morning*: The reports even found their way back to New York, where the *Times* described the ballet as "the last degree of stupidity" in an article published June 8, 1913.

103–104 *In a letter . . . "beautiful"*: CVV to FM, June 4, 1913, Carl Van Vechten Papers, NYPL; Kellner, *Letters of Carl Van Vechten*, 6.

104 *"provocation and event"*: Modris Eksteins, *The Rites of Spring: The Great War and the Birth of the Modern Age* (Boston and New York: Houghton Mifflin, 1989), 15.

104 *"A certain part . . . evening"*: CVV, *Music After the Great War* (New York: G. Schirmer, 1915), 87.

104–105 *"to beat rhythmically . . . ourselves"*: Ibid.

105 *Van Vechten never intended . . . value*: In Modris Eksteins's fascinating exploration of the significance of the first night of *Le Sacre du Printemps* he questions the accuracy of CVV's recollections but not his core assertion that he really was there.

105 *"one must only be accurate . . . fiction"*: CVV to Gertrude Stein, May 17, 1913, Edward Burns, ed., *The Letters of Gertrude Stein and Carl Van Vechten, 1913–1946* (New York: Columbia University Press, 1986), 54.

105 "Au revoir et merci": Dodge Luhan, *Movers and Shakers*, 217.

106 *Van Vechten took to the task . . . conversation*: Muriel Draper, *Music at Midnight* (New York and London: Harper & Brothers, 1929), 121–24.

107 *He praised its . . . "shriek"*: "New York's 'Darktown' Would Do Well on Broadway," *New York Press*, December 14, 1913, CVV scrapbook 9, Carl Van Vechten Papers, NYPL.

107 *"One thing is certain . . . this one"*: Ibid.

107–108 *"is not an imitation . . . to us"*: "Real Thrills in 'Granny Maumee,' " *New York Press*, March 31, 1914, CVV scrapbook 9, Carl Van Vechten Papers, NYPL.

108 *"essentially Negro character"*: CVV, "The Negro Theatre," *In the Garret*, 319.

108 *he was so intoxicated . . . meaning*: CVV to Mabel Dodge, c. October 1913, Mabel Dodge Luhan Papers, YCAL; Kellner, ed., *Letters of Carl Van Vechten*, 9.

108 *Evans had befriended . . . principles*: Evans's unusual personality can be discovered in the strange letters he sent to Van Vechten between 1912 and 1922 in the Carl Van Vechten Papers, YCAL.

108 *"there are in America . . . only"*: Karen Leick, *Gertrude Stein and the Making of an American Celebrity* (New York: Routledge, 2009), 42.

109 *Frederick James Gregg . . . Painters*: Bradley, *Making American Culture*, 133.

109 *"Miss Stein drops . . . Prelude"*: CVV, "How to Read Gertrude Stein," *Gertrude Stein Remembered*, ed. Linda Simon (Lincoln: University of Nebraska Press, 1994), 41–48.

110 *"I have often questioned . . . satisfaction"*: Ibid., 42.

110 *"Her vagueness is . . . qualities"*: Ibid., 47.

110 *"turned language into . . . art"*: Ibid., 42.

110 *"I am very pleased . . . me"*: Gertrude Stein to CVV, October 25, 1914, Burns, *Letters of Gertrude Stein and Carl Van Vechten*, 31.

110 *"favorite genius"*: Phillip Herring, *Djuna: The Life and Works of Djuna Barnes* (New York: Viking, 1995), 93.

111 *Among a crowded itinerary . . . proximity*: CVV notebook, Carl Van Vechten Papers, NYPL. CVV kept a journal of his 1914 trip to Europe, the first such document since his college days.

111 *"intellectual Jewess . . . slippers"*: CVV notebook, Carl Van Vechten Papers, NYPL; Bruce Kellner, "Baby Woojums in Iowa," *Books at Iowa* 26 (1977): 3–18.

111 *It was obvious . . . famously*: CVV notebook, Carl Van Vechten Papers, NYPL.

111–112 *Upon his arrival . . . upset*: CVV notebook, August 1, 1914, Carl Van Vechten Papers, NYPL.

112 *As an old man . . . politics*: The Reminiscences of Carl Van Vechten (May 14, 1960), 263, CCOHC.

112 *When it came to elections . . . standing*: Ibid., 264.

112 *"stupid republican [sic] presidents"*: CVV daybooks, November 7, 1928, Carl Van Vechten Papers, NYPL; Bruce Kellner, ed., *The Splendid Drunken Twenties: Selections from the Daybooks, 1922–1930* (Urbana and Chicago: University of Illinois Press, 2003), 225.

112 *On the day . . . admired*: CVV notebooks, Carl Van Vechten Papers, NYPL.

112–113 *"I've done it all . . . to be"*: CVV, "July–August 1914," *Sacred and Profane Memories*, 119–20.

113 *"a mask of quiescent boredom"*: Dodge Luhan, *Movers and Shakers*, 290.

113 *"Just think . . . again"*: CVV, "July–August 1914," *Sacred and Profane Memories*, 118.

6. IN DEFENSE OF BAD TASTE

114–116 *"exclude stupidity, banality . . . beasts"*: CVV, "The Editor's Workbench," *Trend* 8, no. 1 (October 1914): 101.

116 *"destroy dilettantism and . . . marriage"*: CVV, "War Is Not Hell," *Trend* 8, no. 2 (November 1914): 147.

116 *"That is what the war . . . life"*: Ibid., 150.

117 *"gifted with the most magnetic . . . today"*: CVV, "Away Go the Critics, and On Come the Plays," *Trend* 8, no. 2 (November 1914): 239.

117 *Jolson sought Van Vechten . . . grabbed him*: CVV to FM, November 7, 1914, Carl Van Vechten Papers, NYPL.

118 *"While the alimony . . . dog"*: Ralph Van Vechten to CVV, April 16, 1912, Carl Van Vechten Papers, NYPL.

118 *"Don't fear anything . . . man"*: Charles Duane Van Vechten to CVV, March 26, 1915, Carl Van Vechten Papers, NYPL.

119 *"It was fearfully exciting . . . doctor"*: Louise Bryant to CVV, c. 1915, Carl Van Vechten Papers, YCAL.

119 *"The only place for a writer is prison"*: Mina Loy to CVV, March 12, 1915, Carl Van Vechten Papers, YCAL.

120 *Though Stein had numerous . . . awakening*: Loy's biographer Carolyn Burke maps out the crucial role that CVV played in helping Loy navigate her way between her feminist instincts and the intellectualized misogyny of Marinetti's futurism that so inspired her. Carolyn Burke, *Becoming Modern: The Life of Mina Loy* (New York: Farrar, Straus and Giroux, 1997).

121 *"for his unrestrained guests . . . I didn't"*: CVV, "How I Remember Joseph Hergesheimer," *Fragments from an Unwritten Autobiography*, vol. 1 (New Haven, CT: Yale University Press, 1955), 8.

121 *"Wonderful in their lithe . . . perfection"*: CVV, "On Visiting Fashionable Places out of Season," *Excavations: A Book of Advocacies* (New York: Alfred A. Knopf, 1926), 13.

121–122 *a "primitive jingle . . . sex"*: Ibid., 15.

122 *"wild leaps, whirls . . . Igor"*: Ibid.

122 *"strewn with dried palm . . . cries"*: CVV, "The Holy Jumpers," *In the Garret*, 141–42.

122 *"A young negress . . . still"*: Ibid., 143–45.

123 *"ecstasy of a Negro's sanctity"*: Ibid., 145.

123 *"Americans are easily thrilled . . . Ballet"*: Ibid., 134.

123 *"Americans have little aptitude . . . discussion"*: CVV, "In Defence of Bad Taste," *Merry-Go-Round*, 18.

123 *"it is preferable to be . . . cage"*: Ibid., 17.

124 *"is really distinctively American"*: "Ragtime's Rage a Regular Riot," April 1912, *New York Times,* CVV scrapbook 6, Carl Van Vechten Papers, NYPL.

124 *"has had its day"*: CVV, "Music After the Great War," *Music After the Great War,* 7.

125 *"beyond doubt that music . . . 1914"*: Ibid., 6.

125 *"considerable enjoyment but less sound sense"*: "Music After the War," *Springfield Republican,* March 26, 1916, CVV scrapbook 10, Carl Van Vechten Papers, NYPL.

125 *Modern music in America . . . rebellion*: For a detailed examination of the significance of CVV's work in developing an American critical tradition of modernism in music, see Carol J. Oja, *Making Music Modern: New York in the 1920s* (Oxford: Oxford University Press, 2000), 297–310.

125–126 *"His revolt . . . Greenwich Village"*: H. L. Mencken, "The Tone Art— Snowbirds in Hell, Presbyterians in Paris, Blondes Along the Niger, Musical Critics in the United States!," *Smart Set* (July 1916), CVV scrapbook 10, Carl Van Vechten Papers, NYPL.

126 *"has been in Paris . . . souls"*: Unidentified author and article, *New York Sun,* January 16, 1916, CVV scrapbook 10, Carl Van Vechten Papers, NYPL.

126 *"genial middle ground . . . slang"*: Van Wyck Brooks, *America's Coming of Age* (New York: B. W. Huebsch, 1915), 7.

126 *"the fullest expression . . . cubism"*: Christine Stansell, *American Moderns: Bohemian New York and the Creation of a New Century* (New York: Metropolitan Books, 2000), 6.

127 *"the enemy"*: CVV, "The Bridge Burners," *Music and Bad Manners* (New York: Alfred A. Knopf, 1916), 169.

127 *"even the extreme modern music . . . genius"*: Ibid.

128 *"Music has changed . . . hear"*: Ibid., 193.

128 *"vibrates with the unrest . . . war"*: CVV, "Leo Ornstein," *Music and Bad Manners,* 243.

128 *"not to make the world . . . pessimist"*: Donald Evans to CVV, July 5, 1917, Carl Van Vechten Papers, YCAL.

131 *"narrowly about your case . . . register"*: John Pitts Sanborn to CVV, June 16, 1917, Carl Van Vechten Papers, YCAL.

131 *"It is very exciting . . . converts"*: CVV to Gertrude Stein, April 5, 1917, Burns, *Letters of Gertrude Stein and Carl Van Vechten,* 58–59.

131 *Indeed, according to Van Vechten . . . gutter*: CVV to Gertrude Stein, April 5, 1917, Burns, ed., *Letters of Gertrude Stein and Carl Van Vechten,* 59.

131 *"Lewis F. Muir . . . 2001"*: CVV, "The Great American Composer," *Interpreters and Interpretations,* 270.

131–132 *"complicated vigor of American life"*: Ibid., 279.

132 *"Americans are inclined . . . same"*: Ibid., 281.

132 *"It is no more use . . . of us"*: Ibid., 284.

132 *"a vast body . . . baseball"*: H. L. Mencken, "The National Letters," *Smart Set* (February 1918), CVV scrapbook 11, Carl Van Vechten Papers, NYPL.

132 *"a man may be an American . . . America"*: Ibid.

132 *"He likes what is new . . . appreciation"*: "Interpreters and Interpretations," *Musical America* (July 13, 1918), CVV scrapbook 11, Carl Van Vechten Papers, NYPL.

133 *"It would be much better . . . Ornstein"*: Theodora Bean, "Readable Musical Criticism; A Talk with One Who Writes It—Carl Van Vechten," *New York Morning Telegraph*, February 24, 1918, CVV scrapbook 11, Carl Van Vechten Papers, NYPL.

135 *Upon the publication . . . men*: Charles Duane Van Vechten to CVV, March 19, 1916, Carl Van Vechten Papers, NYPL.

135 *"for musical people . . . people"*: Charles Duane Van Vechten to CVV, September 3, 1916, Carl Van Vechten Papers, NYPL.

135 *"Really it looks to us . . . enough"*: Charles Duane Van Vechten to CVV, August 24, 1918, Carl Van Vechten Papers, NYPL.

135–136 *Marshall's also attracted . . .* Interior: William B. Scott and Peter M. Rutkoff, *New York Modern: The Arts and the City* (Baltimore: Johns Hopkins University Press, 2001), 86.

136 *"Come with me . . . play"*: CVV, "Farfariello," *In the Garret*, 302–303.

136 *"working men in . . . theatre"*: Ibid.

136–137 *"No hysteria or . . . play"*: CVV, "Mimi Aguglia as Salome," *In the Garret*, 292.

137 *"New York . . . unobserved"*: CVV, "La Tigresse," *Sacred and Profane Memories*, 175.

7. WHAT ONE IS FORCED BY NATURE TO DO

138 *"It was an age . . . fun?"*: F. Scott Fitzgerald, "Echoes of the Jazz Age," *My Lost City: Personal Essays, 1920–1940*, ed. James L. W. West III (Cambridge, UK: Cambridge University Press, 2005), 131.

138 *"A young man . . . live"*: Malcolm Cowley, *Exile's Return: A Literary Odyssey of the 1920s* (London: Penguin Books, 1994), 79.

139 *Many decades later . . . apartment*: Donald Angus to Bruce Kellner, undated, Bruce Kellner Papers, YCAL.

140 *As they talked and drank . . . scrutinizing*: Ibid.

142 *"Baby Van Vechten"*: Kellner, "Carlo's Wife," *Kiss Me Again*, 181.

142 *In an echo . . . 1920*: Ibid. Kellner explains that precise dates for the adoption are impossible to ascertain because all the relevant documentation appears to have been deliberately destroyed.

143 *"for the good of your soul"*: Mabel Dodge Luhan to CVV, January 27, 1920, Carl Van Vechten Papers, YCAL.

143 *"has very strong . . . life"*: Ibid.

143 *Every time he received . . . cocaine*: CVV to Mabel Dodge, June 21, 1920, Mabel Dodge Luhan Papers, YCAL.

143 *"Your enhancing appreciation . . . daggers"*: Mabel Dodge to CVV, c. 1920, Carl Van Vechten Papers, YCAL.

143–144 *"held the firm belief . . . novelty"*: CVV, *Red*, ix.

144 *"not only brings . . . readers"*: Ibid., xiii.

144 *"orphic wall of my indecision"*: CVV, *Peter Whiffle*, 12.

144 *"a free fantasia . . . Rhapsody"*: Ibid., 15.

144 *"I have done too much . . . lived it"*: Ibid., 251.

144 *"It is necessary . . . to do"*: Ibid., 250.

145 *Van Vechten was . . . Exquisites*: Alfred Kazin, *On Native Grounds: An Interpretation of Modern American Literature* (New York: Harcourt, Brace, 1942), 227.

145 *The notional figurehead . . . 1919*: Kazin also included Thomas Beer, Elinor Wylie, and CVV's close friend and fellow Knopf author Joseph Hergesheimer in this group.

146 *"Melville's greatest book . . . world"*: CVV, "The Later Work of Herman Melville," *Excavations*, 79.

146 *"cosmopolitan, a sly humorist . . . Washington"*: Ibid., 77.

146 *"Why don't you decide . . . Pepys"*: Mabel Dodge to CVV, c. 1922, Carl Van Vechten Papers, YCAL.

147 *"The Twenties were famous . . . behavior"*: CVV, "How I Remember Joseph Hergesheimer," *Fragments from an Unwritten Autobiography*, vol. 1, 7.

147 *"the splendid drunken twenties"*: Ibid.

147 *During a typical . . . parties*: CVV daybooks, April–May 1922, Carl Van Vechten Papers, NYPL.

148 *"makes a provincial ass of himself"*: CVV daybooks, August 4, 1922, Carl Van Vechten Papers, NYPL; Kellner, *Splendid Drunken Twenties*, 10.

148 *"stood on her head . . . generally"*: CVV daybooks, September 25, 1922, Carl Van Vechten Papers, NYPL; Kellner, *Splendid Drunken Twenties*, 11.

148–150 *an "egotist" of "considerable charm"*: The Reminiscences of Carl Van Vechten (May 2, 1960), 218, CCOHC.

150 *"guide to fast life . . . sense"*: CVV, *The Blind Bow-Boy* (New York: Alfred A. Knopf, 1923), 59.

150 *"the manly American"*: Ibid., 95.

151 *"Ferris wheels . . . education"*: Ibid., 75–76.

151 *"A thing of beauty is a boy forever"*: CVV, *The Blind Bow-Boy*, 117.

152 *"impudent sissies that clutter Times Square"*: Chauncey, *Gay New York*, 308–309.

152 *"that is what any . . . happiness"*: Herbert Armstrong Jaggard, Jr., to CVV, December 3, 1925, Carl Van Vechten Papers, NYPL.

154 *"He knew everyone . . . Day"*: George George to Bruce Kellner, May 29, 1980, Bruce Kellner Papers, YCAL.

154 *"It is impertinent . . . capital"*: Sinclair Lewis to CVV, September 27, 1923, Carl Van Vechten Papers, NYPL.

154 *The reader summarized . . . "pictures"*: Winnifred Reeve to CVV, April 29, 1925, Carl Van Vechten Papers, NYPL.

155 *"The new book . . . know"*: Charles Duane Van Vechten to CVV, August 10, 1923, Carl Van Vechten Papers, NYPL.

155 *Just before Christmas . . . with him*: Charles Duane Van Vechten to CVV, December 17, 1923, Carl Van Vechten Papers, NYPL.

155 *"very clever" novel . . . "yourself"*: Charles Lewis Fitch to CVV, August 13, 1923, CVV Papers, NYPL.

155 *"Very suddenly, out of . . . money"*: The Reminiscences of Carl Van Vechten (May 2, 1960), 202, CCOHC.

155 *The occasion was recorded . . . paid*: CVV daybooks, December 13, 1923, Carl Van Vechten Papers, NYPL.

156 *"The kind of writing . . . better"*: CVV to Ralph Van Vechten, February 7, 1919, Carl Van Vechten Papers, NYPL; Kellner, *Letters of Carl Van Vechten*, 27–28.

156 *"alert intelligence . . . sets in"*: CVV, *Tattooed Countess*, 1.

157 *To his friend . . . "sophistication"*: CVV to Hugh Walpole, October 18, 1924, Hugh Walpole Collection, Berg; Kellner, *Letters of Carl Van Vechten*, 72.

157 *"the Countess was certainly full of pricks"*: CVV to Arthur Davison Ficke, August 30, 1924, Arthur Davison Ficke Papers, YCAL; CVV, quoted by Bruce Kellner in introduction to *Tattooed Countess*, xix–xx.

158 *"a sort of invisible force . . . possible"*: Shirer, *Start: 1904–1930*, 186.

158 *During his visit . . . at once*: CVV to FM, October 24, 1924, Carl Van Vechten Papers, NYPL.

159 *"Carl Van Vechten . . . read"*: CVV, "Some Literary Ladies I Have Known," *Fragments from an Unwritten Autobiography*, vol. 2, 44.

160 *"Beyond a doubt . . . more"*: CVV to Ronald Firbank, October 30, 1923, Carl Van Vechten Papers, Berg; Kellner, *Letters of Carl Van Vechten*, 58.

160 *"title is delicious"*: Ronald Firbank to CVV, November 17, 1923, Ronald Firbank Papers, Berg.

161 *"an autocratic way . . . wanted"*: Mark Lutz to Bruce Kellner, June 11, 1968, Bruce Kellner Papers, YCAL.

161 *"My books are . . . champion them"*: Ronald Firbank to CVV, December 16, 1924, Ronald Firbank Papers, Berg.

161 *"I seemed always to be . . . critics"*: CVV, *Red*, xi.

162 *One evening the following . . . Blue*: CVV daybook, January 17, 1924, Carl Van Vechten Papers, NYPL.

162–164 *"He [Gershwin] has . . . Nègres!"*: CVV to Hugh Walpole, October 18, 1924, Hugh Walpole Papers, Berg; Kellner, *Letters of Carl Van Vechten*, 73.

164 *Even Paul Rosenfeld . . . flaw*: Paul Rosenfeld, *By Way of Art: Criticisms of Music, Literature, Painting, Sculpture, and the Dance* (New York: Coward-McCann, 1928) provides a good overview of Rosenfeld's ideas about jazz, modern art, and America. Carol J. Oja, *Making Music Matter*, has much of interest to say about the differences between CVV's and Rosenfeld's views on jazz and modern music in the United States.

164 *"Jazz may not be . . . hope"*: CVV, *Red*, xv.

8. AN ENTIRELY NEW KIND OF NEGRO

166 *"It was Paul . . . agreeable"*: CVV, *Firecrackers*, 1.

166–167 *"You're too evolved . . . manifestations"*: Mabel Dodge to CVV, September 24, 1924, Carl Van Vechten Papers, YCAL.

167 *"who sleeps with who isn't funny anymore"*: Mabel Dodge to CVV, October 17, 1924, Carl Van Vechten Papers, YCAL.

167 *"a great negro novel"*: CVV daybooks, June 19, 1924, Carl Van Vechten Papers, NYPL; Kellner, *Splendid Drunken Twenties*, 52.

167 *"I had no idea . . . mine"*: Walter White to CVV, August 7, 1924, Carl Van Vechten Papers, YCAL.

167 *The two men . . . immediately*: CVV daybooks, August 26, 1924, Carl Van Vechten Papers, NYPL.

169 *"most Negroes have a talent for acting"*: CVV, "The Negro Theatre," *In the Garret*, 320.

169 *"How the darkies . . . lives"*: Ibid., 316.

169 *He wrote an excited letter . . . about him*: CVV to Mabel Dodge Luhan, c. October 1924, Mabel Dodge Luhan Papers, YCAL.

169–170 *"He speaks French . . . circles"*: CVV to Edna Kenton, c. August 1924, Edna Kenton Papers, YCAL; Kellner, *Letters of Carl Van Vechten*, 69.

170 *"was a hustler"*: The Reminiscences of Carl Van Vechten (March 3, 1960), 20, CCOHC.

170 *"I was never completely sold on Walter"*: The Reminiscences of Carl Van Vechten (May 14, 1960), 266, CCOHC.

170 *"I was no particular . . . to me"*: Ibid., 272.

170 *"he served his purpose"*: Ibid.

171 *"was a miracle straight out of the skies"*: James Weldon Johnson, *Black Manhattan* (New York: Alfred A. Knopf, 1930), 3.

171 *In November, as . . . "pianists"*: CVV to Gertrude Stein, November 15, 1924; Burns, *Letters of Gertrude Stein and Carl Van Vechten*, 208.

171 *"violently interested in . . . addiction"*: The Reminiscences of Carl Van Vechten (May 2, 1960), 193, CCOHC.

173 *"the great black walled city"*: CVV, quoted by Kathleen Pfeiffer in introduction to *Nigger Heaven* (Urbana and Chicago: University of Illinois Press, 2000), xxiv.

174 *"Harlem is laughing . . . home"*: "Harlem Laughs as Night Club Is Smashed Up," *Afro American*, January 25, 1930.

174 *"bright, crowded with . . . laughter"*: Claude McKay, *Home to Harlem* (Lebanon, NH: University Press of New England, 2012), 250.

175 *"adorable, rich, chic"*: CVV to Gertrude Stein, July 24, 1926; Burns, *Letters of Gertrude Stein and Carl Van Vechten*, 131.

175–177 *Small's Paradise, where . . . cocaine*: CVV daybook, March 19, 1925, Carl Van Vechten Papers, NYPL.

177 *"was surely as gay as it was black"*: Henry Louis Gates, "The Black Man's Burden," *Fear of a Queer Planet*, ed. Michael Warner (Minneapolis: University of Minneapolis Press, 1993), 233.

177 *The male writers . . . era*: The cultural historian Ann Douglas poses an interesting thought experiment on the subject. "Try to imagine," Douglas prods, "what the white 1920s generation would have been like if, like the Harlem Renaissance, its most important male ringleaders and spokesmen—say Sinclair Lewis, Mencken, Fitzgerald, and Hemingway—had been homosexual. One almost can't do it; the differences are too immense, too complex." Ann Douglas, *Terrible Honesty: Mongrel Manhattan in the 1920s* (New York: Farrar, Straus and Giroux, 1995), 97.

177 *"they undressed by . . . Beauty"*: Richard Bruce Nugent, "Smoke, Lilies and Jade," *Gay Rebel of the Harlem Renaissance*, ed. Thomas Wirth (Durham, NC: Duke University Press, 2002), 82.

177 *It is worth noting . . . living*: Richard Bruce Nugent to CVV, January 26, 1942, Carl Van Vechten Papers, YCAL.

177 *"Harlem was very much . . . closet"*: Ibid., 21.

177–178 *In one of his first . . . orgies*: CVV daybook, March 10, 1925, Carl Van Vechten Papers, NYPL. Donald Angus gave an account of the incident to Bruce Kellner: *Splendid Drunken Twenties*, 76.

178 *"All around the den . . . busy above"*: McKay, *Home to Harlem*, 31.

178 *"young black entertainer . . . disappeared"*: Chad Heap, *Slumming: Sexual and Racial Encounters in American Nightlife, 1885–1940* (Chicago and London: University of Chicago Press, 2008), 259.

178 *He was part . . . projected*: CVV daybook, January 10, 1924, Carl Van Vechten Papers, NYPL. CVV records that one of those movies was *Strictly Union*, a heterosexual picture notable to historians of the genre for featuring a high-concept story line about the arrival of trade unions in Hollywood—it was made by aspiring mainstream directors who could not get a break with any of the big studios—as well as for being the first known American film to feature graphic close-ups of various sexual acts, such as fellatio and penetration.

178 *he badgered Arthur . . . behalf*: Arthur Davison Ficke to CVV, October 4, 1922, Carl Van Vechten Papers, YCAL; see also the exchange of letters between CVV and Ficke throughout 1922 on this issue, in Van Vechten and Ficke collections at YCAL.

178 *"give a remarkable performance . . . etc."*: CVV daybook, September 29, 1925, Carl Van Vechten Papers, NYPL; Kellner, *Splendid Drunken Twenties*, 97.

179 *"He was extraordinary . . . anything"*: The Reminiscences of Carl Van Vechten (May 2, 1960), 217, CCOHC.

180 *"in great glee . . . as one"*: Ibid., 197.

180 *"a lovely, lovely dry Martini"*: Chris Albertson, *Bessie* (New Haven, CT: Yale University Press, 2005), 172.

180 *"full of shouting . . . sensuous too"*: CVV, "Moanin' wid a Sword in Ma Han'," *Vanity Fair* (February 1926): 61.

180 *"Get the fuck . . . shit"*: Albertson, *Bessie*, 174.

181 *It is worth noting . . . numbers*: CVV daybook, December 4, 1928, Carl Van Vechten Papers, NYPL.

181 *"really thrilling experience"*: CVV to Scott Cunningham, c. January 1925; Kellner, *Letters of Carl Van Vechten*, 74–75.

182 *"the unpretentious sincerity . . . known"*: CVV, "The Folksongs of the American Negro," *Vanity Fair* (July 1925): 52.

182 *"the new American Caruso"*: Martin Bauml Duberman, *Paul Robeson: A Biography* (New York: Alfred A. Knopf, 1989), 80.

182 *To Gertrude Stein . . . Chaliapin*: CVV to Gertrude Stein, June 30, 1925; Burns, *Letters of Gertrude Stein and Carl Van Vechten*, 116.

182–184 *Van Vechten, pained . . . than his*: CVV to FM, May 8, 1925, May 27, 1925, and May 30, 1925, Carl Van Vechten Papers, NYPL.

184 *The evening after she left . . . dawn*: CVV daybook, April 29, 1925, Carl Van Vechten Papers, NYPL.

185 *"Droning a drowsy . . . croon"*: Langston Hughes, "The Weary Blues," *The Weary Blues* (New York: Alfred A. Knopf, 1929), 9

185 *"who sang the blues . . . rock"*: Langston Hughes, *The Big Sea* (New York: Hill and Wang, 1963), 110.

185 *"heritage of rhythm and warmth"*: Langston Hughes, "The Negro Artist and the Racial Mountain," cited in Nathan Irving Huggins, ed., *Voices of the Harlem Renaissance* (Oxford: Oxford University Press, 1995), 307.

185 *"the low-down folks . . . standardizations"*: Ibid., 306.

185 *"people who have their hip . . . go by"*: Ibid.

186 *"I shall write . . . Covarrubias"*: CVV to Langston Hughes, June 24, 1925, Emily Bernard, ed., *Remember Me to Harlem: The Letters of Langston Hughes and Carl Van Vechten* (New York: Vintage Books, 2002), 10–11.

186 *"You're my good angel . . . flying!"*: Langston Hughes to CVV, May 18, 1925, Bernard, *Remember Me to Harlem*, 15.

186 *He worried that . . . sex*: Rampersad, *The Life of Langston Hughes—Volume I: 1902–1941: I, Too, Sing America* (New York and Oxford: Oxford University Press, 1986), 116; Bernard, *Remember Me to Harlem*, 16.

186 *"The influence, if . . . side"*: CVV to Langston Hughes, c. April 1927, Bernard, *Remember Me to Harlem*, 48–49.

186–187 *In his very first letter . . . Haiti*: CVV to Langston Hughes, May 6, 1925, Bernard, *Remember Me to Harlem*, 4.

187 *Soon after, he also . . . doing so*: CVV to Langston Hughes, May 13, 1925, and Langston Hughes to CVV, May 17, 1925, Bernard, *Remember Me to Harlem*, 6–7, 10–11.

187 *"Do not let any lionizers stampede you"*: Rampersad, *I, Too, Sing America*, 119.

187 *"a nice boy"*: Wirth, *Gay Rebel of the Harlem Renaissance*, 226.

187 *"beginning to sound . . . remain"*: Duberman, *Paul Robeson*, 85.

189 *"it was you who made me sing"*: Paul Robeson to CVV, October 21, 1927, Carl Van Vechten Papers, YCAL.

189 *"their independence and . . . indecency"*: Jody Blake, *Le Tumulte Noir: Modernist Art and Popular Entertainment in Jazz Age Paris, 1900–1930* (University Park: Pennsylvania State University Press, 1999), 93.

189 *"strong coffee before the cream is poured in"*: CVV, "Prescription for the Negro Theatre," *Vanity Fair* (October 1925): 98.

189–190 *"a wild pantomimic . . . passion"*: Ibid.

190 *"coining money out of niggers"*: Emily Bernard, *Carl Van Vechten and the Harlem Renaissance: A Portrait in Black and White* (New Haven, CT, and London: Yale University Press, 2012), 119.

191 *"voice, choking with . . . artist!"*: CVV, "Prescription for the Negro Theatre," 92.

191 *"The music of the Blues . . . combinations"*: Ibid., 44.

191 *"Mr. Van Vechten . . . cheers"*: James F. Wilson, *Bulldaggers, Pansies, and Chocolate Babies: Performance, Race, and Sexuality in the Harlem Renaissance* (Ann Arbor: University of Michigan Press, 2010), 139.

192 *He once wrote . . . enjoy*: CVV to James Weldon Johnson, October 11, 1933, James Weldon Johnson and Grace Nail Johnson Papers, YCAL.

192 *According to a report . . . otherwise*: "Author Thought Tiny White Girl Was Colored/Offered to Place 'Brown' Lassie, He Met at Party, in Broadway

Show/LEARNS OF JOKE/Writer Insists Girl Is of Black Origin—Tells Her So; Then She Yells," *Zit's Theatrical Newspaper*, April 7, 1928, CVV scrapbook 22, Carl Van Vechten Papers, NYPL.

193 *By 1927 his . . . population*: John E. Pember, "Race Amalgamation Will Settle American Problem: An Interview with Carl Van Vechten," *Chicago Defender*, March 26, 1927, CVV scrapbook 21, Carl Van Vechten Papers, NYPL.

194 *Hurston believed as fervently . . . relationship*: Robert E. Hemenway, *Zora Neale Hurston: A Literary Biography* (Urbana and Chicago: University of Illinois Press, 1980), 104–33.

194 *"I have taken . . . to be"*: Ibid., 109.

194 *"the guard-mother . . . Zora"*: Douglas, *Terrible Honesty*, 282–86.

194 *Over two decades . . . islands*: Zora Neale Hurston to CVV, various dates between 1925 and 1945, Carl Van Vechten Papers, YCAL.

196 *"the importance—and insignificance—of racial difference"*: Bernard, *Carl Van Vechten and the Harlem Renaissance*, 43.

196 *"You are just . . . or not"*: Harold Jackman to CVV, February 14, 1925, Carl Van Vechten Papers, YCAL.

9. EXOTIC MATERIAL

197 *"a Negro novel"*: CVV to FM, October 23, 1924, Carl Van Vechten Papers, NYPL.

198 *"comparatively easy for me . . . stop-time!"*: CVV to Langston Hughes, June 4, 1925, Bernard, *Remember Me to Harlem*, 17.

198 *The following month . . . setting*: CVV to Gertrude Stein, June 30, 1925, Burns, *Letters of Gertrude Stein and Carl Van Vechten*, 116.

198 *"the nigger book"*: Gertrude Stein to CVV, July 21, 1925, Burns, *Letters of Gertrude Stein and Carl Van Vechten*, 119.

198 *"Title of 'Nigger Heaven' comes to me today"*: CVV daybook, August 14, 1925, Carl Van Vechten Papers, NYPL; Kellner, *Splendid Drunken Twenties*, 93.

198 *"found so good a title . . . write"*: CVV to Scott Cunningham, August 16, 1925, Kellner, *Letters of Carl Van Vechten*, 82.

199 *"primitive birthright . . . emotion"*: Ibid., 89–90.

200 *"men and women . . . evil rites"*: Ibid., 254–55.

201 *Grace Nail Johnson . . . with it*: CVV daybooks, November 25, 1925, Carl Van Vechten Papers, NYPL.

201 *Walter White judged . . . himself*: CVV daybooks, December 1, 1925, Carl Van Vechten Papers, NYPL.

201 *Countee Cullen . . . thing*: CVV daybooks, November 27, 1925, Carl Van Vechten Papers, NYPL.

201 *Van Vechten dismissed . . . people*: CVV daybook, November 28, 1925 Carl Van Vechten Papers, NYPL.

202 *"It had more . . . understand"*: The Reminiscences of Carl Van Vechten (May 2, 1960), 208, CCOHC.

202 *"is freely used . . . resented"*: CVV, *Nigger Heaven*, 26.

202 *"Your 'Nigger Heaven' . . . blacks"*: Charles Duane Van Vechten to CVV, November 28, 1925, Carl Van Vechten Papers, NYPL.

203 *"You are accustomed . . . change it"*: Charles Duane Van Vechten to CVV, December 7, 1925, Carl Van Vechten Papers, NYPL.

203 *On the ninth . . . indulgence*: CVV daybook, January 10, 1925, Carl Van Vechten Papers, NYPL.

203 *He told Hugh . . . again*: CVV to Hugh Walpole, March 7, 1926, Hugh Walpole Collection, Berg.

204 *"the race is getting more popular every day"*: CVV to Gertrude Stein, March 4, 1926, Burns, *Letters of Gertrude Stein and Carl Van Vechten*, 127.

204–205 *"The squalor of Negro life . . . remains?"*: CVV, "The Negro in Art: How Shall He Be Portrayed?," *Crisis* (March 1926): 219.

206 *"shoutin', moanin', yelling . . . jungle"*: CVV daybook, May 23, 1926, Carl Van Vechten Papers, NYPL; Kellner, *Splendid Drunken Twenties*, 120.

206 *During a trip to Virginia . . . Harlem*: CVV to FM, April 20, 1926, Carl Van Vechten Papers, NYPL.

206 *"There is seldom" . . . race*: Robert F. Worth, "*Nigger Heaven* and the Harlem Renaissance," *African American Review* 29, no. 3 (Autumn 1995): 461.

207 *"She says she is . . . for me?"*: CVV daybook, June 25, 1926 Carl Van Vechten Papers, NYPL; Kellner, *Splendid Drunken Twenties*, 125.

207 *"I was having an affair . . . but—"*: Cecilia Garrard, "And the Famous Man Washes Dishes at Home/Wife Says Carl Van Vechten Likes to Do Them," *Brooklyn Eagle*, October 4, 1925, CVV scrapbook 17, Carl Van Vechten Papers, NYPL.

207–208 *Early the next week . . . fitting*: CVV daybook, June 29, 1926, Carl Van Vechten Papers, NYPL.

208 *"between the covers . . . world"*: Advertisement from *Publishers Weekly*, June 26, 1926, CVV scrapbook 18, Carl Van Vechten Papers, NYPL.

208 *"careful observations . . . passion"*: Walter Yust, "Novels by Van Vechten and Pio Baroja," *New York Evening Post Literary Review*, August 21, 1926, CVV scrapbook 18, Carl Van Vechten Papers, NYPL.

208 *"understanding and insight"*: Edwin Clark, "Carl Van Vechten's Novel of Harlem Negro Life," *New York Times Book Review*, August 22, 1926, CVV scrapbook 18, Carl Van Vechten Papers, NYPL.

208 *"lived among the colored . . . think"*: "New Light on Negro Ideals and Destiny," *New York Evening Graphic*, August 21, 1926, CVV scrapbook 18, Carl Van Vechten Papers, NYPL.

208 *"a second-hand dish . . . we are"*: Nathan Irving Huggins, *Harlem Renaissance* (Oxford and New York: Oxford University Press, 2007), 114.

208 *"purity of race"*: M. P. Shiel to CVV, c. July 1926, Carl Van Vechten Papers, NYPL.

209 *To the fashionable white crowd . . . hands*: Sinclair Lewis to CVV, September 20, 1926, and Henry Mencken to CVV, August 4, 1926, Carl Van Vechten Papers, NYPL; F. Scott Fitzgerald to CVV, c. 1926, Carl Van Vechten Papers, YCAL.

209 *"one of the most enthralling . . . Harlem"*: Press advertisement, CVV scrapbook 19, Carl Van Vechten Papers, NYPL.

209 *"the Race . . . aren't they?"*: Arthur Davison Ficke to CVV, August 8, 1926, CVV Papers, NYPL.

209 *The Van Vechtens' housekeeper . . . press*: CVV daybook, September 3, 1926, Carl Van Vechten Papers, NYPL.

209 *"with their noses arched . . . eyelids"*: "Van Vechten's Book," *Norfolk Journal & Guide*, September 23, 1926, CVV scrapbook 19, Carl Van Vechten Papers, NYPL.

210 *"You mean to say . . . nigger?"*: Eden Bliss, "This Harlem," *Afro American*, CVV scrapbook 19, Carl Van Vechten Papers, NYPL.

210 *"We don't care . . . exaggerated about"*: Lewis Baer to CVV, September 28, 1926, Carl Van Vechten Papers, NYPL.

210 *"somebody does something . . . immediately"*: The Reminiscences of Carl Van Vechten (May 25, 1960), 354, CCOHC.

212 *"The cries of protest . . . Paris"*: Nora Holt to CVV, August 17, 1926, Carl Van Vechten Papers, YCAL.

212 *"breach of the peace . . . men"*: Hubert Harrison, "Homo Africanus Harlemi," *Amsterdam News*, September 1, 1926. Reprinted in Jeffrey B. Perry, ed., *A Hubert Harrison Reader* (Middletown, CT: Wesleyan University Press, 2001), 341–44.

212 *"It is the surface mud . . . sadism"*: W.E.B. DuBois, "Books," *Crisis* (December 1926): 81–82.

212 *Shortly after the first bad . . . mob*: CVV daybook, September 4, 1926, Carl Van Vechten Papers, NYPL.

213 *"make a stir . . . sympathy"*: Charles Johnson to CVV, August 10, 1926, Carl Van Vechten Papers, NYPL.

213 *"colored people the rare tribute . . . puppets"*: James Weldon Johnson, "Romance and Tragedy in Harlem—A Review," *Opportunity* 4, no. 26 (October 1926): 316, 330.

213 *With a dash of pride . . . criticizing it*: CVV to James Weldon Johnson, September 7, 1926, James Weldon Johnson and Grace Nail Johnson Papers, YCAL.

213 *Hubert Harrison's review . . . society*: L. M. Hussey, "Homo Africanus," *American Mercury* (January 1925): 83–89.

214 *"Harlem's new and . . . publicity"*: Harrison, "Homo Africanus Harlemi," Perry, *Hubert Harrison Reader*, 83.

214 *"the vogue for . . . other book"*: Gwendolyn Bennett, "The Ebony Flute," *Opportunity* 4, no. 26 (October 1926): 322.

214 *"Sightseers, visitors and . . . around"*: Gwendolyn Bennett, "The Ebony Flute," *Opportunity* 4, no. 27 (November 1926): 357.

214 *In fact, librarians . . . his books*: Charles Chesnutt to CVV, September 7, 1926, Carl Van Vechten Papers, NYPL.

215 *"Can it be possible . . . classes?"*: Florence Thompson to CVV, April 15, 1928, Carl Van Vechten Papers, NYPL.

215 *"all the other characters . . . fine"*: Joseph Epstein to CVV, February 9, 1927, Carl Van Vechten Papers, NYPL.

215 *"who go to Negro homes . . . equals?"*: Lilian Wang to CVV, February 12, 1927, Carl Van Vechten Papers, NYPL.

216 *"The things that I said . . . 'Heaven'"*: Walter White to W.E.B. DuBois, November 26, 1926, Carl Van Vechten Papers, NYPL.

216 *"misdirected a genuine poet"*: Allison Davis, "Our Negro Intellectuals," *Crisis* 35 (August 1928): 268; and Hughes's response: Langston Hughes [letter to the editor], *Crisis* 35 (September 1928): 302.

216 *Claude McKay's 1928 novel . . . begun*: In 1924, frustrated that he could not find a publisher willing to handle his gritty depiction of black life, McKay had burned his manuscript of *The Color Scheme*. Wayne F. Cooper, *Claude McKay: Rebel Sojourner in the Harlem Renaissance* (Baton Rouge: Louisiana State University Press, 1996), 193–222.

217 *"powerful . . . daring and even sensational"*: Advertisement for *Sweet Man* in unidentified newspaper, CVV scrapbook 24, Carl Van Vechten Papers, NYPL.

218 *"I pay no attention . . . opinion"*: The Reminiscences of Carl Van Vechten (May 25, 1960), 342, CCOHC.

219 *Marinoff was desperate . . . infected him*: FM to CVV, January 5, 1927, Carl Van Vechten Papers, NYPL.

10. CRUEL SOPHISTICATION

220–221 *"long, lone, uninspired Kansas . . . New Mexico"*: CVV daybook, January 1, 1927, Carl Van Vechten Papers, NYPL; Kellner, *Splendid Drunken Twenties*, 145.

221 *"naïve—yet blood stained . . . breasts"*: Mabel Dodge Luhan to CVV, April 12, 1920, Carl Van Vechten Papers, NYPL.

221 *"How can you like . . . more"*: Mabel Dodge Luhan to CVV, c. June 1920, Carl Van Vechten Papers, NYPL.

221 *"tall and slight . . . pince nez"*: Mabel Dodge Luhan to CVV, October 8, 1920, Carl Van Vechten Papers, NYPL.

222 *"Couldn't you pick out . . . of them"*: Flannery Burke, *From Greenwich Village to Taos: Primitivism and Place at Mabel Dodge Luhan's* (Lawrence: University Press of Kansas, 2008), 29.

222 *Mabel acquired a new type . . . Lujan*: Although Tony Lujan spelled his name the traditional Spanish way, Mabel Anglicized the name for her own use after they married, styling herself as Mabel Dodge Luhan.

222–224 *"finally overcome all . . . environment"*: Mabel Dodge Luhan, *Edge of Taos Desert* (New York: Harcourt, Brace, 1937), 177.

224 *"like the dawn of the world"*: Mabel Dodge Luhan, *Lorenzo in Taos* (London: Martin Secker, 1933), 15.

224 *His letters to Marinoff . . . Fifth Avenue*: CVV to FM, January 8, 1927, Carl Van Vechten Papers, NYPL.

224 *"I got very drunk . . . at 3"*: CVV daybook, July 1, 1927, Carl Van Vechten Papers, NYPL; Kellner, *Splendid Drunken* Twenties, 150.

224–225 *"His face was . . . moonshine"*: Dodge Luhan, "Twelfth Night," 11, Mabel Dodge Luhan Papers, YCAL.

225 *"cruel sophistication"*: Ibid., 14.

225 *"two overgrown schoolboys"*: Ibid., 17.

225 *Van Vechten wrote Marinoff . . . week*: CVV to FM, January 14, 1927, Carl Van Vechten Papers, NYPL.

225 *A further letter . . . Fania*: CVV to FM, January 16, 1927, Carl Van Vechten Papers, NYPL.

225–226 *One evening he and Tony . . . of thanks*: CVV to FM, January 14, 1927, Carl Van Vechten Papers, NYPL.

226 *"Not even Louis . . . thinking"*: Dodge Luhan, "Twelfth Night," 13, Mabel Dodge Luhan Papers, YCAL.

226 *The "Indians" of Taos . . . surface*: CVV to FM, January 14, 1927, Carl Van Vechten Papers, NYPL.

226 *After only five days . . . natives*: CVV to FM, January 6, 1927, Carl Van Vechten Papers, NYPL.

226–227 *A couple of days before . . . "moodiness"*: CVV daybook, January 11, 1927, Carl Van Vechten Papers, NYPL; Kellner, *Splendid Drunken Twenties*, 151.

227 *"Mr. Van Vechten was disappointed . . . Harlem"*: Dodge Luhan, "Twelfth Night," 17, Mabel Dodge Luhan Papers, YCAL.

227 *"The air was all clear . . . singing"*: Ibid.

227 *she wrote him a letter . . . his stay*: Mabel Dodge Luhan to CVV, March 4, 1927, Carl Van Vechten Papers, YCAL.

228 *suggested to his friend . . . good*: CVV to Max Ewing, December 13, 1925, Max Ewing Papers, YCAL.

228–229 *who wondered aloud why . . . changed*: Mordaunt Hall, "Strange Parcel of Mirth Serves as Miss Negri's Latest Vehicle," *New York Times*, December 20, 1925, CVV scrapbook 17, Carl Van Vechten Papers, NYPL.

229 *"more money, more . . . dissatisfaction"*: CVV, "Fabulous Hollywood," *Vanity Fair* (May 1927): 54.

229 *Van Vechten worried . . . city*: CVV to FM, January 19, 1927, Carl Van Vechten Papers, NYPL.

229–230 *Aside from the Fitzgeralds . . . above*: CVV, "Fabulous Hollywood," 54.

230 *"often late in the afternoon . . . night"*: Ibid.

230 *"Say that I am one author . . . around"*: Gilmore Millen, "Carl Von [sic] Vechten in L.A. Tells His Ideas of Authors," *Los Angeles Evening Herald*, January 20, 1927. Clipping included in a letter from CVV to FM, January 22, 1927, Carl Van Vechten Papers, NYPL.

230–231 *"an astonishing sight" . . . hills*: CVV daybook, January 19, 1927, Carl Van Vechten Papers, NYPL.

231 *The very next morning . . . command*: CVV daybook, January 20, 1927, Carl Van Vechten Papers, NYPL.

231 *"as much intensive study . . . Earth"*: CVV to FM, January 24, 1927, Carl Van Vechten Papers, NYPL; Kellner, *Letters of Carl Van Vechten*, 92.

231 *meeting every significant person . . . master*: CVV to FM, January 24, 1927, Carl Van Vechten Papers, NYPL.

233 *For* Vanity Vair *. . . "humanity"*: CVV, "Hollywood Royalty," *Vanity Fair* (July 1927): 38.

233 *As the three of them entered . . . ovation*: Ibid.

233 *"the power of satisfying wishes"*: Ibid.

233 *"accompanied by nude Nubians with torches"*: Ibid.

234 *"I am swimming among movie stars"*: CVV to FM, January 24, 1927, Carl Van Vechten Papers, NYPL; Kellner, *Letters of Carl Van Vechten*, 93.

234 *Like a tourist . . . roll call*: CVV, "Hollywood Parties," *Vanity Fair* (June 1927): 47.

234 *"Never before . . . Hollywood"*: Ibid.

234 *"which may have been something . . . concerned"*: Ibid.

235 *she told Carl bluntly . . . together*: FM to CVV, January 19, 1927, Carl Van Vechten Papers, NYPL.

235 *She received assurances . . . teetotal*: CVV to FM, January 24, 1927, Carl Van Vechten Papers, NYPL.

237 *"incredible, fantastic, colossal"*: Van Vechten, "Fabulous Hollywood," *Vanity Fair*, 54.

237 *"walls of the Hollywood houses . . . hollow"*: CVV, "Understanding Hollywood," *Vanity Fair* (August 1927), 78.

11. A QUITE GAY, BUT EMPTY, BUBBLE THAT DAZZLES ONE IN BURSTING

238 *she sent letters home . . . end*: See letters from FM to CVV throughout April and May 1927, especially a lengthy one dated May 13, 1927, Carl Van Vechten Papers, NYPL.

238–239 *a new sense of menace . . . Cummings*: CVV daybook, entries from April and May 1927; the references to the violence at Bob Chanler's appear on April 5, 1927, and April 14, 1927, Carl Van Vechten Papers, NYPL.

239 *although the movie producer Arthur Hornblow . . . story*: CVV to FM, April 18, 1927, Carl Van Vechten Papers, NYPL.

239 *In an attempt to get him . . . next*: FM to CVV, April 29, 1927, Carl Van Vechten Papers, NYPL.

240 *"embarked on a party that lasted three months"*: Sara Mayfield, *Exiles from Paradise: Scott and Zelda Fitzgerald* (New York: Delacorte Press, 1971), 119.

240 *"Charles Lindbergh arrives . . . aircraft"*: CVV daybook, May 21, 1927, Carl Van Vechten Papers, NYPL; Kellner, *Splendid Drunken Twenties*, 166.

240 *"From the depths . . . drunkenness"*: Zelda Fitzgerald to CVV, May 27, 1927, Carl Van Vechten Papers, YCAL.

240 *"a gas range . . . dining room"*: Zelda Fitzgerald to CVV, May 29, 1927, Carl Van Vechten Papers, YCAL.

240 *"way of life didn't appeal to me"*: The Reminiscences of Carl Van Vechten (May 2, 1960), 226, CCOHC.

240 *"they both drank . . . excessive"*: Nancy Milford, *Zelda Fitzgerald* (London: Penguin Books, 1985), 110.

242 *"You need a change . . . see you"*: Hugh Walpole to CVV, April 22, 1927, Hugh Walpole Papers, Berg.

242 *He was now gaunt . . . escapades*: CVV daybook, June 12, 1927, Carl Van Vechten Papers, NYPL.

242 *Ralph passed away . . . June 28*: CVV daybook, June 28, 1927, Carl Van Vechten Papers, NYPL.

242 *phlebitis in his leg*: Problems with CVV's leg, for which he was given a number of diagnoses and treatments, persisted for years.

242 *"I adore having Marinoff . . . alive"*: CVV daybook, July 4, 1927, Carl Van Vechten Papers, NYPL; Kellner, *Splendid Drunken Twenties*, 170.

243 *He wrote Mabel . . . tranquillity*: CVV to Mabel Dodge Luhan, October 10, 1927, Mabel Dodge Luhan Papers, YCAL.

243 *a depressing experience . . . problems*: CVV to Aileen Pringle, December 19, 1927, Aileen Pringle Papers, YCAL.

244 *"Van Vechten Follywood . . . Bursting"*: Anthony J. Casey, "Van Vechten Follywood a Quite Gay, but Empty, Bubble That Dazzles One in Bursting", *Brooklyn Eagle*, August 26, 1928, CVV scrapbook 23, Carl Van Vechten Papers, NYPL.

244 *"My revulsion towards . . . complete"*: CVV daybook, March 6, 1928, Carl Van Vechten Papers, NYPL; Kellner, *Splendid Drunken Twenties*, 199.

244 *"I listened for two hours . . . knees"*: Gilmore Millen, "C. Van Vechten Wants to See Aimee, Fox," *Los Angeles Herald*, February 29, 1928, CVV scrapbook 22, Carl Van Vechten Papers, NYPL.

245 *"I only hope that you didn't . . . damn"*: H. L. Mencken to CVV, March 3, 1928, Carl Van Vechten Papers, NYPL.

245–246 *Somerset Maugham wrote . . . "water"*: Somerset Maugham to CVV, July 21, 1928, Carl Van Vechten Papers, NYPL.

246 *"You just can't beat . . . later"*: FM to CVV, July 30, 1928, Carl Van Vechten Papers, NYPL; Jack F. Sharrar, *Avery Hopwood: His Life and Plays* (Jefferson, NC: McFarland, 1989), 195.

247 *Van Vechten scribbled in his notebook . . . turn*: CVV notebook from 1928, Carl Van Vechten Papers, NYPL.

248 *A few days after spotting . . . company*: Ibid.

248 *when he met Greta Garbo . . . immediately*: CVV to FM, February 26, 1928, Carl Van Vechten Papers, NYPL.

248 *"That was almost my fate . . . Harlem"*: The Reminiscences of Carl Van Vechten (May 2, 1960), 206, CCOHC.

248 *"You'll find little Harlems . . . it all"*: Langston Hughes to CVV, May 8, 1929, Bernard, *Remember Me to Harlem*, 64.

249 *Paul Robeson's highly praised . . . Theatre*: Sheila Tully Boyle and Andrew Bunie, *Paul Robeson: The Years of Promise and Achievement* (Boston: University of Massachusetts Press, 2001), 192–206, provides a useful account of Robeson's popularity in Britain at the same time.

249 *"It was their first party" . . . Astaire*: CVV to Gertrude Stein, November 27, 1928, Burns, *Letters of Gertrude Stein and Carl Van Vechten*, 184.

250 *Van Vechten passed several long nights . . . rent boys*: CVV daybook, various entries for June, July, and August 1929, Carl Van Vechten Papers, NYPL.

251 *"Exhausted by wars . . . themselves"*: Alfred A. Knopf advertisement for *Parties*, c. August 1930, CVV scrapbook 24, Carl Van Vechten Papers, NYPL.

251 *"hot asphalt, a distinct . . . streets"*: CVV, *Parties* (1930; repr., Los Angeles: Sun & Moon Press, 1993), 141.

251 *"most of which . . . years ago"*: Ibid., 142.

251 *"what is new . . . is old"*: Ibid., 140.

252 *"that interest in America . . . Europe"*: Jack Campbell, "Speaking of Beaux-Arts . . . Carl Van Vechten Returns," *New York Herald* (Paris edition), August 10, 1930, CVV scrapbook 24, Carl Van Vechten Papers, NYPL.

252 *"bootlegger, speakeasy, buffet-flat . . . ecstasy"*: CVV, *Parties*, 185.

252 *"the expression of electricity and living movement"*: Ibid, 186.

252 *"It is so funny ... country"*: Ibid., 260.

252 *"'Parties' scared me ... upsetting"*: Mabel Dodge Luhan to CVV, September 22, 1930, Carl Van Vechten Papers, YCAL.

252 *"strange" and "disquieting"*: Joseph Hergesheimer to CVV, November 10, 1930, Carl Van Vechten Papers, YCAL.

252 *Marinoff was less diplomatic ... home*: CVV daybook, April 23, 1930, Carl Van Vechten Papers, NYPL; FM diary, April 22, 1930, Carl Van Vechten Papers, YCAL.

252 *"they have so much in common ... Freud"*: H. O., "Freud and Van Vechten on Our Attempts to Escape Unhappiness," *Baltimore Evening Sun*, September 13, 1930, CVV scrapbook 24, Carl Van Vechten Papers, NYPL.

252–253 *In time he came ... achieved*: In a letter to Reverend Peter Francis O'Brien, S.J., written one week before his death, CVV described *Parties* as his best novel. CVV to Reverend Peter Francis O'Brien, S.J., December 14, 1964. Letters in the possession of Reverend Peter Francis O'Brien, S.J.

253 *"He was getting on ... fifty"*: CVV, *Parties*, 238.

253 *On August 22 ... lesbians*: CVV daybook, August 22, 1930, Carl Van Vechten Papers, NYPL.

253 *the Silhouette, a favorite ... ties*: See Florence Tamagne, *A History of Homosexuality in Europe, 1919–1939* (New York: Algora Publishing, 2004) and Mel Gordon, *Voluptuous Panic: The Erotic World of Weimar Berlin* (Port Townsend, WA: Feral House, 2000) for vivid details of the clubs Van Vechten visited during his trip.

254 *"I am very sad ... place"*: CVV daybook, August 28, 1930, Carl Van Vechten Papers, NYPL; Kellner, *Splendid Drunken Twenties*, 299.

254 *On May 18 ... research*: CVV to FM, May 18, 1931, Carl Van Vechten Papers, NYPL.

255 *"rotten act"*: CVV to FM, May 21, 1931, Carl Van Vechten Papers, NYPL; Kellner, *Letters of Carl Van Vechten*, 122.

255 *"already forgotten ... flowers"*: CVV to FM, May 22, 1931, Carl Van Vechten Papers, NYPL; Kellner, *Letters of Carl Van Vechten*, 122.

12. PAPA WOOJUMS

256 *he telegrammed Marinoff ... airborne*: CVV to FM, October 10, 1931, Carl Van Vechten Papers, NYPL; CVV to Gertrude Stein, October 19, 1931, Burns, *Letters of Gertrude Stein and Carl Van Vechten*, 246.

257 *"tinkers with planes ... liked it"*: Joseph Mitchell, "Mrs. Van Vechten, 'Tired of the Speakos,' Becomes Fania Marinoff of Stage Again," *New York World-Telegram*, January 12, 1932, CVV scrapbook 25, Carl Van Vechten Papers, NYPL.

257 *"Taylor Crump is ... there"*: Hunter Stagg to CVV, August 15, 1926, Carl Van Vechten Papers, NYPL.

257 *When they first spoke ... high-handedness*: Mark Lutz to Bruce Kellner, June 29, 1967, Bruce Kellner Papers, YCAL.

258 *In one of his notebooks ... nature*: CVV notebook, undated, Carl Van Vechten Papers, NYPL.

258 *put Lutz in touch . . . trial*: For commentary and analysis of Hughes's response to the Scottsboro Boys incident, see Rampersad, *I, Too, Sing America*, 216–31; Langston Hughes and Susan Duffy, *The Political Plays of Langston Hughes* (Carbondale: Southern Illinois University Press, 2000).

258 *"It was disappointing . . . yesterday"*: Mark Lutz to CVV, December 16, 1944, Carl Van Vechten Papers, YCAL.

259 *"I settled down . . . MILLUN"*: Mark Lutz to CVV, June 20, 1945, Carl Van Vechten Papers, YCAL.

259 *"bright winter Saturdays"*: Prentiss Taylor to Bruce Kellner, May 21, 1980, Bruce Kellner Papers, YCAL.

261 *"Great photographers are born, not educated"*: "Born to Use a Lens," *New York Herald Tribune*, October 16, 1938, CVV scrapbook 27, Carl Van Vechten Papers, NYPL. CVV gave his opinions on what makes a great photographer in his review of Walker Evans's seminal collection *American Photographs*.

261 *As early as February . . . hold an exhibition*: CVV to Gertrude Stein, February 28, 1932, Burns, *Letters of Gertrude Stein and Carl Van Vechten*, 252.

261 *struggling to decide . . . good*: CVV to Max Ewing, February 7, 1932, Max Ewing Papers, YCAL.

261 *By June he was . . . talent*: CVV to Mabel Dodge Luhan, June 10, 1932, Mabel Dodge Luhan Papers, YCAL.

261 *"My first subject . . . O'Neill"*: J. M. Flagler, "The Talk of the Town: Van Vechten," *New Yorker* (January 12, 1963), 21.

261–263 *the volume of celebrated people . . . shoot*: Prints of all these photographs can be found in Carl Van Vechten Papers, YCAL.

263 *"a few glasses . . . self-consciousness"*: Mark Lutz to Bruce Kellner, June 29, 1967, Bruce Kellner Papers, YCAL.

263 *"in about a twentieth of a second"*: The Reminiscences of Carl Van Vechten (May 18, 1960), 306, CCOHC.

264 *"She began to cry . . . laughing"*: Ibid.

264 *"There are no good photographs . . . of her"*: Ibid.

264 *he used much of the same . . . "documentary"*: CVV to Mary Seymour, October 19, 1942, Kellner, *The Letters of Carl Van Vechten*, 187; The Reminiscences of Carl Van Vechten (May 14, 1960), 232, CCOHC.

265 *"The revolutionary poems . . . ever"*: CVV to Langston Hughes, March 4, 1933, Bernard, *Remember Me to Harlem*, 103–104.

265 *"the only person one can improve is oneself"*: CVV to Noel Sullivan, February 13, 1940, Kellner, *Letters of Carl Van Vechten*, 172.

265–266 *On March 7 . . . Germany*: FM diary, March 7, 1934, Carl Van Vechten Papers, YCAL.

266 *She spent a good deal . . . marriage*: FM diary, April 1935, Carl Van Vechten Papers, YCAL.

266 *In the summer of 1933 . . . Taos*: Prints of this series of photographs are in Carl Van Vechten Papers, YCAL.

267 *Even on December 31 . . . time*: FM diary, December 31, 1935, Carl Van Vechten Papers, YCAL.

267 *"elegance in the ordinary"*: Lincoln Kirstein, "An Unpublished Eulogy for Carl Van Vechten, December 23, 1964," Carl Van Vechten Papers, YCAL.

267–268 *"first saw an American ballet . . . ballerinas"*: Ibid.

268 *In May 1933 . . . "good"*: CVV to Gertrude Stein, May 1, 1933, Burns, *Letters of Gertrude Stein and Carl Van Vechten*, 266.

268–269 *"only gave real loyalty . . . to her"*: Andrea Weiss, *Paris Was a Woman: Portraits from the Left Bank* (London: Pandora, 1995), 98.

269 *"a tinge of jealousy"*: CVV to Gertrude Stein, October 23, 1933, Burns, *Letters of Gertrude Stein and Carl Van Vechten*, 282.

269 *"OUR Three Lives"*: CVV to Gertrude Stein, September 21, 1933, Burns, *Letters of Gertrude Stein and Carl Van Vechten*, 277.

270 *"I am getting very excited"*: Gertrude Stein to CVV, February 5, 1934, Burns, *Letters of Gertrude Stein and Carl Van Vechten*, 294.

270–271 *"I haven't seen a crowd" . . . day*: CVV to Gertrude Stein, February 8, 1934, Burns, *Letters of Carl Van Vechten and Gertrude Stein*, 295.

271 *Henry-Russell Hitchcock . . . tears*: Steve Watson, *Prepare for Saints: Gertrude Stein, Virgil Thomson, and the Mainstreaming of American Modernism* (Berkeley: University of California Press, 2000), 279.

271 *he also implied that . . . in 1933*: CVV, "A Few Notes About Four Saints in Three Acts," Gertrude Stein, *Four Saints in Three Acts. An Opera to Be Sung, etc.* (New York: Random House, 1934), 7.

271 *Thomson maintained his . . . elsewhere*: Watson, *Prepare for Saints*, 199.

272 *On her first night back . . . them all*: FM diary, October 24, 1934, Carl Van Vechten Papers, YCAL.

273 *The scholar Tirza True Latimer . . . rival*: Wanda M. Corn and Tirza True Latimer, *Seeing Gertrude Stein: Five Stories* (Berkeley and London: University of California Press, 2011), 149.

273 *On receiving the Virginia . . . "happy"*: Gertrude Stein to CVV, March 12, 1935, Burns, *Letters of Gertrude Stein and Carl Van Vechten*, 411.

273 *A matter of weeks into the tour . . . time*: CVV to Mabel Dodge Luhan, c. November 1934, Mabel Dodge Luhan Papers, YCAL.

275 *"Thornton Wilder has got me . . . PLEASE!"*: CVV to Gertrude Stein, 1935, Corn and Latimer, *Seeing Gertrude Stein*, 150.

275 *"I always wanted to be . . . baby on"*: Gertrude Stein and CVV, "A Message from Gertrude Stein," *Selected Writings of Gertrude Stein* (New York: Vintage Books, 1990), vii.

277 *"It is violent and gentle . . . genuine"*: Douglas Gilbert, "U.S. Is 'Violent and Gentle,' Miss Stein's Parting Shot," *New York World-Telegram*, May 4, 1935, CVV scrapbook 26, Carl Van Vechten Papers, NYPL

13. YALE MAY NOT THINK SO, BUT IT'LL BE JUST JOLLY

278 *"Im [sic] in a big show . . . notice!"*: CVV to Langston Hughes, November 29, 1935, Bernard, *Remember Me to Harlem*, 133.

278 *"literature's loss is photography's gain"*: Henry McBride, "The Leica Exhibition," *New York Sun*, November 30, 1935.

278 *Man Ray, who was . . . work*: Man Ray to CVV, September 14, 1934, Carl Van Vechten Papers, YCAL.

278–280 *"They are damn swell . . . few"*: Alfred Stieglitz to CVV, September 25, 1933, Carl Van Vechten Papers, YCAL.

280 *"cold sober and . . . mood"*: CVV, "Memories of Bessie Smith," *Jazz Record* (September 1947): 7.

280 *"I got nearer her real personality . . . exist"*: Ibid., 29.

280 *"I hadn't planned to meet . . . saw him"*: Milford, *Zelda Fitzgerald*, 347.

281 *"a nice, sober . . . side"*: Frances Scott Fitzgerald Lanahan to CVV, August 7, 1948, Carl Van Vechten Papers, YCAL.

281 *"the glamour . . . years ago"*: Zelda Fitzgerald to CVV, December 29, 1940, Carl Van Vechten Papers, YCAL.

281 *"one red, one white . . . Americans"*: Hughes, *The Big Sea*, 254–55.

281–282 *"I always said . . . amusing"*: The Reminiscences of Carl Van Vechten (May 14, 1960), 270, CCOHC.

282 *"tolerant of unorthodox behavior . . . advice"*: Bernard, *Carl Van Vechten and the Harlem Renaissance*, 214.

282 *a bronze statue . . . requested*: For an illuminating analysis of this episode, see Bernard, *Carl Van Vechten and the Harlem Renaissance*.

283 *"Walter was never . . . Johnson was"*: The Reminiscences of Carl Van Vechten (May 14, 1960), 266, CCOHC.

283 *"to induce others to make . . . collection"*: CVV, "The J. W. Johnson Collection at Yale," *Crisis* (July 1942): 222.

284 *"and no doubt verge toward the grandiloquent"*: Langston Hughes to CVV, October 30, 1941, Bernard, *Remember Me to Harlem*, 193.

284 *"Don't be selfconscious about Yale . . . halls"*: CVV to Langston Hughes, April 11, 1941, Bernard, *Remember Me to Harlem*, 196.

285 *"was all white people's . . . places"*: The Reminiscences of Carl Van Vechten (May 18, 1960), 294–95, CCOHC.

285 *"I am mad over . . . segregation"*: CVV to Arna Bontemps, December 31, 1943, Arna Bontemps Collection, YCAL; Kellner, *Letters of Carl Van Vechten*, 199.

285 *"The use of riches . . . level"*: George Santayana, *The Last Puritan: A Memoir in the Form of a Novel* (London: Constable & Co., 1935); CVV notebook, Carl Van Vechten Papers, NYPL.

286 *In the entry for . . . page 14*: James Weldon Johnson Collection Catalogue, written by CVV, 411, 70, James Weldon Johnson Collection, YCAL.

286 *"so much in your debt . . . for you"*: Mahala Dutton Benedict Douglas to CVV, March 26, 1936, Carl Van Vechten Papers, YCAL.

287 *"With great pleasure . . . sympathizers"*: CVV to Dorothy Peterson, December 4, 1939, Dorothy Peterson Collection, YCAL; Kellner, *Letters of Carl Van Vechten*, 169.

287 *he noted that C.L.R. James's . . . writer*: James Weldon Johnson Collection Catalogue, written by CVV, 466, James Weldon Johnson Collection, YCAL.

288 *He told Dorothy Peterson . . . "week"*: CVV to Dorothy Peterson, October 23, 1942, Dorothy Peterson Collection, YCAL; Kellner, *Letters of Carl Van Vechten*, 188.

288 *telling Pearson that he made it . . . "Negroes"*: CVV to Norman Holmes Pearson, September 28, 1948, Kellner, *Letters of Carl Van Vechten*, 237.

288 *"cultivate the art of living"*: Santayana, *The Last Puritan*, 552–53.

289 *"I am understood by . . . fewer"*: George George to CVV, July 24, 1943, Carl Van Vechten Papers, YCAL.

289 *George came to idealize . . . grand*: George George to CVV, January 18, 1944, Carl Van Vechten Papers, YCAL.

291 *By 1947 Hoover . . . existed*: Jennifer Terry, *An American Obsession: Science, Medicine, and Homosexuality in Modern Society* (Chicago and London: University of Chicago Press, 1999), 323.

291 *between 1947 and 1955 . . . homosexuals*: Ibid., 324–25.

292 *The article in question . . . assault*: "Whipping of Boy Starts Hunt for Harry K. Thaw," *New York Times*, January 12, 1917, CVV scrapbook 11, Carl Van Vechten Papers, YCAL.

294 *"Dad Praises Courage of Son-Turned-Daughter"*: "Dad Praises Courage of Son-Turned-Daughter," unidentified newspaper, c. December 1951, CVV scrapbook 9, Carl Van Vechten Papers, YCAL.

294 *The inclusion of . . . noted*: Jonathan Weinberg, "Boy Crazy: Carl Van Vechten's Queer Collection," *Yale Journal of Criticism* 7, no. 2 (1994): 25–49.

295 *Into his seventies and . . . woodpeckers*: CVV to Aileen Pringle, September 22, 1953, and May 21, 1953, Aileen Pringle Papers, YCAL.

297 *"pornography in the family mailbox"*: Paul S. Boyer, *Purity in Print: Book Censorship in America from the Gilded Age to the Computer Age* (Madison: University of Wisconsin Press, 2002), 297.

297 *"occupy key positions . . . FBI"*: William N. Eskridge, *Gaylaw: Challenging the Apartheid of the Closet* (Cambridge, MA: Harvard University Press, 2002), 75–76.

297 *"Dear Carl . . . CURIOSA!"*: CVV scrapbook 8, Carl Van Vechten Papers, YCAL.

297 *"we should exchange . . . here"*: Max Ewing to CVV, c. December 1932, Carl Van Vechten Papers, YCAL.

298 *"some of them have worn . . . cold"*: Max Ewing to CVV, July 22, 1932, Carl Van Vechten Papers, YCAL.

298 *"Note the influence of 'Freaks'"*: Ibid.

298 *"my African model"*: CVV to Langston Hughes, February 10, 1941, Bernard, *Remember Me to Harlem*, 185.

301 *"Grace in suffering . . . St. Sebastian"*: Charles Darwent, "Arrows of Desire," *Independent* (February 10, 2008).

302 *George wrote a fellow . . . beauty*: George George to Bruce Kellner, December 7, 1979, Bruce Kellner Papers, YCAL.

302 *"life more easy in a concentration camp"*: CVV to Arthur Davison Ficke, December 18, 1940, Arthur Davison Ficke Papers, YCAL; Kellner, *Letters of Carl Van Vechten*, 175.

302 *"Yale May Not . . . Jolly"*: CVV scrapbook 3, Carl Van Vechten Papers, YCAL.

EPILOGUE: THE ATTENTION THAT I USED TO GET

303 *Months before its . . . published*: CVV to Charles R. Byrne, c. June 1950, Kellner, *Letters of Carl Van Vechten*, 240–41.

303 *"most of the Negroes . . . read it"*: CVV, *Nigger Heaven*, "A Note by the Author."

304 *asking the Scottish academic . . . kilt*: CVV to Bruce Kellner, c. June 1955, Bruce Kellner Papers, YCAL.

304 *"segregation is being dealt . . . Negro"*: CVV, *Nigger Heaven*, "A Note by the Author."

306 *"My relations with . . . to get"*: The Reminiscences of Carl Van Vechten (May 14, 1960)," 274, CCOHC.

306 *"was that Gertrude . . . chew"*: CVV, "A Few Notes à Propos of a *'Little' Novel of Thank You*," Gertrude Stein, *A Novel of Thank You*, vol. 8 of *The Yale Edition of the Unpublished Writings of Gertrude Stein* (New Haven, CT: Yale University Press, 1958), vii.

306 *Aged seventy-eight . . . boys*: CVV to Bruce Kellner, April 12, 1959, Bruce Kellner Papers, YCAL.

307 *The artist Wynn Chamberlain . . . too far*: Elwyn Chamberlain, interview with the author, July 2012.

307 *"Very few Americans . . . engaged in"*: Elwyn Chamberlain to CVV, September 9, 1954, CVV Papers, YCAL.

307 *"between sensitive and creative people"*: Ibid.

308 *"one of the city's most . . . Negroes"*: Flagler, "The Talk of the Town: Van Vechten," *New Yorker*, 21–22.

Select Bibliography

• •

A NOTE ON PRIMARY SOURCES

The Columbia Center for Oral History, Columbia University owns the transcript of a lengthy interview that William Ingersoll conducted with Van Vechten in 1960. In this Van Vechten gives a meandering account of his life and his experiences in New York during the first half of the twentieth century.

The bulk of archival material relating to Van Vechten's family life, including his letters to and from Fania Marinoff and his diaries, are in the Carl Van Vechten Papers, at the Manuscripts and Archives Division of the New York Public Library. The Berg Collection of English and American Literature at the New York Public Library houses numerous other Van Vechten documents, including his correspondence with the English authors Ronald Firbank, Hugh Walpole, and Somerset Maugham. The theatrical scrapbooks that Van Vechten compiled as a boy are at the Billy Rose Theater Division of the New York Public Library.

Van Vechten's relationships with fellow artists are best documented in the letters and photographs that form the Carl Van Vechten Papers at the Beinecke Rare Book & Manuscript Library, Yale University. This collection also contains the scrapbooks in which he documented his sexual interest in men and his male nude photographs. Other collections within the Yale Collection of American Literature contain hundreds of letters from Van Vechten to many of his closest friends, including Mabel Dodge, Gertrude Stein, and Langston Hughes.

The breadth and depth of his connection to African-American culture are extensively documented in the letters, photographs, phonograph records, and various other materials in the James Weldon Johnson Collection at the Beinecke Rare Book & Manuscript Library.

Numerous other institutions in New York and elsewhere in the United States own prints of Van Vechten's photographs; most notably the Library Congress has a collection of 1,395 Van Vechten prints, all in the public domain. The Museum of the City of New York has a smaller collection of Van Vechten's photographs of the city, its celebrities, and other inhabitants. The Metropolitan Museum of Art holds prints too, as well as a large collection of his multicolored neckties and other pieces of clothing that help bring the force of this remarkable man's personality to life.

PUBLISHED WORKS BY CARL VAN VECHTEN

BOOKS OF ESSAYS

Excavations: A Book of Advocacies. New York: Alfred A. Knopf, 1926.

Fragments from an Unwritten Autobiography. Vols. 1 and 2. New Haven, CT: Yale University Press, 1955.

In the Garret. New York: Alfred A. Knopf, 1920.

Interpreters and Interpretations. New York: Alfred A. Knopf, 1917.

The Merry-Go-Round. New York: Alfred A. Knopf, 1918.

Music After the Great War. New York: G. Schirmer, 1915.

Music and Bad Manners. New York: Alfred A. Knopf, 1916.

Red: Papers and Musical Subjects. New York: Alfred A. Knopf, 1925.

Sacred and Profane Memories. London: Cassell & Company, 1932.

NOVELS

The Blind Bow-Boy. New York: Alfred A. Knopf, 1923.

Firecrackers: A Realistic Novel. New York: Alfred A. Knopf, 1925.

Nigger Heaven. Introduction by Kathleen Pfeiffer. Urbana and Chicago: University of Illinois Press, 2000. First published 1926 by Alfred A. Knopf.

Parties. Los Angeles: Sun & Moon Press, 1993. First published 1930 by Alfred A. Knopf.

Peter Whiffle: His Life and Works. New York: Alfred A. Knopf, 1922.

Spider Boy. New York: Alfred A. Knopf, 1928.

The Tattooed Countess: A Romantic Novel with a Happy Ending. Introduction by Bruce Kellner. Iowa City: University of Iowa Press, 1987. First published 1924 by Alfred A. Knopf.

ARTICLES, INTRODUCTIONS, AND PREFACES

"A Few Notes About *Four Saints in Three Acts*." In Gertrude Stein, *Four Saints in Three Acts. An Opera to Be Sung, etc.* New York: Random House, 1934, 5–10.

"A Few Notes à Propos of a *'Little' Novel of Thank You*." In Gertrude Stein, *A Novel of Thank You.* Vol. 8 of *The Yale Edition of the Unpublished Writings of Gertrude Stein.* New Haven, CT: Yale University Press, 1958, vii–xiv.

"Away Go the Critics and On Come the Plays." *Trend* 8, no. 2 (November 1914): 233–39.

"The Black Blues." *Vanity Fair* (August 1925): 57, 86, 92.

"Fabulous Hollywood." *Vanity Fair* (May 1927): 54, 108.

"George Gershwin." *Vanity Fair* (March 1925): 40, 78.

"Hollywood Parties." *Vanity Fair* (June 1927): 47, 86.

"Hollywood Royalty." *Vanity Fair* (July 1927): 38, 86.

"How to Read Gertrude Stein." *Trend* 7, no. 5 (August 1914): 553–57. Reprinted in Linda Simon, ed., *Gertrude Stein Remembered.* Lincoln: University of Nebraska Press, 1994, 41–48.

"Introducing Langston Hughes to the Reader." In Langston Hughes, *The Weary Blues.* New York: Alfred A. Knopf, 1929, 9–13.

"Introduction." In Edward Jablonski and Lawrence D. Stewart. *The Gershwin Years.* Garden City, NY: Doubleday, 1958, 21–26.

"Memories of Bessie Smith." *Jazz Record* (September 1947): 6–7, 29.
"Moanin' wid a Sword in Ma Han'." *Vanity Fair* (February 1926): 61, 100, 102.
"Negro 'Blues' Singers." *Vanity Fair* (March 1926): 67, 106, 108.
"Portraits of the Artists." *Esquire* 18 (December 1962): 170–74, 256–58.
"Prescription for the Negro Theatre." *Vanity Fair* (October 1925): 46, 92, 98.
"Rogue Elephant in Porcelain." *Yale University Library Gazette* 38, no. 2 (October 1963): 41–50.
"Salome: The Most Sensational Opera of the Age." *Broadway Magazine* 17 (January 1907): 381–91.
"The Editor's Workbench." *Trend* 8, no. 1 (October 1914): 100–01.
"The Folksongs of the American Negro." *Vanity Fair* (July 1925): 52, 92.
"The J. W. Johnson Collection at Yale." *Crisis* (July 1942): 222, 223, 226.
"The Negro in Art: How Shall He Be Portrayed?" *Crisis* (March 1926): 219.
"Understanding Hollywood." *Vanity Fair* (August 1927): 45, 78.
"War Is Not Hell." *Trend* 8, no. 2 (November 1914): 146–52.

SECONDARY SOURCES

Abbott, Karen. *Sin in the Second City: Madams, Ministers, Playboys and the Battle for America's Soul.* New York: Random House, 2008.
Addams, Jane. *The Spirit of Youth and the City Streets.* New York: Macmillan Company, 1909.
Albertson, Chris. *Bessie.* New Haven, CT: Yale University Press, 2005.
Argyle, Ray. *Scott Joplin and the Age of Ragtime.* Jefferson, NC: McFarland, 2009.
Baskin, Alex. *John Reed: Early Years in Greenwich Village.* New York: Archives of Social History, 1990.
Beard, Rich, and Leslie Cohen Berlowitz, eds. *Greenwich Village: Culture and Counterculture.* New Brunswick, NJ: Rutgers University Press, 1993.
Bennett, Gwendolyn. "The Ebony Flute." *Opportunity* 4, no. 26 (October 1926): 322–23.
———. "The Ebony Flute." *Opportunity* 4, no. 27 (November 1926): 356–58.
Bentley, Toni. *Sisters of Salome.* New Haven, CT, and London: Yale University Press, 2002.
Bernard, Emily. *Carl Van Vechten and the Harlem Renaissance: A Portrait in Black and White.* New Haven, CT, and London: Yale University Press, 2012.
———, ed. *Remember Me to Harlem: The Letters of Langston Hughes and Carl Van Vechten.* New York: Vintage Books, 2002.
Biel, Steven. *American Gothic: A Life of America's Most Famous Painting.* New York and London: W. W. Norton & Company, 2006.
Blake, Jody. *Le Tumulte Noir: Modernist Art and Popular Entertainment in Jazz Age Paris, 1900–1930.* University Park: Pennsylvania State University Press, 1999.
Boehm, Lisa Krissoff. *Popular Culture and the Enduring Myth of Chicago, 1871–1968.* New York and London: Routledge, 2004.
Boyer, Paul S. *Purity in Print: Book Censorship in America from the Gilded Age to the Computer Age.* Madison: University of Wisconsin Press, 2002.
Boyle, Sheila Tully, and Andrew Bunie. *Paul Robeson: The Years of Promise and Achievement.* Boston: University of Massachusetts Press, 2001.

Bradley, Patricia. *Making American Culture: A Social History, 1900–1920*. New York: Palgrave Mcmillan, 2009.

Brooks, Van Wyck. *America's Coming of Age*. New York: B. W. Huebsch, 1915.

———. *The Wine of the Puritans: A Study of Present Day America*. London: Sisley's, 1909.

Burke, Carolyn. *Becoming Modern: The Life of Mina Loy*. New York: Farrar, Straus and Giroux, 1997.

Burke, Flannery. *From Greenwich Village to Taos: Primitivism and Place at Mabel Dodge Luhan's*. Lawrence: University of Kansas Press, 2008.

Burns, Edward, ed. *The Letters of Gertrude Stein and Carl Van Vechten, 1913–1946*. New York: Columbia University Press, 1986.

Caffin, Charles. "Henri Matisse and Isadora Duncan." *Camera Work*, no. 25 (January 1909): 17–30.

Canby, Henry Seidel. *The Age of Confidence*. New York: Farrar, Straus and Giroux, 1934.

Carbone, Gerald M. *Nathanael Greene: A Biography of the American Revolution*. New York: Palgrave Macmillan, 2008.

Chambers, John Whiteclay. *The Tyranny of Change: America in the Progressive Era, 1890–1920*. New Brunswick, NJ, and London: Rutgers University Press, 2000.

Chauncey, George. *Gay New York: The Making of the Gay Male World, 1890–1940*. London: Flamingo, 1995.

Clark, Emily. *Innocence Abroad*. Westport, CT: Greenwood Press, 1975. First published 1931 by Alfred A. Knopf.

Coleman, Leon. *Carl Van Vechten and the Harlem Renaissance: A Critical Perspective*. New York and London: Garland Publishing, 1998.

Commager, Henry Steele. *The American Mind: An Interpretation of American Thought and Character Since the 1890s*. New Haven, CT: Yale University Press, 1959.

Cooper, Wayne F. *Claude McKay: Rebel Sojourner in the Harlem Renaissance*. Baton Rouge: Louisiana State University Press, 1996.

Corn, Wanda M., and Tirza True Latimer: *Seeing Gertrude Stein: Five Stories*. Berkeley and London: University of California Press, 2011.

Cowley, Malcolm. *Exile's Return: A Literary Odyssey of the 1920s*. London: Penguin Books, 1994.

Crunden, Robert M. *American Salons: Encounters with European Modernism, 1885–1917*. New York and Oxford: Oxford University Press, 1993.

Crunden, Robert M. *Body & Soul: The Making of American Modernism*. New York: Basic Books, 2000.

Darwent, Charles. "Arrows of Desire." *Independent* (February 10, 2008).

Dell, Floyd. *Homecoming: An Autobiography*. New York: Farrar & Rinehart, 1933.

———. *Love in Greenwich Village*. Leipzig: Tauchnitz, 1926.

DiMeglio, John E. *Vaudeville U.S.A.* Bowling Green, OH: Bowling Green University Popular Press, 1973.

Dizikes, John. *Opera in America: A Cultural History*. New Haven, CT, and London: Yale University Press, 1993.

Dodge Luhan, Mabel. *Edge of Taos Desert*. New York: Harcourt, Brace, 1937.

———. *European Experiences*. Vol. 2 of *Intimate Memories*. New York: Harcourt, Brace, 1935.

———. *Lorenzo in Taos*. London: Martin Secker, 1933.

———. *Movers and Shakers*. Vol. 3 of *Intimate Memories*. New York: Harcourt, Brace, 1936.

Douglas, Ann. *Terrible Honesty: Mongrel Manhattan in the 1920s*. New York: Farrar, Straus and Giroux, 1995.

Dowling, Robert M. *Slumming in New York: From the Waterfront to Mythic Harlem*. Urbana and Chicago: University of Illinois Press, 2007.

Draper, Muriel. *Music at Midnight*. New York and London: Harper & Brothers, 1929.

Dreiser, Theodore. *Sister Carrie*. New York: Bantam Books, 1958.

Duberman, Martin Bauml. *Paul Robeson: A Biography*. New York: Alfred A. Knopf, 1989.

DuBois, W.E.B. "Books." *Crisis* (December 1926): 81–82.

Edwards, Justin D. *Exotic Journeys: Exploring the Erotics of U.S. Travel Literature, 1840–1930*. Hanover, NH: University Press of New England, 2001.

Eksteins, Modris. *Rites of Spring: The Great War and the Birth of the Modern Age*. Boston and New York: Mariner Books, 2000.

Erenberg, Lewis A. *Steppin' Out: New York Nightlife and the Transformation of American Culture, 1890–1930*. Westport, CT, and London: Greenwood Press, 1981.

Eskridge, William N. *Gaylaw: Challenging the Apartheid of the Closet*. Cambridge, MA: Harvard University Press, 2002.

Fitzgerald, F. Scott. *My Lost City: Personal Essays, 1920–1940*. Edited by James L. W. West III. Cambridge, UK: Cambridge University Press, 2005.

Flagler, J. M. "The Talk of the Town." *New Yorker* (January 12, 1963): 21–22.

Gabauer, Peter A., et al. *Annals of Psi Upsilon, 1833–1941*. New York: Psi Upsilon Fraternity, 1941.

Gates, Henry Louis, Jr. "The Black Man's Burden." In Michael Warner, ed., *Fear of a Queer Planet: Queer Politics and Social Theory*. Minneapolis: University of Minneapolis Press, 1993.

Glaspell, Susan. *The Road to the Temple*. London: Ernest Benn, 1926.

Gordon, Mel. *Voluptuous Panic: The Erotic World of Weimar Berlin*. Port Townsend, WA: Feral House, 2000.

Hapgood, Hutchins. *A Victorian in the Modern World*. New York: Harcourt, Brace, 1939.

Harrison, Hubert. "Homo Africanus Harlemi." *Amsterdam News*, September 1, 1926. Reprinted in Jeffrey B. Perry, ed. *A Hubert Harrison Reader*. Middletown, CT: Wesleyan University Press, 2001, 341–44.

Heap, Chad. *Slumming: Sexual and Racial Encounters in American Nightlife, 1885–1940*. Chicago and London: University of Chicago Press, 2008.

Hemenway, Robert E. *Zora Neale Hurston: A Literary Biography*. Urbana and Chicago: University of Illinois Press, 1980.

Herring, Phillip. *Djuna: The Life and Works of Djuna Barnes*. New York: Viking, 1995.

Hoffman, Michael J., ed. *Critical Essays on Gertrude Stein*. Boston: G. K. Hall and Company, 1986.

Huggins, Nathan Irving. *Harlem Renaissance*. Oxford and New York: Oxford University Press, 2007.

———, ed. *Voices of the Harlem Renaissance*. Oxford: Oxford University Press, 1995.

Hughes, Langston. *The Big Sea*. New York: Hill and Wang, 1963.

———, and Susan Duffy. *The Political Plays of Langston Hughes*. Carbondale: Southern Illinois University Press, 2000.

———. *The Weary Blues*. New York: Alfred A. Knopf, 1929.

Hussey, L. M. "Homo Africanus." *American Mercury* (January 1925): 83–89.

Hutchinson, George. *In Search of Nella Larsen: A Biography of the Color Line*. Cambridge, MA, and London: Belknap Press of Harvard University Press, 2006.

Imbs, Bravig. *Confessions of Another Young Man*. New York: Henkle-Yewdale House, 1936.

Jablonski, Edward, and Lawrence D. Stewart. *The Gershwin Years*. Garden City, NY: Doubleday, 1958.

Johnson, James Weldon. *Black Manhattan*. New York: Alfred A. Knopf, 1930.

———. "Romance and Tragedy in Harlem—A Review." *Opportunity* 4, no. 26 (October 1926): 316–17, 330.

Joiner, Thekla Ellen. *Sin in the City: Chicago and Revivalism, 1880–1920*. Columbia and London: University of Missouri Press, 2007.

Kazin, Alfred. *Bright Book of Life: American Novelists and Storytellers from Hemingway to Mailer*. New York and Toronto: Little, Brown, 1973.

———. *On Native Grounds: An Interpretation of Modern American Literature*. New York: Harcourt, Brace, 1942.

Kellner, Bruce. "Baby Woojums in Iowa." *Books at Iowa* 26 (1977): 3–18.

———. *Carl Van Vechten and the Irreverent Decades*. Norman: University of Oklahoma Press, 1968.

———, ed. *Keep A-Inchin' Along: Selected Writings of Carl Van Vechten About Black Art and Letters*. Westport, CT: Greenwood Press, 1979.

———. *Kiss Me Again: An Invitation to a Group of Noble Dames*. New York: Turtle Point Press, 2002.

———. *The Last Dandy, Ralph Barton: American Artist, 1891–1931*. Columbia: University of Missouri Press, 1991.

———, ed. *Letters of Carl Van Vechten*. New Haven, CT: Yale University Press, 1987.

———, ed. *The Splendid Drunken Twenties: Selections from the Daybooks, 1922–1930*. Urbana and Chicago: University of Illinois Press, 2003.

Kendall, Elizabeth. *Where She Danced*. New York: Alfred A. Knopf, 1979.

Klatt, Wayne. *Chicago Journalism: A History*. Jefferson, NC: McFarland, 2009.

Larson, Erik. *The Devil in the White City: Murder, Magic and Madness at the Fair That Changed America*. London and New York: Doubleday, 2003.

Leick, Karen. *Gertrude Stein and the Making of an American Celebrity*. New York: Routledge, 2009.

Levin, Joanna. *Bohemia in America, 1858–1920*. Stanford, CA: Stanford University Press, 2010.

Levine, Lawrence W. *Highbrow/Lowbrow: The Emergence of Cultural Hierarchy in America*. Cambridge, MA: Harvard University Press, 1988.

Lewis, David Levering. *When Harlem Was in Vogue*. New York and Oxford: Oxford University Press, 1989.

Locke, Alain, ed. *The New Negro*. New York: Touchstone, 1997.

Lorenz, Larry. "The Whitechapel Club: Defining Chicago's Newspapermen in the 19th Century." *American Journalism* 15, no. 1 (Winter, 1998): 83–102.

Lott, Eric. *Blackface Minstrelsy and the American Working Class*. New York and Oxford: Oxford University Press, 1993.

Loy, Mina. *Becoming Modern: The Life of Mina Loy*. New York: Farrar, Straus and Giroux, 1997.

Lueders, Edward. *Carl Van Vechten*. New York: Twayne Publishers, 1965.

——. *Carl Van Vechten and the Twenties*. Albuquerque: University of New Mexico Press, 1955.

Mayfield, Sara. *The Constant Circle: H. L. Mencken and His Friends*. New York: Delacorte Press, 1968.

——. *Exiles from Paradise: Zelda and Scott Fitzgerald*. New York: Delacorte Press, 1971.

McKay, Claude. *Harlem: Negro Metropolis*. New York: Harcourt Brace Jovanovich, 1968.

——. *Home to Harlem*. Lebanon, NH: University Press of New England, 2012.

McKenna, Neil. *The Secret Life of Oscar Wilde*. London: Random House, 2011.

Milford, Nancy. *Zelda Fitzgerald*. London: Penguin Books, 1985.

Moore, Lucy. *Anything Goes: A Biography of the Roaring Twenties*. London: Atlantic Books, 2008.

Mumford, Kevin. *Interzones: Black/White Sex Districts in Chicago and New York in the Early Twentieth Century*. New York: Columbia University Press, 1997.

Neihart, Ben. *Rough Amusements: The True Story of A'Lelia Walker, Patroness of the Harlem Renaissance's Down-Low Culture*. New York: Bloomsbury Publishing USA, 2008.

Nugent, Richard Bruce. *Gay Rebel of the Harlem Renaissance*. Edited by Thomas H. Wirth. Durham, NC: Duke University Press, 2002.

Oja, Carol J. *Making Music Modern: New York in the 1920s*. Oxford: Oxford University Press, 2000.

Okrent, Daniel. *Last Call: The Rise and Fall of Prohibition*. New York: Scribner, 2011.

Padgette, Paul, ed. *The Dance Writings of Carl Van Vechten*. New York: Dance Horizons, 1980.

Pells, Richard. *Modernist America: Art, Music, Movies and the Globalization of American Culture*. New Haven, CT, and London: Yale University Press, 2011.

Rampersad, Arnold. *The Life of Langston Hughes—Volume I: 1902–1941: I, Too, Sing America*. New York and Oxford: Oxford University Press, 1986.

Rosenfeld, Paul. *By Way of Art: Criticisms of Music, Literature, Painting, Sculpture, and the Dance*. New York: Coward-McCann, 1928.

Ross, Steven J., ed. *Movies and American Society*. Oxford: Blackwell Publishers, 2002.

Salisbury, William. *The Career of a Journalist*. New York: B. W. Dodge and Company, 1908.

Santayana, George. *The Last Puritan: A Memoir in the Form of a Novel*. London: Constable and Co., 1935.

Scott, William B., and Peter M. Rutkoff. *New York Modern: The Arts and the City*. Baltimore: Johns Hopkins University Press, 2001.

Sharrar, Jack F. *Avery Hopwood: His Life and Plays*. Jefferson, NC: McFarland, 1989.

Shepherd, Jean, ed. *The America of George Ade*. New York: G. P. Putnam's Sons, 1960.

Shindo, Charles J. *1927—and the Rise of Modern American Culture*. Lawrence: University of Kansas Press, 2010.

Shirer, William L. *The Start, 1904–1930*. Vol. 1 of *20th Century Journey: A Memoir of the Life and the Times*. New York: Simon and Schuster, 1976.

Simon, Linda. *The Biography of Alice B. Toklas*. Lincoln: University of Nebraska Press, 1991.

Singh, Amritjit, et al., eds. *The Harlem Renaissance: Revaluations*. New York and London: Garland Publishing, 1989.

Souhami, Diana. *Gertrude and Alice*. London: I. B. Tauris, 2010.

Smalls, James. *The Homoerotic Photography of Carl Van Vechten: Public Face, Private Thoughts*. Philadelphia: Temple University Press, 2006.

Sochen, June. *The New Woman: Feminism in Greenwich Village, 1910–1920*. New York: Quadrangle Books, 1972.

Spinney, Robert G. *City of Big Shoulders: A History of Chicago*. DeKalb: Northern Illinois University Press, 2000.

Spurling, Hilary. *The Unknown Matisse: The Life of Henri Matisse: The Early Years, 1869–1908*. Berkeley: University of California Press, 2001.

Stansell, Christine. *American Moderns: Bohemian New York and the Creation of a New Century*. New York: Metropolitan Books, 2000.

Steffens, Lincoln. *The Shame of the Cities*. New York: Peter Smith, 1948.

Stein, Charles W., ed. *American Vaudeville as Seen by Its Contemporaries*. New York: Alfred A. Knopf, 1984.

Stein, Gertrude. *The Autobiography of Alice B. Toklas*. London: John Lane, The Bodley Head, 1933.

———. *Four Saints in Three Acts. An Opera to Be Sung, etc.* New York: Random House, 1934.

———. *A Novel of Thank You*. Vol. 8 of *The Yale Edition of the Unpublished Writings of Getrude Stein*. New Haven, CT: Yale University Press, 1958.

———. *Portrait of Mabel Dodge at the Villa Curonia*. Ann Arbor, MI: University Microfilms International, 1994.

———, and Carl Van Vechten. *Selected Writings of Gertrude Stein*. New York: Vintage Books, 1990.

Sterns, Harold E., ed. *Civilization in the United States: An Enquiry by Thirty Americans*. London: Jonathan Cape, 1922.

Strauss, Richard. *Recollections and Reflections*, trans. L. J. Lawrence. London: Boosey & Hawkes, 1953.

Strong, Josiah. *Our Country: Its Possible Future and Its Present Crisis*. Cambridge, MA: Crisis Belknap Press of Harvard University, 1963.

Susman, Warren I. *Culture as History: The Transformation of American Society in the Twentieth Century*. New York: Pantheon Books, 1984.

Tamagne, Florence. *A History of Homosexuality in Europe, 1919–1939.* New York: Algora Publishing, 2004.

Terry, Jennifer. *An American Obsession: Science, Medicine, and Homosexuality in Modern Society.* Chicago and London: University of Chicago Press, 1999.

Tetrazzini, Luisa. *My Life of Song.* London: Cassell & Company, 1921.

———. "The Story of My Operatic Career by Luisa Tetrazzini." *Cosmopolitan* (June 1908): 49–51.

Toklas, Alice B. *What Is Remembered.* New York: Holt, Rinehart and Winston, 1963.

Trav, S. D. *No Applause—Just Throw Money: The Book That Made Vaudeville Famous.* New York: Faber and Faber, 2005.

Trimberger, Ellen Kay, ed. *Intimate Warriors: Portraits of a Modern Marriage, 1899–1944: Selected Works by Neith Boyce and Hutchins Hapgood.* New York: Feminist Press at the City University of New York, 1991.

Van Laer, A.J.F., ed. and trans. *Minutes of the Court of Rensselaerswyck, 1648–1652.* Albany: University of the State of New York, 1922.

Vogel, Shane. *The Scene of Harlem Cabaret: Race, Sexuality, Performance.* Chicago and London: University of Chicago Press, 2009.

Washburn, Charles. *Come into My Parlor: A Biography of the Aristocratic Everleigh Sisters of Chicago.* New York: National Library Press, 1936.

Waters, Ethel. *His Eye Is on the Sparrow.* London: Jazz Books, 1958.

Watson, Steve. *The Harlem Renaissance: Hub of African-American Culture, 1920–1930.* New York: Pantheon Books, 1995.

———. *Prepare for Saints: Gertrude Stein, Virgil Thomson, and the Mainstreaming of American Modernism.* Berkeley: University of California Press, 2000.

Weiss, Andrea. *Paris Was a Woman: Portraits from the Left Bank.* London: Pandora, 1995.

Wertheim, Arthur Frank. *The New York Little Renaissance.* New York: New York University Press, 1976.

Wetzsteon, Ross. *Republic of Dreams: Greenwich Village: The American Bohemia, 1910–1960.* New York: Simon and Schuster, 2002.

Wilson, Edmund. *A Literary Chronicle: 1920–1950.* New York: Doubleday Anchor Books, 1952.

Wilson, James, F. *Bulldaggers, Pansies, and Chocolate Babies: Performance, Race, and Sexuality in the Harlem Renaissance.* Ann Arbor: University of Michigan Press, 2010.

Worth, Robert F. "*Nigger Heaven* and the Harlem Renaissance." *African American Review* 29, no. 3 (Autumn 1995): 461–73.

Acknowledgments

· ·

First, I should like to thank Genevieve Pegg and Jon Elek, whose help at the very start of this project was crucial to its continuation. Thanks also to Chris Parris-Lamb at the Gernert Company for showing such belief in the book in its infancy and for helping me tell the story I wanted to tell. For similar reasons, I am indebted to Jonathan Galassi at Farrar, Straus and Giroux. Thanks also to Alexander Star at FSG, but in particular to Chris Richards for his hard work and erudition and for fielding my dozens of confused queries so phlegmatically. Without his sharp critical eye this book would not have been published.

It was a pleasure to have worked with some fascinating archival materials stored at the Schomburg Center for Research in Black Culture and the Billy Rose Theatre Division of the New York Public Library. Staff at these institutions and at the Columbia Center for Oral History, the Bass Library at Yale University, and the Boatwright Library at the University of Virginia helped me with innumerable issues, large and small. I must reserve a special mention for the staff of the Beinecke Rare Book & Manuscript Library, as well as for Thomas Lannon, Tal Nadan, and all the staff at the Manuscripts and Archives Division of the New York Public Library for their invaluable help and expert guidance. I should also like to say a word for the British Library, where much of this book was written and where I first discovered Van Vechten's writing.

My research was aided enormously by the patience and generosity of many people. Wynn, Sally, and Sam Chamberlain gave their time to help me further my understanding of Van Vechten in his later years, as did Reverend Peter Francis O'Brien, S.J., who also responded to my inquiries with great enthusiasm and thoughtfulness. Nobody has done more over the last fifty years to keep alive interest in Van Vechten and his works than Bruce Kellner, Successor Trustee of the Carl Van Vechten Trust, whose scholarly efforts proved extremely useful to me during my research. Rosa Vieira de Almeida and Erik Cronqvist offered a rare combination of hospitality and research assistance. Darryl Pinckney showed great kindness by offering advice and introductions; Emily Bernard gave similar help and shared her tremendous knowledge and insight as I researched and wrote the manuscript. Karen Abbott helped clear up some issues about the bordellos of nineteenth-century Chicago, for which I am grateful, and Hannah Kauders did a terrific job in providing research assistance. I also owe thanks to those who gave their permission to reproduce text and images throughout the book: John Pennino at the Metroplitan Opera Archives, María Elena Rico Covarrubias, Wynn Chamberlain, Mimi Muray, Andrea Beauchamp at the Hopwood Room at the University of Michigan, and Nancy Kuhl and the Yale Committee on Literary Property.

Various friends and colleagues on both sides of the Atlantic pretended—sometimes quite convincingly—not to be bored when I rambled on, yet again, about Carl Van Vechten. They also offered help, advice, and critiques, all of which were greatly appreciated. I should like to say special thanks to Chris Levy and Andrew Bainbridge for hours of conversation about the book and for the repeated use of their sofa beds, while Robert Portass gave much-needed counsel and encouragement at various points. Mary Bralove and Peggy Mitchell served up steak dinners, club sandwiches, and support when I first arrived in the United States, and Sue Jones did a passable impersonation of The Great Soprendo, pulling rabbits out of hats just when I needed them most. Simba Bhebhe merits a line of thanks for indirectly stoking my interest in Van Vechten's life and work.

The biggest thanks of course go to my family for their help in ways too numerous to list here. In particular, I owe my parents, John and Patricia, an enormous debt for their unfailing support during the writing of this book and the twenty-odd years that preceded it.

Index

The name Carl Van Vechten has been abbreviated as "CVV."
Page numbers in *italics* refer to illustrations.

Illustration Credits

130 H. L. Mencken, c. 1913 (Photographer unidentified. Yale Collection of American Literature, Beinecke Rare Book & Manuscript Library, Yale University)

134 Carl Van Vechten, c. 1925 (Photograph by Nickolas Muray. © Nickolas Muray Photo Archives. Manuscripts and Archives Division, The New York Public Library, Astor, Lenox and Tilden Foundations)

141 Donald Angus, aged nineteen, c. 1919 (Photograph by Claridge Studio, Yale Collection of American Literature, Beinecke Rare Book & Manuscript Library, Yale University)

149 Tallulah Bankhead, c. 1934 (Photograph by Carl Van Vechten. Library of Congress, Prints & Photographs Division, Carl Van Vechten Collection, LC-USZ62-134171 DLC)

153 Max Ewing, c. 1932 (Photograph by Max Ewing. Yale Collection of American Literature, Beinecke Rare Book & Manuscript Library, Yale University)

163 George Gershwin, c. March 1937 (Photograph by Carl Van Vechten. Library of Congress, Prints & Photographs Division, Carl Van Vechten Collection, LC-USZ62-126699 DLC)

168 Walter White, c. March 1942 (Photograph by Gordon Parks. Library of Congress, Prints & Photographs Division, FSA/OWI Collection, LC-USF34-013344-C)

172 James Weldon Johnson, c. 1920 (Photograph by James Calvin Patton. Yale Collection of American Literature, Beinecke Rare Book & Manuscript Library, Yale University)

176 Nora Holt, c. 1930 (Photograph by James Hargis Connelly. Yale Collection of American Literature, Beinecke Rare Book & Manuscript Library, Yale University)

183 Paul Robeson, c. 1933 (Photograph by Carl Van Vechten. Library of Congress, Prints & Photographs Division, Carl Van Vechten Collection, LC-USZ62-59725 DLC)

188 Langston Hughes working as a busboy at the Wardman Park Hotel, Washington, D.C. (© Bettmann/CORBIS)

195 A caricature of Carl Van Vechten as a black man by Miguel Covarrubias, entitled *A Prediction* (© María Elena Rico Covarrubias. Yale Collection of American Literature, Beinecke Rare Book & Manuscript Library, Yale University)

211 Zora Neale Hurston, c. 1938 (Photograph by Carl Van Vechten. Library of Congress, Prints & Photographs Division, Carl Van Vechten Collection, LC-USZ62-79898 DLC)

223 Mabel Dodge Luhan, c. 1934 (Photograph by Carl Van Vechten. Library of Congress, Prints & Photographs Division, Carl Van Vechten Collection, LC-USZ62-106861 DLC)

232 Carl Van Vechten at the Famous Players-Lasky studio, Los Angeles, January 30, 1927. From left to right: Frank Case, Van Vechten, Flora Zabelle, Emil Jannings, Bertha Case, Jesse Lasky (Photographer unidentified. Henry W. and Albert A. Berg Collection of English and American Literature, The New York Public Library, Astor, Lenox and Tilden Foundations)

236 Lois Moran, c. 1932 (Photograph by Carl Van Vechten. Library of Congress, Prints & Photographs Division, Carl Van Vechten Collection)

241 F. Scott Fitzgerald, c. 1937 (Photograph by Carl Van Vechten. Library of Congress, Prints & Photographs Division, Carl Van Vechten Collection, LC-USZ62-118643 DLC)

260 Carl Van Vechten, self-portrait, c. 1934 (Photograph by Carl Van Vechten. Library of Congress, Prints & Photographs Division, Carl Van Vechten Collection, LC-USZ62-124551 DLC)

262 Anna May Wong, c. 1932 (Photograph by Carl Van Vechten. Library of Congress, Prints & Photographs Division, Carl Van Vechten Collection, LC-USZ62-42509 DLC)

274 Gertrude Stein, January 4, 1935 (Photograph by Carl Van Vechten. Library of Congress, Prints & Photographs Division, Carl Van Vechten Collection, LC-USZ62-103680 DLC)

276 Carl Van Vechten and Gertrude Stein aboard the SS *Champlain* as Stein waves farewell to the United States, May 4, 1935 (© Bettmann/CORBIS)

279 Bessie Smith, 1936 (Photograph by Carl Van Vechten. Library of Congress, Prints & Photographs Division, Carl Van Vechten Collection, LC-USZ62-124517 DLC)

293 The dancer Al Bledger, c. 1938 (Photograph by Carl Van Vechten. Library of Congress, Prints & Photographs Division, Carl Van Vechten Collection, LC-USZ62-114506 DLC)

296 A sketch by Wynn Chamberlain at some point during the mid-1950s that Van Vechten put in his scrapbooks. Chamberlain identifies this as a preparatory sketch for *Doorway*, a painting that was subsequently bought by Lincoln Kirstein. (© Elwyn Chamberlain. Yale Collection of American Literature, Beinecke Rare Book & Manuscript Library, Yale University)

299 Allen Juante Meadows, c. 1940 (Photograph by Carl Van Vechten. Library of Congress, Prints & Photographs Division, Carl Van Vechten Collection, LC-USZ62-114425 DLC)

300 Hugh Laing, c. 1940 (Photograph by Carl Van Vechten. Library of Congress, Prints & Photographs Division, Carl Van Vechten Collection)

305 Carl Van Vechten, c. 1960 (Photograph by Oscar White. © Bettmann/CORBIS)